Symbolic Communication

MIT Press Series on Organization Studies
John Van Maanen, general editor

Symbolic Communication
Signifying Calls and the Police Response

Peter K. Manning

The MIT Press
Cambridge, Massachusetts
London, England

This book was set in Palatino by Asco Trade Typesetting Ltd., Hong Kong, and printed and bound by The Murray Printing Company in the United States of America.

Library of Congress Cataloging-in-Publication Data

Manning, Peter K.
  Symbolic communication: signifying calls and the police response / Peter K. Manning.
    p.   cm.—(MIT Press series on organization studies; 9)
  Bibliography: p.
  Includes index.
  ISBN 0-262-13234-6
  1. Communication in police administration—Great Britain. 2. Communication in police administration—United States. 3. Police communication systems—Great Britain. 4. Police communication systems—United States. 5. Semiotics. I. Title. II. Series.
  HV7936.C79M36   1988   363.2′014—dc 19   88-17533

Dedicated to Rodney Needham and Erving Goffman

Contents

Preface and Acknowledgments

Signifying Calls unfolded in East Lansing, Guilford, Surrey, and Oxford, in Balliol and Wolfson Colleges, in Quarry House and Rowin. It is a two-way mirror. It speaks to a general problem, transmission of messages between people within an organizational context, and about my experiences of such processes. This book abstractly represents aspects of encounters with people in organizational roles communicating to me about communication. It adopts the perspective of police "on the ground" as they saw, represented, gestured, dreamed, and fantasized about essential and trivial communication. It is a rendition from observation, interviews, and records of a police account of communication among themselves and between themselves and the public. It was heard in cars, rooms, pubs, living rooms, offices, and diverse shabby restaurants in "Centreshire" and "Metro City," transcribed and drafted in East Lansing and written for the most part in Oxford.

In the course of the work, I heard, reheard, and disattended much. I often listened when I felt a deep need to talk, to explode and express my contained feelings. In time I became less patient, open, and sensitive and somewhat more distracted. Perhaps my interviewing, probing, and observation became less perceptive and penetrating. On reflection, age and my experiences changed me: I possessed somewhat more refined and firm opinions on a range of topics, felt driven to dominate conversations, and less tolerant of often rambling and disconnected discourse. I was 32 when I began the first volume in this triology. I am now 47. One might now see a less "boyish" and parochial person, one much less like the young police officers with whom I shared drinks, tea, and chat in London in 1973.

Several fellowships, leaves, and grants enabled me to pursue this research. Michigan State University granted several leaves, including a sabbatical, and funded an All-University Research Initiation Grant. The Law Enforcement Assistance Administration funded research on crime control with Mary Ann Wycoff of the Police Foundation (grant 79-NI-AX-0095), and the National Science Foundation supported an investigation of the potential impact of information technology on crime control. The University of Surrey provided a Johnsons Wax Fellowship in 1979, and the Centre for Socio-Legal Studies, sponsored by the Economic and Social Research Council (ESRC) in England, at Wolfson College, Oxford, provided fellowships in 1981 and 1982. I was honored to have been awarded a Visiting Fellowship at Balliol College, Oxford, for the Michaelmas and Hilary terms, 1982–83. Wolfson College also honored me as a College Fellow in 1984–86. I am grateful for these often graciously offered opportunities.

I am particularly indebted to W. Donald Weston, dean of the College of Human Medicine, who made it possible for me to remain at Michigan State and to pursue my research elsewhere for substantial periods. Norbert Enzer and Don Williams empathetically encourage me to realize my aspirations. I also thank Jay Artis, Tom Conner, and Chris Vanderpool. Asher Tropp, the chair at Surrey, Don Harris and Dick Markovits, codirectors of the Socio-Legal Centre, and John Boal, also of the Centre, were congenial, understanding, helpful, and supportive.

In Oxford from mid-1981 to early 1986 Keith Hawkins and Dick Markovits were friends and colleagues. Elaine Player, to whom I owe more than I can say, was a loyal intellectual and personal companion. Rodney Needham entertained, provided imaginative tessellations, and taught much on many gray mornings in the Wharton Room of All Souls College, Oxford. If more scholars combined such wisdom, insight, and intensity, we would all be better positioned to be judged. I draw on his pellucid prose to set a mood for this volume. Comments on drafts punctuated more by spilled coffee than by well-placed commas were provided by Betsy Cullum-Swan, Charles Lemert, Elaine Player, Paul Rock, John Van Maanen, and Mary Ann Wycoff. Erving Goffman rejected a previous working title.

Industrious work for which I am grateful was undertaken by Roxie Damer, Kimberly Bancroft, Michele Carrier, Tammy Dennany, Fanny Kuhn, Karen Kay, Sara Randazzo, John Wells, Betsy Cullum-Swan, and Mahendra Singh at Michigan State and by Nöel Blatchford, Jennifer Dix, Linda Peterson, Rosemary Stallan, and Joan Watson in Oxford.

Research access and support were provided from time to time, in significantly variable degrees and in widely separated times and places, by officers of the two departments who cannot be named, Anthony Butler, former chief constable Maurice Buck, Inspector Harold Johnson, Eva Buzawa, and chiefs of police in St. Petersburg and Tampa, Florida, and Rotterdam, the Netherlands.

I thank those who truly cannot be repaid: Marilyn and family, Terry Stein, Elaine Player, Coline E. S., mom and dad, Lawrence Brown, and everyone at Sunday soccer at Hannah over the years and at Sunday softball at Wolfson. Those who made this book possible are Jennifer Hunt, Ellen Greenman, Michael Hobbs, and Barrie Biven. I know now to anticipate problems when I take a cab: I carry a liter of petrol. Without the sometimes kind assistance of E. Manual Autoglyph, whom once I met at a conference and entrusted with significant papers, I doubt if I could have transformed this object into a mere job. Once again, as always, thanks Kerry, Merry, and Sean Peter.

Portions of this manuscript, in earlier drafts, were published in the following journals and books: "Organizational work: Structuration of the environment," *British Journal of Sociology* (1982), 33:118–139; "Producing drama: Symbolic communication and the police," *Symbolic Interaction* (1982), 5:223–241; "Organizational control and semiotics," in *Control in the Police Organization*, M. Punch, ed. (Cambridge, Mass.: MIT Press, 1983), 169–193; "Queries concerning the decision-making approach to police research," in *Proceedings of the British Psychological Association* (Criminal and Legal Division), J. Shapland, ed. Sheffield: British Psychological Association, 1983), 50–60; "Police classification of the mentally ill," in *Mental Health and the Criminal Justice System*, L. Teplin, ed. (Newbury Park, Cal.: Sage, 1984), 177–198; "Limits upon the semiotic structuralist perspective upon organizational analysis," in *Studies in Symbolic Interaction*, N. Denzin, ed. (Greenwich, Conn.: JAI, 1985), vol. 6, 79–111; "Signwork," *Human Relations* (1986), 39:283–308; "Texts as organizational echoes," *Human Studies* (1986), 9:287–302.

Introduction

My impressions of the communications center remain vivid and powerful. It was a smelly, smoky, poorly lit room reeling under the glare of harsh flickering fluorescent lights. Windowless, stuffy, with restricted exit and entry, few amenities. Nervous anxiety and worry was the prevalent tone. Operators answered calls sequentially and quickly sent them on. I shared the daily round with one of the 911 operators. Perched on a chair, my eyes watering from dense cigarette smoke, my nose running, my rear end aching from sitting on a hard seat, and my ear raw from contact with the ear piece I had jammed in one ear, I have rarely endured such an upleasant fieldwork experience. The supervisors were helpful in the way that precludes or closes off access to potentially illuminating information. As we checked in and out of duty, I found that on breaks operators did not so much talk about the substance of the work as reiterate their complaints, fear of errors, dread of supervisors, and the anticipated consequence of making a mistake. There prevailed an obsessive concern with the need for rigid compliance with formal rule and procedures. Overlooked by no less than seven distinct monitoring means, there was little fun, little life, and little enjoyment to be had in that confining coffinlike area high in a dirty, noisy, deteriorating building in the middle of a rotting and disintegrating city. "How *did* they do this job?" I thought.

Set out here is an ethnographically based descriptive account of symbolic communication, the precise intent of which is to identify, formulate, and demonstrate how selected factors in addition to message content ("information") pattern organizational communication.[1] Drawing on a variety of perspectives, I make the case that meaning is socially constructed from the occasioned relevance of "message content" in an organizational structure and through interpretative work. Telephone calls made to the police are an important window on organizational communication. "Organization" is a background against which a message is normally projected. This usual figure-ground relationship is systematically altered in this analysis. A comparative design incorporating observations drawn from two police organizations, one in Britain (the BPD) and another in America (the MPD), permits analysis of differences between the two communicational systems and those found among and between organizational segments. Some practical consequences of computer-based systems for theory and for administration and service are addressed in the final chapters.

How and why the police "understand" calls as they do is practically relevant, for these variegated processes of signification convert human cares, worries, dread, anxiety, and obligations into a form that allows the police to display their obligation to serve the public. The interpretative possibilities are vast, but by channeling calls into symbolic forms, they produce routine actions. The police thus engage in a subtle dance that traces their organizational needs on the demands and problems of various publics.

The arguments presented here interpolate semiotics, structuralism, and information theory. They provide a point of origin for analysis much as semantics does for pragmatics (Levinson 1983, pp. 13–21).[2] That is, they permit one to explicate aspects of meaning that cannot be accounted for by the truth value of a proposition.[3] Meaning in organizational communication is produced by four interrelated social factors: Technology that drives the informationally based communication system, coding of requests, interpretations made of communicational units at various points in the organization, and roles and tasks of members of the organization. These four factors are part of the constraints necessary to maintain formal communication in ecologically dispersed collective enterprises, whereas the social relations that emerge from the interaction of these communicational matters and social structure form ritual constraints (Goffman 1981).

Organizational communication employs visual, tactile, aural, and written channels that are conflated during message processing. A cultural basis for understanding how these various forms are embedded in organizational discourse is required. This cultural base for knowledge precipitates enstructuration (Giddens 1984), even as it integrates action. Although the social patterning of communication, primarily in the guise of discourse and texts, is the focus here, it is assumed that the practices that constitute the patterning pin it to contexts (Lyons 1977, p. 574) that indicate its character as organizational discourse (Bittner 1965) and suggest the observer's role.[4]

Not all readers will bring the same interests or desires to this text, and a variety of subtexts can be read from the following chapters. Julio Cortazar provided an apodictic outline for presumed readers of *Hopscotch* suggesting various lines of reading and envisioning one, two, three, or more "books" depending on the several nontransitive, not mutually exclusive choice sequences. Similar approaches are found in Italo Calvino's *Castle of*

Crossed Destinies, If on a Winter's Night . . ., and *Invisible Cities*, and Primo Levi's *Periodic Table*. A looser sort of ordering is found in Borges's *Book of Imaginary Beings* and the short story, "Tlön, Uqbar, Orbis Tertius" in *Ficciones* and in Vargas Llosa's *Aunt Julia and the Scriptwriter*.

Let us imagine that a person with criminal justice and policing interests reads the book. An agenda of chapters 7, 4, 5 and 3 in that order might be satisfying with chapter 1 held out as an appetizer. A person with interests in organization theory might read chapters 1 and 2, 7 and 8, and then 3 through 6. An ethnographer would dive into chapters 3 and 4, chew on 5, and consider 6. That strange continental beast, the structuralist, might read this introduction and chapters 2, 4 or 5, savor 6, and pass on to 8. Are these three or more books here? Of course, one might choose to read chapters 1 through 8 in order and see this book as part of a triology.

The book is a revision, emendation, and continuation of my previous work on policing. In *Police Work* (MIT Press, 1977) and *Narc's Game* (MIT Press, 1980), the orienting query was the relative contribution of information, rationality, and predetermined policy, planning, and scientific administration to the governance of public service organizations and particularly to "scientific policing." In each book I sought to identify the physical and social constraints on police action, processes of environmental definition, and sources of relative sensitivity to objects and events disclosed to police view. The internal structuring of the police environment was described as a coding system that patterns the resultant flow of information. The internal uses of information and its role in the maintenance of authority systems and the capacity of information to shape strategies and tactics of the organization were also addressed.

Narc's Game [and *Police Narcotics Control* (Washington, D.C.: Government Printing Office, 1979)] focused rather more sharply on internal constraints, organizationally shaped communicational processes and definitions, and uses of this information. *Police Work* set the stage for this analysis, arguing on the basis of ethnographic research on one London subdivision that social bases of communication shape and pattern police action and organization. Although the informational basis of policing is enduring, authoritative, and fundamental, it remains in constant tension with organization structure and occupational culture. Other symbolic aims, such as expressing and marking social order and continuity and maintaining enduring authority relations, and many traditions of policing also shape information processing.

How does organized rationality interface with the variegated dilemmas and perplexities of human communication? These abstract and formal concerns mirrored my aim to clarify the role of information and rationality in modern life and to identify some limits on rational discourse. In *Narcs' Game* I suggested that "beneath" organizational forms, hierarchies, rules, and plans lie diffuse feelings, emotions, and even passions (Manning 1980a, p. lx). These are perhaps encoded in language and social relations and are not discernibly distinctive matters but ways of seeing. Any experience is transformed by reflection and is thereby made external, exclusive, and potentially a source of the "otherness of meaning" (Barthes 1981, p. 65). But given that rationality is also characteristically human, it can provide a substitute for imaginative understanding, a false mirror, a mere streetcar that anyone can adapt to any situation (paraphrasing Heidegger). One danger is substitution of *pseudorationality*, in the form of technocratic language, for political, moral, and administrative discussion. I distrust the sense of false clarity that the ponderous language of information theory and other formalisms can induce. Such vocabularies and methods for representing thought decontextualize human experience and threaten to further reduce its vibrancy and resonance. Computer-based police processing of calls edges toward this kind of decontextualization.

Several working assumptions organize this book. They can be cast in rather more grand terms than merely "working assumptions." It seems to me that the fundamental dilemma of people in modern societies is meaning: creating, transforming, and reproducing for others subjectively intended credible messages. Modern societies, especially the political leaders of these societies, have sought to fill the gap created by meaning that is eroded, confused, or lost by the imposition of authoritative power. This in turn produces the sting or the resistance to command that reverses its purpose (Canetti 1962; Cooper 1983a). The escalation of authority, with correlative lies and deceptions, further erodes fragile ties. Machines of various kinds, the technology of communication in particular, have been falsely seen as the source of new and binding meaning. They have been seen as an independent source of societal unity and cohesion. This is as false a hope as is the search for authoritative meaning, what Fromm (1941) termed the escape from freedom. Shared meaning, the tacit, unspoken personal, and situated as well as the explicit, spoken, and transituational come into conflict as systems of imposed meaning (such as computer language) compete with locally situated communicational speech communities. The broadening of the ambit of "computerese," with its ugly, ponderous, and assaultive and dehumanizing tones, is one aspect of the decline of literacy and the dominance of the visual. People, especially Americans, confuse talk with communication and view silence with mistrust. Ortega y Gasset (1932) suggested that this was one manifestation of the process of massification of society. The grand structures of power and knowledge assembled at the top of Western societies speak to the decline of debate and differentiation of coherent opinion. Mindless journalists become the "intellectual leaders" of the country appearing on television nightly to pronounce on the nature of truth. If language is reduced to a mere tool, badly used, equally used, and an inadequate source of dreams, hopes, wishes, feelings, and strivings, a mere collection of object names with nouns converted into verbs to provide the "action," then language is not the solution but the problem. The wish to find answers to all problems and the belief that there are answers to all problems is a technological conceit. Nothing can completely tidy communication, ensure meaning and precision, and reduce the ambiguity of life.

There is a humanistic aim of this analysis. Growth in the degree of self-knowledge requires a deeply felt intuitive understanding of the complexity of human relations and rests on nuanced vocabularies, rich embodied experience, and a breadth of vision. In segments of society based on the view that technology alone can solve human problems and conflicts, where meaning is falsely fabricated on every side and amplified by the media, self-knowledge is elusive. It is ironic that many feel alone in an informationally complex, highly reflexive environment in which machines and information can variously simplify, increase, and distort the quality of human communication. Isolation can drive one to accept false credos, to engage in empty rituals, to profess faith in "progress" by means of improved technologies. Deeply held feelings may thus be unarticulated, denied, displaced, or invested mistakenly in machinery (Weizenbaum 1976). One can strive to understand and control the empty echoes of mechanistic logics and reject the fallacy that conceives of persons as value-neutral robots, as well as that habit of mind that confers human properties to machines. Words represent connections that permit explication, exploration, and renewal of primordial human links. They index the worlds of feeling that can be variously shared.

Men do not reason often; they do not reason for long at a time; and when they do reason they are not very good at it.——Rodney Needham, *Primordial Characters*, p. 69

One of the first ways to characterize human beings is to say that they are sentient beings, and I take it to be true that what we think of as our "real" lives is characteristically an account of our feelings.——Rodney Needham, *Circumstantial Deliveries*, p. 99

The depths of love, the transports of ecstasy, the sundering pangs of grief, and other such supreme affections in our personal intercourse, are precisely those of which we readily say that they are inexpressible; and the very fact that they are inexpressible is a distinctive sign of their quality.—— Rodney Needham, *Belief, Language and Experience*, p. 229

I

Metaphors

1

The Police Communications Problem

Human society is based on symbolic communication; yet communication is assumed to do its work much like the increasingly complicated technological infrastructure that carries television, radio, telephone, and microcomputer signals between large, loosely linked networks. All modern institutions are communication dependent, and those that serve the public must channel and mediate with limited resources the potentially undiminished demand of citizens. Here, communication is viewed as problematic.

The police face a communications problem: how to anticipate, respond to, mediate, and filter rising citizen demand with a controlled and calculated strategy. Police forces are based on complex communications systems and are dramatic, quasi-judicial organizations structured to allocate and deploy officers across time and space. They actively intervene and intrude increasingly in private spaces and stand ready to respond to diversely organized, highly uncertain events. When reacting, they must for the most part rely on citizens' information, cooperation, goodwill and actions in order to accomplish their defined tasks. Policing in Anglo-American societies has evolved a structured capacity for technologically mediated accessibility.

As the technology of police communications systems makes the police more accessible, increasing citizen demand and police workload, it also strains traditional modes of supervision and control, motivation and reward, and carefully monitored response to events. The increased message flow processed by these new technologies (computer-assisted dispatch, information retrieval, allocation and distribution of personnel, the two-way radio, three-digit telephone numbers, and centralized collection of calls) is not self-sufficient but organizationally embedded. It is accommodated within traditional role structures, classified in quasi-legal codes in line with emergent and accepted practices based on the occupational culture, and disposed in accord with traditional police procedures. The police have evolved technologically sophisticated equipment to cope with increased citizen demand, but messages are received, interpreted, processed, transformed, and allocated for resolution within socially patterned relationships. Social relations, coding procedures, interpretative practices, and working rules, derived in part from the occupational culture, shape, constrain, and pattern messages regardless of their informational content and form.

This last proposition goes to the heart of communications and organization theory, which together address the nature of the connections between organizations and environment. What patterns a message? It suggests further that symbolic communication, whether in the police or elsewhere, requires a science, *semiotics*, or the science of signs, by which to analyze these connections (Saussure 1966; Peirce 1931; Culler 1975; Hawkes 1977; Eco 1976, 1979, 1984). With the strands of organizational and communicational theory and semiotics in hand, in the following pages I weave together an analysis of communications between the police and the public in two police organizations in two cultures.

Semiotics provides a set of assumptions and concepts that permit the systematic analysis of symbolic systems. A sign is something that represents or stands for something else in the mind of someone. A sign is composed of an expression and a content. The connections made between expressions and content and among signs are mental. For example, a rose is conventionally an expression linked with romance as a content. Smoke is linked to fire, and the American flag to courage. The nature of the link can be indexical, semantic, or iconic. The process of linking or connecting expression and content is social and depends on the perspective of the observer. Peirce (1958) has argued that every sign is incomplete because it requires an "interpretant," something that links the expression (the signifier) and the content (the signified). Because interpretants change, signs change meaning. There is no reality behind a sign, no "real world" against which the sign can be checked. The interpretant of a sign is another sign, and that sign is validated by yet another sign, and so on.

Semiotics depends on a "primitive phenomenology"; that is, a meaningful connection between the expression and the content must be socially constructed. Typically these connections are shared and collective and provide an important source of ideas, rules, practices, codes, and recipe knowledge called culture (Culler 1975). These connections or contexts are sometimes called paradigms. The arrangement of signs that is meaningful can be syntactic (based on order), syntagmatic (based on proximity), or metaphoric (based on similarity in meaning). Several domains of meaning, when collected, constitute a field. A field can be mapped onto larger social structures of signs as well. A code provides the social connection between the components of a sign, a set of signs clustered as texts, and even signs assembled as discourse. These distinctions are moot and not conventionalized in semiotics generally (Hawkes 1977; Culler 1975; Leach 1976; Pettit 1977).

To some degree, the volatile and unstable contextual nature of meaning is reduced by shared rules and codes employed within a culture to make sense of fields of signs. Once a set of signs is recognized by an analyst, the task is to reduce the data to a pattern, a set of rules, or typifications. The structure of meaning can be represented by concepts that contain the potential for generalization, such as codes. Furthermore, because all meaning is found within context, a matter of contrast, opposition, transformation, and marking of differences, signs are always a product of some form of contrast, such as the contrast between the first sounds of the words "cat" and "hat" or the contrast in the light waves that provide our sense of the colors red and green. Thus signs are a function of difference and similarity in context.

Throughout this book I use the concept of rules variously. At times I use rules to describe a procedural guideline for the police, such as "All calls must be given at least one classification"; at other times I use rules to gloss an observed action in a decision situation, such as "Send everything down"; at still other times I use rules to draw general inferences about the structure of beliefs and practices, such as those used to analyze the occupational culture of police in chapters 4 and 5. The word "rules" captures different aspects of organizational action in each of these contexts, and yet it is a useful pointer.

Rules are not an explanation for an action choice. They conflate, or represent, a number of social factors. Individuals do not look to rules to guide practice but act and at times refer to a rule or written conventional justification for their actions. All verbal statements presuppose a set of common understandings in part captured in grammatical knowledge, knowledge of syntax, semantics, and commonsense typifications of behavior. They are a portmanteau of concepts applicable to everyday life. Thus shorthand rules such as "Describe an incident in the least possible words" or "Cover your ass," build on and assume such unexplicated and often shared commonsense understandings (Giddens 1976, pp. 88–91, 107).

Rules arise, as I will show, for contingent complexities. Rules are few and clearly defined in highly homogeneous societies and are used in differentiated societies in which an official statement is required to cover public variations from acceptable procedure (Bourdieu 1977, p. 14). In chapters 3, 4, and 5 I discuss rules as rationalizations and justifications for decisions displayed in repeated actions. As a result the analysis may obscure the extent to which Gidden's term "knowledgeability" (Giddens 1984) captures the sense of events for these organizational actors. What is unspoken, assumed, accepted, or seen to be accepted mobilizes action but may not be fully captured by such concepts as rule-following behavior or rule-guided action. Knowledgeability can only be partially captured by the sociologists' concept of rule-based action. Any attempt to reduce complex assessments to rules raises functionalistic and normative images of social action. In the section on occupational culture, I suggest a sketch, not a normative paradigm. I do not mean to suggest that policing is done by "tacit consensus" around normative or behavioral principles [see Sykes and Brent (1983)]. My argument, in short, is a tentative and inferential outline not based on repeated systematic observations of police behavior in "domestics."

On the whole, the concept of a rule indicates actors' sense of rules rather than official rules or even the officialization of discourse discussed by Bourdieu (1977, ch. 1). However, the actors' sense and the official meaning of rules are in some kind of reflexive relationship because actors' sense of rules provides the resources for justification of action in official terms. Sociological analysis far too often deals with a universe of precon-stituted discourse and meanings and rules eliding complexity and inter-prets both of these within theoretical schemes, mediating technical and ordering language. In the final chapter I make some effort to clarify the argument concerning rule-guided behavior by using the concept of meta-rules as a sensitizing notion reflecting the double articulation of sociological analysis and the reflexivity of individual discourse.

In this study, I examine the symbolic transformation of communication: how communicational units are produced and reproduced, how they are defined, and the background understandings that make message pro-cessing possible. I illustrate how communication is mediated by classifica-tion systems, technology, roles and tasks, and interpretations. In this analysis I compare two organizations with similar communications sys-tems in two cultures. It is a work about how people think and feel about thinking, feel and think about feelings, and turn all such matters into mere organizational products. The background is the foreground of this analysis: How do institutionalized structures develop the images, techniques, and shorthand interpretations and indexes that make brief and elliptical calls for "service" routine messages? All these ideas and practices occur before officers take any action at a scene. I report symbolizations and representa-tions of anticipated events but not behavior on the scene. That is another book, one that has been written already.

The Police and Communication

The communications problem of the police is a shared one; to a striking degree highly industrialized societies are technologically driven and tech-nologically dependent (Bell 1973; Nora and Minc 1981). The problems of defense, such as the "star wars" defense system proposed by the United States in 1985, electronically controlled fragile missile launching networks

(Ford 1985), and underwater submarine counterattack forces, are defined technologically as are those of health, industry, and education. The technological conceit provides the mirror by which problems are defined and thus technological solutions sought. The capacity to provide a similar technological infrastructure for defense, policing, and industry has produced ineluctable associated problems as well as solutions (Ford 1985; Bracken 1983).

The police communications problem is somewhat more than a merely technological one requiring a technological approach. Technology may increase access, reduce processing time within organizations, and provide more accessible and immediately extant records, but it also produces its own unresolved or heightened difficulties. Consider the following:

1. Every year in America and Great Britain large police organizations (serving about 2 million people) receive between 0.29 and 0.77 calls per year per person (Bercal 1970; Hough 1980a; Shearing 1984).

2. Many calls arise from three-digit numbers (911, 999), are centrally processed by computerized command and control systems, and are allocated in accord with highly sophisticated systems for dispatch, data storage and retrieval, tactical deployment, and strategic planning (Tien and Colton 1979).

3. These calls vary widely in time of day, day of the week, and month of the year in which they arise, in the channel on which they arrive (alarm, citizen emergency, citizen information given or requested, internal management systems maintenance), content (crime, noncrime, information, emotional reassurance, status of officers), length (from a few seconds to several minutes), priority, political and social significance, and communal relevance [see, for example, Ekblom and Heal (1982) and Shearing (1984)].

4. These calls also vary in information, redundancy, and meaning (MacKay 1969). They vary in the amount of "new" information provided, what is previously known, and what, in any case, the call signifies or communicates about social relations (Davis 1983).

Police communications technologies have been adopted also as a means of organizational surveillance, guidance, and control: nominal control of police officers, especially those at the bottom of the discretionary pyramid, and ostensive control of the external environment (Bordua and Reiss 1967). They have become increasingly acceptable, viewed as "modern" and progressive techniques, scientific means to increase policing effectiveness. They are assumed to enhance the image and prestige of the police. These and other unproven assumptions wedded to a crime control ideology have driven the police in Anglo-American societies to demand public support for ever-greater expenditures for computer technology.

Until about ten years ago there were few systematically gathered facts for evaluating the claims made for police communication technologies [see Tien and Colton (1979) for the finest such review]. Available evaluations strike consistent chords that, taken together, suggest that technology alone does not alter the fundamental constraints on policing.[1] These organizational, occupational, political, legal, and informational constraints are differentially amplified and depressed in salience by communications technology in different types of police work. The juxtaposition of this research, police presumptions, and the claims of technocrats sets the stage, somewhat strewn with discarded ideas like a picnic ground after a drunken Fourth of July celebration or a failed family reunion, for the description of the two police organizations and their technology. First a word on technology.

Technology and Police Work

Techne, a Greek word, means an art, craft, or skill. Technology is defined in Webster's as (1) "a technical language," (2) "an applied science" or "a technical means of achieving a practical purpose," and (3) "the totality of means employed to provide objects necessary for human sustenance and comfort." Although these terms imply systematic and logical method, technology is used in several nonexclusive yet specialized senses in the organizational behavior literature (Zey-Ferrell 1979). The assumption is that no social variable contributes more to the determination of organizational structure than technology. Work processes and flow are said to shape organizational structure, and work processes to a greater or lesser degree are patterned by technology. However, there is no agreement in the organizational literature about the phenomena to which technology refers:

> The concept of technology has been operationalized in terms of the extent of task interdependence, automation of equipment, uniformity or complexity of the materials used, and the degree of routineness of the work.... There seems to be general agreement that organizational technology involves either the mechanical or intellectual processes by which an organization transforms inputs, raw materials, into outputs. (Zey-Ferrell 1979, p. 108)

Important distinctions are made between types of technology. Operations technology involves sequencing and equipping the activities in the work flow or the ways in which inputs are processed and output is produced and distributed. Material technology has to with the physical characteristics of the materials used. These materials are quite variable, from people to prunes, from gas to gastronomes. Knowledge technology refers to the characteristics of the knowledge used in the work flow. The amount, quality, and specificity of the relevant knowledge utilized in production may vary. These analytic types of technology can coexist in an organization; they may be in conflict or be compatible, or they may increase or decrease integration of the various subsystems, producing structural differentiation and autonomy.

Technology is the means by which an organization transforms raw materials or inputs into processed outputs (Zey-Ferrell 1979, pp. 108ff). I make several further distinctions. The police presently use a non-routinized, tacitly articulated technology (Manning 1980b; Manning and Hawkins 1987). Police technology is mirrored in the ways the police work. Knowledge or information shapes the technology and is transmitted through or worked on by technology. Tasks are subcomponents of the work process, accomplished by means, or technology, that can be modified. Whether modification of a task by technology means that a new technology has been applied or that the task has been redefined is difficult to answer. Work flow is the sequencing of tasks. Bureaucracy consists of the formal rules of procedure, offices, functions, and the associated structure of authority. The term "police technology" refers both to traditional, rather disorderly technology and to new technologies. When one speaks of technological innovations in policing, one is referring to the attempt to introduce new means of defining and interfacing with the environment and of processing the "product." Thus the innovations are found in operations (such as in the development of new case processing schemes in detective work), materials (such as the use of computers and centralized radio dispatching), or knowledge technology (such as the development of new models or strategies of enforcement and deployment of resources).

The traditional technology of the police is nonroutine; the material means are limited, and they are applied to people; and the knowledge in use is nonsystematic and situational or tacit rather than theoretically derived and causal (see Thompson (1967) and Manning (1980b)]. Historically the police eschewed the formal technologies found in manufacturing; they utilize semiroutinized processing. Higher forms of technology (that is, rational routine types found in mass production or material technology used in large batch work) are also associated with rational legal bureaucratic forms. In the police force, bureaucratic organization of a special sort is combined with low routinization, a limited amount of material technology, and a quasi-logical or commonsense theory of policing.

Police: Shaped and Shaper

A police organization is a particular sort of bureaucratically organized, ecologically dispersed public service organization responding to highly diverse events appearing in an uncertain pattern, with high discretion at the bottom. The police organization is shaped by and the shaper of the communications problem.

Both functionally and politically, police organizations create and display a public image of service and paramilitary discipline while maintaining a backstage version of their activities in which they filter demand, act with discretion, refuse to respond, selectively allocate officers to functions, and differentially reward activities. Both images convey a partial view of policing (Goffman 1959; Holdaway 1983). My research tries to convey the reality of both images.

The conditions under which organizations respond to demand cannot be established independently of the operations of the organization in encoding, processing, and decoding the flow of environmental stimuli (Weick 1979). Because in the case of policing a "response" seems to be a function of the meaning assigned to "problems" in the environment (originally existing as a set of behavioral events) and these are in effect transformed internally by the information-processing system, the meaning of events does not arise as a result of a change in the logical orientation of the information-processing system (MacKay 1969). The level (quantity) of the external stimuli is undifferentiated from the perspective of information receptors in the organization.

Police organization in large urban areas in Anglo-American societies has been based historically on patrol, later on responding to citizen calls, and increasingly on producing a fairly rapid and differentiated response to important calls (Clark and Sykes 1974). The police make claims of success on the basis of rapid response, especially in life-threatening or crime-related incidents. The ecological-organization strategy of the police is firmly rooted in this mandate. Although the police are mandated to respond in some fashion to promote and protect the public collective good, they are not legally required to respond to all requests; nor are they legally or even morally a "service organization" in the sense that they serve individual citizens. They serve the state and the state's interests (Brogden 1982; Manning 1977, ch. 3; Manning 1981).

Nevertheless, the police are in constant intermittent contact with the various social worlds from which messages arise. The primary channel by which information reaches the police is the telephone (Reiss and Bordua 1967), and evidence from citizen-police encounters suggests that much police work is initiated by citizen calls. The self-generated "stops" crucial to policing (Reiss 1971; Ericson 1982, p. 216) present the active and intrusive face of policing. Direct communications, given the discretion valued in policing, the supervisory system, and the ecological dispersal of officers, are a form of *demand* shaped little by the formal system of control and authority symbolized by the quasi-military facets of police operations (Jermier and Berkes 1979). These calls, as I will describe in detail later, are normally received at a communications center, answered by operators or operator-dispatchers, and processed (accepted, refused, referred; given a classification, priority, forwarded, or held).

These arrangements for processing calls to the police are the focus of the analytical concept, the police communications system. Ethnographic data in later chapters detail the particular character of two police communications systems but the system is the center of the analysis. Some calls, the proportion of which varies from organization to organization, are sent to officers for observation, investigation, comment, or disposal. Calls are subject to a number of influences or *filters*, such as citizen decisions to call, number and kinds of operators, dispatcher and officer discretion, mechanical and computer failures, lost calls resulting from telephone malfunction, periodic overloading, queuing and missing information.[2]

Background
Police organizations, within the limits of personnel, ecology, technology, and social organization, receive, filter, interpret, allocate, respond to, and otherwise dispose of demands for their service. This means that the loyalty and command questions are tightly linked with the communication problem. How officers are motivated, educated, committed, rewarded, punished, and mobilized in a predictable and rational manner is increasingly seen as a communications and technological problem.

The communications problem for the last fifty years seems to have been solved by the development of a series of applied technologies: the telephone, then the two-way radio system, then centralized call systems (three-digit emergency numbers), and then computerized dispatch and monitoring systems. It has been argued that the communications system represents a systematized microcosm of the police problem. It facilitates the control of crime by lawful means; it produces accountability because the telephone is a democratic instrument by which citizen preferences are expressed and to which the police are obligated to respond (and to be seen to have responded); it enhances the level and quality of citizen response and participation in crime control and order maintenance. Because the line of communication seen in the police communications system is visible, reproducible, and monitored and directly replicates the chain of command (dispatches are defined as "orders"), the internal accountability and supervision problem is also changed in character. It enables the policing in theory to gear response to demand in a subtle, ongoing, and evaluated fashion, thus potentially improving the quality and efficiency of police as well as improving the quality of life.[3]

New technologies have been examined from engineering, administrative (Wilson and McLaren 1972), and governance standpoints (equality of service). Unfortunately these studies virtually treat the actual communications system as an unexplicated "black box" (Tien and Colton

1979). Few studies examine the workings of the police communications system, and they largely focus on output, such as response time, equality of service, patterns of incidents received and/or responded to, and citizen satisfaction.

As I show in the following chapters, the claims for technologically sophisticated command and control systems have not been carefully evaluated, and when they have, they have been shown to be underutilized, marginal to operational and strategic considerations, and marginal to tasks viewed as central to the police organization.[4]

These analyses of the communications problem of the police are complemented by a handful of studies that examine the context within which information is received by the police. They seek to describe information-processing technology, information processing, and what results from this activity. Inevitably, they reveal how matters such as social organization, ecology, and the symbolic nature of communication forcefully pattern what is done (Hough 1980a, 1980b; Jorgensen 1981; Hulbert 1981a; Ekblom and Heal 1982; Shearing 1984). These studies focus on an aspect of the process, such as the allocation of calls, dispatchers' decision processes, or cognitive understandings, but each is partial [see Manning (1980b) for an overview of police organizations and technology]. Previous research has not combined a concern with message content with influential non-message aspects of the communication process in policing, including technology, roles and tasks, coding, and interpretative work. My aim is to do so in order to increase social science and administrative understanding of symbolic communication in a police organizational context.

2

Message Processing: From Environment I to Environment II

Message processing is conceptual work. It involves the transformation of messages about events in the everyday world into objects and organizational communicational units, a partial basis for police response. This work is described initially as if there were no errors, feedback, lost messages, failures in the technology, and the like. Figure 2.1 is a model of communication that shows how the environment is enacted within the police. We begin as does the caller, in the social world (environment I), and return to that social world, redefined as environment II by the police who received the message.

The Social World

The social world is composed of ongoing processes delineated perceptually, subjectively, and cognitively and individually and collectively. The social world and the physical world are not seen as mere moving molecules or physical causalities but in terms of phenomenological causality or primary frameworks. Perception is dualistic; items, sounds, and concrete chunks of reality are organized and patterned into schemata, organizing ways of seeing so that what is felt, heard, and seen is integrated with plans and intentions. The character of the intentions permits generalization about the structure of experience. In the social world, as Goffman has argued (1974, p. 21), *primary frameworks* are a means for organizing experience in a semipermanent fashion, a basis for "guided doings." These are socially structured means by which perception is stabilized. In environment I there exists a world of *events*, which are labeled or named using *prototypes*. For crime some common prototypical terms are "rape," "murder," and "burglary" (bear in mind that these probably overlap in content with legal terms and refer, as Wittgenstein reminds us, to different matters referenced by the same name). The primary frameworks may contain a hierarchy, or taxonomy, or have other undiscovered formal properties. For the purposes of this analysis it is adequate to note that the vocabulary of crimelike *events* exists and orders experience. Some events in the world become the

Time ⟶
Movement of communicational units ⟶

|———— Boundary 1 ————| |———— Boundary 2 ————|

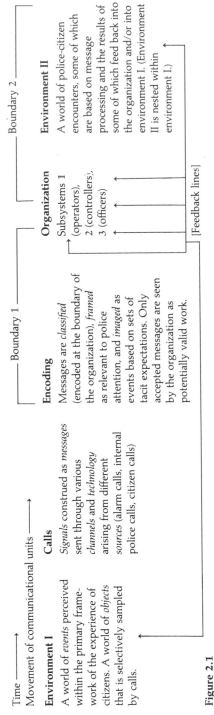

Environment I	**Calls**	**Encoding**	**Organization**	**Environment II**
A world of *events* perceived within the primary framework of the experience of citizens. A world of *objects* that is selectively sampled by calls.	*Signals* construed as *messages* sent through various *channels* and *technology* arising from different *sources* (alarm calls, internal police calls, citizen calls)	Messages are *classified* (encoded at the boundary of the organization), *framed* as relevant to police attention, and *imaged* as events based on sets of tacit expectations. Only accepted messages are seen by the organization as potentially valid work.	Subsystems 1 (operators), 2 (controllers), 3 (officers)	A world of police-citizen encounters, some of which are based on message processing and the results of some of which feed back into the organization and/or into environment I. (Environment II is nested within environment I.)

[Feedback lines]

Figure 2.1
Transformations of communications to and within police communication systems. The mechanics of the movement of calls through the two systems is depicted.

A *signal* is the physical embodiment of a message, which is a sign event or an instance of a sign type. A *message* is an ordered selection from an agreed set of signs intended to communicate information. When a call is made about an event or object, it is a signal, a sign event. It becomes a message when encoded, that is, when it is transformed from one representation to another by operators applying coding rules to classify a message. A *channel* is a communication vehicle. Police *technology* includes radios, telephones, computers, recorders, telex and teleprinters, and visual display units. It is a means of sending and receiving messages across boundaries 1 and 2, between the organization and environments I and II, and within the organization from subsystem to subsystem. It is also used to send messages from subsystems to environments I and II. The sources are variously social organized and informationally based networks (Leaf 1972).

The framing in the encoding stage is both literal and figurative. Physically a message becomes a police call when it passes boundary 1, and it becomes an instance in the cognitive world (a signifier) when placed within the classification system.

It is useful to think of the signal becoming a message call in subsystem 1, an incident in subsystem 2, and a job in subsystem 3. A record is created in subsystem 1 and is transformed as it moves form that subsystem to subsystem 3. It can be recycled and transformed if it is fed back into environment I and reenters the organization as a call signal. The object-even-call-incident-job-record transformation is not necessarily linear, because face-to-face communication with a citizen can be a basis for undertaking a job and incidents can be created without calls. The basic forms of the communicational flow should be understood as cognitive partitions of a process and as organizational fictions for freezing this process.

basis for a notification of the police; a sample of them become *objects* cast out for police attention.[1] An object is an event cast in a new social form selected for transmission to police attention as defined by the caller. It is selected from among the range of events coming to the caller's attention. Environment I, from which calls arise, is the world of primary experience or the commonsense world (Schutz 1964).

The world of signs and sign systems is differentially organized, and these systems vary in their degree of coherence and stability (Guiraud 1975; Needham 1978, 1979, 1980, 1981).[2] Signs may be placed in new contexts and thus transformed in meaning.

This *transformational* or interpretive problem is unsolved in semiotic analyses. It is not known, for example, how precisely sign systems in which the signifier-signified links are relatively context bound, such as everyday conceptions of crime and morality, are interpolated with formal sign systems, such as the legal code or police classification systems [see, for example, Sudnow (1965), Cicourel (1968), Reiss (1971), and Waegel (1981)]. Even translation of crime categories in various segments of organizations is not well understood (Kitsuse and Cicourel 1963; Hulbert 1981a, Jorgensen 1981; Bottomley and Coleman 1980; Ekblom and Heal 1982). The task here, in part, is to sort out the transformation of one set of codes into another using calls from the public to the police and observations and interviews. Let us consider calls more specifically.

An Example

A caller rings the police, reports "my house has been broken into," and gives a name and address. The call is framed as a message and typed onto a visual display unit (VDU) according to a set format in a given order. The key item in the format (one of some eleven syntagms in the organization studied) is the category it is given by the operator. There are thirty categories used by the police studied (it can be double-categorized and/or recategorized). This is the basis for further assignments by police controllers, who are sent the message from the operators. This call will be given an "11": burglary house/dwelling. The connection between the classification system and the encoding done by a given operator, that is, how this operator decides the call is about a burglary, is informal and tacit, but there is a systematic relationship between the units and the classificatory system or code (Manning 1985). The work of establishing connections, or hearing "11" as burglary or "06" as assault, is done by implicit understandings or contrasts between the expressions (the categories) and the contents (the words) and differences between expressions and other expressions and contents and other contents. "11" (a content) is linked to burglary (an expression); they denote each other. Established conventions within the police mean that one is heard and seen as the other.

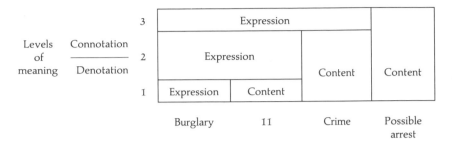

Figure 2.2
An example of denotative and connotative meanings of the sign 11/burglary in the BPD.

As seen in figure 2.2, the sign (11/burglary), a combination of expression and content, can act as an expression for yet another content, crime. Crime is a more connotative meaning supplied by officers in the fields. "Crime" can then become an expression for another content, possible arrest. Each of these linked sets, layered one on the other, is part of a signifying chain. Seen as a whole, however, the message 11/burglary can be placed into a cognitive grouping of other similar calls or put within an associative context or paradigm. The associative context may have to do with the action requirements of the call, its potential for good police work, or what was done to dispose of it. The most obvious distinction or context is crime and noncrime calls, because crime calls are much sought and well regarded by officers.

Through this work of encoding, formatting, interpreting, and placing in context, police message processing converts or transforms calls into jobs (see figure 2.1) and produces a layering of meanings that moves a long way from the social world of the caller. It is precisely this process of text-message production that a semiotic analysis deciphers.

A call from environment I (see figure 2.1 under "calls") is a *signal* construed as a *message* (see figure 2.1 caption). The phone is one of several channels by which a signal can arrive: walking into a police station, contacting an officer on the street, letters, etc. Other channels are used to transmit the message through the organization. The number of calls reaching the center is patterned by social arrangements and by the number and capacity of channels available to carry messages, the number of personnel available to answer and dispose of calls, and the workload (number of calls per hour per person per phone line). The conditions under which any call on any channel actually "penetrates" the several boundaries of the police organization is partially a function of the character of the environment the police define and enact and partially a function of other aspects of the physical and social environment not under direct police control.

The technology conveys communications arising in variously organized sources to the police (Leaf 1972). The police, as a general type of information-processing system, receive messages from both highly organized and loosely organized social *networks*. These are linked systems of relationships along which communication flows. From a communications theory perspective the police mostly process messages from loosely organized information-sending systems. They are loose in the sense that the few links that connect people in the networks tend not to overlap and are used infrequently (Granovetter 1973). Messages arising from loosely organized social networks are therefore quite diverse. Noise is anything that interferes with a valued signal. Noise and equivocality, doubt on the part of the receiver concerning the content of the message, exist in both loosely and tightly structured networks. Information, for the moment considered the choice one has when choosing a message from a set (Shannon and Weaver 1964, p. 9), is a function of selection and construction and exists in both internal systems (organizational subsystems) and external systems. Internal communication is also accompanied by noise and equivocality, which vary by segments within the organization. The MPD and the BPD are capable of receiving, processing, and producing messages with high information value because the internal system allows a wide latitude of choice among possible communicative acts. Furthermore, the choice of one communicative act does not determine the choice of another.

The idea of a message is conceptual. Some of the extended complexities of the notion are examined later. However, once a message is seen as phenomenological [an ordered selection from an agreed set of signs intended to communicate information (Cherry 1978, glossary)], a number of issues present themselves. A message can be defined positively by saying what it is and providing criteria about which arguments can be made: What is "ordered"? By whom? How are they selected? What degree of agreement is involved and between what parties? (Linguistics uses the fiction of the ideal speaker-hearer dyad). What is "intention," and how is it displayed? Information, however defined, is still only one aspect of a communicational sequence or act. A message can also be defined negatively, as what it is not—the social stimuli, setting, assumptions, and expectations of participants that surround the message.

Not all calls, visits, radio receptions, and transmissions are recorded, even though this is required by police regulations (McCabe and Sutcliffe 1978; Smith and Gray 1983). This suggests that other matters operate in the definition of what will be considered a message. One organizationally based definition is: *A message is something for which a result must be shown to have been produced* (Smith and Gray 1983, pp. 27–28). The message system is intended to ensure that, once entered and acted on or not, a result will be shown. The system depends on prior unrecorded decisions made about whether a call, bit of information, telex, or advisory will be recorded. Conversely, if someone decides that nothing will be done or an incident arises about which one does not want to act or record an action, it will not be officially entered. Recorded messages do not signify what sort of information determined why they were recorded.

In some sense a message is an analytic fiction because the message context, or the social stimuli and assumptions that surround the message, and the resultant text become elided in the course of movement of communicational units through the police communications system. However, separation of the message from noise, activities, and context is a primary concern in all three subsystems (operators, controllers, officers), as is ascertaining the salient facts of a given message.

Messages can be viewed as infinitely varied and complex. The structure of a police communications system can be considered a rational means for producing decisions. They are contexts for the working out of the relationships between infinity and rationality. Luhmann (1980) defines rationality, following Leibniz, "as highest variety combined with nevertheless reliable order." Rationality, Luhmann contends, means "utilizing infinity without losing the possibility to decide." Furthermore, it would appear that organizational structures represent different ways of coping with infinity and different ways of proposing rationality. The capacity of the organization to structure itself to respond to the degree of complexity of the environment is in part a function of the degree of social organization of the message sources or networks to which it routinely responds (Simon 1982; Weick 1979).

Sources of Calls: Network and Response

There are three types of call sources:[3] (1) Calls from citizens at large can enter police communications centers from either the 911 or 999 number (defined as "emergency numbers") or from the other "nonemergency" seven- and eight-digit numbers. These calls can include a wide range of bits of information. The set of messages emitted by citizens, seen as a source or socially organized network, is characterized by high entropy. These are high-information calls from poorly organized networks or sources. (2) Calls can be received within the communications centers from subdivisions or precincts from other locales within the police telecommunications systems. Calls from the public are transferred by a switchboard to the center from general police lines. These calls are issued from more organized entropic networks and are considered semiorganized sources. (3) Calls can be received from single message channels, alarms,

Table 2.1

Processing of messages from variously organized sources: Information, meaning, and predictability of behavioral response to calls

Message source[a]	Level of information	Meaning	Action	Resultant sequences of behavior
Highly organized (low entropy)	Low	Various, conventionalized, restricted, and explicit.	Ritualized	Highly predictable
Semiorganized (medium entropy).	Medium	Semiconventionalized, limited, and implicit.	Semiritualized.	Predictable
Poorly organized (high entropy).	High	Complex, elaborated, and implicit.	Instrumental, practical.	Unpredictable

a. Noise and equivocality accompany transmissions from all three sources.

fire and ambulance calls, and from other direct line "customers" such as the state government, banks, and large commercial establishments. These are low-information calls because the source is highly organized, the set of messages produced is extremely limited, and the call either is made, in which case action is required, or not. The channel or mode of communication inself—the direct line—is strongly marked and differentiated from other sources.[4]

In table 1, note that highly organized sources yield low-information messages, whereas poorly organized sources yield high-information messages. Because there are several channels operating into and out of the central control rooms, any measure of uncertainty must take into account the number of channels and the number of messages. Following the progress of messages from highly organized sources further, as shown in table 2.1, one can see that the meaning of most messages is "vacuous" or highly conventionalized because of the nature of the source. These messages produce a highly predictable, nonproblematic, and ritualistic response and are associated with highly predictable action sequences. Response to an alarm call is set by policy, and procedures are written, stipulated in detail, and carefully monitored. Messages from internal or somewhat organized sources contain medium information, semiconventionalized meanings, and some implicit or context-bound particulars and tend to produce a selection of known behavioral sequences. Messages from poorly organized sources yield with greater probability the likelihood of high-information messages, those that are meant to convey meanings derived from the contrast between messages. These calls tend to be associated with practical instrumental acts and to arrive in unpredictable sequences.

Once calls cross the organizational boundary and become a part of the police communications system, they are *encoded* or classified using general procedures, thereby producing greater certainty in their subsequent handling. They are also given a priority and a preliminary subclassification. Assignment of the call as a classified incident further reduces uncertainty. Action and disposition of the job by the officer completes a call cycle.

Table 2.1 also glosses the nature of the social organization of response to calls. The most frequent types of calls, emanating from low-organization high-information sources, cross organizational boundaries and are encoded as organizationally relevent messages. This involves *classification*, or deciding what rules exist for making sense of such messages. The operations of the center in effect place greater constraints on the message and reduce the uncertainty of the messages forwarded to the controller. Messages received there can be seen in terms of the information sent in the incident format. The potential number of items of information is at this point infinite. At the dispatch level the meaning of the message changes as a result of the interface between the controller and the officers. If passed on by the operators, messages are increasingly limited in information content, because for each message, viewing an incident as a message, constraints are produced by the items required and the format used. The range of possible actions is established in part by the status-activity codes for units or officers (their current tasks) and by event classifications.

Under the "Encoding" column in figure 2.1 are listed the effects on incoming messages as and when they cross boundary 1, which is the symbolic line between environment I and the organization. When messages are received at boundary 1 of the police organization, they are received within a context of *assumptions* based on the police and organizational culture; they are given a *form* based on these assumptions about the nature of the world of events reported in the objects formulated in the calls. This is the work of constituting the object world of the citizen, a fundamental yet invisible transformation that converts one set of signs into another and so converts events in one social world into signs located in another social world, the police organization.

Thus far the source and type of messages arising in environment I producing *general* police response have been described. A complex process of further differentiation occurs within the organization. Messages are processed as a set and as discrete separable and noncontexted communicational units. In what follows I integrate the social organization of cognition with technology, roles, ecology, and organizational procedures. First, I describe the nature of the objects of police concern as seen in environment I. Events in environment I are constituted in the police organization with the following character:

1. All events reported or encountered are problematic and constitute a selected sample of all such events that have recently occurred. If reported, the reasons for such a report are not intrinsic to the event itself but are the result of a combination of social forces that lie behind the reporting, for example, social values and interests, hidden agendas, emotions such as revenge and envy, and the event proper.

2. All events are uncertain as to when they will appear, the sequence or order in which they appear, the frequency with which they appear, and their consequences and content.

3. All events change temporally and spatially. They are shaped by inter-personal forces, are phenomenologically variable, and continue to change regardless of what actions are taken, what is said to have been done, or what is seen to have been done. Their interpretative contours are a function of observers' perceptions, interests, and perspectives.

4. All events communicated in a call or description to the police are problematic in the sense that events are on the ground *and* because the caller expresses a form of self-interest in making the call and may distort, omit, forget, lie, fabricate, conflate, or otherwise confuse the details of the tale. Such processes are always present to an unknown and variable degree.

5. The event, as it reaches the attention of police, unless directly observed by the officer to whom it is referred or by a trusted colleague, is assumed to have been processed or encoded imprecisely (written, classified, encoded, characterized) by observers (especially civilians) who are not likely to have brought the proper degree of doubt to the observation, recording, and classification of the event as reported in the call. The event could have been related in another form with other details and other salient features. Garfinkel (1967) notes that there is always more or less that could be said about a given event.

6. The ever-changing event is altered in character with each change in segment in the organization, each form of technology, and each passing moment. Stylistic aspects are added to the processes of distortion. The event as received must always be "read off" as having been transmitted through a system and interpreted. Signifiers are variables rather than fixed entities, as are the signified.

7. Calls and incidents, as recorded, have a problematic relationship to the actual event. The written record, the job, the incident, the call, and the event are phenomenologically distinct and differentially coded social objects.

8. Events given formal names and classified are seen as being taken out of context, or "decontextualized." They cannot be easily reconstituted or "back-translated" into the code of the street or into everyday observed experience. They have a tentative and problematic status vis-à-vis the reported events, the call, the incident as processed, a formal record, and the event as observed when the officer arrives on the scene. Unlike a videotape, the picture cannot be reversed to review the scene as it actually happened. Everything changes and is changed, except the fact of the preeminence of this rule of fluid interpretation.

This outline for the description of events is an abstract gloss of the fundamental grounds for the relevant social constitution and nature of the world as seen by the operators, dispatchers, and officers. The objects so constituted float in the unseen world beyond the immediate experience of those who process calls. Events reported in calls await precise classification, and classification is an organizational matter. They are problematic in this special fashion as events to be considered relevant.

The organization always stands in some symbolically mediated relationship to events; events are presented as sets of signs. It is the precise nature of this symbolic mediation that requires further explication. No "deeper" truth lies "behind" or "under" this symbolic system; there is no question of peeling back a layer of reality to penetrate more "closely" or "deeply" toward "truth." It is patently unavailable.

When a call crosses boundary 1 and is encoded, it moves from one system of discourse to another or between overlapping and multiple discourses [compare Goffman (1974) with Derrida (1976)]. This alters the nature of the objects constituted in the observational fields.[5] It would appear further that there is a functional aspect to marking such transitions and in marking messages within discourse systems. Bateson (1972, pp. 177–193) uses as an example the message "This is a play" (a message about a message), noting that animals signal that what follows is not real fighting but play at fighting. He argues that this communicative skill is shared with humans.

Bateson shows that communication between persons is *framed* in such a way that people can differentiate types of experience and understand the rules that apply for ordering it, transforming it, and communicating that knowledge to others. This framing is metacommunication (Jakobson 1960), or communication about the relations between the message and the code. Framing, for example, is done verbally in one force studied, the MPD, when a call is answered, "Police, where is the problem?" It assumes that there is a problem, that there is a police-relevant problem, one that can be "solved" by such a call, and that the caller is "motivated" by the wish to have the police respond to the reported event. Framing produces a context patterned through time, insofar as messages sent to the police are processed and thus transformed from one sort of story or message into another. The context, all that is recognized by the communicators and is not the message, frames the message and places it in a social relationship with other communications. The inability to recognize changes in logic and changes in code can create "double binds," or the simultaneous relevance of two contexts that are, in turn, not discriminated as "different" in meaning and therefore contain different action implications (Bateson 1972, pp. 201–227).

A boundary may be a "rim" (Goffman 1974, p. 82), a physical anchor such as the ecology of a police station (Holdaway 1980) or shifts in roles and tasks by location. Frames can be voided or violated as a way of communicating the negation of the assumed context, as when Van Gogh painted yellow chrysanthemums on the "frame" as well as on the "canvas" or when novels are written in indented short phrases and highly associative and metaphoric poetic style.

Once in the organization, messages are subject to *interpretative work* that involves message handling. Message handling requires delineating the message from noise and the field and supplying an ordering frame. *Internal message analysis* involves establishing the meaning of a message, or how to "read" a message. These elements of interpretative procedures seem to be minimally relevant for the kind of interactional competence necessary for the production of everyday social structures. They provide a link between sociolinguistic activities and cognitive processes (Cicourel 1973, pp. 168–169).

The socially relevant cognitive properties of messages animate the analysis of message processing; they are not formalized or written but understood even though they are not given in the semantics, syntax, or grammar of the communication. They are used to understand these matters and how they are to be seen in relation to the social world (Levinson 1983). They may be related to certain contexts or to the relevant aspects of the social and psychological world that the user assumes in a given time (Levinson 1983, p. 23); these may include cognitive attributions, such as matters of how to choose level of formality, topic, speaker, next speaker, subject matter, and topic of a talk. Context gives talk its spatial and temporal location when utterances do not contain specific references to these matters. Context-derived cues are used to understand past references and future references of talk and to normalize violations and exceptions in order to maintain contact. Assumed properties of talk are used to link short- and long-term memory of topics and information, general rules, and particular cases and overall are the background against which information and meaning are articulated within organizational context. As such, they are used to transform communicational units.

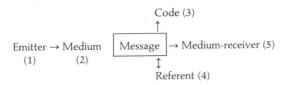

Figure 2.3
Jakobson's (1960) functions of the sign.

Internal Message Analysis

Messages, communicational units inside the organization, are social forms processed regardless of content and have an internal structure and meaning that is constituted and reconstituted through time. This suggests the utility of a model of communication.

The problem of orientation to communication can be traced following a semiotic model introduced by Jakobson (see figure 2.3). The function of the sign according to Jakobson is to communicate ideas. These can be grouped as messages. This implies, according to Guiraud (1975, p. 5), a referent or object, a sign, a code or set of rules for interpretation, a means of transmission or channel, a sender, and a receiver. Figure 2.3 shows that any one of functions of the message, or indeed several, can operate at the cognitive level. Unfortunately the abstract character of this model omits the social context within which such messages are created, communicated, interpreted, and/or misunderstood.

The numbers indicate the modes of cognitive orientation or functional aspects of the message. Orientation to the sender-message connection is the emotive function (1); orientation to the receiver-message connection (2) is the cognitive function; orientation to the message itself is the poetic function (3); orientation to the objects to which signs refer (if they do) is the referential function (4); and orientation to communication itself, as a framing of meaning or ritual act, is the phatic function (5). Semiotics itself is a framework for analyzing communication, especially the metalinguistic function or communication about communication.

A series of problems results from using a linguistic and semiotic model of the communication system. How are the participants *oriented* to the messages? There are five modes in addition to the message itself. Second, what are the possible channels of communication within the various segments of the police organization? What are the effects or consequences of each orientation on the message in the communications system? If speakers are oriented, for example, to the informational aspects of the message, what aspects of human communication (affective symbolism, contact among people, shared values) are depressed in salience? What metalinguistic (social) aspects of the communication operate in an organization to allow people to know what code is being used? This is particularly important in police-public communications, in which at least some shared understanding is essential to providing a response.

Although I am concerned primarily with message processing regardless of content, internal message analysis with an emphasis on content and form occupies some of the discussion. Police messages are formal narratives with instrumental purposes organized and structured by classification, social organization, and technology.

The analytic form of processed messages is a product of the level at which messages are seen within the organization. At one level messages are produced within an organizational format. At another level messages contain bits of information (syntagms) that can be organized and reorganized as to salience and connections made with bits of information in that message or another. They may be reorganized analytically to create other messages.

Once the units and their relationships are sorted out, another level of analysis is possible, a level suggested by formal analysis of literary texts.[6] In searching for the narrative and deep structure of police messages, it is assumed that alternative surface structures can be produced by the same deep structures and that a limited sample of messages can suggest some of these patterns. A given statement can yield diverse surface structures, each presenting an interpretative problem. A structural analysis of messages cannot eliminate alternative readings of deep structure.[7]

The rules governing the production of observed multiple meanings are unknown. Analysis can only represent them in several paradigmatic formulations.[8] Even given a range of codes [such as those identified by Barthes (1974)] and associated constitutive conventions, islands of agreement are known to have been mapped. My analysis has the advantage of exploiting a point of view or modality of discourse that is partially and publicly shared by participants in the police communications system. This is now described.

When questions of surface and deep structure are examined within an institution, some known and shared connections linking experience, plans, and conventions for communicating and understanding messages can be discovered (Halbwachs 1980; Douglas 1986). Messages are nested within shared conventions about communication, narrative modalities, genres, and institutions. Police calls are made meaningful because they draw on knowledge and experience with "calling the cops" and related culturally sanctioned sources of organized meaning.[9] Internal messages analysis views the message as the *textual unit*, which is format based. A set of syntagms or units of meaning are derived from the notion that every message contains a proposition or action carried out by a named person, object, or thing directed toward, away from, or about another that is modified by various descriptions. It is told in the first instance from a point of view (the caller reports to the operator) and subsequently translated into police-neutral third-party present-tense modality. The resultant discourse uses the symbolic repertoire of members of the occupational culture of policing; thus calls about events become incidents in a rhetorical stream of police discourse. Stories of human woe, for example, become mere instantiations of classification. From a linguistic point of view this constitutes an analysis of narratives, or stories: "everyday communication devices that provide for the development, climax and denouement of action in the context of a defined collection of actors, means, motives and scenes" (Bennett and Feldman 1981, p. 7). Stories tell about a critical event normally assumed to be in the object world using a narrative perspective, a plot (sequence of cumulative events with a tacit outcome), and a central point or focus around which lie the inferential connected or supporting elements.[10] From these detailed analyses of text understanding spring the bases for the criticisms of technologically based police communications systems and, more generally, technology in organization context.

The processing of messages, encompassing first distinguishing the message from noise and the field and placing it in an ordering conception or frame, is not based exclusively on message content. Subcultural or setting-specific connotative meanings are also associated with message processing. Internal message analysis assumes the effects of message handling. Internal message analysis shifts focus rather more to content. It seeks to work with and through examples of deep and surface structure relationships to depict types of messages. The deep structure of messages is further explored in terms of formulaic conceptions in the subsystems of the MPD and the BPD. The derivation of "deep structure" is based on identification of units, assigning them to syntagmatic units and paradigmatic categories (associative contexts), discovering the salience of each of the units for organizing the action implications of the message, and relating these units, categories, and salience rankings to surrounding understandings or tacit knowledge.

Although interpretative practices, the pragmatics of message processing, reify cognition, knowledge, understanding, and the like, making the message socially real, internal message analysis shifts attention to what the message is thought to contain. These practices are attached to various roles and tasks but are not synonymous with them. Therefore internal message analysis is affected by the subsystem within which it occurs. It is possible to identify the sytagms and paradigms used in each subsystem and to see how in a given selected set of messages they are given salience. Surrounding understandings may alter the salience of the units as well as what units are taken into account in action decisions.

In subsequent chapters, especially chapters 4 and 5, I examine the movement of messages within each subsystem. It is something like showing a series of pictures or slides of message processing in each of the subsystems in the BPD and the MPD. In chapter 6, however, I analyze the cumulative aspects of message movement *across* the three subsystems. I build on and presume the knowledge of organizational structure but detail a "counterstructure" or imagery that arises from the problem of imagining a communicational unit to have been transformed and to have stable, enduring features.

Content and Logic

In the previous chapter I claimed that the police require frequent and extensive communications with the public yet must control and discriminate among types of demand. Technology is seen as a solution to this communication problem. The result is that the police are increasingly technology dependent. The police argued that additional technology will "solve" the communications problem and many other operational problems faced by large urban forces. However, features of police organizations, occupational culture, and communications systems constrain new modes of technologically based command and control.

I outline the background of police communication, the setting of the MPD and the BPD, and methods employed in the study in chapter 3. I include a brief summary of the development of police communications and the communications technology in the two forces. I also describe the processing of communication in the two organizations. The primary focus of analysis is the police communications system that disposes of internally and externally sourced calls and other communications. I argue that the workings of the organizations are a fusion of thought, action, and technology.

The Logic of the Analysis

The logic of the analysis organizes the chapters that describe the two police organizations. The scheme is shown in figure 2.4. Chapters 4 and 5 compare the British BPD and the American MPD, with a focus on the place of the police communications system in the two. Each system is seen as being composed of three subsystems: (1) operators, (2) controllers/dispatchers, and (3) officers. The four variables of the subsystems are coding and classification, technology, roles and tasks, and interpretative practices. Within each organization the subsystems are the context for analyzing the effect of the four variables on communicational units that pass through. There are five communicational units or forms that a message takes when moving through the system: a telephone call, an incident, an

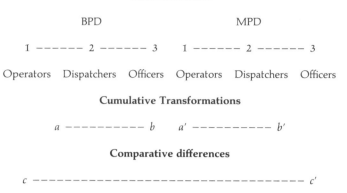

Figure 2.4
The logic of the analysis.

assignment, a job, and a record. At times the term "message" is used to gloss these, as is the term "communicational unit."

My overall aim is to clarify how the variables affect the communicational units within the subsystems and what happens when messages move from the world of everyday life of the caller to the police communications system and across it. This is undertaken in two modes: a synchronic mode, used in chapters 4 and 5, and a diachronic mode, used in chapter 6. Chapters 4 and 5 address sets of relationships one at a time, whereas chapter 6 attempts to examine the process of movement itself, providing a new context for the diachronic analysis.

Chapters 4 and 5 contain the ethnographic materials bearing on transformations and cumulative transformations. Each of the four variables is considered for each of the three subsystems in order. Although this format may be a bit tedious and rigid and perhaps somewhat repetitive despite efforts to reduce reiteration and reference to previous discussions, it is necessary to establish these detailed ethnographic facts in order to build the case for comparative analysis. A mere combination of chapters 4 and 5 would have highlighted the similarities and reduced the differences between the BPD and the MPD. However, I want to demonstrate the subtle cumulative differences in message processing that can be identified with organizational structures and the conferral of meaning independent or regardless of the nature of the message set and message content.

The movement of any set of communicational units from subsystem 1 to 2 and from subsystem 2 to 3 in both organizations is effected by classification, technology, roles and tasks, and interpretative practices and is called a transformation. There are two transformations in each subsystem, indicated by the lines drawn between subsystems 1 and 2 and 2 and 3 on figure 2.4. They show the movement of the units from operators to dispatchers and from dispatchers to officers in both systems. These transformations occur regardless of the size of the message set and, most important, regardless of the level and meaning of the information contained in the message. The analysis of transformations examines the impact of the four variables within the subsystems on message units. Transformations across subsystems are system properties and make the transmission and processing of any communicational unit possible. The most subtle analytic problem arises in understanding interpretative practices, where content becomes relatively important in the sense that differences between message and field and between message and noise and in the ordering frame employed by operators, controllers, and officers are sought. Within-message variation is a focus.

The transformations summed, or cummulative transformations (see figure 2.4), result from the movement of the communicational units from subsystem 1 to subsystem 3 or the movement shown by the lines drawn from a to b and from a' to b' in the two organizations. The inference is that the full movement across the police communications system in each organization is more than the additive effects of the individual transformations.

Having established the noninformational effects on message movement within the organizations, it is possible to compare them. Comparison of the differences between the two organizations with respect to transformations and cumulative transformations is called the analysis of comparative differences (see figure 2.4). They result from comparison of the differences between the differences cumulated within the communications systems of the two police organizations and are indicated by the lines drawn from c to c'.

The informational and noninformational effects on message processing is defined here as primarily an organizational question. The purpose of the elaborate analytic framework is to decompose the effects within these contexts and then to assess the overall organizational effect(s) of the variables, subsystems, and processing activities. The organizational comparison, indicated in figure 2.4 by the line between the two organizations and subsuming the previous inferences, are usually glossed by terms such as "organizational structure," "organizational effects," or simply "organization." Organizational comparisons require an analysis of change as it occurs across organizations and how that change is contrasted with stability.

Chapter 6 is devoted to diachronic analysis of message processing in which sources of stability and change in the message-processing system are analyzed. In order to understand change, one requires a stable background of those matters taken to maintain stability or order. These are not matters explained by the message-processing system itself. To some degree, message and workload do affect processes of stability and change in meaning, but they are assumed to vary and not to exceed the normal limits that are the context of this analysis. Through this analysis of police communications systems, one begins to see that organizations and society have continuing and important shaping effects on message processing and that this in turn allows one to glimpse the limits of a purely informationally driven or technologically determined model of message transmission.

In chapter 7 I assess the ethnographic material, a brief case study of the uses of technology, in terms of technological conceit (the notion that police communication problems can be solved finally by technology) and explore the transparent constraints on computerized information-based systems of command and control. In chapter 8 I examine the utility of structuralism for the analysis of organizational communication.

Limits on the Analysis

I have a precise focus, and this could be an important limitation. I assume that transformations of data from the event to the record are loose and limp and far too complicated to describe entirely in variable terms. My view is closer to that advocated by Weick (1979), Garfinkel (1967) and Kitsuse and Cicourel (1963) than to studies that attempt to trace the flow of information from the public to the police organization (Spelman and Brown 1981). The aim of my analysis is not to trace the "attrition" of data from event to call to message to incident to job assignment, and record but to describe phenomenologically all that constitutes the background that makes possible such notions as transformation, tracing, flow charting, and input/output analyses and models of such matters called cost-benefits or cost-effectiveness studies (Clark and Hough 1984).

My conceptual focus means that no data are presented on such matters as the time lapse between various stages in the process of message transmittal (the questions addressed in response-time research), the pattern of attrition from events to records or at any two stages in between, or the correlations between units at different stages (for example, correlations between types of events based on victim reports or calls with assignments completed). Within the categories no data are presented on the distribution of events, calls, messages, etc. at any stage in the subsystem of the two organizations. I present some data on level of work, types of calls, and classifications. These are meant to point to a direction or sort of base for action. I also present categories or types of data seen to be relevant at each stage, such as the workload of the controllers, but I give the empirical distribution only to indicate some of the boundaries on choice rather than to characterize the overall nature of the level of work in the two organization.

There are many sound theoretical reasons why such data were not gathered and, if gathered, not presented. Studies that take any set of indicators, such as police response time based on types of call, are misleading. For example, they rarely compare the classifications made by operators of the calls and the actual events discovered by the officers or the officers' interpretation of the call as they hear it contrasted with the information provided to them by the dispatcher. Studies that describe the process of "dispatching" as a series of binary choices made on the basis of police allocation procedures, hazard formulas, and workload rarely take into account the situated nature of the decision process [for an exception, see Lineberry (1977)]. Such studies as Scott and Percy's (1983) in my view mistakenly posit undemonstrated decision bases and *assume* that call classifications, either by their scheme or as used by the police, affect the decisions to send a car, priority decisions, and resource allocation. Because no evidence demonstrates how this takes place, a black box view of police work results.

Many studies take the distribution of calls or the types of assignments undertaken to be indicative of the workload of the police (Cumming et al. 1965; Wilson 1968; Lilly 1978). Unfortunately no studies have addressed the question of how categories of police calls are construed by officers at various points in the process. Thus the researchers project call classifications forward and backward *as if* they were nonproblematic in character, reliable, and valid. Researchers have noted the invalid nature of police classifications (Ekblom and Heal 1982; Davis 1983) or have reclassified police data into their own schemes (Scott and Percy 1983). However, the relationship between these classification systems and other aspects of the police operation is assumed rather than examined.

I provide no data on "outcomes" or results of the calls; nor do I attempt to measure or compare the distribution of types of calls of various sorts across or between organizations. I am not studying the effect of various symbolic transformations on what the police do in the field. I am studying facets of police officers' behavior. Because I am concerned primarily with the police communications system for processing citizen-based calls to the police from less-organized networks, I do not speak to the relationships between this system and other systems of control within the police. For example, many units have little contact with police communications systems and operate on their own (specialized squads, detective units, and ranks higher than sergeant).

Background, Settings, and Method

The phenomenological analysis of organizations emphasizes the role of organizations in absorbing, processing, and producing symbols in the form of messages.

Organizations

The primary context within which metaphors, systems of interpretation, or sign systems are found in complex society is organizations. Several characteristics of organizations as systems of codes and signs are critical to the argument. Organizations are a means by which "nature" or the multivocal external world is converted into a "culture," in this case the organizational domain. Organizations have an ecological location, a physical reality in specific settings, times, and places. They posses permeable boundaries and technologies and manifest resultant sociotechnical activity systems. Organizations avidly seek communicational materials, obtain, enfold, and produce symbolic differentiation, and so structure themselves. This is their symbolic work. In a sense organizations convert raw experience into messages; they see, grasp at, disclose, sort out, classify, and symbolically mark these messages and transform them from one code into another. Organizations are not only semantic but also syntactic processing systems, for they convert message sequences according to rules and principles of communication.

Police organizations are drama absorbing, drama processing, and drama producing; they assign new signifieds to old signifiers. Police organizations in particular collect and transform messages received from the public: They maintain a binocular vision, converting calls for help into classified incidents. The police possess, reflect, use, and manipulate systems of signs that produce culturally and socially meaningful differentiation and constraint. The police map onto the social world their implicit vertical and horizontal rankings and their understandings of social causation, justice, truth, obligation, duty, and the character of social and juridically bounded relations. The primary products of police organizations are thus symbolic—

messages conveying statements to social groups about their moral well-being, their social position (horizontal and vertical rankings), identity, and status—and the degree of their acceptance often passes for news on American television. This imagery requires unpacking to reveal a number of facets and their origins.

A Working Definition of Organization

These arguments suggest that organizational work is self-referential activity sometimes glossed as product, production, or output. The gloss results from the reflexive and recursive nature of the organization-environment interchange: Meanings arising within the organization are enacted in the everyday actions of the organization, a bounded system of systematic and repeated interaction that is relatively permanent in time and place. The cognitive mapping of the organization and the environment by members is based not only on information but also on typifications based on organizational perspectives rooted in a powerful fashion in what members of segments are required to do. Organizations are phenomena, representations of the meaning of membership, lenses by which the problem of the external world are routinized and made available to members, and power systems. To some degree organizations define, structure, and shape the environment in which they operate. They must try to define the reality of the external world, mobilize strategies that are seen to address the relevant aspects of the external world, and engage in confirmatory and validating operations. They tacitly and formally encode the environment, process it, decode it, and socially affirm its salient features. The "social construction" of the environment results as the interpretative work of organizational members is accomplished: They are socialized into organizational motives, contingencies, and teamwork such that they can collectively make sense of negotiated situations; they engage in interactional sequences that serve to differentiate and integrate organizational segments; they absorb tacitly shared assumptions and emergent definitions of contingent situations; and they learn the principles, working rules, and practices thought to be the commonsense basis of the occupation.

Organizations are also resources for conceptualizing, assessing, and coping strategically with perceived threats from the posited environment and in many respects therefore are political entities. Organizational members create and maintain the fiction of the existence and reference of a particular sort of environment, especially in people-processing organizations, in order to protect, expand, or consolidate a mandate or political domain. They will, for example, manipulate performance figures, distort intelligence and misuse it systematically and intentionally to create "crime waves," and develop new, often self-serving strategies in response to their own assembled environmental creation. These actions are based on male bonding, "shared misunderstandings," and the like that flesh out the contours of the external world while affirming its existence and defining as constraining the ways in which it demands strategic solutions. Inevitably the organization stands as a representation of what is posited and maintains a recursive existence. From the perspective of the persistent ambiguity in the nature of the external-internal division, one can examine the centrality of the interplay among an occupational culture, internal rules and controls, and a posited environment. They remain locked in a powerfully determined play.

Information, which shapes police organizations, police function, and police imagery (what is expected by the public of the police), is central to the character of organizations. In this chapter I move closer to the actual operation of police communications systems to examine in detail the process of interpreting messages: calls to the police and how they are defined, what they signify, and the organizational consequences of this message processing.

From a symbolic point of view the multivocality of messages cannot be compressed between organizational doors; nor can human feelings, pain, anguish, concern, lust, and violence be shattered, transmogrified into the awkward and vulgar language of information or system, or classified once and for all as a matter of record. There are some things about which one cannot easily speak. The struggle for unity of experience, faced repeatedly by many, at once both logical and aesthetic, is, like language itself, something that one might construe as a panhuman characteristic. The struggle from my perspective is found in organizations, symbolic machinery that is mostly working out of sight of commonly guided observing.

Police Communications

The dispersal of officers in space, their diverse duties, the wide range of situations that they are expected to encounter, and the "temptations" of the job have always been thought of as impediments to full and proper control and supervision of the police (Reith 1956; Miller 1977; Radzinowicz 1968). The wish to overcome the taint of application and control of violence, the absence of other alternatives, and the potential for corruption lead to the appeal of the quasi-military model of police discipline (Bittner 1970, pp. 52–54). But the thin thread that draws together, integrates, coerces, and otherwise binds the loyal person to the organization subtlely has weakened in the past hundred years. The basic work, a set of tasks, outlooks, and public encounters, has changed little.

It would appear that the initial notion that character combined with control would yield a coercible and tractable force (Miller 1977, ch. 1) was altered as notions of moral character changed and the environment of policing become ethnically diverse and politicized in new ways in American cities [see Fogelson (1977) and Bittner's brilliant review of it (1978)]. The hope became increasingly one that organizational control and decoupling from urban political machines would produce prudence and discipline. Tensions between the two arose, for close adherence to rules and regulations were counterproductive to other achievements expected of members of the organization, for example, as indexes of diverse activity (Bittner 1970, ch. 8). In the 1920s, with the rationalization of modern police administration occurring in and through the writings of L. Fuld, Raymond Fosdick, August Vollmer, Bruce Smith, O. W. Wilson, and others (Stead 1977), technological conceit came perniciously into its own. Goldstein, in a perceptive summary article, claims: "Indeed, the emphasis on internal management [in the writings of Vollmer, et al.] was so strong that professional policing was defined primarily as the application of modern management concepts to the running of a police department" (Goldstein 1979, p. 238).

With this emphasis in the early twentieth century, an important transformation was initiated. Although the hopes of the first commissioners of the London Metropolitan Police lay in recruitment, training, supervision, and clear statements of police powers and the role of the constable at common law (Marshall 1965) in the context of organizational rules and regulations, modern twentieth-century police administrators turned first to organizational and then to technological solutions. In the period best chronicled by Fogelson (1977), the transition to a professional, scientifically administered, well-managed, and politically neutral and distant police force based on objective statistical information emerged. It was later to be represented by Chief William Parker's Los Angeles police (Brown 1981). In the post–World War II years the development and application of several technological innovations were seen as the solution to the ever-perplexing problem of gaining, using, and expanding public trust. Police communications, including first the telephone and then the two-way radio and later the computer and associated systems, were seen to fill the need to maintain internal control (discipline, supervision, accountability, and command direction) and external effectiveness (the eradication or at least the regulation of crime and the maintenance of the status quo).

Each of these innovations is marked in the police communications literature. Tien and Colton usefully summarize several of the more important developments:[1]

In 1877 Albany, N.Y. had five telephones installed connecting the mayor's office with police precinct stations. Thus began the development of modern police command and control procedures. The telephone, first simply and auxiliary to the telegraph, gradually allowed the public to gain voice access to the police department as well as to give the department better means of communication with and control of its personnel.

In 1923, the Pennsylvania State Police adopted teletype machines. In 1928, Detroit deployed police cruisers equpped with radio receivers. Two-way police radio came to Boston in 1934. Transistorized circuitry, in the 1960s, gave police smaller and more reliable radios. Progress in communications technology was even more dramatic in the following decade. (Tien and Colton 1979, p. 294)

A new set of factors, however, increased the appeal of technology in the period following the invention and marketing of the first commercially available computer, Univac, unveiled at the University of Illinois in 1951. Aside from its connection with scientific management and "profession-alization" (a misconception contributed to by social scientists and others who use the presence of computers per se as an index of professionaliza-tion and "efficiency"), there are a number of other reasons why technology has maintained such a strong appeal for police administrators in both the United States and in England, including prominently the wish for the prestige associated with science, businesslike procedures and appearances, and high-energy technology. Technology was imported from areas in which it had achieved considerable success. As Hough (1980a) puts it, it was assumed that the police might stand to benefit from technology because their problems were defined as being analogous to those of the military and the fire service.

Technological solutions provide an option supported by commercial pressures and, when placed in the context of operations research and sys-tems theory, can be persuasive to those burdened with complex and en-during problems of organizational control and direction. The impetus for innovation or "technology transfer" also arose from the dying aerospace industry, a result of reduced defense spending after the Vietnam War, and the fear of redundancy in high-technology industries. Some have claimed that the growing crime crisis of the late 1960s, begun by President John-son when he appointed the President's Crime Commission and exploited savagely by President Nixon in the 1968 election and in the ensuing years, drove the willingness to innovate, provided the money through the Law Enforcement Assistance Administration (LEAA), and sanctioned exploration of new technologies (Harris 1970; Epstein 1977; Feeley and Sarat 1980). The crisis in policing, riots, public fears of crime, and symbolic urgings and sponsorship by the government increased interest in and the adaptation of computer technology by police agencies (Tien and Colton 1979; Colton 1978; Hough 1980a, 1980b).

There is an argument to be made for the utility of command and control systems, and indeed Reiss and Bordua (1967) and Bordua and Reiss (1967) have argued that radio has been one of the most significant sources of change in the capacity of the police to become more bureaucratically organized, more centralized with respect to decision making and supervision, and more responsive to citizens' demands. When coupled with high rates of telephone use and reporting, this is seen as a source of both improved policing and improved responsiveness to citizen demands and needs (Broome and Wanklin 1980). It has been claimed that computer technology is the single most important innovation in policing in America and perhaps in Western Europe (Barnett 1978).

It was perhaps this combination of a perceived need on the part of police administrators and the level of public concern that led to the emphasis on experimentation with new computer-based technologies that appeared in the President's Crime Commission *Task Force Report on Science and Technology* issued in 1967.[2] In the 1967 report and in the National Advisory Commission on Criminal Justice Standards and Goals report in 1975 it was concluded that there was little storage and feedback of information to and from police communications centers, that the location of police cars was only crudely known, that communications, it could be assumed, affected response time and that a reduction in response time might reduce crime and increase citizen satisfaction, and that radio congestion impairs communication between dispatchers and officers (President's Crime Commission, 1967; *National Strategy* 1975, pp. 258–260). This became what Hough aptly terms the "conventional orthodoxy" for a number of years. This orthodoxy first posited problems and then posited ameliorative effects of the advocated innovations, especially in information-processing technology (Hough 1980b, p. 350).

Such innovations were directed primarily to internal management concerns such as supervision, direction command and control, resource allocation (which in effect means the allocation and deployment of officers), and gathering and storing of data. All were designed to increase the probability of compliance of officers with administrative decisions. It is now possible to review some of the specific claims made for computer technology and research bearing on those claims. Then we can explore the social organization of policing as a source of insight into what must to this point be viewed as a decade of self-deception amplified by commercial interests and sanctified by operations researchers whose profound ignorance of the managerial problems of police are now fully apparent.

Claims and Aims

One must note that in general the claims for the performance of systems such as the two-way radio are made on the basis of *capacity* rather than of performance. Kelling (1978) lists, for example, some claims that have been made for the two-way radio in police vehicles. Radio dispatch was meant to produce rapid mobilization of active force for emergencies, instant communication with individual units, patrol units informed almost immediately of calls for service, patrol officers reports of progress on the handling of events and requests for assistance and supervision, rapid adjustment of number and kind of personnel needed as a result of changes during emergencies, and constant monitoring of police officer activity.

The general aims and objectives of the radio and its extension, computerized dispatching, coupled with three-digit numbers are not defined operationally (by the police or others) such that decisions can be reached about the contribution of this new technology to crime control, resource allocation, or improved policing. It has been argued, for example, that a three-digit number (911 or 999) when combined with centralized collection and dispatching has these advantages [summarized by Wells (1979)]:

1. A three-digit number is simpler and easier to dial than a seven-(or eight-) digit number. In addition, many seven-digit police numbers are not easily remembered.

2. A three-digit number can be used nationally; people in strange towns or those who are not sure which of several departments to call can call and leave subsequent allocation and disposition of the call to the police.

3. A three-digit number reduces dialing time and the likelihood of dialing mistakes.

4. Once a call is channeled to a specific center, it can be assigned to the nearest and most appropriate agency and thus produce better coordination and less duplication of effort and service in a given area.

5. Three-digit numbers can reduce response time.

6. A three-digit number allows the citizen to call for assistance and leaves to the agency the determination and the assignment of the type(s) of service needed (fire, police, ambulance).

It should be noted, however, that agencies in centralized number areas, including the police, continue to receive calls on numbers other than 911 and alarm calls. The single largest source of calls that constitute the workload of operators is internal police calls (Scott 1981). These are increased by more sophisticated phone networks and may well be inversely related to the capacity to respond to externally sourced demand. Capacity for systematization permits the integration of command functions and adds a secondary capacity of collating information, planning and longer-term management, allocation and deployment of resources. Computer technology can also act as an integrative force, tying together several logically distinct aspects of police command, communication, and control (911, centralized computerized dispatch, automatic vehicle monitoring, etc.). The popular and widespread primary computer functions link centralized number and call processing (911 and 999), computer-aided dispatching (CAD), and management information systems (MIS). Ancillary functions, such as mobile computers, automatic vehicle monitors, and regional communicational schemes, are rarely used (Tien and Colton 1979).

There is a belief that such systems will increase effectiveness and efficiency of policing by reducing response time, producing more equitable distribution of resources, and ensuring more balanced workloads across subdivisions. There is also a wish that such systems will produce tighter integration of the organization through increased communication, greater compliance with directives, and increased capacity to monitor and/or reconstruct the behavior of officers. Ideally this integration would also make possible greater responsiveness to public demands [Tien and Colton (1979), summarizing the President's Crime Commission (1967)].

The aims of computer-aided dispatching systems are to (1) assist dispatchers in aligning given resources (vehicles, officers, other resources such as dogs, scenes of crime vehicles, equipment) to given calls; (2) to maintain "on-line" information on the status of available units; (3) to know at a moment's notice the available resources for the entire force by their function and divisional assignment and the present activities of officers; (4) to retrieve quickly and review events processed during the previous twenty-four hours, present (in-process) incidents, and the workload for any given officer at present and over the past twenty-four hours; (5) to exercise centralized control of selected events from central command at police headquarters, a mobile control center, or the communications center itself; (6) to maintain a record of previous decisions and allocations and a time-process record of these actions; and (7) to permit the monitoring of the handling of any ongoing event by officers both for accountability and for review of decision. The overall purpose of a CAD system is to align spontaneous demand for police with available resources such that the most efficient and appropriate response is made consistent with the potential threat of the event(s), the law, and extant current knowledge.

These seven points might be called the *primary functions* of a command and control system. The *secondary functions* involve analysis of these data to make low-level generalizations about workload trends and to measure the relationships between workloads and resources. A *tertiary function* of the system is to create data to use in modeling workloads, testing policy options, shifting personnel, making decisions about the effectiveness of certain strategic deployment and allocation options, and developing planning and intelligence functions. In theory, it makes it possible to devise and test environmental impacts resulting from modifications in policing strategies. [These options are summarized from Hough (1980b) based on a Home Office study of the Strathclyde system.] Although any command and control system has the potential, with respect to the storage and reduction of data and analysis techniques, to implement a variety of rational adjustments in organizational responses to the environment, these are contingent on the successful acquisition of an adequate database, interest, and skill that might permit experimenting with the scheme (Hough 1980b). As has been noted by such perceptive observers and advocates of computerization as Tien and Colton:

The large majority of computer applications by police remain "routine"—straight-forward repetitive information processing activities such as traffic records or maintaining real-time patrol and inquiry files. Non-routine use such as resource allocation models of computer assisted dispatching (CAD) systems, in which the machine has become a tool for decision-making and strategic planning, has been disappointing. (1979, p. 296)

Within the police the most common computer applications are such things as payroll, record keeping, data storage, and on-line day-to-day monitoring and adjusting of calls, units, their present function, level of activity and ostensive location, and resource availability. In other words, the police computerize routine functions previously carried out by roughly the same number of individuals with less expensive technology.

Police organizations emphasize command, control, and supervision, not evaluation. The police are dependent on public communication and eager to filter, control, and limit demand and to ration their services (Lipsky 1980). In these respects and others the two departments I studied resemble each other. In what follows I discuss the access, methods, backgrounds, rationale, and operation of the two police communications systems in the MPD and the BPD. These background descriptions will permit a closer look at the diachronic and synchronic aspects of message processing found in chapters 4 through 6.

Access and Method

British Police Department
In July 1979, having been challenged to do a study of the BPD,[3] I spent a long day conferring with the assistant chief constable (ACC) of the BPD in charge of communications, had a tour of the headquarters, and the communication center, and met an officer who had just completed a higher degree who served under the ACC. The study was agreed to, providing that I would summarize my findings for the chief constable.

I was introduced to an administrator who was carrying out an evaluation of some of the policies and practices of the force. He suggested that I study at "Queen's Fields," a subdivision composed of mixed West Indian, Pakistani, and Indian ("Asian") groups, with a large middle-class white population on its borders.[4]

My data collection began in earnest when I returned to England in late November 1979. I gathered a set of official publications, the 1978 and

1979 annual reports of the Chief Constable (Chief Constable, 1979, 1980), descriptions of the command and control system of the BPD, and several reports of research done within the BPD by other scholars. I obtained a copy of the entries in the Queen's Fields incident book for March 20–23, 1979, and files for four major incidents that occurred between July 30 and November 25, 1979. Major incidents are controlled by the communications center, and files contain all relevant actions taken in regard to a declared major incident.[5] I also obtained a set of printouts of incidents for an hour on June 12, 1979, and on January 25, 1980, and a tape recording of calls for one hour on January 25 received at the center and forwarded to the Queen's Fields Subdivision.

Intensive fieldwork began in mid-November 1979 and extended until mid-December 1979; I revisited the force for two brief periods in mid-December 1980 and late February 1983. During this time I gathered some sixty interviews ranging in length from fifteen minutes to three hours; I interviewed officers at all ranks. In addition, I interviewed two computer experts employed by the force to install, operate, and evaluate the command and control system, two researchers in the Home Office who had done a parallel study of communications in several forces in Great Britain, an economist whose research involved police efficiency and measurement thereof, and three other researchers who were at the time of my work also engaged in research in the BPD. I applied my own coding system to the raw data for analysis.

I spent some 135 hours in police settings gathering raw data. These included the communications center on X division, the control rooms of Queen's Fields and two other subdivisional offices, the headquarters of Traffic Control [a separate system of dispatching that is not analyzed here but parallels the command and control system described (Braslavsky 1982)], and BPD Headquarters. I also observed and did interviews in a variety of other settings, such as police vehicles, other subdivisional premises, private homes, and various pubs, clubs, and restaurants, and while walking. I twice attended the subdivision's annual Christmas disco. The bulk of my observational time was spent in controllers' offices in Queen's Fields and several other subdivisions.[6] The results of the analysis have been presented in several analytic memos, oral presentations at meetings and seminars, and various publications.

Midwest Police Department

I was invited to tour the communications center of the MPD by a former student now teaching in the Police Academy. The tour was unremarkable, punctuated by my seizing on an opportunity to acquire a return invitation. I was fascinated by the operators and dispatchers processing calls. Other contacts led to permission being given for some observations of patrol in a central city precinct.

Intensive fieldwork began in late January 1979 and extended to March 1980. I gathered printouts for dispatching for one zone, the training and procedures manual for operators, a 300-page book that is constantly updated and revised, and several research publications (Ashton 1981; Wilde 1972; Buzawa 1979). Since 1974 I had collected clippings on the department from Metro City's press and in 1978 began to keep clippings on police communications centers.

From January to mid-March 1979, I spent some sixty hours in the communications center, the headquarters building, one precinct, and police vehicles. I returned in March 1980 for further observation, interviews, and checking of my previous inferences with key informants. At this time I interviewed a former head of the communications center and several officers in the training division of the MPD. During this period I interviewed twenty-three officers, from deputy chief to officer, for a few minutes to two hours. I interviewed five operators whom I had observed in order to verify, expand, or disconfirm inferences I had drawn from observation.

As I had done with my notes for the BPD, I coded the raw data for the MPD and replicated the diagrams, flow charts, floor plans and algorithms. The fieldwork and data gathering in the MPD were woven around parallel fieldwork undertaken in England. An alternating pattern of work resulted —USA (January–February 1979), England (July 1979, November–December 1979), USA (March 1980), England (December 1980, February 1983).

Description of the British Police Department

The BPD as of 1979 had an establishment of some 6,509 officers (the Home Office sets the size limit for the force) but actually employed 6,160.[7] There were also 1,922 nonpolice employees. The establishment limit in the past has been met rarely because of loss or "wastage" and in ability to recruit acceptable officers. It is now not problematic because of the massive rise in police salaries, around 200% since 1972, and related expansion in promotion opportunities. The constabulary was formed to police a large metropolitan area and was created by the amalgamation of several forces. The force is roughly 85% white males. It is organized traditionally with a chief constable accountable to the local police authority. The force is funded jointly by the Home Office (50% approximately) and the local county council. A deputy chief constable and five assistant chief constables are responsible for operations, crime, staff services, organization and development, and support and staff services. Other ranks are, in order, chief superintendent, superintendent, chief inspector, inspector, sergeant, and officer. Roughly 70% of the force is in the uniform branch, about 5% in the Crime Investigation Division (CID; that is, detectives), and 8% in traffic. These figures could be expanded or contracted depending on definition by at least five percentage points. There were 147,350 crimes in 1979, a figure that was slightly down (2.95%) from 1978 according to the annual report of the chief constable (Chief Constable, 1980).

The metropolitan area, which is in one of the most industrialized sections of England, contains manufacturers of vehicles and heavy metal products and large engineering works. The area has suffered from declining population, rising unemployment, and the loss of industrial jobs generally. It is also one of the most ethnically diverse areas outside London. In 1979, some 2,729,000 people lived in about 222,400 square acres, producing a ratio of 2.38 officers per thousand citizens.

Background

Policing in metropolitan London set the pattern for policing in the provinces and cities outside London and was from the beginning territorially based. In order to facilitate supervision, each officer is expected to walk a set pattern and cross fixed points. This scheme was modified by the unit-beat scheme widely adopted after 1964 in Great Britain. The present BPD scheme, command and control and computer-assisted dispatch, is overlaid on and builds on tacit understandings that are a product of past practices.

The fixed-points system, in wide use in Britain until 1964, is succinctly described by Chatterton (1979, pp. 87–88). Under the fixed-points system a police subdivision is divided into foot beats assigned to a police constable. The assigment is rotated every six weeks. Emergency calls from the public are received by a central information room at headquarters and filtered, and those viewed as requiring a quick response are then relayed to one of the mobile units patrolling the division. Officers are little directed by the radio man in the reserve or information room. Technological support, including such now commonly assumed wherewithal as two-way vehicle and personal radios, the vehicles themselves, and specialized mobile units (for example, scenes of crimes vans, dog vans, and special patrol units), are minimal. Much emphasis is placed on individual skills of handling incidents, getting to know one's "patch" and, indeed, avoiding calling for assistance. This is considered, except in the case of a large crowd or pub fight, to be a failure on the part of the bobby. Judgments of competence are local in origin and based on interpersonal skills, knowledge, and relationships.

The system is designed to routinize the patrol activities of constables and to make them and their supervisors accountable. There are four fixed points numbered in a clockwise sequence, point 1 to point 4, at specified locations on each beat.

The patrolmen were required to arrive at or "make" [a set of] fixed points at specified times during each tour of duty in order that the section sergeant could make contact with them. The section sergeant was responsible for supervising three, sometimes four, beatmen, and their beats represented his section. He was required to make at least two visits to each beatman during a shift, preferably once before and once after the refreshment period. He had to record each visit in the constable's notebook—known in the divisional argot as "signing his book" —and also enter it in his own pocket-book and in the station visits book which was kept in the police station....

The patrol-variation was changed every shift.... The system required each patrolman to work his beat in strict accordance with the patrol-variation, to keep within the boundaries of his own beat and to make his points punctually. These rules were backed by the discipline regulations. (Chatterton 1979, pp. 87–88)

The fixed-points system, even when modified into the unit-beat concept, provided what can now be considered an enduring and lasting imagery by which officers continue to conceive of their work. In many respects the fixed-points system still serves as a kind of model or invisible paradigm. It currently embeds modern policing in the United Kingdom for officers above the rank of inspector. Officers with more than fifteen years service (this varies by the force) continue to view police work within this model of visible, routinized, almost mechanical coordination and supervision.

Even as these patterns of policing persisted in large urban areas, the effects of technology were eroding and transforming the role of the police. Although, as I will show, new technologies are integrated in some ways with old practices, traditional habits and customs, and power relationships, they also work to modify a number of the more visible surface features of the work. And like a gray cloud that suddenly shifts, bursts, and moves on, technology cast a constant shadow on police work since the first 999 calls were made in Centreshire in 1923 and in London in 1937.

Centralized systems for receiving calls for service were more quickly developed and standardized in the United Kingdom than in the United States. After World War II the British Home Office engaged in numerous experiments in applied technology. Many of these were stimulated by the work of Sir Eric St. Johnstone, chief constable of Lancashire and later Her Majesty's Inspector of the Constabulary (HMI) (Johnstone 1978). With the introduction of unit-beat policing elaborated by the use of small vehicles that transport officers between points and to calls and the personal radio, either held by the officer or installed in a vehicle, more sophisticated systems of communication were possible.

Unit-Beat Policing

Unit-beat policing was intended to be based on a number of "home" or "permanent beat" officers living in an area they policed, maintaining community contact, and feeding diverse and richly relevant information to a collator in the subdivisional station. The collator, in turn, was to systematize this information for the use of all subdivisional officers in the CID, uniform and specialized units. In most forces the notion that an officer (HBO, or home beat officer) would live in the area, set his or her own times for working, and maintain a flexible schedule was abandoned, and a walking and/or "permanent beat" officer (PBO) was substituted. In addition, small minicars ("pandas") were to cover two beats, transport officers, answer calls, or even patrol larger areas in order to be a visible and available deterrent. Large area or "wireless" cars, linked in most forces both to VHF or force radio and a UHF or subdivisional radio, were the most flexible and were meant to cover two panda beats (four unit beats).

The original intent of unit-beat organization was to combine flexible response with community relations and crime information coordination. Panda car drivers and unit-beat officers were instructed to park the cars frequently and walk. The development and use of the lightweight personal and car radio, vehicles, and radio-teleprinter-telephone links from the communications center to ecologically based officers decreased the gap between communications centers and officers. For example, in the Metropolitan Police two quite different systems of communication link the subdivisions and the central force. The first is the central force radio, which broadcasts calls from the 999 number in Central London, sends calls needing speedy responses to area cars, and follows this assignment with a telex later to be received in the subdivision concerning the assignment to one of the subdivision's area cars. The second is the local subdivision radio, which allocates some matters sent by telex, some arising on the subdivision, and some received by walk-in or calls direct to the subdivision. The net effect was an increase in social distance between the police and the public and a shift of the definition of the police role. Even in Centreshire the growing domination of policing by central communication was enhanced by the appeal of the car and driving over walking, the status that came from attending calls seen as "emergent" or crime related, and the growing influence of American-style fast-response specialized policing.

As the insightful work of Holdaway (1983) has shown and assessments of the Brixton riots in south London demonstrate (Scarman 1981), the rise of communications technology and motor-powered mobility subtlely, almost invisibly, shifted police concern and emphasis from discipline and control and contact with the public in relatively diverse situations to increased availability, speedy response, and reaction to public demand as filtered through centralized call collection and distribution systems [see on this theme Holdaway (1979a, 1980, 1983), James (1979) and Scarman (1981)]. In fact, the association of "professional" policing and advanced management and police administration and technology is most dramatically seen in an examination of the history of the command and control system in the BPD. Other forces in the United Kingdom, including the Metropolitan Police, have been led in these matters by the BPD.

The BPD's command and control system is one of the most innovative in the United Kingdom. The force has long been on the forefront of introducing refined technological advances into policing. It has attempted to combine operations technology with British interest in carefully supervised, accountable, and citizen-oriented policing. In that sense it has represented in the last two decades or so an interesting amalgam of Anglo-American developments in policing. In 1970 Home Secretary Roy Jenkins went to Chicago to view their computer-assisted dispatch system. Subsequently the Home Office Scientific Development Branch decided to adopt experimentally a system similar to the NYPD's SPRINT system. The system was installed in late 1971 in Centreshire with four remotely operating visual display units (VDUs). When amalgamation took place in 1974, a city force and two constabularies were combined to form the British Police Department with headquarters in Centreshire. There were initially three control rooms and three separate traffic control rooms. Computerized dispatching was phased in gradually over five years, and the last division to be included became fully operational in February 1979. System modifications introduced in April 1979 are incorporated in my descriptions.

System Rationale in Centreshire

The philosophy of the multifaceted police communications system is to combine central control room receipt of 999 and other calls to avoid queuing while continuing to place responsibility for level, type, and speed of response on the thirty-one local subdivisions. Nine divisions are composed of three subdivisions; two are composed of two subdivisions. Each division has about 350 officers; each subdivision has around 110. These officers rotate in four units or sections (A, B, C, D) of about twenty-five persons. Each unit is assigned in rotation a "turn" or "shift" (early, 6 A.M.– 2 P.M.; late, 2 P.M.–10 P.M.; night, 10 P.M.–6 A.M.). One unit is on leave. On any given turn, there are in theory one or two area or Zulu cars, two to four pandas, and five or six other variously assigned officers.[8] There are in addition in each unit an inspector and three sergeants, one of whom has been specially trained and serves as the controller.

Telephone calls, some screened by police operators, are received at the communications center, further screened, and allocated to the appropriate location (almost always a subdivisional controller). All 999 calls, including alarm calls, are preliminarily filtered by British Telecommunications operators. The present rate of calls received is about 800,000 per year (Chief Constable, 1979). About 1,800 incidents a day are processed.[9]

The aim of the 999 system is to direct the greatest number of calls through the central 999 number, receive alarm or "hard line" (direct calls), filter them, and disperse them to the subdivision for disposal. Calls can be monitored by supervisors by listening to the radio on either VHF or UHF channels or to tape recordings made at the control center and by recalling finished incidents previously placed on tape or disk. Another purpose of this filtration and dispersal system is to hold out the possibility of high-level command control over major incidents, for example, disasters, large traffic accidents, significant murder investigations, and demonstrations.

The variable response to calls results from three sources: the individual officer, the subdivisional controller, and the central control room. The system is relatively closed with respect to input because the central control room is isolated physically, symbolically, and organizationally: All calls for service shunted through this system are handled semiofficially. Relatively few incidents are controlled at the center (around 100 in 1979, some 0.00125% of the calls received).[10] The supervisory consoles have special functions. They can be used to cut into any transmission and can add information to any incident. Incidents not defined as major incidents cannot be altered by any console except the originating one. Supervisors can monitor the two-way radio transmissions of any of the consoles because any VHF or UHF radio channel can be monitored at any console.

Most of the work generated for the subdivisions passes through this center. It is claimed (estimated) that about 40% of the work on the subdivision is locally generated and that about 60% originates from the central control room. Priorities are informal and are set in the control room at the subdivisional controller's desk and by individual officers who receive requests from the controller. The subdivision in effect controls the vast majority of incidents and can call for needed divisional, force, and extra force assistance. The direct lines to the subdivisions receive less than five calls per hour, even in the busiest times. Not all are actionable. The rarely used phone numbers of the subdivisional controllers who use the VDU-computer-teleprinter-phone-radio system are unlisted. Most of the calls received on these lines involve internal police business. The assumed convenience of the 999 number (the subdivisional number, although listed and used, is a seven-digit number)[11] reduces the number of direct calls that might be otherwise received at the subdivisions.

Communication Channels

The communications center has seven distinct communication channels: radio, telephone, teleprinter, telex, telegraph, the Police National Computer, and dictaphone. The radio connects through five VHF channels the operator-dispatchers with officers in the first- or fast-response cars (Zulu cars), the dog vans, and cars in traffic or at headquarters control and with the operating rooms of the three adjoining county forces. UHF radios connect panda and Zulu cars to indicate their activity status and emergency but the system is not presently fully functional.

There are ten incoming telephone lines for 999 calls, and twenty for area-based calls made on six- or seven-digit numbers in the BPD area. Calls received at the general switchboard (those made using the seven-digit police general number) at BPD headquarters can be transferred directly from there to the control room. Outside lines connect callers with the twenty-three consoles in the central control room; twelve accept "emergency calls" by means of 999; three process inquiries for the Police National Computer (PNC) at Hendon; four accept general public inquiries, and three are used for supervision. One is reserved for major incident control. Direct silent alarm calls are received by means of an outside directory number; some of these calls are monitored by private security companies and then transferred. Other alarm calls come by means of an automatically dialed call to 999 and are screened by Telecoms operators and directed to a console. Direct calls also arise from the Bank of England security in Centreshire, the local prison, or the British Transport Police. There are also three ambulance and two direct fire lines. Internal calls of various sorts arise from subdivisions, from headquarters, from various support services, etc. The allocation of calls between the emergency and the routine inquiries desks is problematic because calls are not easily distinguished either by line or content. 999 calls, fire brigade calls, and ambulance calls are screened by operators working for British Telecoms [formerly called the GPO (General Post Office)]. They ask for the caller's number, ask them to hold, and transfer the call to the police at the communication center. When the center operators answer, they are given the number by the Telecoms operator, and they, in turn, answer the caller, "Police, may I help you?"

The fifty teleprinters in most departments of the force and in each subdivision are also linked to the computer consoles and to the VDUs. VDUs are used to enter and show the received incidents thought by central operators to require an incident report. The telex is also used to distribute messages throughout the force. The telegraph is used to communicate messages to the center and to external forces and agencies. The Police National Computer, which stores criminal records and information on vehicle ownership and registration and driver's licenses, can be accessed either through the center or directly from subdivisions. In addition to the twenty-three VDUs in the communications center, there are four in traffic control (a semi-autonomous division that controls traffic incidents), one in the command center at police headquarters, and thirty-one in subdivisions (assigned letters B through M). In addition, all incoming calls to the center are recorded by two-reel tape-recorder. One tape is always available for immediate playback and monitoring.

Ecology

The communications center in the BPD is located in a large second-story room in the headquarters building of the Queen's Fields subdivision. It has restricted access. The operator and dispatchers sit in a large, airy, light-filled area that is entered through an anteroom containing the telex, tele-printer, and telegraph equipment.

Half of the operators are civilians; the other half are officers. There are about eight operators per shift, and they are rotated together as a unit through the three shifts, serving twenty-eight days on each. About 25% are female. On any given shift, not all the consoles are in operation. Operators are seated at consoles that contain a VDU, a radio-telephone, a telephone equipped with a foot pedal and headset (to free their hands while answering), and a radio circuit switchboard by which one can monitor one or more of the fifty-four available channels. The console also includes a speaker, a clock, and buttons indicating direct alarm calls and other incoming calls. Above the operators is a red light that flashes when a 999 call is received. Controllers, all male sergeants, sit at a similar desk or control panel in the subdivisions. They are equipped with a computer keyboard and screen, a radio-telephone for subdivisional transmittals, a direct phone from the communications center, and a telephone normally equipped with two lines (this varies from subdivision to subdivision) for outgoing and incoming calls. Usually the console and attached desk form a semicircle that acts as a physical and symbolic barrier to the intrusion of officers and civilian clerks who wander in and out of the controller's room. Informal interactions are usually work-related banter and gossip. This center is the functional equivalent to the old "radio" or "reserve" room occupied by the reserve officer under the previous system. The clerical office and the window and barrier at which the public is met is usually nearby. There is frequent communication between the public desk and the controller by telephone, in person, or when telex messages are passed from the clerks to the controllers. The controller's room is a focus for informal interactions and may include making and drinking tea and coffee, eating, and checking difficult or problematic paperwork. It is also an important place for the exchange of advice, favors, gossip, and informal information. Within its confines, work is surrounded by duties, the working out of the official versions of reports and other paperwork, and arrangements for refreshment breaks and days off. Critical negotiations between sergeants and constables take place around the controller's desks (Van Maanen 1983).

Flow of Calls through the System: Process Description of Operations

A flowchart depicting call processing in the communications center of the BPD is shown in figure 3.1 and described here in further detail. Figure 3.2 is a task-role operations chart.

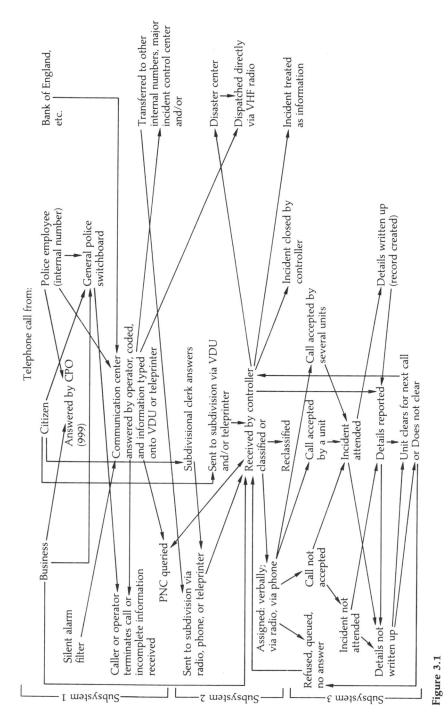

Figure 3.1
Flow chart of call processing in the communications center of the BPD (December 1979).

System A

Telephone calls from telecoms lines (999), internal lines, alarm and other direct lines (fire, ambulance) (queue formed only on telecoms lines where initial screening is done)

Subsystem 1: 8 Operator-dispatchers (civilian and sworn officers) plus 4 on-duty supervisors (2 sergeants, 1 inspector, and 1 chief inspector per shift)

Operations/tasks
 Receiving stimuli (calls)
 Establishing the credibility of call
 Selecting and sorting facts: refuse, refer, or accept call

Constructing an image of the event

Encoding-writing on VDUs
 11 items in format

Transmission channels (all 2-way)
 VHF: dog vans, area cars, other process
 UHF: pandas, walkers, subdivisions   54 Radio Channels Available
 teleprinter, telex
 VDU: computer
 phones: telecom lines, internal lines
 CYFAS (vehicle status indicator)
 Police National Computer (PNC) (Hendon, near London)

Subsystem 2: 31 Controllers (sergeants, one for each subdivision) (11 divisions, 9 with 3 subdivisions, 2 with 2)

Operations/tasks
 Receive phone messages (external and internal lines), VDU messages, teleprinter messages, verbal messages
 Selecting and sorting facts

Constructing an image of the call and of the event

Decoding of message elements
 Message Analysis: 11 items in incident format and adding "context"
 Verbal assignment of incident to unit

Figure 3.2
Functions and tasks in the BPD. Subdivisions, the basis of English policing, are composed of four areas, or unit beats. Two beats are covered by a panda, four by a Z or area car. A typical subdivisional shift or turn is composed of one Z car (two officers), one panda (one officer), two to four permanent beat officers, and one or two foot officers. There are approximately 150 officers in a subdivision and about 350 on a division.

The initial classification can be modified twice if necessary. All classifications made are included on the incident form.

The assignments attempted and made are entered in the incident format by time, as are the arrival time and the time completed. The incident remains unfinished and the computer will "bleep" to remind the controller until all data are entered. This means that the controller is accountable for officers reporting details of actions taken. The outcome of the incident is reported and written up (in the VDU) if it is entered.

Transmission channels
  Two-way radio to cars: UHF only to walkers, pandas, dog handlers
  Teleprinter
VDU: computer to central control room and PNC

Subsystem 3: 25 (approximately) Officers with area responsibilities

Operations/tasks
  Receiving, sensing, and sorting of messages

Constructing an image of the incident, call, and event

Reclassification possible

Decoding message
  Analysis: 11 items and "context"

Transmission channels
  Telephone, e.g., from public call box
  Radio VHF: Z cars, dog vans
  Radio UHF: pandas, walkers, dog handlers
  Verbal

Action outcomes/disposition of the job reported
  Verbally or over radio

Status reported (in or out of service)
  Content feedback required

Figure 3.2 (continued)

In general, control room personnel tend to enter calls received on the VDU as incidents, although they can dissuade the caller, refuse to accept the call as an emergency or as police business, refer the caller to another source of assistance, or answer the question on the phone without sending the incident on for further screening at the subdivisional level. Once a call is accepted by operators, they are expected to fill in the facts in an established format on the VDU for transmission.

The format in which information is recorded is used to order the items included in the VDU and, subsequently, if necessary, on the teleprinter printout of the information. There are thirteen required types of information: date, time, incident, location, caller, message, action by control room operator, action by subdivisional controller, result and remarks, reporter, beat on which the incident occurred, and grid reference or location. Incidents are classified using a set of thirty categories, which can be changed. Up to three categories for an incident may be used. A final classification is assigned by the controller after results are known. Actions can be taken by the control room and by the subdivision. (Figure 3.3 gives the classification and resource summaries used by the BPD.)

The Final Classifications of Incidents and Resource Summary Codes, BPD
The list can be obtained on screen by sending after entering the reporting officer's number. (In a "CHANGE FINAL CLASS" option in a recall the list can be displayed by entering a question mark in the data field.

01	RTA Injury	11	Burglary D/house	21	Illness
02	RTA Noninjury	12	Burglary other	22	Injury
03	Alarm arrest	13	Damage criminal	23	Sudden death
04	Alarm no arrest	14	Damage other	24	Drunk
05	Alarm false	15	Theft of cars	25	Trespass
06	Assaults	16	Theft from cars	26	Alcotest
07	Sex offenses	17	Other thefts	27	False/Malicious
08	Disorder	18	Other crimes	28	No trace
09	Domestic disputes	19	VEHS OBST or ABND	29	Messages
10	Missing persons	20	Fires	30	Miscellaneous

Up to three can be entered, each separated by a space. If a change final class option on a recall is used then new codes will overwrite the previous. If appropriate, therefore, reenter the previous code(s) with the new.

Resource Summaries

Use of code + RS will produce the format as below from which displays of resources of the type shown can be produced. For options 1 and 2 enter divisions, options 3–5, enter subdivisions; options 6–11 are force-wide totals.

RS1	Resource availability	–	S-DIV cars	(Enter Div)
RS2	Resource availability	–	Traffic vehicles	(Enter Div)
RS3	Resource availability	–	Beat cars	(Enter Sub-Div)
RS4	Resource availability	–	PBOs	(Enter Sub-Div)
RS5	Resource availability	–	Foot patrols	(Enter Sub-Div)
RS6	Resource availability	–	Special cars	
RS7	Resource availability	–	Motorway vehicles	
RS8	Resource summaries	–	S-div cars	
RS9	Resource summaries	–	Traffic vehicles	
RS10	Resource summaries	–	Beat cars	
RS11	Resource summaries	–	Totals	

Choice [   ]   Division or Sub-Div [   ]

1–5 TYPE   + RS/CHOICE/DIV OR SUB-DIV
  11 TYPE   + RS/CHOICE

Figure 3.3
Classification and resource summary displays of the BPD.

The operator must decide to which subdivision to send the message. Calls are generally sent through the VDU to the subdivisional controller. Some calls may bypass the subdivision and be sent directly to the fast-response cars or dog vans over one of the VHF channels. These calls cannot be monitored by the subdivision.

The communication channels are telephone (external and internal lines); radio (VHF, UHF, and CYFAS car locator); teleprinter, telex, and telegraph; VDU link to PNC; and verbal (which may occur from a mobile command spot). Although there is a programmed capacity to send a message by location automatically to the correct subdivision for processing, it is not yet functional. Control room operators use a combination of areal listings and their divisional locations, a street directory, advice from other operators, and their own personal knowledge to select a subdivision. A large street map of the area, called the ground, is on the wall and is also used to locate general outlines of subdivisional areas, adjoining police areas, and public buildings. Incidents occasionally are dispatched incorrectly to subdivisions. Controllers then have to decide whether to respond to the call, send it back, or put it in a queue for later handling. The time spent assessing and forwarding incidents is rather small in proportion to the time required at the subdivisional or controller's level.

Once the message is dispatched, either it appears on the VDU or a quiet "bleep" is heard announcing that a message is waiting in the queue. The ways in which the command is sent and received are isomorphic. The modes of response assigned to these calls are in large part determined by the subdivisional controller. Typically the controller makes an assignment of the incident to an officer either verbally or by radio and then "buries" the incident (places it in the computer memory, leaving the screen available for subsequent calls) until results are reported. When the report is completed, the controller can retrieve the incident, enter missing data, and include the beat and grid reference (location). Some data are entered automatically. When new action is initiated, pages are continued so long as no results are entered. The role of the controller, the person who operates the "board" on the subdivisions, is crucial. By force regulations the controller must be trained in computerized dispatching technology and be at least a sergeant.

The controller can select from several options: (1) bury the incident by viewing it and returning it to storage [depending on the priority (high or low) with which it was sent, it will "bleep" for attention within a given period of time]; (2) decide that it does not require police attention; (3) treat it as a message, acknowledge it, and carry on with other business; or (4) assign someone to the task. Inquiries, such as PNC inquiries, are formatted but need not take the form an incident report. Incidents can also be handled without written record, by means of a note scribbled on the pad next to the controller or by placing the incidents in the log and on the VDU; these are not mutually exclusive modes of processing incidents.

No binding formal priorities are conferred on calls at any level of the system. The bases on which an incident can be accepted as valid, entered on the VDU or on paper, and passed on for action are tacit, social, and experiential and are not stipulated in writing. Few decisions are guided directly by policy or law. If a call is accepted, some controllers will write out a brief note in the incident book, enter it on the VDU, and attempt to assign it. The number of the unit or officer to which it is assigned is entered on the VDU and remains as assigned to that incident unless and until the operator clears with the controller. The time of completion, the final classification of the incident, the grid reference number (referring to a cross-coded area within the subdivision), and any remarks are then entered in the VDU. The incident is then stored in memory as finished. Unfinished incidents can be viewed by recalling them to the screen.

The options for responding to a given call, given a normal staffing pattern at the subdivisional level include doing nothing, assigning local resources, or assigning extraforce resources. Resources involving more than the subdivision are usually initiated as a request through the command structure to the control room in headquarters or to the chief inspector in the communications center. Combinations of resources at the divisional level are frequently called on, often informally.

These actions can be seen as a set of *task operations*. One can imagine perhaps the flow of calls through the communications system, conceptualized as a set of subsystems, using figure 2.1. There are three loci of decision making or subsystems in which technology interfaces with the social environment of the work: the control center, the subdivisional controller's office, and the officers.

The control room operators must sense whether the call is credible (this is also done by the operators who screen calls before sending them on to police operators). They must decide whether the address is valid in two senses: whether it is in the police area and whether the call is "false and malicious." When encoding the call on the VDU, the operators prepare to send it for assignment to subdivisional controller.

Once the call is sent to a subdivision, the second subsystem, it is received on the VDU. Except in rare cases in the subdivisions observed, there was no queuing of calls or any overload. There was no perceived need to establish formal priorities. Incidents are given an informal priority, sorted out, and assigned to the officers available by area and their present location. Some assignments are based on remarks found at the bottom of the screen. These actions are the basis for a *reconstructed image* in the mind of the controller concerning the incident: what is happening to whom, where, why, and with what degree of danger and urgency. The easiest calls to rank are perhaps the alarm calls,[12] and the least demanding are calls for accompanying an ambulance or attending road accidents where the police are not obliged to attend unless they believe injuries have or might have resulted or where there might be allegations of criminal behavior. Traffic vehicles can independently be sent to and attend any incident (Braslavsky 1982).

In the third subsystem officers receive calls verbally or over the radio and set functional priorities in terms of their own sense of the urgency of the call, their personal interests in such types of calls, and/or other idiosyncratic definitions of the situation. Informal priorities determine the order in which calls are dispatched and who accepts them. The officer is the most likely to actually *see* the event about which information is originally received. Actions are produced by the officers in concert with the public, and these actions are variable and selectively reported to the controller and written up in reports or in the officer's book. In general, the required status report is transmitted to the controller, who uses it to close the incident. The controller must also decide, given the verbal report of the officer, how and what to include in the incident report on the VDU. Other formal paperwork, if required, is executed on "the officer's own time." If the controller does not close an incident, it continues to generate audible signals and reappear on the VDU screen, literally demanding attention. The record is entered in the VDU, kept in the communications center on a disk for twenty-four hours, and then transferred to tape and kept for several months.

Description of the Midwestern Police Department

The MPD[13] is a force of some 5,703 officers (all data are as of 1979 unless otherwise noted) and 715 civilians (Annual Report, 1979, p. 66). The force is divided by ethnicity and sex as follows: 35.6% minority, 85% male (60% white, 25% black), and 15% female (4.4% white, 9% black) (Buzawa 1979).

The MPD is traditionally organized with a chief who was appointed in 1976, one of the first black chief executives in the country. Deputy chiefs and twenty-two commanders command the fourteen precincts. The ranks from that level down are inspector, lieutenant (189), sergeant (869), and officer (3,861). Thus the two lowest ranks constitute 94% of the force.

The standard metropolitan area (SMSA) policed in 1970 had 1,512,893 people (a total that had declined to 1.2 million by 1980) and covers approximately 143 square miles. The ratio of officers to population is 2.63 per thousand while the national average (1980) is 2.5. It is a large force in one of the largest, most heavily industrialized cities in the country. The MPD serves a community that is deeply divided by drugs, violence, and crime by race, class, and ethic loyalties (Ashton 1981). The city's population is about 6% black, and the city is heavily industrialized (steel, vehicle manu-facturing, light industry). It also contains the national headquarters of a number of corporations in its center and nearby suburbs. The surrounding political areas are largely white and lower to upper middle class, marking a stark contrast to the shrinking black and mixed ethnic population in the center city area.

The department itself is known for its close political ties to the local black city administration controlled by a black mayor. It has been char-acterized by political turmoil, frequent changes in chiefs, and high racial tension (Wilde 1972). Although it has been known as a conservative and nonprofessional department [according to Wilson's (1963) schema], it has nevertheless undergone massive changes in the last twenty years.

In the period of the research and since, this change and related tension has been shown in a series of developments related to affirmative action policies for promotion and hiring within the department. These trends were exacerbated by the decline in crime over the period 1978–1980, the decrease in inner city population, movement to the suburbs, economic chaos, and some calming of the city after riots in the late 1960s and again in mid-1970. Economic disasters in the state's economy led to large layoffs in 1976 (800 officers, some of whom were rehired) and again in 1980–1983, when 255 officers were laid off. The general decline of the automobile industry, the center pin in the local economy, affected the area and led to further budget reductions in the department and retrenchment in the city and the state. The state led the nation in unemployment for several years after 1979. As a result of the economic changes, despite the influence of a black mayor and police chief, many of the advances made in the late 1970s (an increase in black police officers from 18% to 32% of the force) were lost because seniority was used as a basis for the layoffs (es-tablished as valid in several court cases) and rehiring.[14] In addition, several suits were brought challenging "racial quotas" in hiring and promotion and, for example, a goal set for blacks to constitute 50% of the depart-ment's lieutenants by 1990. The suits alleging "reverse discrimination" were resolved in favor of the department.

In spite of this, some innovations have been made. Two-hundred mini-computers were added to squad cars from 1979 to 1983; a special car is used to cover low-priority calls, possibly reducing the number of calls for which no dispatch is made. The communications center itself has been seen as a model for training, procedures, supervision, and technology. New York and San Francisco sent delegations to observe the operations and to copy some of the innovations for their own 911 centers in 1979.

The period between 1976 and the present has, in sum, been fraught with political change and economic decline—the loss of federal funds that established the central communications center, fluctuation of city budget support, and reduction of personnel levels. The department no longer has the capacity to coordinate services across the entire metropolitan region but continues to dispatch all EMS, fire and police calls within the municipal boundaries.[15]

Background

Policing in America is based, perhaps since the late eighteenth century, on two images. The first is the image of territorial obligation, which allocates areas into "beats," or personally designated "turf" that individual officers work and to which they are somewhat formally assigned. This notion, in turn, is based probably on the social organization the ward and watchman system of early nineteenth-century London. Here the watch obligations were neighborhood based, and citizens served on a rota basis to watch the houses of fellow citizens. In time, the number of persons living above or near the shops was so few that alternative paid systems had to be devised (Radzinowicz 1968). The second image on which the organization of policing has evolved is that of a tightly controlled formal communication command system highlighted by the introduction of two-way radio (Leonard 1938; Tobias 1974).

On the one hand, the allocation of responsibility is regional, neighborhood based, or crime based and, on the other hand, is increasingly rationalized by workload schemes such as those introduced by O. W. Wilson and by centralized communications. The dilemmas and ironies introduced by this dual organization of policing are noted by such acute observers as Van Maanen (1974), Rubinstein (1973, ch. 3), and Walker (1984).

Police officers have a commitment to "keep out of trouble" and to make sure that their own beat is well policed. Work emanating from the central communications system is a potential for error, work, paperwork, and command direction that restricts choice of movement and action. The level of work per se is not the problem, although it is highly variable. As Pepinsky (1976) describes, increasingly communications from the center may be a source to which officers turn for information and direction. Although direction or advice may be desired once the job is sent and received, in the absence of calls that may not be sought, autonomy is the primary aim of patrol.

In the last fifty years in the large cities of the United States, introduction of the personal radio and vehicle two-way radio has placed the radio control system in a central symbolic position in policing. It has also been elevated to a central position in the literature on police management. Bordua and Reiss (1967) consider the two-way radio command and control system to be one of the most important sources of centralization of authority within policing. It has surely become one of the central premises of the administrative model of policing (Manning 1977, ch. 4).

These developments, as they do in England, overlay formal control on previous patterns of patrolling based on local and territorial knowledge, close community relations, and corruption (Lane 1967; Wilson 1968; Clark 1968; Miller 1977). The extent to which this traditional "watchman" style is used throughout the United States, rather than restricted to the Eastern seaboard, is still to be ascertained (Reppetto 1978). It can be assumed, however, that in the past the degree of autonomy of the officer, contacts with the community, political role and importance, violence, and dispensation of on-the-spot justice far exceeded the present degree, even in traditional old Eastern cities [compare Wilson (1968) with Brown (1981)].[16]

Furthermore, perhaps stimulated by Bittner's (1967) brilliant ethnographic description of the police on skid row and Rubinstein's (1973) shrewd, watchful, rational, cold, tragic cop figure, much literature on policing exaggerates the knowledge, skill, capacity, and insights of police officers (Fielding 1984, forthcoming). Even Muir (1977), in an otherwise insightful and evenhanded book, tends to grant to officers far more legal and political authority and legitimacy in the broad sense than they actually possess. One can say, based on the detailed work of Van Maanen (1974, 1983) and Rubinstein (1973), that the social organization of police work is opposed to the rational or administrative organization symbolized by command and control systems [see also Ianni and Ianni (1983)]. The occupational culture, nurtured by the organization, is the most powerful force determining police behavior and is much less accessible to scrutiny than official records.

Increasingly, overlaid on this occupational culture, this set of practices, knowledge, detailed contacts with some members of the community, and a practical attachment to one's territory is a formalized, radio based, dispatching, and motorized response. Concomitantly, organizational specialization and the formal designation of roles arrived: a sharper division between staff and line and between generalist and specialist officers. Officers in Metro City are assigned to vehicles nominally based in a precinct. All general calls are meant to be shunted over the radio to the vehicles, and the force maintains the capacity to dispatch simultaneously specialized vehicles (tactical units, dog squads, etc.). The dominant image of policing remains that of territorial affinity and obligation; "intrusion" by specialized units and officers are considered poaching from the patrol officers' perspective. This invisible paradigm, like that in Centreshire, is based on the previous mode of policing that involved contact with citizens and an area, despite the fact that because of rotation of officers, the introduction of new tactics of policing (for example, in Metro City of local ministations and scooter units), and the high turnover and recruitment of new officers in the last ten years, there is little local knowledge. Furthermore, officers may not even ride in or drive the same car in the same area from one shift to another.

The MPD was one of the first American departments with radio-controlled vehicles and, later, centralized dispatching. The present system emerged, somewhat like the system in the BPD, as a response to a felt need within the metropolitan area to integrate services. Political arguments included a wish to centralize dispatching, to reduce time in providing the services to minimize tax costs, to centralize administration, to increase accountability, and to provide a single structure for receiving, processing, and allocating calls for police, fire, and emergency medical services (EMS). The fragmentation of service in the county was expected to be solved in 1970 by establishing an area-wide 911 emergency number. In theory, the citizen calling 911 would either have a request refused, accepted, or referred.

The network of services did not result as envisioned in 1970. A number of anomalies remain in the provision of police services in the metropolitan area, and the overall system remains incomplete: Calls for fire service must be transferred to a fire department for disposition; calls for medical service are transmitted to EMS, where they are processed; and calls for police in suburban areas are referred to agencies in those areas. One independent city remains in the middle of the metropolitan area. Callers giving addresses located in that city when they call 911 are given the number of their local police department and told to call there. Federal funds once paid for "hard wire" between the eighteen suburban areas and the communications center; this enabled 911 operators to transfer calls directly. Since the funds were terminated, only the incoming capacity remains. Finally, one suburban police department has contracted with the MPD to supply certain specialized services. Some calls from that locale are referred there, and some calls are accepted and vehicles dispatched by the MPD dispatchers.

System Rationale in the MPD

The administrative rationale for the centralized call collection system of the Midwest Police Department is that all calls are received centrally rather than at a precinct level and that all requests for police are routed from the precincts to the center, from where they are returned to these same precincts. This facilitates administrative control and supervision of the allocation of resources, reduces discretion in theory at the precinct level, and centralizes the control over level and kind of response. Slack resources can be used to meet demand unknown to the peripheral precincts, for example, a large-scale traffic accident, hostage situation, weather disaster, or riot. Calls are queued in the center and tracked by a computer. Calls can be monitored by supervisors at consoles, handled by a sergeant at the master or control desk in the dispatch segment, or handled by supervisors in the operator's room at the supervisor's desk. Calls, radio communications, and informal interaction can be monitored, and computers monitor all calls, radio transmissions, and telephone messages.

Once sent from the operator through the dispatcher to the precinct or specialized unit, the responsibility for response lies at the local level. Each precinct in theory has about ten scout cars and about twenty-eight officers who must staff five to ten "inside" positions and three to six cars (two officers per car). Patrol car areas are named by the precinct and the car number combined, for example 10:92 (car 92 in the tenth precinct). Three to six cars are actually on duty in a given day. Variations in staffing level are introduced because of repairs to vehicles and differential allocations of vehicles by shift, holidays, and days of the week (Sundays are generally lightly patrolled). Differential availability is also due to transfer of units and sick days, which are handled initially at the center. There is an additional factor that complicates the determination of the number of cars available at any given time. Law requires that prisoners be transported to several courts within the city for arraignment, and prisoners, especially on Monday, must be moved from cells they have occupied over the weekend. Transport from the precincts to the courts must be provided separately for men and women and for juveniles; this may demand one to three cars and may require several round trips to court from the precinct. Because precincts phone in their strength to the communications center at the beginning of a shift, there is a tendency to conceal or show cars out of service so that they can be used to transport prisoners. During periods seen as high-crime periods, tactical units and other cars may be assigned to precincts to assist. This description omits any temporal variations in availability resulting from variations in demand or special events such as a parade, a demonstration, or a "crime crackdown," which require additional personnel. Thus the *actual* strength on a given shift varies widely, as does the assigned strength. Officers rotate through three shifts in four units of about twenty persons. One of the units is always on leave. These units are the basis of the social organization of policing at the precinct level.

Telephone calls are received directly by operators in the communications center, located in the central police station, screened by operators, and passed on to dispatchers and hence to officers. There are some fifty-two trunk lines coming into the room, and calls received are answered (within eight seconds) by the operators, the number of which depends on shift, time of day, day of week, and variations in personnel availability. Some work is generated by the response of the computers, and there are telegraphs and teleprinters in the communications center. All communication to the precincts is done over the telephone or radio. In theory, certain calls can be handled by the supervisor of the dispatcher section, a sergeant, the lieutenant on duty, or the inspector in charge of the communications center itself. These are rare emergency incidents. Theoretically all work comes through the center, because even calls from the precinct to officers must be received and passed on, for example, "Please advise Officer Smith to call the precinct." Response is by either a specialized unit sent directly from the center or a nonspecialized unit assigned by the center. There are no official responses arising from and settled in the precinct itself. The center controls all calls coming to the center and those referred to it and can call on individual, precinct, zone, or force-level or extra-force-level assistance (the county police, the state police, the Federal Bureau of Investigation, the Drug Enforcement Agency, etc.). Data are stored in the computer for twenty-four hours, on tapes for approximately twenty-four hours, and on permanent printouts for ninety days.

In 1979 operators received and processed some 1,548,336 calls. This is an average of some 129,000 a month, 4,232 per day, or about 177 per hour. The operators, about 13 of them, although there may be as many as twenty-one on the late afternoon shift (4 P.M.–midnight), handle about fourteen calls each per hour, or about one every three minutes. The calls vary in length, but essential facts can be obtained in less than thirty seconds. No data are kept on calls arriving directly at the precincts and handled there; nor are data from scout car logbooks kept centrally.

Communications Channels

The communications center has nine distinctive communication channels: radio, vehicle locator, telephone, written records, electrowriter, verbal messages, tape recorder, load flow indicator, and silent alarm. The radio connects by means of VHF channels dispatchers with detectives or officers in scout cars, tactical vehicles, dog vans, and ministation vehicles (patrol cars funded by federal monies working from neighborhood "walk-in" bases). UHF radio transmits to personal radios carried by each officer and the detective unit, and a force-wide radio transmitter can broadcast to all units and precincts simultaneously.

The vehicle locator, which is rarely used, transmits a signal indicating a vehicle in trouble. The signal appears on the screen in the center. The idea is that an officer in trouble pushes the button to indicate distress when there is little time to make a radio transmission. Unfortunately the absence of information on precise location means that little can be done until the officer radios a location or is located using dispatcher's records, other officers' hunches about where the car is, or other information.

Perhaps the dominant channel with respect to workload and symbolic importance for the operators is the telephone. Some fifty-two lines come into the operators' consoles (usually twelve to fourteen are staffed), carrying 911 calls. Calls that cannot be answered because staff are engaged are automatically answered by a recorded message, put in a queue by a computer, and shunted to the next available operator. City government lines are also available for general use. One line with a seven-digit city number is reserved for general service inquiries. Two operators answer telephone requests from dispatchers and officers directly. Requests from precincts for information from the State Department of Motor Vehicles computer (vehicle registration, driver's license numbers, and license plate numbers) and the national FBI computer for records checks and outstanding federal warrants are also answered. Several hundred internal police lines connect dispatchers and operators with the rest of the force. Internal lines are occasionally used by officers to call in information to operators or dispatchers when a radio is jammed or malfunctioning or when they wish to communicate with dispatchers avoiding taped 911 lines.

Written records, or printouts of computer files, include output such as traffic tickets, arrests, warrants served, vehicle logbooks, and officers; notebooks. Computer printout is produced of dispatches made the previous day based on dispatchers' notes written on incident cards. This shows when each call was received, when dispatched, when a unit accepted the call, the unit to which it was assigned, when the car called in as "clear" or back in service, the address, location, and event classification. A computer keeps data on minicomputers used by some cars. A computer also monitors telephone calls made to the center (number, length, operator who answered the call, seconds per hour the operator was in service, and, conversely, the length of the operator break).

The electrowriter is a machine encasing a sheet of paper on which one writes. The machine "reads" the message and transmits it electrically to a receiving screen. In this case the operators are connected by electrowriters with the EMS center, which dispatches ambulances, and with police zone controllers or dispatchers. The latter connection is used only when the computer is not working.

Verbal communication takes the form of informal face-to-face interactions between members of subsystems 1 and 2, rarely between subsystems 2 and 3, and almost never between subsystems 1 and 3 (see figure 2.1).

There are two types of tape recorder used in the center. One, at each console, contains about sixty minutes of tape and is intended for brief use and quick replays of calls. The other is a two-reel master tape machine recording all transmissions in and out of the center by phone on 911 lines and radio.

Two load-flow indicators are used for internal administrative control. One is a board with a set of lights, one for each console, showing whether a call is being answered at that time, and the other is a set of three lights indicating the current workload level. A green light indicates that up to four calls are waiting in the queue formed by the master computer; a yellow light indicates that five to nine calls are waiting, and a red light indicates that ten or more calls are waiting. Up to fifty calls can be stored and queued.

There are also silent alarm calls accepted in the dispatchers' section. The dispatcher who controls the city-wide desk, normally a sergeant, has responsibility for the silent and bank alarm system and the police helicopter when it is airborn. The dispatcher may also control any "crisis" that exceeds the boundaries of a given zone, for example, a high-speed chase, or requires force-level attention, for example, a hostage situation, demonstration, or shooting.

Ecology

The communications center of the MPD is located on the seventh floor of the police headquarters in the center of Metro City. It has restricted access monitored by closed circuit television and a buzzer system for entry; it can be approached only by elevator.

The operators sit in a small room at consoles in tiny cubicles wedged next to each other. There are no outside windows. About 90% of the operators are female and most are black. All are civilians. They are not allowed by union contract to ride in police vehicles, and most never have. They do not interact with police officers except in the operators' lounge, where they retire for fifteen minutes each hour (by contract), or when dispatchers or supervisors observe them. The consoles at which they are seated contain a VDU and a keyboard for entering data into the computer, an electrowriter, a telephone with several lines, a small tape recorder that can be played back, and a small note pad. The operators cannot see each other easily unless they stand or lean back, and such movements are impossible because of the length of the telephone cord. The noise level is high because of the frequency of the calls and the number of persons in the room. The supervisors sit at a desk that can aurally monitor any console (the desk does not have a VDU), above which is the set of workload warning lights. Interactions are limited to off-duty chats and the occasional conversation between operators or between operators and dispatchers by telephone and nonverbal gestures seen through the glass barriers.

The control center office adjoins the dispatchers' space, and off of that are the offices of the inspector in charge of the communications center, the lieutenant in charge during the shift, and the training sergeant.

The dispatchers, sitting just across from the operators, are mostly male police officers. About 95% are white (this varies by shift and time of day). They sit at small desks that have switchboard consoles and wear headsets connected to a radio-telephone (which can be operated by hand or with a foot pedal). The small desk holds cards on which are printed the calls they are currently assigning. On the left is a larger ledger in which the dispatcher signs in and out and enters the time he reads out the call numbers of the department's radio station (required by federal law). On the right is a set of wooden slots into which the dispatcher slides assignments once made, and somewhat further to the right is the IBM printer that issues the copies of the incidents typed up by the operators on the VDUs. The dispatchers can listen to other zones on the radio, can broadcast their transmittals on the air in the room through amplifiers, and can use the telephones for internal and external calls. Above the desk is a map of the zone for which the officer dispatches. The calls sent to him or her are automatically sent there by the computer, but the map is sometimes used to give directions to lost officers or to check the location of cars when they call in. Dispatchers take ten-minute breaks every hour and are relieved by other officers. There is a casual atmosphere in the room, and people call back and forth to each other. They can see some of the other dispatchers. They have a broader vista than the operators. The officers attached to the communications center wander in and out and chat with the dispatchers, and they share a coffee break room and a locker room off the hall to the rear of the operators' area.

An unused computer sits in a glass-encased room next to the operators. It is occasionally turned on by computer salespeople but is otherwise unused. It is intended to serve as the backup computer for the present system, which is located in the basement of the city-county building nearby, and for the car minicomputers.

The officers are dispersed in vehicles throughout the city. They are connected to the communications center only by radio or interact with each other primarily on the scene of certain events, over the radio, or on breaks in or out of the precinct. They are isolated from the communications center and from the operators and dispatchers. They interact as strangers with the dispatchers and have no contact with the operators.

The isolation of the dispatchers and operators from the officers in the field means that, unlike the situation in the BPD, where there is interaction in the subdivision between officers and the controller, there is no face-to-face contact, duty related or not, between the communications personnel and the officers in scout cars. This has a number of consequences, which are outlined in subsequent chapters.

Flow of Calls through the System: Process Description of Operations
A flow chart of call processing in the 911 center in the MPD is shown in figure 3.4. A task-role operations chart (figure 3.5) is the basis for the following description.

Operators at the center are under strict instructions, one could almost call them orders, to enter every call on the VDU as an incident for which

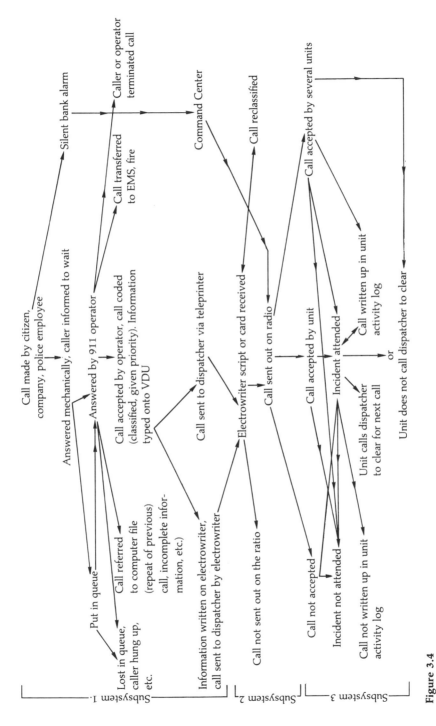

Figure 3.4
Flowchart of call processing by subsystem in the 911 center of the MPD.

System B

Telephone calls from 911 lines, alarm lines and internal lines (calls automatically answered and placed in computer queue if overload occurs)

Subsystem 1: 13–21 Operators (civilian), plus 2 supervisors (1 sergeant and 1 civilian per shift)

Operations/tasks
  Receiving stimuli (calls)
  Establishing the credibility of call
  Selecting and sorting facts: refuse, refer (EMS, fire), or accept

Constructing an image of the event

Encoding: writing on VDUs
  Entering a location
  Classifying the event
  Establishing a priority
  Entering any remarks

Transmission channels (all 2-way)
  Phone: Bell telephone and internal lines
  VDU: Computer
  Electrowriter
  Voice
  Nonverbal

Subsystem 2: 7 Dispatchers zone controllers (sworn officers) (4 zones with 2 precincts; 2 with 3; 1 city-wide desk)

Operations/tasks
  Receive hard-copy or electrowriter-script from operators,
  Calls (internal) and commercial alarm signals
  Selecting and sorting facts

Constructing an image of the call and of the event

Figure 3.5
Functions and tasks in the MPD. Some of the elements in this model are adapted from Eldridge (1979), which in turn is based on Ross (1977).

Although transmission in subsystem 1 is by computer, which prints out for the dispatcher what the 911 operator has written or typed, dispatchers and operators can also call each other by telephone for clarification and can be in visual contact. They work in two rooms divided by a plate glass window. On breaks, dispatchers may briefly come into the 911 room to chat. When the computer is down, all transmissions are written on the electro-writer, which will transmit hard copy to dispatchers. EMS dispatches are always sent by electrowriter.

Dispatchers (subsystem 2) cannot officially be called by officers in precincts except in special circumstances. All calls must go through either a service desk or 911 before being routed to a dispatcher. Dispatchers make few outgoing calls but do receive numerous phone calls, primarily from precincts and 911 operators.

Decoding of message elements
  Location
  Priority
  Reclassification (?)
  Entering any remarks and adding "context"

Verbal assignment of incident to unit

Transmission channels
  Computer to department of motor vehicles, FBI (NCIC)
  Two-way VHF radio to cars, multiple channels

Subsystem 3: 130 scout cars with areal responsibilities (varies with shift and days of the week)

Operations/tasks
  Receiving, sensing and sorting of messages

Constructing an image of the incident, call and event

Decoding message
  Elements and "context"

Transmission channels
  Telephone, e.g., from public call box
  Mobile computer (some vehicles)
  Radio VHF (personal and vehicle)

Action outcomes/disposition of the job reported
  Any of above channels, principally radio

Status reported (in or out of service)

Figure 3.5 (continued)

The police patrol system (subsystem 3) is composed of zones, precincts, and scout car areas and is a series of partially overlapping areal responsibilities. All precincts, except one, have ten scout car areas, not all of which are patrolled on a given day because of vehicle or personnel shortages. Precincts also have two or three federally funded ministation vehicles and may have other special units (supervisors, detectives) based at a precinct or city-wide (tactical squad, plain clothes, vice, dogs, four officer cars). There are also foot beat patrol officers in some precincts. Because cars can leave their areas for calls and do not have to report arrival at a call, it is in fact impossible to know the location of cars in or out of service, even when they are requested to give a location.

In subsystem 3 officers can -call 911 operators or dispatchers on the phone or over the two-way radio or talk to them in person (rare). In general, neither 911 operators nor dispatchers know what the outcomes of their actions are beyond the receipt of their transmission by a member of the linked subsystem. This means that virtually all feedback loops are weak, unofficial, and ad hoc. and that the links between the subsystems and between the communications system and the environment are loose.

there is a valid address at which the problem is said to be happening.[17] In general, operators activate the computer by means of the VDU immediately on hearing a call. As soon as they hear a click in their headset, they access it to enter an address so that the computer will accept further information. They can terminate without recording nuisance calls, incomplete calls, or those that repeat earlier requests. They can also refer a call or transfer it to EMS or the fire department.

In subsystem 1 the operators receive a phone call answering, "Emergency Center, where is the problem?" They must do "sensing", that is, decide if the call is credible [many calls are terminated by the operators ("Go play in the freeway")], decide if the address or location is valid, and ascertain what the nature of the problem is, selecting and sorting from the message, for example, taking cues from voice, speed, accent, language used, and their own commonsense knowledge or imagery of such events ("That doesn't sound like a women who's afraid."). Then they must encode the message. It will automatically be given a priority. The operators must decide at that time whether to refer. If the location is in another jurisdiction, they can refer the call by asking the caller to phone another police department, providing the seven-digit number. If it should be sent to another municipal agency, that number is given. If the information is not complete at the time of the call, for example, the caller hangs up, the operators refers it to the computer's memory bank. They also must decide to what unit, if any, to send any valid service request: fire, EMS, or police. Sometimes more than one unit must be sent by law, but if one is requested by the 911 operator, the caller is told only that "a unit will be or has been requested." If a call is valid and not referred, they then send the message to a dispatcher in the adjoining room.

The format (see the incident codes list in figure 3.6) is fairly simple and is used to order the items for transmission to the dispatcher. There are roughly five required types of information entered on the VDU by operators: (1) address; (2) type of dwelling—single, apartment, or multiple occupancy unit—and, if an apartment, where in the building the apartment is located; (3) classification (1 nonchangeable category out of 245 possibilities) and priority (predetermined by the incident code); (4) remarks, for example, whether a weapon is present; and (5) unit requested (police, EMS, fire, or some combination thereof). The caller's name is not requested, but the machine automatically enters an incident number, numbers indicating the receiving console and the operator, and the time, day, and date.

Once the call is coded in 1 of 245 categories, the operator sends it automatically to the zone controller in subsystem 2. The incident is sent to the controller for the area of the city in which the address is located. The incident can be retrieved in the future by address, number, date, or operator's

Incident Codes

Note: The number (1 thru 5) in front of the incident code designates the suggested priority of the code. However, runs are dispatched by seriousness, urgency, growth rate, and availability of resources.

31. Homicide/Death
1-3100 Homicide (kill another)
1-3111 Att. suicide in prog.
2-3112 Suicide just happ.
2-3119 Suicide rept.
2-3120 Dead person (nat./acc.)

32. Sex
1-3201 Rape in prog.
2-3202 Rape/just happ.
2-3203 Rape att/just happ.
3-3209 Rape rept.
1-3211 Molesting in prog.
2-3212 Molesting just happ.
2-3213 Molesting att/just happ.
4-3219 Molesting rept.
3-3221 Exposing in prog.
3-3222 Exposing just happ.
4-3229 Exposing rept.
2-3241 Other sex in prog.
3-3242 Other sex just happ.
3-3243 Other sex att/just happ.
4-3249 Other sex rept.
4-3251 Disorderly couple in car

33. Robbery
1-3301 RA in prog.
2-3302 RA just happ.
2-3303 RA att/just happ.
3-3309 RA rept.
1-3311 RNA in prog.
2-3312 RNA just happ.
3-3313 RNA att/just happ.
3-3319 RNA Rept.
1-3321 Purse snatch in prog.
2-3322 Purse snatch just happ.
3-3323 Purse snatch att/just happ.
3-3329 Purse snatch rept.
1-3331 Extortion in prog.
2-3332 Extortion just happ.

3-3333 Extortion att/just happ.
4-3339 Extortion rept.

34. Assault
1-3401 FA in prog.
2-3402 FA just happ.
3-3409 FA rept.
1-3412 Shooting just happ.
1-3422 Cutting just happ.
1-3431 Person w/weapon there now
2-3432 Person w/weapon just left
2-3441 Shots h/f now
3-3442 Shots h/f just happ.
4-3449 Shots h/f rept.
1-3451 Kidnapping in prog.
2-3452 Kidnapping just happ.
2-3453 Kidnapping att/just happ.
3-3459 Kidnapping rept.
1-3461 A&B in prog. (no weapon)
4-3469 A&B rept.

35. Burglary
1-3501 B&E business in prog.
2-3502 B&E bus. just happ.
3-3503 B&E bus. att/just happ.
3-3509 B&E bus. rept.
1-3511 B&E dwelling in prog.
2-3512 B&E dwell just happ.
2-3513 B&E dwell att/just happ.
4-3519 B&E dwelling rept.
1-3531 B&E auto in prog.
3-3532 B&E auto just happ.
4-3539 B&E auto rept.
1-3541 B&E other in prog.
2-3542 B&E other just happ.
3-3543 B&E other att/just happ.
4-3549 B&E other rept.
2-3551 Glass breaking
2-3560 People away/lights on
3-3570 Investigate building

Figure 3.6
Incident codes for the MPD.

2-3580 Open door
3-3590 Enter w/o permission

36. Larceny
2-3601 Larceny in prog.
3-3602 Larceny just happ.
3-3603 Larceny att/just happ.
4-3609 Larceny rept.

37. Automobiles
2-3701 UDAA in prog.
2-3702 UDAA just happ.
4-3709 UDAA rept.
3-3711 Tamp w/auto in prog.
4-3719 Tamp w/auto rept.
4-3720 Recovered auto
2-3731 Stripping auto now
3-3740 Investigate auto
3-3750 One over wheel

38. Miscellaneous Crime
3-3801 MDP in prog.
3-3802 MDP just happ.
4-3809 MDP rept.
2-3820 Cab & fare
3-3830 Defraud innkeeper
2-3841 Bad check in prog.
4-3842 Bad check just happ.
4-3849 Bad check rept.
2-3851 Stolen CR/card in prog.
3-3852 Stolen CR/card just happ.
4-3859 Stolen CR/card rept.
3-3860 Gambling
2-3871 Forged Rx in prog.
3-3873 Forged Rx att/just happ.
4-3879 Forged Rx rept.
2-3881 Narc. in prog.
3-3882 Narc. att/just happ.
4-3889 Narc. rept.

39. Family Trouble/Domestic Violence
1-3900 F.T. homicide
1-3901 F.T. FA in prog.
2-3902 F.T. FA just happ.
3-3909 F.T. FA rept.
1-3911 F.T. shooting j/h
1-3921 F.T. cutting j/h

1-3931 F.T. person w/weapon
2-3932 F.T. person weapon J/L
1-3941 F.T. fight
1-3951 F.T. person screaming
1-3961 F.T. A&B in prog.
3-3969 F.T. A&B rept.
3-3971 F.T. MDP in prog.
3-3979 F.T. MDP rept.
3-3989 F.T. Spouse abuse law-injunction/
        peace bond

80. Alarms
1-8000 Bank alarm
1-8010 Hold up alarm
1-8014 Hold up alarm—M.O.W.
1-8020 Hold up alarm (Monitored)
1-8030 B&E alarm
1-8034 B&E alarm—M.O.W.
1-8040 B&E alarm (Monitored)
1-8050 Police alarm
1-8060 Automated dial alarm

81. Traffic
1-8100 Auto X—injury
2-8110 Auto X
3-8119 Auto X rept.
3-8130 Towing
4-8140 Parking
5-8151 Hot rods
4-8160 Aid motorist
2-8170 Xing-school/Rush
3-8180 Misc. traffic

82. Disturbance
4-8200 Boys
3-8210 Crowd gathering
3-8220 Disorderly gang
3-8230 Fight
3-8250 Landlord/tenant trouble
3-8260 Neighbor trouble
3-8270 Disturbance/trouble
1-8280 Person screaming
3-8290 Noise/radio, etc.

83. Disaster/Fire
3-8300 Fire
1-8310 Fire dept. needs help

Figure 3.6 (continued)

1-8322 Fire bomb just happ.
2-8323 Fire bomb att/just happ.
4-8329 Fire bomb rept.
1-8330 Bomb threat
1-8331 Explosive device
1-8340 Explosion
4-8350 Tree/wire/pole down
3-8360 Gas/other odors
1-8370 Disaster/hazard

84. Persons
3-8400 Meet person
3-8401 Meet the baliff
3-8410 Drunk
2-8420 One down
2-8430 Pt. out wanted person
3-8440 Investigate person
2-8441 Holding person
2-8442 Holding shoplifter
2-8450 Prowler (window peeper)
1-8461 Missing serious (age/mental)
4-8469 Missing rept.
5-8470 V.R.M.
3-8480 Holding missing/runaway

85. Medical Service
2-8500 Meet EMS
2-8510 Mental run
2-8520 Blood run
3-8530 Aid invalid
4-8549 Misc. X-rept. (pers/pub prop)

86. Animals
2-8600 Animal bites
3-8610 Other animal compl.

87. Miscellaneous
3-8700 Unlisted: See remarks
4-8720 Recovered property
5-8730 Publish/litter

90. Officials/Calls
1-9000 Officer in trouble
3-9010 Meet officer
4-9020 Call station BZ
5-9021 Call station in-service
4-9030 To station BZ
5-9031 To station in-service

4-9040 Dial BZ
4-9050 Special detail
4-9060 Station security
2-9070 Man the auto

91. Vehicle maintenance
5-9100 Car wash
5-9110 Gas BZ
2-9120 Flat tire
5-9130 Vehicle inspection
3-9140 Radio repair
3-9150 To garage
3-9160 Car trouble

93. Other
2-9300 Arrest
2-9302 Attempt to arrest
1-9310 Court
5-9320 Deliver msg/info
5-9330 Lunch
5-9340 Serve papers
2-9350 Demonstration
3-9360 Strike
3-9370 Transport prisoner
3-9380 Transport witness
4-9390 Transport property

50. & 51. EMS Codes
5000 Sick
5001 Sick
5002 Sick
5010 Injured
5011 Injured
5012 Injured
5020 Unconsciousness
5030 Heart
5040 Stroke
5041 Stroke
5042 Stroke
5050 Seizure/convulsion
5051 Seizure/convulsion
5052 Seizure/convulsion
5060 Bleeding/external
5061 Bleeding/external
5062 Bleeding/external
5070 Bleeding/internal

Figure 3.6 (continued)

5080	Poisoning	5130	Obstetrical
5090	Burns	5131	Obstetrical
5091	Burns	5132	Obstetrical
5092	Burns	5140	Bites
5100	Breathing	5141	Bites
5110	Diabetic coma	5142	Bites
5111	Diabetic	5150	Accidental cutting
5120	Drug overdose	5151	Accidental cutting
5121	Drug overdose	5152	Accidental cutting

Figure 3.6 (continued)

console position, but the responsibility of the operator ends at this point. No further information about the call is given to the operator, and, unless another call about the event is received or the caller recalls, that is the last the operator hears of the incident. A crisis in the handling of the event or feedback from the dispatcher about some detail of the transmission may cause it to be recalled by the operator. Other transmission channels are rarely used.

Once the incident is sent on to the dispatcher or zone controller, it is printed out. The dispatcher then sets a priority for the call and attempts to assign it. The available and nonavailable cars are represented by the slots to the right of the controller. The type of response made by the police is shaped primarily at this point by the controller, who sets priorities, juggles cars, areas, and units, and verbally seeks (over the radio) a unit to accept the incident. Allocation to a unit, as explored in detail in the following chapters, is based on features and imagery of the incident and call and the context within which the controller is working. Once he has made an assignment, he writes the precinct and car on the card and places it in the appropriate slot.

Although a dispatcher might verify a message or parts of it by phone with a 911 operator, it is generally sorted out using knowledge of the cars available in the zone to which the call is sent. It will then be decoded with reference to priority (and may be disregarded by the dispatcher), code type (this may be revised on the basis of checks with a 911 operator or be done independently by the dispatcher), location (cars are generally assigned to an area but may leave it, be "off-duty," or "out-of-service," thus requiring other cars to be assigned), and finally the verbal remarks of the caller typed in by the 911 operator ("woman says she fears ex-husband may kill her.").

On the basis of these data and perhaps as a result of conversation with officers in the cars, 911 operators, or even other dispatchers or a supervisor, the original imagery of the event provided on the basis of the dispatcher receiving the printed copy may be modified and reshaped. This transformation is critical in the decision concerning whether to dispatch, what to dispatch, and with what priority and label or code. The dispatcher does not simply forward the request as received by 911 operators from citizens, nor as it is forwarded to him by 911 operators.

It is important to recall here that unlike the British system, there is no assignment or reassignment of calls at the precinct level. All assignments based on citizen requests are handled through the center and directed to vehicles in the precincts. Unfinished work, in the form of the 4 × 6 cards printed out, are placed in slots on the desk of the controller before official assignment. These provide a quick review of the present workload of that controller for a relief dispatcher or supervisor. Data from these cards are entered into the computer the next day and each "run" or assignment is printed out by precinct and time of day.

In the third subsystem, the scout car officer system, the message is received over the radio. Officers must sense and sort out the call. They code it or give it a rough priority with respect to their present duties, location, the time of day, their past experience with these types of event, and official or departmental procedures for handling such calls. These variables are important in decoding messages (Van Maanen 1974). A reconstructed image of the event based on auditory data is shaped by the officer(s) in the car. But most important, only officers in the scout car subsystem actually see the reported event if they arrive on the scene and are able to revise and reconstruct the meaning of the situation on the basis of their own sensory data. Finally, action outcomes are produced by officers frequently in concert with citizens, and these are variably and selectively written up in activity logs and reported verbally to dispatchers.

Conclusion

The history of the BPD in Centreshire and the MPD in Metro City suggests a slow and steady growth of technology and slight shaping of police duties and supervision by the machines and by citizen expectations and habits. In the following chapters I analyze message flow synchronically and then diachronically and compare the two systems explicitly.

II

Workings

The British Police Department: Synchronic Analysis

Ethnographic data, observations, interviews, and records are presented here utilizing the conceptual framework previously outlined. I start by discussing the effects of coding, technology, roles and tasks, and interpretative practices on messages by subsystem (operators, controllers, officers).

Operators: Codes

Assigning codes involves placing information within an organized, usually formal scheme. The phone rings, and the operator answers, "Hello, police, can I help you?" or something simpler, for example, "This is the police." The call may have been transferred from the British Telecoms operator, in which case it is "double-framed." This frames the call as a call to the police and makes it ostensibly a matter of police business. The answer "Police" affirms or disconfirms the caller's intention of reaching the police but, once affirmed, marks the message on that channel and sets it apart as police relevant. The answering procedure reflexively marks it as a police call.

This marking is done in seven ways: (1) the presumed intention of the caller to call using this channel; (2) the answer of the operator as a police representative labeling the call request; (3) the prospective willingness of the operator to listen to the narrative and to grant it credibility; (4) the request for specific data (name of caller, address, description of the "trouble," district or area) if the call is deemed credible and police relevant; (5) Promising to "send someone to come and have a look"; (6) the act of requesting that information be repeated—"What's that address?" "How do you spell that?" (for a street name or person's name)—or asking the caller to "speak up" or start over (because the caller began talking before the operator put the call through) to orient the speaker to phatic aspects of the message but also to frame it as a *kind* of message communicating help seeking and a potentially helpful reply; (7) the active seeking of information *not* offered, such as asking, "What's the trouble?"

The BPD operators allow people to talk fairly extensively without attempting to constrain their narrative to an established format or to force it into a preset order. They do attempt at some point to elicit the essential format-required facts.

Actions of fact seeking (4, 6, 7), helpful "attitude" (5), and prospective receptivity (3) also serve to orient speaker-hearer dyads to the phonetic and referential aspects of talk and, conversely, to reduce in salience the emotive and poetic potential of a message. Although a caller may occasionally indicate (mainly by tone of voice) an emotive aspect of the message, receivers rarely exhibit a conative emphasis (they do, however, occasionally express irritation at the level of volume, speed of message transmission, or demanding tone in caller requests).

Key words, once seized on to characterize a message, are related to an image of the event about which the call is made.[1] A type of event is thus established. The process of "seizing" is detailed in the section on internal message analysis, but "imagining" can be described and exemplified.

Image formation acts to link verbal stimuli and action (encoding). Identifying the image is a turning point in the analysis. Four empirical examples are useful to illustrate the operators' image of events.

1. A caller (37)[2] referred to a "robbery" of his home. After he was connected by an operator, the police responded, saying "attempted break-in, was it sir?"

2. A caller (7) phoned for someone else. "I'm phoning in behalf of Mrs. W. She's too upset; she's had a robbery." "A robbery, you mean they broke in her house? What's her address?" After receiving the address, the operator continued, "Can you tell her not to touch anything? I'll send the police 'round."

3. Some calls are refused as not being emergency calls without a reason being given, suggesting that some tacit sense of emergency is being employed. A caller (27) asked, "Is this the X police [local station]?" and was told "No, you've rung 999, the emergency number."

4. The caller (40), a child, reported a lost dog and wanted to know if there was a local kennel. The operator responded," Do you require the police in an emergency? I would suggest that this is not an emergency call. You can ring your local police station about it. I'll give you the number of the local police, and you can ring them.... But it isn't an emergency call, you see."

Thus a caller who presents the requisite cues to image emergency but not the correct label is connected, but one who gives incorrect cues is refused, being told it is not an emergency. When not viewed as an emergency, inappropriate use of the 999 line is used as a gloss for "police relevant" in some cases, whereas clearly nonemergency calls such as break-ins that occurred the night before in a shop reported the following morning *are* viewed as police relevant and accepted on the 999 emergency line. When accepted, format constraints are applied; operators interrupt callers' narratives to obtain the format-necessary facts in order: address and district or general area name if the call is seen as something other than "information received." The nature of the event reported (for dispatching) has often already been presented. The characteristic sequence of an accepted call is thus a blunted narrative interrupted by operators who seek address, district, and name and closed with a promise to send someone.

The image is also indexed by formatting the responses of the caller, by interruption, and by repeated reflexive and phatic remarks designed to classify facts of location, name, district, and the reported event. Metalinguistic comments, such as those connecting a caller's use of the term "robbery" to "breaking" or "attempted breaking," are also used once the call is framed as a police call and the operator has decided to format it. These actions, in turn, involve the imagining of future sequences of police action, namely, the assignment of the call, the police searching for a location and address and seeking a particular caller, and the controller requiring information from a constable on the scene to fill in or suggest a type of event for the "remarks" section. The chunking that goes on involves a reference to short-term memory of details of the narrative (actors, actions, setting, and scene) while connecting this to long-term memories of similar events and how they were coded, responded to, and solved and their dynamics. The bits of relevance are held, for example, the victim, the address, the caller (if not the victim), the items stolen. These facts are stored while other events are compared to these facts and a connection drawn between them and between caller and call. The caller and the victim or the caller and the event are also compared while proceeding with the manual task of typing in these selected facts.

Three kinds of meaning are implicit within the message. First, there are facts, opinions, observations, and asides framed as irrelevant by police answers—such things as, "I was just coming home from work" (5) or "I'm calling from the florist's shop" (35) (when reporting a traffic accident). Second, some meanings are known but not stated to callers, such as the fact that automatic alarms sounding between 8 and 10 A.M. are almost invariably false, a result of shopkeepers failing to turn off the alarm before opening the shop. A call may be made to check the veracity of the alarm, but on other occasions the message is sent to the subdivision to be managed by the controller. The third implicit meaning is that communicated by inflection of the voice—lowered in concern or words spoken in a reassuring tone (45)—or by specifically conative words of consolation, such as the police operator saying, "Oh dear," when hearing that a woman's house has been broken into (10).

Most calls are controlled by the operator ending the conversation: "I'll send someone around to talk to you" or "This is not an emergency call." These are metalinguistic counterparts of the opening ritual.

Encoding into the police scheme of things minimally constrains callers at the time, because any category is subject to negotiation when and if officers and/or the CID arrive. It does presumably constrain controllers. Furthermore, the pattern of decisions made by operators about calls to the police contributes to a theory of codes or encoding, for coherence and order emerge regardless of the content of the calls.

Calls vary in form, length, content, and degree of ambiguity (a feature of content). Some calls are brief, terse, almost elliptical, or redundant: "Mrs. Jones at Tesco supermarket is holding a prisoner." This is redundant because Mrs. Jones is known to be the manager of the Tesco. She normally calls when she has a shoplifter in hand, and the action implications of the name, the place, or holding a prisoner are the same: Send an officer in a car or the van to pick up the person being held. Other calls are rambling, convoluted, and characterized by multiple starts and stops, restarts, and hesitations and are both confused and confusing.

The following five features of natural decision making and rules for coding incoming calls characterize the first level of understanding.

1. When calls are ambiguous, this ambiguity must be resolved: All calls must be referred, accepted, or refused. If accepted, they must be classified. Apparently ambiguous calls are enacted as cases of calls to the police about which something will be done by a series of operations of analogical reasoning, based on presumptions held by the operators about the nature of such events. Calls are both, maybe, something like, and "as if" they were a certain category within the classification system. The coherence of the message is based on tacit knowledge. This tacit knowledge takes the form of a posited underlying order of which successive calls are taken to be representatives rather than unique ambiguous problems.

2. Analogical reasoning governs decisions about calls. The scientific literature depicts decision using a model of rational decision making in which the decisions are discrete, binary, or digital (on or off, present or absent), separated in time, and sequential in nature (easily represented in flowcharts, diagrams, decision trees and the like). [See Leonard (1938) and Tobias (1974); for the basic model, see Simon (1976, 1982). For a critique of this view, see Emerson (1983), Waegel (1981), Weick (1983a), Feldman (forthcoming), and Manning and Hawkins (forthcoming)]. There are reasons to support an alternative view and to suggest that decision making is analogical in character, that one decision affects the next (and that caseload affects sets of decisions), and that decisions fold back and affect others. The focus on discrete cases or units is misleading.

Needham has argued that classification need not be based on notions of hierarchy (categories arrayed in vertical order) and mutually exclusive categories based on a single dimension producing terms at the same level of generality and abstraction (1980, pp. 42–56). Rather, sets of categories may be juxtaposed and arrayed—"extended so as to comprise a range of qualitatively disparate objects and attributes" (p. 45). They may overlap in implicit meaning, and the relations between the units are analogous, whereas the items are merely homologous to each other. Futhermore, Needham argues on the basis of study of many diverse classification systems that *relations* may be defined by indigenous values (not formal and abstract properties of the items), that context defines the relations between items, and that even oppositions, because of connotative meanings, may be quite different.

The BPD classification system is used as a background grid against which individual calls are seen. No single feature of calls make them encodable; the basis is their relation to police work as a practical activity. As Needham has convincingly argued, the categories are themselves polythetic in character when jumbled into a classification group, and the movement of the message produces "serial or sporadic resemblances" (Needham 1980, p. 56).

3. Belief always embeds facts. Facts are context dependent. Certain key defining characteristics set a context within which a call is heard. Operators make judgments about the credibility of the caller based on the source of the call (whether it is from a recorded alarm that automatically rings the police and plays a tape, such as "This is the Royal British Legion Club on Bogside Splash," or from a 999 line), the tone of voice (age, sex, ethnic background), and the time when the call is received (calls first thing in the morning, in Britain around ten o'clock, from people identifying themselves as shopkeepers are consistent with past experience; such a call about a burglary at 4 P.M. is not). These characteristics give the call *face validity* and frame what follows as "shopkeeper-rings-about-a-burglary type of call." Conversely, calls from outside lines made by children at five o'clock are distrusted as nuisance calls, regardless of content. Once these characteristics of the call and the caller are recognized, other beliefs come into play. For example, shopkeepers who report that "the shop has been broken into" (regardless of whether the caller labels this event a "larcency," "burglary," or "robbery") are told not to move anything or clean up the shop until an officer arrives to take a statement and gather the evidence, even when the caller has not reported any breakage, mess, or damage. The view that the shop has been burgled as reported is based on operators' assumptions or beliefs about what the shopkeeper has seen, namely, that the shopkeeper or someone at the scene can read iconic signs that indicate

burglary and differentiate it from "vandalism," "robbery," or "attempted breaking."

Because the operator characterizes the call in a certain way, makes assumptions about the caller's acuity, the occurrence of the reported event, and trusts the information, the burglary classification is used. The opposite would lead to the call not being accepted, but the existence of these contextualized facts does not mean that "burglary" is seen as the solely apposite category that might have been employed. Margalit summarizes this process of belief as the context within which facts are heard:

The information one receives must be relative to what one already *knows* about possibilities at source. This knowledge occurs on both sides of the definition. K knows that s is F if and only if, given what K knows about the relevant alternative states of F, the information that s is F causes K to believe that s if F. (Margalit 1982, p. 1170).

This is a more formal statement of the anticipatory nature of facts and their appearance once a context is defined.

4. The logic of differences does not apply in call coding. The logic of difference and identity, the basis for classic Aristotelian logic, does not operate in call classification. The case has already been made for the relevance of context, which defines the nature of the relationship between properties. The argument can be made from another position. In the BPD calls can be double classified and reclassified on the basis of officers' investigation; priorities are not observed or changed without informing others. A given call can be simultaneously low priority and high priority in different subsystems. The phenomenological definition of all calls is that they are made tentatively, "as if" for all practical purposes, and are given a silent question mark which has a kind of anaphoric function. A call that becames an incident initially categorized as a "burglary" is viewed as a possible burglary (it could be a burglary, or it could be something else, or it could be a burglary *and* something else). All calls are sent forward or "down" regardless of content, so that the appearance of a call labeled "burglary" does not itself mean a crime call of high priority.

A decision is thus not one part of a cumulative, transitionally or transitively coded series but is subsystem specific. The decision(s) involved in classifying an event as a burglary are *not* reiterative because the classification in the first instance is not reviewed on factual and informational grounds but is transferred across subsystems on the basis of trust in the source and the sender. It is believed that it is a burglary because the *source* is credible (messages become more credible if police processed) and because classification is believed to produce actions subsequently that will not contradict the classification.

5. Tacit knowledge is used to organize calls. A set of required items orient the operators: time, place, nature of the complaint. Little additional questioning of callers take place. There are several relevant aspects of tacit knowledge, or knowledge based on feelings and intuition that is nonsystematized, shared and taken for granted, and often affectively laden. Although tacit knowledge is predictable in form and underlying structure, it is resistent to formulation (Needham 1981). Tacit knowledge is used to "connect" talk and events in the social and physical world, functions to make sense of deictic and anaphoric references ("It's going on now"; "He hit me"), and surrounds the message. This knowledge is not written down by operators, broadcast by them, or typed into the VDU for transmission. Aspects of tacit knowledge known to the operator about the call or caller are not included. Other information given to operators, such as the caller's wishes, the history of the development of the incident, and its duration and potential for further development, is also omitted. Ekblom and Heal, in research in an English force, listened to tapes of calls and concluded:

Controllers frequently seemed … to make judgments on the basis of unspoken assumptions. It was clear, for example, that they generally allowed the importance, time dependence and veracity of a reported occurrence to remain implicit in the caller's account, unstated and unchecked. They sought only rarely to confirm with callers their impression of the urgency of an incident by the interpolation of such questions as "Is the prowler still outside now?" (1982, pp. 16–17)

The assumptions made by the operators about the call may not be those made about it by others in subsequent subsystems, and they have little opportunity to check them unless feedback leads to questioning. Tacit knowledge is assumed to be shared within the communications system and makes the calls like each other and internally consistent and coherent despite the absence of detailed facts elicited from the caller or present in the incident as received. Tacit knowledge serves to connect islands of fact or logic.

Coding Effects

Coding effects are alterations in the number of words used to describe an event, the level of abstraction produced, the ordering of items, and the categories into which talk can be placed resulting from the transformation of a call into an incident. The coding has effects resulting from the process of assigning codes. Coding is in part a matter of the logic of images. Coding effects result from six factors: format-supplied constraints, ordering constraints, interactional constraints, and priority, item, and informational constraints.

Format-supplied constraints depend on six "semimechanical" operations. First, the computer automatically enters the date, time, the controller's collar number (equivalent to a badge number in the United States), and the grid reference or location of the event (assigned by the computer once an address is entered on the VDU). Second, the computer leaves open classification of the incident (up to three categories can be used), location, caller's name, message, action taken (by the operator, later by the controller and/or the officer). Later actions are entered on the VDU by the controller. Third, each action *reduces* the number of options available to the operator. Initially there are six options; each one filled reduces the range of the next choice. Fourth, the subchoices given by each category are constraining: The BPD operator has thirty subcategories from which to choose; location is *binary* (present or absent) as are "caller," "remarks," and "message." Fifth, classification of the event, the most uncertain operation, in this linear, logical, formal, binary, referential fashion orders the environment as a set of logically articulated facts. They occupy one time and one space, are formally situated, and have meaning only as a set of facts referring to other facts rather than to imaginary features or the quality of interactions within caller-answerer dyads. This replicates the attitude required of the operators toward human misery.

The internal constraints on the next action, given the first in the format, are reproduced in ordering operator's actions and in constraining caller's talk. The way in which a call is constituted phenomenologically is consistent with the format requirements of giving information in order, regardless of the chaos of the caller.

Thus, in a way, internal constraints also produce interactional constraints. That is, they generate what can be heard as relevant and accepted as part of a call, the need to classify the call as an incident, and what is requested and asked for next from the caller. This sequence is set by the operator's questions and indicates the power of the operator to set the agenda and to control pacing and order.

Coding also serves to set an explicit or implicit *priority* on the event. This is done either mechanically or implicitly by sending the call down to subsystem 2 (the controller) for further consideration. Its arrival signifies a need for organizationally thematized and sanctioned action. Not sending a message also gives it a priority, seen only when one message and not another is sent down.

The particular classification rendered within the thirty possible has an effect. On the one hand this is revealed when interpretative practices are discussed. It can be discussed from a coding perspective inasmuch as there are code ramification effects of an incident constraint. That is, a given category suffuses the incident so that further information is more or less likely to be acquired. There are three types of constraint-producing codes on nonalarm calls. These can be ranked by the degree of constraint they produce on operators: Crime-probable categories, order-related categories, and metacommunicative categories.

Crime-probable categories (06, 07, 11–13, 15–18, and 23 in figure 3.3) set orientations to further developments and information, have action-resolution potential, and key the high probability of not only dispatch but also attendance at the scene, paperwork, and further transactions. Order-related categories (08–10, 19, and 23) set orientations to further developments and information, have high action but low resolution potential, and key the probability of "sponge" classifications, and variable outcomes required. These are the most frequently used categories into which events are elided. Metacommunicative categories are categories that communicate about other categories within the code (26–30). These have a tendency to close off action or to be highly routinized in consequence. The actions required are predictable, and resolution and type of resolution are already certain or they merely serve to redefine previously taken actions. These classifications indicate something about what has been or will be sent to other subsystems.

Finally, the amount of information given by the caller relative to classification requirements varies the effect of the code. If little or no information is given—the caller hangs up or refuses to talk—no code can be assigned. If the caller omits details of the incident or the location, no coding can be done. If, however, these two bits are given, other information either can be supplied or is not needed.

Operators: Technology

Information technology sets limits and is a limit on and the source of expanded opportunities. Although the operator receives messages from eight channels in the center, from the point of view of frequency of message transmission and channel use, four channels are relevant to operators: radio, telephone, VDU, and the PNC. CYFAS is almost never used; telegraph and telex messages are always handed to the operator and thus are once mediated; teleprinter messages are flashed on the VDUs if relevant to operators' decisions or for their information. Each channel is affected by (1) credibility, (2) the form of messages sent and received, (3) fringe meanings associated with the channel on which the messages were sent, (4) patterns of feedback, (5) the absence of presence of the caller, (6) channel alternation effects, (7) ambiguity, (8) single-channel dominance, and (9) the degree of mediation of the message by technology.[3]

Regardless of content or interactional features of the talk, all messages are affected by the channel on which they are received. Credibility refers to the extent to which the message is trusted as a rendition of the event (figure 2.1). The most credible and trusted channels are those that most frequently carry police sourced messages (police calls on internal lines, radio messages directly from controllers or officers reporting their opinion or behavior, VDU messages, and PNC reports). This means that the closer to a police source, the greater the credibility of the channel used and the message sent. A police source itself can be graded in credibility from person-centered judgments to subdivisional judgments, if one knows the "ground" or person sending the message, to force judgments (one's own force, local regional forces, then the Metropolitan Police about which there is the greatest distrust and mystery). This means that the trust effect operates directly with social distance, so that the largest source of calls, the public, is the most distrusted, regardless of caller or call content.

Technology gives a message form. Direct messages received verbally from supervisors are rare, usually associated with coordination of a major incident, and are temporally ordered. Those received from other channels are spatially and linearly ordered; they extend in a controlled, fixed, formatted fashion.

Message form has symbolic fringe meanings associated with it. They "surround" or embed any message sent by this channel and received in this form. If one focuses on the symbolic meanings of the written record that is considered the most significant basis on which one can evaluate performance, it should be understood that all written records are transformations of spoken information (for example, statements taken by detectives, notes made on calls for service, or the incident as written for transmission over the computer-VDU link, or the written report submitted by the officer). The contrasts between written messages and spoken languages have been noted by a number of researchers concerned with the place of the written word in the development of civilization (Goody and Watt 1963; Goody 1977). Goody, for example, has argued that written words can be *stored* (they have a degree of permanence that the spoken word does not have, even when stored on tape) and looked at again. The written word can be *reexamined* in different contexts (in comparison to other written material on the same topic, to things written in other languages, or in different styles); the written word can be *reorganized* and reordered and can be understood, in short, *outside* the context of the conversational situation. The message can be decontextualized or extracted from one context and placed in another. Written signs are treated in the command and control situation *as if* they were formulaic and had a trans-situational meaning, whereas they are seen by operators, controllers, and officers as highly situated, that is, best understood by those who participate in the communicative transaction.

Feedback takes several shapes. Unless the caller calls again, there is little second feedback to the caller from the operator. (The first feedback is given at the time of the call: "I'll send someone to see you") There is occasional feedback from officers in subsystem 2 or 3 to operators about a call, initiated by either actors in subsystem 1 or other actors in subsystem 2 or 3 (figure 2.1). This sequence occurred when a woman called a second time to ask if the police were on the way (7). The operator first informed the caller, "Oh, yes, hold on my dear, I think there's somebody on the way there." The caller replied that she lived next door to the number given. The operator checked the VDU status-activity pages and replied, "Well, yes, my dear, there's somebody there now." The caller said they were not there. The operator responded, "Well yes, but they won't have come to you. They have gone to see if the woman's all right. Hold on a minute and I'll see what's happened." The operator asked the controller to get on the radio to ask the officer attending to "go and see the woman who's reporting this." He answered that he'd pass the message on. She then returned to the caller and said, "Hello, my dear. Well, the police should be with you any time now. All right? They'll come and see you, I've asked them to." The caller replied, "Yes, all right." Such feedback circuits are rare and involve all three principal channels—radio, telephone, and VDU.

When the PNC is queried, it is usually in the following manner:

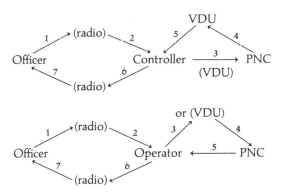

This can be seen as a fairly closed feedback loop, usually initiated by the officer and returning to officers.

Other feedback capacities exist. Operators can dispatch a call directly to a unit in the field by VHF or UHF radio, the most commonly used channel, and can monitor events directly from their console. They can speak with officers and enter data on their status and activity as they develop. Operators can also alert controllers that a message is coming down by VHF when they view it as urgent or when the computer is flagging. (At times, the demand for power from other sources is so great that the computer-VDU glows dimly and is slow in registering new data, responding to queries, and shifting format.) Operators may also be involved in the control of an incident from their console if the incident is major can be in repeated contact with constables, subdivisional controllers, higher ranked officers, and other officials, for example, telecommunications workers, police surgeons, or the fire brigade.

It should be noted that feedback in this subsystem is largely internal to the system rather than citizen initiated. Citizens whose calls are accepted are given a ritualistic or routine response (that a unit is being dispatched) unless they call again, in which case the action is checked. There is little or no feedback either to or from citizens initiated from this subsystem after the fact of police intervention.

Absence of presence means that the verbal communication is accepted as an index of complex events taking place elsewhere. Absence of presence effects are those that result because operators must form a "full version" of the person calling in order to judge the credibility of the message, its relevance to police business, and the relationship of the person to the message being transmitted. Conversely, a present person communicates nonverbally. When a message is only heard, all visual, tactile, aural, and olfactory cues are absent. The hearer must construct these features and their connection to the social world. A reader must construct all but the visual cues. All other data (nonverbal gestures, postures, facial expressions, individual attributes, and location) and prosodic features of talk (speed, register, dialect, accent) and its stylistic, poetic, or self-referential aspects are suppressed. The construction of these absent particulars gives a person presence. This construction is the result of the absence of a embodied person. The absence of presence effects result from the constructions or filling in or out of a "real person." Channels differentially omit matters relevant to this construction process. Thus telephone and radio channels omit context particulars and nonverbal matters, whereas VDUs and the PNC omit verbal or aural data, context particulars, and nonverbal matters.[4]

Channel alternation effects occur in several ways. Primarily they result from the cues associated with a given communication channel and change when the channel changes. Alternation effects are a consequence of the change from aural to visual to aural channels during the transformation of the event as an incident. If a message arrives by telephone, it is "pure sound," which must be transformed into text. This involves the image formation process, which links the sound image or signifier with the signified. "Translation" must occur, such as that noted by Cicourel when signers watched a videotape of a sign language user and wrote out a narrative of what was indicated by the signer (1973, ch. 4). Lamination of message meaning occurs as a result of remarks that refer to "non–English speaker," which imply editing and "cleaning up" of the syntax and grammar of the message. The actual changes are not specifically indicated and are invisible except to the operator. In other words, new signifiers are shaped while the signifieds are assumed to remain the same. The entire sequence of talk is collapsed into a linear sequential format. This differs from the format effect in that it specifies embeddedness. Semioticians call this intertextuality. The spoken words are both partially absent and partially present in the written text sent by the operator (Kristeva 1980). They are, however, missing when the message is sent to the dispatchers, and its once-present nature is lost. Notes are indexical. Often operators will take notes on a call in the form of scrawls on a pad indicating the name of the caller or a bit of "core" information, such as "weapon present"; these will be used rather than the VDU to review a call once sent. These indexical signs represent already chunked information that bears a syntactic relationship to the aural signs and the other iconic signs on the VDU. This is understood by actors' unreviewed interpretation of these condensations and displacements.

Technological ambiguity is caused because a channel has characteristic noise, failure, "gremlins," or the like. Perhaps the channel most plagued with this is the personal radio carried by officers. Each channel produces effects derived from the ambiguity or uncertainty about the message associated with the transmission modality itself. That is, the receiver cannot decide on the basis of the message received whether information is absent, withheld, equivocal, or masked by noise associated with technology. The first source of ambiguity is introduced by reliance on a single dominant channel, the telephone, in the communications center. The second is absence of presence, with the additional factor that in this absence no feedback is permitted to *connect* "misreadings" resulting from "filling-in" typical attributes, biographical features, nonverbal matters, and setting-derived factors in social action. The feedback-omission factor may be further amplified by technologically produced ambiguity. This may result when, for example, the assumption that a call from a child is a "nuisance" call cannot be checked or verified because the phone line is busy at the number given by the Telecoms operator or because the caller did not distinctly utter the number from which the call was made. The VDU, radio, and computer also each produce these effects. When messages are sent to the PNC and returned, they are highly trusted, so that an error in punching in a license number, a programming error that produces the wrong owner of a vehicle, will not be verified by a second check.

VDUs can be used to enter the status activity of officers, but, when the computer is affected by power drains, it is slow in returning information and the operator cannot determine which officers are in or out of service by relying exclusively on VDU-sourced information.

If it is assumed that a vehicle has been dispatched and the radio is used to call to establish whether the car is on the scene, a radio message cannot in itself establish the whereabouts of the officer replying to the call or which officer answers. The "corrective features" of radio are limited by the channel-specific nature of the messages sent and received. These effects are produced by technology of a particular sort and amplified, given certain other conditions.

Technological failure can be both a known or unknown impediment to work. When telephone lines are out of service, calls cannot be received. When multiple calls are made, lines are overloaded; in the BPD no queue is created. Messages and calls are presumably "lost" when callers do not call back or when calls are lost in transfer from Telecoms to police lines or when callers "talk over" during the transfer (call 17).

When power is low because of other power demands, VDUs are dim and slow to function. When they are "down," they affect messages in several ways. If they lose all power, all times entered on subsequent records will be wrong. If an officer was dispatched at 10:15 and called in at 10:30 as finished while the computer was down, he would still be shown as on that job when power returned, or, if he was still on the job, the cumulated time shown on the computer would be incorrect because it would omit the time during which the computer was inoperative. If the local terminal PNC is down, records checks can be made by alternative use of the telephone to the PNC site, producing long delays, uncertain responses, citizen irritation at being kept waiting, and lack of early feedback on checks made.

The effect of a single channel for receiving incoming messages, the telephone, has been noted. However, the dominant single-channel effect derives from the reflexively significant fact that, once a channel is used routinely for sending messages of a certain type, the channel itself has a "marking" effect on all messages sent on that channel. In the communications center messages arriving on commercial or private alarm lines or alarm lines from special services (the Bank of England, Railway or Transit Police) and messages from controllers or officers on radio and telephone lines are marked as more important than those on the telephone lines serving the general public. For the operator the dominant channel varies: It is the radio or telephone for outgoing messages and the telephone for incoming messages.

Operators, unlike controllers and officers, are isolated ecologically and socially, and the only source of information they have about environments I and II arises from technologically mediated sources. Operators talk with each other about current calls or incidents they are processing, more or less as "asides," or on refreshment breaks, but virtually never with officers in person. About half of the operators are civilians who lack contact with policing on the ground and therefore lack biographical context within which to consider calls they receive. More important, perhaps, technologically sent messages are viewed as more equivocal than personally delivered (or sent) ones; once-mediated messages are less equivocal, however, than twice-mediated ones. This means that the average doubt concerning a message's validity increases the more it has been processed.

Personal experience may, of course, validate a given claim and reduce the equivocality of a message. It may thus override the technology mediation effects.

Operators: Roles and Tasks

Once a call is accepted, seen as credible, and had its relevance established, it must be typed or classified. This enables operators to construct the phenomenology of intent of the call and caller. An algorithm of calls (figure 4.1) suggests that only those calls that involve potential crime events and involvement lead to further questions about callers' intent in the BPD. These processes are a microversion of controllers' and officers' speculations about the call, caller, intent, event, and message.

It should be noted that the dilemma in the operators' world is between efficiency (the greatest result for the lowest cost in effort and time) and avoiding a type II error (a false negative or a call that is *not* given a high priority or dispatched when it should have been; this is generally only known after the fact). This dilemma, seen in EMS, police, fire, and medical care more broadly, is closely related to the occupational values and organizational principles of the police. Support is found in the occupational culture for action, second-guessing is denigrated, and a clinical notion of the work is maintained ("You had to be there."). The implications of this are discussed in detail, but the operators' practical solution is to put a fine point on priorities only when the workload is heavy. As is seen here, the organizational effects or constraints of the MPD are greater than those of the BPD, thus reducing operators' risks but also radically reducing their autonomy.

Selecting and sorting of facts involves the important capacity to project one's thought into the social world and to understand its features. Because both systems are predicated on establishing the *location* of the problem, projection requires spatial imagination.[5] There are quite a number of assumptions necessary for the operation of such a system because the name of the caller is not required. Recall that there are a number of loosely linked features of a call as a signal interpreted as a message by these operators. The caller must be seen as located in the social world with a capacity to interpret it along the lines Cicourel (1973, pp. 169–170) has said are required for conversational interaction. The callers need not have seen the event in the world. His car may be missing; she may be reporting what someone else told her; he may have only heard a noise, some light, a moving person; she may be calling for someone else who may also be inferring a whole set of facts about the social world. Thus some calls involve a caller informed by a second person telling a third, the operator on the telephone, about the event. The caller need not be at the location at which the problem is said to be located. The caller may be calling about an event

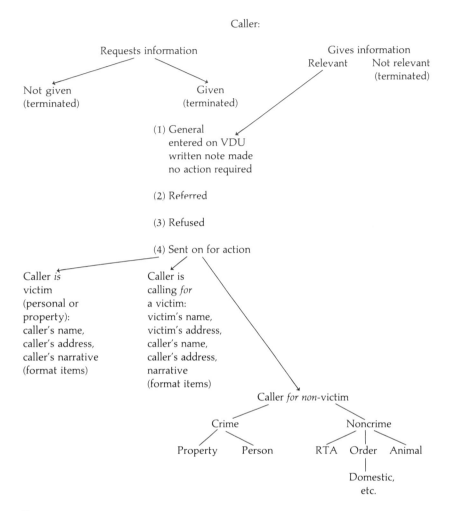

Figure 4.1
Taxonomy of spontaneous demand: BPD operators.

that happened in the past. This may be up to several months in some cases, such as when people return from vacation to discover that their house has been burgled. The caller may not trust what has happened to him, been told to him, or what he has seen or heard with reference to the event. A call is an analogue, something like a verbal photograph (Barthes 1981).

In the BPD, addresses must be located in subdivisions using personal knowledge. Sending a call to a subdivision leaves implicit the question of the correct subdivision, but feedback, either from the subdivisional controller by radio or telephone or the VDU, will reveal whether the message has been accepted by the subdivision. Such sending down of a message may involve a logical unpacking of the transformations outlined in figure 2.1 or those made in later stages of the communications system, but it will certainly involve prospective understandings of subsequent actions and sensitivity to the occupational culture.

Because all calls are answered as they arrive, there is no discretion involved in their receipt with respect to priority, order of disposition, emergent nature, or potential at the operator level. It is claimed that operators "send everything down." This pattern combines high individual decision-making authority and a sense of its absence, leading to a variety of stresses, rituals, and systematic avoidance behavior. This relative lack of discretion is important. Discretion increases as one moves away from the operators. It is preempted by major incident decisions taken by chief inspectors in the center. Discretion is probably a function not only of subsystem location but also of the current workload of each subsystem of the BPD. Because encoding, imaging and rating actions are conflated in the practical action of entering the call in the VDU as a incident *and* sending it by VDU, radio (VHF or UHF), or phone or all three, little differentiation is seen in the roles and tasks associated with any given set of message-call-incident.

There are few collective effects on call processing. The primary consequence of individualistic work done at a single console, in isolation with separate headsets, lines in and out, and frequent supervision is to make salient the autonomous nature of the work in this subsystem and the decisions that are taken.

Operators: Interpretative Work

I move now from message processing to message analysis and interpretation. Message processing includes mechanical movement of the message in time and space and the attribution of meaning to the message from sources other than its content. Thus message processing can be considered an analysis of metameaning because there is a reflexive relationship between the content meaning if or once known and message-processing meaning. Message analysis focuses attention on the cognitive processes by which messages are divided into bits or units of meaning arrayed as to significance and salience, interpreted in connection with the central theme or point of the message, and labeled of continuing police concern.

Message-Handling Processes
The Noise-Message Distinction

The noise-message distinction is based on the fact that, whatever is defined as a message is considered to be a signal. Noise thus contrasts with it. Both noise and signal are defined with respect to social values (Klapp 1978, p. 191). What is considered to be noise from a social perspective is anything that interferes with the receipt of and action on a valued signal. At times, then, a call sent from the communications center to the controller can be noise (for example, when the operator has already dispatched an officer to the call as a result of a direct call to the station), as can a call from the controller to an officer when an officer is attempting to complete overdue reports. The same call when one is eager to "do something" is a signal. A signal arriving at the "wrong time," "wrong place," in the wrong amount, with the wrong content according to the receiver's needs can be noise. Likewise, "bad redundancy" (Klapp 1978) can result when repeated messages are sent that are irrelevant or when a message conveys something about which the officers believe they personally can do little (for example, messages reminding the control room that certain divisions are under strength on a Sunday morning or that a boy has absconded from an approved school some miles distant and off the ground).

Stylistically unacceptable messages, for example, an operator who speaks too quickly or slowly or transmits a radio call in an idiosyncratic fashion, are also noise. In an important sense informal interactions in the center can be viewed as either information or noise. Some operators ignore nearly all informal interaction around them, whereas others participate in joking and banter, even while handling calls. Some ask each others' advice on addresses, subdivisional boundaries, and phone numbers. Various adaptive styles are used, and these styles may involve tolerating different kinds and levels of noise.

Technology produces noise that is ignored in calls, such as the "clicks" of calls being transferred from the Telecoms operator to the police operator, faulty lines filled with static, the dull tapping of VDU keys, the noise of people in the background of a call, and traffic noise (when calls are made from a phone box). When a 999 call is received, a red light goes on in the center. Even though the call is shunted automatically to one console, it becomes noise to those who do not answer it (because they ignore it). Because telephones select for the loudest noise and transmit it and the headsets direct sound to the operator, these are relatively easy to separate from the call. Noise from the social environment is considerable: comments from fellow operators, supervisors' advice, conversations with clerks wandering through the center.

Because of the low workload of the BPD (average of 9.5 calls per operator per hour), more time is spent reading the newspaper, doing crossword puzzles, or chatting with others than answering phones. Phones can be seen at that point as noise. This is in fact "timing noise" based on involvement in other activities at the time of the call.

Field-Message Distinction

The social field is constituted by all the activities in a subsystem around the key message receiver and sender that are neither message nor noise. If noise is disvalued communication, it can be located in a social field of activities of others, expectations of other operators as perceived by them, and personal stylistics expectations of self. These are both internal and external to the actors' subsystem location. For example, an operator in subsystem 1 is "internal" to that subsystem, and the two other subsystems are "external" to that subsystem but in that field.

BPD operators ignore a set of physical and social features of the setting. They differentially attend to social activities. The message can be either these activities or the phone ring, depending on the definition of the situation by the operators. The expectations of other operators intrude during shift or break periods. When general chat takes place, when an issue crosscuts consoles, or when a major incident is unfolding, collective interests replace individual task-based interests, and messages relating to these concerns take momentary precedent. Personal style is less obvious among operators than controllers, if this is defined as how messages are accepted, given priority, and passed on, which ones are sent immediately to cars, bypassing subdivisional controllers, the speed with which one handles a message, and knowledge of the ground (location of addresses, subdivisional boundaries, local physical details). Components may result from informational or noninformational sources. The effects are fewer here because of the physically fixed location, the one after the other sequencing of calls, and close supervision. When the style of the operator conduces to less speed, then the operator receives fewer messages, thus having further consequences for the next call received.

Any aspect of the field can intrude and become the message at any given time, but messages do not flow outward and destroy the field. Thus the message is more or less field dependent whenever these types of activities, expectations, and stylistics come into play.

The question arises, then, as to precisely those constraints that focus attention of the operators on the call and not the field. These would appear to be the shaping of situated demand by the pull of excitement implicit in listening to police calls, in solving personal dilemmas, in counseling people, and in the power inherent in requesting police to attend any scene anywhere in a huge metropolitan area. The presence of headsets and the direct action of the call in the ear of the operator makes the stimuli of the call both compelling and constraining. There is a reflexive effect of answering calls and hearing oneself answer, "Police, may I help you," the mutual association of "Police," "I," and "help you" that differentiates and stratifies caller and answerer. Repeated calls for this or another problem act to define the role of the answerer.

Answering the call thematizes the role of the operator and that of the caller and frames the message apart from the field. Luhmann (1981) writes of this general process in a perceptive fashion: "All communication takes place under normative premises. It assumes structures that are counterfactually stabilized, i.e., structures which continue to maintain their validity in the face of individual violations" (p. 241). This permits understandings of the form of language despite violations in use and asserts the relevance of general normative constraints even though the current here and now is confusing and changing (Luhmann 1981, pp. 237–239). The existence of norms depends on citation, framing, and dramatization. They must be, in Luhmann's phrase, thematized or woven into the situation, shaping and highlighting certain relevant features of the situation coming under those chosen and displayed norms. The answering sequence acts as a separation and a boundary sign, a transitional mark and a message frame, and distinguishes field from message.

The Ordering Frame

Operators receive messages in order, one after the other. They may be dealt with as a combinable sequence or a *syntagmatic chain*, in which one message is viewed as a part of an associated string. If dealt with in this fashion, the messages are viewed as being linked only by proximity, regardless of other meanings or similarities the content might suggest. If, on the other hand, calls are dealt with as a substitutable sequence in which similarity in message content is the basis for order, the clusterings or orderings derive from a paradigmatic view. They are linked as calls of a certain type. These are not mutually exclusive orientations for observers or participants.

The ordering frame arises only if the operator is oriented to meaning other than that derived from the sequence itself, mere syntactic relations among the calls. If the operator turns from a one-after-the-other orientation and is indeed concerned about content (for whatever reasons), then he or she also changes orientation to the content of the message and closes off functions other than the referential function of the communication. At this point the operator seeks out defining key words or syntagms that incorporate the central features of the message. This might be called the "defining point of the call." The orientation to messages as a syntagmatic chain governs the discussion in this section.

Consider the following list of calls using the BPD classification system (figure 3.4): road traffic accident (RTA) (02), other crime (18), fire (20), false/malicious call (27), car theft (15), disorder (08), domestic (09). These calls can be ordered or framed variously.[6] First, calls can be ordered by their arrival as listed. Second, they can be ordered numerically by classification codes: 02, 08, 09, 15, 18, 20, 27. This sequence is strictly arbitrary because the assigned numbers have no intrinsic meaning. Both of these orderings are syntagmatic because they involve a metonymic ordering, or one based only on proximity or temporal sequence, regardless of content. Other possible orderings are based on the mental creation of similarities of various kinds (paradigmatic associations).

Individual operators attend one call at a time, although they can "bury" a call they have entered on the VDU. If this happens and the call is recalled or automatically reappears, a string of calls is created and questions of type and priority arise. The likelihood of such a sequence of queuing increases as one moves from subsystem 1 to subsystem 3. The autonomy to produce and act on metaphoric clustering is a sign of power. The more that metaphoric associations are the basis for action, the more choice possible (Crozier 1964, p. 164).

The constraint placed on the operators produces syntactic regularity in that all signs (gathered into message clusters) are treated as equal, equally thematized as police-relevant matters for classification, and constant in meaning. It also produces what might be called semantic regularity on the surface of the code insofar as the meaning of the sign in that context or field is restricted to its meaning in that situation (MacCannell and MacCannell 1982, pp. 56–64).[7] A full development of the sign requires both a syntactic and a semantic dimension as seen *temporally*. To have noted semantic and syntactic regularity in processing is simply to note at this point the inadequacy of such concepts for a full analysis of message handling across subsystems.

Internal Message Analysis

I now proceed from an outline of the form or structure of messages, as influenced by the source and the networks in which they arise, to a structural analysis. The syntagms and paradigms available to the BPD operators are used to surface the deep structure of such messages. This set of diagrams is a first approach to the cognitive substructuring of police thought.

In order to discuss the internal features of calls, one must make a first approximation of the axial distinction within the police organization gen-

erally between action-consequential calls and non-action-consequential
calls. This probably extends to all messages, calls, memos, advisories, rules,
and regulations. The calls demanding most interest are those that are seen
as possessing action potential and as containing the seeds of active intervention and resolution. They are located in the field of the moment. The
salient question arises: What do I do about, with, or to this call? If viewed
within this context, the call is seen within an *action paradigm*. Other calls
are seen within the information or metainformation paradigm and are not
seen as actionable. This distinction holds across the three subsystems as
well as across the two organizations.

Partitioning the Message into Units

Eight types of calls arrive in the center from three sources:

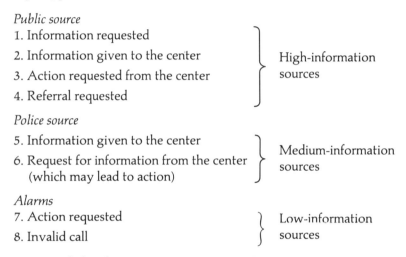

Public source

1. Information requested

2. Information given to the center

3. Action requested from the center

4. Referral requested

High-information sources

Police source

5. Information given to the center

6. Request for information from the center
   (which may lead to action)

Medium-information sources

Alarms

7. Action requested

8. Invalid call

Low-information sources

Internal classification actions are most relevant to call types 2 through 6.
In order of priority of internal content are calls containing action request,
information given, information requested, referral, and information given.
Information given or information requested often do not qualify as messages and are not entered or acted further once information is received or
provided. Invalid calls are not seen as messages, whereas action requested
by an alarm call is treated as a signal: The channel, the source, and the
actions to be produced are seen as "the same thing." They are encoded
when they flash on the operator's board and require little internal differentiation. The location and the place are provided in the call, and the alarm
tapes (with the message to be played) must be approved by the police.
Receiving a call is heard as equivalent to a decision to send an officer to
that location to investigate.

I have selected five completed calls to be examined further; these calls
were made to the BPD communications center on January 25, 1980:

1. An owner of a shop calls to say that, when he arrived this morning, he found his shop broken into.

2. A citizen calls to say that there has been a recent accident on the motorway that has dumped a sheep on the road. The caller asks that the BPD contact the motorway police.

3. There is an automatic alarm call from the Youth Center saying that suspects are on the premises and giving the address and telephone number of the center.

4. A woman calls for her neighbor to report that the neighbor says that two dogs have been "put into her garden" and "they're ripping everything up." The caller's name and address are obtained as well as the address of the house with the problem.

5. Mrs. Johnson calls to report that a dog has been run over in front of her house (999 call) and asks, "Who deals with dead dogs?"

These summaries do not reproduce the order of items as given, the language of the caller unless in quotes, the elicitation procedures of the police, or any of the actions or talk of the telecoms operators who screened calls 3 and 5.

Turning to table 4.1, note that the calls arrive from public sources, some of them screened initially by Telecoms operators. The time of the event reported is of interest because in calls 1 and 3 it is not clear whether or not the event is in progress, when it happened, or whether in the case of the alarm if it is false. It is entered and investigated. The actions are also to some degree a reconstruction of the operator in the case of the first three calls. Similarly it is not clear from the calls who acted in any of the events ("someone," "suspects," "someone put them in," and an unseen vehicle). All are sent down for police action except call 2, which is transferred to the motorway police by radio.

Operators gather information, not necessarily in order, about the caller, the caller's location, and the number or address as well as information about the event being reported. Operators promise action, saying "I'll get someone to come down and have a look." Despite an apparent attention to detail and seeking information, the practical actions are virtually always the same: refer or "send it down." No questions of priority, resource allocation, or grading of response, based on precision in probing the event for its potential for development, increase in scope or danger, or community relations are seen as relevant for interrogating callers.

Each of these calls requires a degree of reconstruction and prefiguration, but the work is far less than that engaged in by the controllers and the officers. Operators send "down" everything they define as a message. Thus there is no need to predict what the officer will see other than to

Table 4.1
Syntagms for the five calls to the BPD

Syntagm	Call 1	Call 2	Call 3	Call 4	Call 5
1. Source	7 digit	7 digit	999 (alarm)	7 digit	999
2. Caller's name	Mr. Smith	Mr. Holman	—	Mrs. Jones for Mrs. Brown	Mrs. Joseph
3. Caller's location	371 Merry Rd. (shop)	Home, 111 West Pl.	Youth Center	151 Crank Pole Rd., Coalsley	2 Closely. St., Beacon
4. Location of the event	371 Merry Rd. (shop)	Motorway exit	Youth Center	151 Crank Pole Rd., Coalsley	Front of her house
5. Time of the event	Last night	In progress	In progress	In progress	In progress
6. Actions/event	Broke in	Accident, sheep dead in road	Broke in/ false	Dogs in garden	Dead body in road
7. Persons acting	Someone	Cars braking, Changing lanes	"Suspects"	"Someone put them in"	Car ran over
8. Toward whom/what	Shop	Possible accident (refer)	Youth Center	Mrs. Brown's garden	Dog

determine that something might be there to be seen or that it should be registered as something the police think is a problem. Whether the police actually think it is worth looking into, to what degree, and whether they think anything could or should be done on the scene is not a consideration of the operators. Thus, unlike the controllers, the operators do not engage as a professional matter in reconstruction of events unless they distrust the caller. Their predictions are therefore that the controller should decide whether to send an officer to the incident. They take a fairly practical view of the job at hand.

The operators engage in little rich, detailed, and complicated interpretation of the meaning of events: They do not create an elaborate cognitive map of the call because they are not responsible for sending an officer to the situation. If there are no questions of priority or resource strain (which they would not be aware of in any case unless they queried the computer about the status activity of officers on a particular division), they do not have to take into account the relative importance of the call.

The Salience of the Units

It has been argued previously that operators are concerned about the salience of a unit of information only with respect to "filling in the boxes," a kind of unthinking and mechanical wish to complete a task to show that it is done, but without interest in whether the content of the boxes is correct, reliable, or carefully produced. The interest of the operator furthermore is in characterizing the call about the event, not the event per se or the consequent actions of the officers on the scene (environment II). Thus typically the units of interest in order of salience, are when the event reported occurred, location of the event (address, place, named site), actions taken, to whom/what (source of call is given), persons acting, caller's name, and caller's location. The material used in assigning codes provides a rationale for how these seven items are understood and placed within the format. The order or rank is fairly stable within subsystems.

Surrounding Understandings

Surrounding understandings refer to nonmessage matters that alter the salience of given syntagms within the message and therefore may alter what is taken to be the central point of a message. Given a set of units, syntagms, and paradigms, events external to the message system can alter the salience of the units. If "understandings" is shorthand for "what is taken for granted by members as normal and routine," then surrounding understandings are events perceived as external to the message system that bear on the existence or salience of a syntagm. Alterations in surrounding understandings can produce independent restructuring of the ranking of the salience of bits and therefore of incidents of a given type. For example, during a series of "terrorist" bombings attributed to the IRA, any message containing reference to an "abandoned car," "car parked blocking a drive, entrance, or street," or a "suspicious vehicle" would be seen as a potential bombing incident. The item referring to car blocking a drive would be salient, core, or thematic, and the entire incident would be viewed as first priority urgent by operators, controllers, and officers. Similarly, calls concerning sexual or violent offenses, especially those in given areas, can become salient if a series of rapes has been reported in an area and public attention has been focused.

Controllers: Codes

The controller manages twice-processed messages that have existed first as calls to the police about events and then converted by operators into incidents. The signals embodied first in the call, received as a message, and transformed into an incident can appear to the controller from one or more of four distinctive sources: as an incident on the screen (or as a call on the radio *and* an incident on the VDU, as a call followed by an incident appearing on the screen of the VDU, as a radio call, or as an in-person report from an officer. The coding effect must be treated separately for each of the four sources of work received by the controllers. All the problems of coding in the initial instance by operators are reproduced and amplified for controllers.

Assigning Codes

The first source is messages routed through the center received at the subdivision. The encoding of the event constrains the controller. He has few ways in which this incident can be handled; he acts *as if* the coding were "real" for the present purposes and can only add a classification to the event or remarks or notes of his attempts to assign the incident. This cannot be done until new information is given to him by either the Center or an officer who has accepted the incident as a job.

Uncertainty is reduced because the next action available to the controller is established by the mode of receipt and the encoding of the call as an incident at the Center. This format-coding effect thus constrains the modes of choice for the next action by the controller. It should be noted that the indicated phenomenological and interpretative practices of the controller are not obviated or altered by these code restraints. In coding terms the formal fiction of the existence of the event and object configuration in the world is reified when a coded incident is passed on by the controller.

With respect to the second mode of receipt of messages, the radio-incident combination, the coding effect remains the same. The effect merely amplifies the immediacy of the need to handle the event with care, not for formal features of the incident. These do not change.

If the incident comes to the attention of the controller over the phone, a call to the subdivision from the center, then the channel effect noted for the receipt of phone (single-channel) messages occurs, but the coding operations replicate the pattern described for operators receiving a call.

If the incident arrives in the controllers' office over the radio from an officer in the field, the picture of the event is shaped by the trust in the officer, the practical knowledge that whatever the officer does will be what is reported and entered in the VDU. An *immediacy effect* is created. This works to activate the presumption that the event as reported is the event that is being dealt with and will be entered as having been dealt with in that fashion, thus giving subsequent information a prospective credibility.

If the incident comes directly to the attention of the controller through a verbal statement of an officer made in the controller's office, then the encoding practices of the operators are absent and irrelevant. In addition, the effects of face-to-face communication and the trust context of the message described are brought into play. The encoding and the receipt of the incident are one and the same operation and produce isomorphic effects in the coding and handling of the incident by the controller.

The image work described for operators is depressed in salience in subsystem 2 because all communications arriving at the controllers' office have been processed once, thus reducing the uncertainty in the message, because the messages have been formatted and coded into the police classification scheme, and because an effect is produced by the channel (VDU, radio) of receipt itself, which alters the implicit credibility of the message. Formally, coding has occurred, and it has no additional consequence unless it is changed in the course of the investigation of the incident.

What coding does is not apparent to controllers. What is concealed is the *prefiguration* of the event by the controllers, who call on previous experience of the area, neighborhood, time of day, perhaps the actual caller, and past contact with events perceived as being of this type. This parallels the coded incident as it is constructed.

Coding Effects

Coding effects on messages in the controllers' subsystem derive from format, ordering of data, priority, reclassification possibilities, and the particular classification rendered.

The format limits on the range of data provided operate only when data are received by means of the VDU, in which case the options for adding information are reduced to three items: reclassification, remarks, and actions taken. These are the action domains because altering other aspects of the formally constituted message is prohibited. Furthermore, the actions previously taken are closed off, the priority given by the center is taken as tentative, and the incident is reassessed into terms of the practices and priorities of the controller. Because the classes are so gross, few incidents are actually reclassified, but some are given an additional category once they have been investigated.

The particular classification has an effect in that controllers tend to cluster calls into paradigmatic groups based on classification types. Three types of classification produce constraint. Those involving crime are generally of most interest and most constraining with regard to the next action. Those involving order and order-maintenance calls are of less constraint, and those involving messages are seen as information-only communications that require little action. Other messages are not constraining and can be dealt with variously by the controller.

Controllers: Technology

Controllers are powerful actors in creating meaning in the message system. Officers on the ground act on the implications of messages sent by controllers. Controllers receive messages from four channels: radio (VHF and UHF), telephone (from the center, outside lines, and the headquarters switchboard), VDU, and personal face-to-face verbal and nonverbal communication from clerks who pass on telex, teleprinter, telephone, and messages taken from citizens at the desk and from police constables.

Each source has an effect on the aspects of message processing: the credibility of the message, the form in which the message is sent, fringe meanings surrounding the "core" meanings of the message, patterns of feedback, technologically produced ambiguity, and the salience of the dominant channel or source.

From the perspective of frequency of message transmission and channel use, the VDU is the most used, followed by the radio, personal sources, and the telephone. In many respects the insulation of the controller from direct contact with environment I is high, and environment II is present only in the shape of communication with officers and feedback from them. Thus, more than any other member of the communications system, the controller is engaged in sign work, in imagining the prospective and retrospective meaning of the troubles he encounters. He is swimming in a pool of images in a leisurely, circular fashion.

The channel on which a message is sent has varying capacity to confer credibility on whatever message is either sent or received on it. All messages to the controller are police sourced or at least mediated once by police handling, but variations nevertheless can be identified. The most trusted sources for BPD controllers are personal communications embedded in face-to-face knowledge or contact. This means that once-mediated messages passed on by clerks are more like VDU, telephone, and radio messages than "personal messages." Next most trusted are direct phone and/or radio calls from other officers or from the center. The least trusted are routine VDU calls transmitted from the center. The trust gradient is inversely related to the frequency with which the controller must deal with messages on that channel. This means that the "pull" of the most frequent source, the VDU, is contradicted by the interpersonal relations it indexes and that the most controlling source is the least trusted and rewarding with respect to reciprocity of response and interpersonal dependencies.

The form of the message coming to the controller varies by channel (technology), with face-to-face orders likely from either same-rank (lateral orders) or higher-rank (inspectors or above) sources; mechanically mediated messages arrive from the center. Fringe meanings also accompany a message's translation into action terms.

Feedback is an important source of redefinition of messages. It is best discussed with respect to source. Personally conveyed messages come from clerks in the reserve room and generally are messages received from the center intended for general information, for example, a stolen car that may be coming in the direction of the subdivision or a school absconder reported missing by parents. Little feedback is produced or required. Similar messages generally require no feedback, such as indication of an arrest by the officer in the first instance and reported to the controller to enter on the VDU. Other messages require only acknowledgment or are for information only; these are initiated by the center and sent out by VDU, telex, or teleprinter. Still other messages require some feedback, such as calls to confirm the arrival of the divisional surgeon to draw a blood sample for a sobriety test or to check an injured prisoner or messages to be passed on to the officers by the controllers. These must be pursued until feedback is obtained from the officer but are generally not put on the VDU. Other personal messages are opened and closed in the setting, such as when officers inform the controller of something and are given an immediate response.

VDU messages from the center to the controller and back and to the PNC and back most resemble what might be called a constant feedback model in which subsequent messages redefine and clarify the meaning of the message. These can also involve double loops in which officers request information on a possible stolen car from the controller, the controller uses the VDU to signal the PNC, the reply comes back on the VDU, and the controller uses the radio to contact the officer with the information. Other one-and-a-half loops are produced by officer-controller interaction that leads to a request that the controller enters in a book (for example, "Call for scenes of crimes vehicles") and asks CID to attend. The controller may report that he has requested a unit, but may not know whether that the unit arrived. Conversely, the arrival of other nondispatched units is not reported, so no feedback about their actions on arrival is possible. What is not the subject of feedback is as important as what is. Most important, of course, at this stage in the process is that no feedback is given to the citizen unless the citizen calls the operator again.

Radio messages are both the most frequently handled and those for which there is the highest proportion of feedback. Here is a rather lengthy example [this material originally appeared in Manning (1984)].

It was approximately 10:08 A.M. when a message appeared on the VDU screen in the controller's office at Queen's Fields subdivision. It read (format is indicated by items in italics)

Serial number	Time	Date	SD	Class
1525TCl	10:08	23 08 83	B #3	11

Location
77 Linds Rd., Ballbrook

Remarks
Lady reports possible items stolen, believes someone is still in the loft.

The controller looked at the message and decided to query the central communications center to discover if they had established whether anyone was there now. After typing in the inquiry, placing it in the "pipeline, and sending it to the communications center for verification, he sent a message to the Police National Computer (PNC) about an abandoned vehicle just reported by a constable. He thought that there might be further information on file, such as the owner and whether it had been reported as stolen.

A reply from the center appeared on the VDU in regard to 1525TC1, "She doesn't know; that's why she phoned us."

The controller laughted at the uselessness of the returned information and scanned the VDU display of reported "status activity," which shows officers on duty and their present obligations. The display revealed that the permanent beat officer (PBO) for that area was not on duty. The controller decided to send the incident to a radio car (Bravo Mike or BM) and picked up the headset-radio-telephone and said, "This is Bravo Mike 3 calling Bravo Mike 22. Bravo Mike 22?" BM 22 answers, "Yes, Bravo Mike 3. This is Bravo Mike 22." "Could you have a look at 77 Linds Rd., Ballbrook? She's reporting items stolen, believes someone is sleeping in the loft" [laughs].

"Doubts if they're still there? [laughs] Thanks, sarg" [sarcastic tone].

The controller turned to [me] and opined, "I always send these calls as requests ... [but] I don't get refusals ...."

Another voice came on the radio, "Sarg, I finished that job. I think there was a boy reported missing in that road. A teenage boy. He could be in the loft."

The controller noted this and entered on the VDU that BM 22 had been dispatched to the incident at 10:24.

A soft sound was emitted from the console. This bleep announced that a reminder has appeared on the screen about the status of a PBO. He had exceeded the time notionally assigned by computer engineers for the tasks assigned. Auto-matically entered by the computer once a classification entry has been made for the task and a time of assignment entered, these signals are routinely ignored.

Another officer called in on the radio phone and announced that he had com-pleted his inquiries at 131 Kings Rd.

An officer radioed in from elsewhere in the subdivisional building to say that he would soon be "out and about." The controller acknowledged this and asked when he would be out. The officer replied, "I'll be out in five minutes." The status activity screen had shown him as being on refereshments in the office. The con-troller updated the status activity display.

5187 (collar number of an officer) called in to book on.

A reminder with sound accompaniment appeared. Another officer, on a task more than twenty minutes, had exceeeded status activity limits. The controller reassigned the officer, indicating him as being en route, thus giving him another twenty minutes before another reminder appears.

A police constable (PC) walked in to report verbally on his inquiries about a missing boy (these were previously assigned inquiries). The PC did not have a radio while carrying out these duties; the controller had attempted serveral times to reach him. He explained that he had been serving as relief officer in the "nick" (the jail, literally, but synecdochically it refers to the subdivisional offices). The results of the inquiries were not entered on the VDU because the sergeant ex-plained that a full written report would be required to be made in time. He altered the PC's status to available.

The VDU bleeped and the incident at 77 Linds Rd. appeared, showing "action field incomplete" at approximately 1100. This indicated that the officer had ex-ceeded the permitted limits for such a task, and the controller had failed to obtain the required data to close the incident.

Two WPCs (women police constables) strolled into the controller's office and began to chat, asking about whether certain officers on the shift had been asked whether they wanted curry on Friday night. They were going to cook it and re-quired an estimate of the number of people on duty who wanted the meal. The inspector suddenly appeared and asked if he could join in eating the curry.

The phone rang.

Another PC appeared in the office.

BM 22 appeared and began to talk about a volunteer parachuting jump that will yield a charity contribution from the BBC. They discussed the merits and de-merits of the duty, who had been "volunteered" for the duty by the superinten-dent, and whether it was worth the money offered. The officers arriving were asked whether they wanted curry on Friday.

At 11:07 there were eight people in the room (including me). The controller [and I] were discussing the relative merits of the German scheme of radio dispatch and the fact that, according to the controller, the German public, to his warm ap-proval, did not call in domestics. He also volunteered that the radio room in Baltimore, Maryland, which he had seen on holiday, was superior to that of the Centreshire Police. The others in the room discussed in loud tones whether cer-tain people had been contacted about the curry.

The PNC reply reported on the "abandoned car."

There were six people in the room.

The sergeant explained to [me] the limits on recall of certain information from the computer. He asserted that the use of the machine varies from controller to controller, as does the conception of what it is meant to do.

The officers in the room asked the controller (sergeant) to produce the duty roster listing those who would be on duty Friday night. All discussed who had been contacted about the curry, guesses were made about whether absent others wanted curry, had been contacted, and whether they might want one or two portions.

The controller asked one of the officers in the room to check on the key holder of an establishment on the High (main street) "across from Woolies" (Woolworth's).

At 11:20 the curry discussion was still in process. BM 22 leaned over the desk and casually said that they had a look at "the old girl's loft' and that he and his partner had found "only cobwebs and a big golden void." (He had been in the office casually chatting for nearly twenty minutes.)

At 11:25 the controller closed the incident. He typed in as a result: "Mentally disturbed woman. PBO will be advised." [I] ask if a teleprint will be made of this for the PBO. The controller answered that the officer who dealt with the incident will leave a note for the PBO. [The implications of this example for "processing the mentally ill" are taken up in Manning (1984).]

At 11:30 There were only two people in the office. It was again very quiet.

Feedback loops routinely arise in multiple calls made in reference to a job, such as getting a police surgeon[8] to attend the scene of a murder and seeking a key holder to open a shop and turn off an alarm. Such duties absorb an enormous amount of time and phone calls and often result in dead-ends.

The greater the number of transformations in the message, for example, from one code to another, from one channel to another, or from one subsystem to another, the greater the potential for lamination of meanings of the message. This occurs regardless of content. Each message form contains a set of subjectively attached meanings surrounding it. This produces a channel alternation effect.

For each form of technology utilized, there are effects, primarily from the ambiguity or uncertainty produced in the message by the vagaries of the technological vehicle. That is, the receiver cannot decide on the basis of the message received whether the information is missing or withheld or whether noise and/or equivocality are operating. Technology exerts less control at the controller level than at the operator or officer level because the sergeants serving as controllers have more face-to-face contact with the officers who handle the incidents, past experience with events, and frequent verbal feedback from officers.

Technologically produced ambiguity is derived from the use of each of the channels: VDU, radio (UHF and VHF), PNC, and telephone. The fewest contingencies are produced by the telephone, which is relatively predictable and produces little more than an amplifying effect on messages sent from the center. Virtually no call-related jobs are produced for the controller from phone calls, so that the telephone generally decreases uncertainty. For the radio, special problems are found. Calls "break up" frequently—cannot be heard by either the controller or the officer. Certain areas of all subdivisions are difficult to reach by radio, usually because of physical or natural obstructions. Car or personal radios may fail or the batteries may be low and thus unable to amplify a call properly. Other radio communications may interfere with the transmission. Officers may either purposely or unintentionally leave their radio switched on, thus creating "white noise" blocking the channel and reducing power in the system. They may switch off radios while attending a call, to obtain a few moments peace, to engage in surveillance, or to take an uninterrupted break. Specialized units and CID personnel may not carry personal radios. Given an inability to raise an officer on the radio, it is not possible to distinguish technological malfunction from human error or intentional work avoidance. Noise can be produced by nature, humans, or the machinery. Officers do not answer for each other or "lie" over the radio in the BPD (unlike the situation in the MPD), although by silence or refusal to answer a call questions may be raised about the loyalty of the officer [see Manning (1977, pp. 170–174) for a discussion of this matter in London].

The most confusing situations of this kind are when the personal knowledge of the controller and the machine-shown information contradict. The controller must trust the officers for most of the information given to him because he has a limited number of channels through which to gather information independently of an event in environment II; sources may in fact be limited to the officer assigned or others who have been there or seen the officer in question. If an officer requests to be cleared, is shown as available for additional calls, or reports she is clear, the controller cannot know what has been done, except as reported by the officer, and will show her as clear.

The technological effect is less on the VHF radio than on the UHF (the panda cars and the walkers) because the dispatcher deals less frequently with specialized units. They are often called directly by the center. The VHF radio is more reliable over longer distances. The UHF is most likely to malfunction, be full of static and other noise, malfunction unpredictably, and be unable to reach certain places on the ground.

When the technology fails, several consequences can be noted. When the VDU fails or when the computers are down, the sergeant keeps rough track of what people are doing in the same way as before the advent of the technology—by asking other officers in the station, by contacting officers when they come into the station, and by using the telephone to seek information.[9] The controller cannot control or supervise the officers by direct visual contact as could the sergeant in the fixed-points system and the unit-beat system before computer-assisted dispatch. Rather, the controller must rely more on the station and patrol sergeant to inform him of movements and activities of the officers. The temporary absence of technology thus reduces the workload normally created by the machinery and does not increase the usual and necessary information monitoring of officers by the controller. These "failure" situations tend to make the officers and the controllers cynical about the contribution of command and control technology to good policing. When the radio fails, aproximately the same thing occurs, except that it is rare that both VHF and UHF fail. (I did not observe such a situation but saw many instances of the computer system failing.) Telephones operate in a generally ancillary fashion to the day-to-day work of the subdivision except when they result in messages being brought by the clerks to the controller.

The salience of the dominant channel varies. The channels on which messages are received are more varied for controllers than for the participants in either of the other two subsystems. They receive messages from four channels and transmit primarily on two. The radio is used secondarily. The dominant modes of message receipt are face-to-face communication and by the VDU, but the radio is by far the most dominant for transmitting, far exceeding face-to-face messages in terms of the power or demand effects on officers.

Because both environment I and II are frequently indexed for the controller, he is "in touch" with them in an immediate fashion not possessed by any other participants in the BPD communications system. But several implications of this should be appreciated. Controllers' impressions are always once mediated unless they are interacting in a double loop, and they primarily respond to signs about signs formulated by others, principally operators who have coded citizens' calls. They are constantly interpreting signifier-signified relationships that result from temporal changes. The contradictions between channel-sourced messages must be solved. Usually this is done by referring to the original speakers', that is, the constable's impressions. This may or may not result in checks with citizens. The dominant channel effect interacts with several other roles and tasks of the controllers and their interpretative practices.

Controllers: Roles and Tasks

The controller receives messages from several sources and executes both physical tasks and mental operations. When a message arrives as an incident on the VDU from the center, the only formal question that must be answered and be shown to have been answered is; Is this incident on the ground? Even if not, the job is usually assigned, because it is often located near the borders of the ground. Calls from the center are neither rejected nor referred; therefore issues taken up by the operators are irrelevant here.

The facts selected and sorted are of three kinds: address, type of incident, and previous actions taken (if any). These orient the controller to the action aspect of the incident.

The type of incident can be described in a crude taxonomy based on interviews with controllers in three subdivisions (figure 4.2). The determinant facts of most interest are, in order of priority once location is known, injury, injury potential, possible crime in progress, crime scene (live), crime scene (dead), active nuisance, passive nuisance, information inquiry, etc., fait accompli, and metacommunications (for information only).

All calls are queued if necessary but are certainly ordered or given a priority with respect to the fundamental question—Is police presence required? [See Bittner (1974) on this question.]

Selecting and sorting facts is limited by the facts provided, the perceived credibility of the incident, and the controller's imagery of the event. This imagery is in turn linked to the retrospective construction of the relationship between objects, events, and calls issuing from environment I and the incident as communicated across the boundaries of the organization. This process involves constructing an image of the object, event, call, and incident and the relevance of these matters to police action under the controller's review. Once this information is in place, the incident must in effect be decoded. The rules that govern the mapping of locations onto place and verbal data into categories and incidents and the insertion of remarks are reviewed. A new structure of relevance must then be created to assign the incident to an officer, refuse it, put it in the queue, or close it with a summary action.

With these tasks completed, the sergeant attempts to assess the present obligations of the officers—their previous workload, their skills at such work, their present (or imaged) location on the ground, their mobility (whether walking or not), their age and sex (relevant to certain calls more than others), the number of officers needed, previous assignments by the center (for the particular incident, and the present overall workload on the subdivision.

In practice, this is simply done, for better or worse, by controllers. It is assumed that any job could have been done otherwise, that misinformation and deception are variable but always present to some degree, that unknown factors are at work in any dispatching decisions (for example, that certain people will be given certain types of calls regardless of their workload or current activities and that some officers will be given few) and that all such "data" can never be fully processed in some computerlike fashion (and probably should not be) and that, even if the requisite minimal information were available, other factors constantly intrude to make

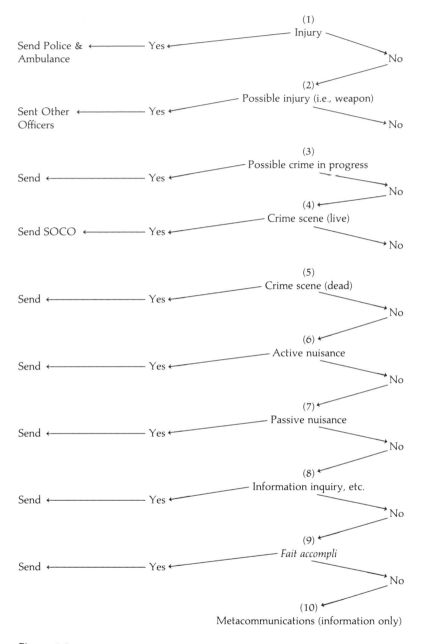

Figure 4.2
Controller's priority algorithm in the BPD, Queen's Fields subdivision.

such rational decision making impossible. There are other factors, such as cars that break down, unexpected jobs that arise in the course of tending to an assignment, personal favors and obligations that must be respected, and other untoward events.[10]

The controller then attempts to set his readings of the priority of the incident. Given that he decides to act or to send an officer, he attempts to determine from his imagery and his decoding of the event the priority it should be given and then attempts to make the assignment. This is based largely on assumptions about the incident as received in the controller's office. The following material draws on the vignette about the woman who thought someone was sleeping in her loft. Four major assumptions are made by controllers: limited information, action decisions, construction (and reconstruction) of actions of the officer, and reclassification and closing.

Limited Information   A message contains only a brief and stylized summary, a format effect. However, a decision must be made; something must be shown to have been done. When the incident appeared, the controller could not discern from the message the degree to which the caller and the operator believed that it was likely that someone was actually on the premises. The controller queried the center to attempt to establish if there was further information, formal or informal (he could also have done this by radioing the center). The controller reported that, *if* there was someone there, he would want to send two PCs. Sending two officers would have a series of implications for workload and personnel level, as many people were on break and others were unavailable because they were relieving those on breaks or on assignments. He wonders: Are there children present at the residence? Is this situation dangerous to the person or her property? Will support (more personnel) be required? He acts on inference.

Action Decision   The controller must decide whether to send officers, who and how many to send, where, with what speed, and to what sort of event. He receives no feedback. He decides to request one car (two officers) to the woman's house.[11] Message-noise and message-field distinctions are maintained.

The controller must decide what type of message he has. In this case the controller is dealing synchronously and sequentially with each call as it arrives. He does not delay or queue calls or bury any calls in the computer queue. He dispatches them one at a time as they arise. The controller treats this call as a crime call initially, sending an area car with two PCs to the address. He also assumes that it is not a crime call, that no evidence of burglary will be found, that no person will be found sleeping in the loft, and that it is reported by a woman who is too frightened to investigate the loft personally.

Construction (and Reconstruction) of the Actions of Officers   The controller assumes that the officers in the field assume that he is to be informed as and when information is relevant to the controller's responsibility for processing the message. Therefore the controller continues to "bury" the incident when it reappears on the VDU and does not continue to query the officers who accepted the call. This was true even though an hour passed without a report from them. He waited from 10:24, when the incident was entered and shown on the VDU as having been officially assigned (actually some seven minutes after it had been verbally assigned by radio to BM 22), to 11:25. He assumes that they are en route or otherwise legitimately engaged, will attend and investigate, and will report relevant actions for selective entry on the VDU.

Reclassifications and Closing   The controller received the report verbally from the officers who attended and apparently took much from their tone of voice, posture, smiling faces, and the manner of reporting. Officers said (punned?) that they had found "nothing but cobwebs and a golden void" (in the loft and in her head?). The result, "mentally disturbed," was added as a remark to the incident. The controller altered the original classification of the incident as a possible burglary. The understanding was that the PC who made the call would leave a note for PBO: "The PBO should be advised." [12]

The assignments attempted and made, by time, are required to be entered on the VDU in the incident format, as must the arrival time and time completed, or when the officer is "clear." The incident remains in the computer queue as "unfinished" until closed, and the computer bleeps quietly, reminding the controller of incomplete incidents. All data must be entered and the incident closed and sent to the computer memory before the computer will rest. This means that the controller is accountable to the machine for officers' reporting their results or progress until the incident is closed. These safeguards are quite effective for incidents entered in the computer and assigned officially to officers in this way.

This detailed work of assignment must take into account the occupational culture (described later) with reference to officers [see also Manning (forthcoming)]. This is a shared culture, differentiated by ecology, social roles and tasks, and, to some degree, rank, age, and gender. Because all actors involved in communications between subsystems 2 and 3 are police, internal schisms based on the listed variables are significant.

Reporting outcomes to the controller by officers is discretionary and is based on a number of considerations: Is it on the VDU now such that it will remain open until closed? Does it involve other units (scenes of crimes, CID, traffic, etc.)? Does it require further paper action such as a report by the officer involved? Is there likely to be a subsequent investigation of this event (by the CID or supervisors)? If so, the controller will print the incident from the VDU. Otherwise the records are kept on computer tapes.

Controllers are variously influenced by their lower-level colleagues, seldom by supervising officers, and almost never by fellow controllers. They make their decisions individually, as sergeants have done traditionally, with little advice or consultation (Van Maanen 1983). It can be said, then, as opposed to the patterns of the operators, that controllers are oriented to both the metaphoric and the metonymic aspects of message flow as a condition of their task-role obligations. Management of these matters is discussed along with their interpretative work. The organization permits choice in order of action on tasks (jobs), which is denied to operators. In this sense, as in many others, controllers stand midway between operators and officers.

Controllers: Interpretative Practices

Message-Handling Processes
Noise-Message Distinction

For the controller, technologically produced types of noise are the most important.[13] Noise, because it is socially defined, is also a function of the timing of a call for controllers, either when they are busy or when they have already handled a call. A call of unacceptable style to the controller from the clerk, an officer, or the center, for example, one that is spoken too quickly, mumbled, incomplete, uttered with an unacceptable accent or tone, is also noise. Informal interactions in the controllers' office can be noise in both the physical sense and the social phenomenological sense—they can be distracting, masking other desired sounds (from the VDU, the radio, or the telephone), and they can be socially annoying or burdensome. They compete for positive social valuation. The social environment is auditorily complex and presents issues of social definition, personal tolerance, and, in the end, the occupational culture. Some controllers welcome joking, banter, and talk, asking only occasionally for quiet or dismissing visitors in order to attend to the board, whereas others desire quiet, allow few people to drift in and out, and prefer to do crossword puzzles or read when it is quiet.[14]

A number of conflicts in processing messages are focused on the role of the controller and his tolerance of noise, demand, and social obligations. There are conflicts between the handling of present messages and the taking of new ones that appear or call for attention on the VDU and between the role of the controller as a kind of supervisor and the station and the patrol sergeants who expect the officers to complete paperwork, bring in prisoners, and "keep up the stats." Ironically these tasks take more time than handling routine calls. There is a potential tension between the formal ordering of calls and the preferences and personal priorities of the controller. The controller's role as keeper of the machinery and as informal adviser to young PCs who need advice and assistance in their current and past duties (for example, their paperwork) creates a role conflict. The controller as the center of communication is expected to provide expressive and moral links connecting shifts, sergeants, and officers who are rarely seen by others; the controller acts as the moral center of the subdivision and the commander of machinery with instrumental obligations. The classic dilemmas of the supervisor or the middleman are layered onto this technological-social split that is so obvious to officers in the subdivision.

The various orientations of the actor to the message are replicated in this subsystem, although in general the constraints introduced by the primary channel (the VDU), idiosyncratic particulars of communicants, and phatic functions of messages tend to be overshadowed by the referential aspects of the process as conceived by the controller.

Finally, there are matters of style in handling messages. This is partially a matter of discretion and partially a matter of the controller's definition of his role. Some controllers prefer to hold jobs in a queue and to assign them in block fashion to officers; other prefer to immediately assign jobs when they appear on the VDU. Some controllers prefer to use the telephone to deliver messages to citizens, for example, shopkeepers, whereas others assign these duties to officers or clerks in the reserve room. Some delegate almost all work using the VDU; others prefer to keep notes beside the VDU on a pad, using them to assign calls, make inquiries, and then enter information at a later time if need be. They refer to these notes from time to time rather than use the VDU to recall such data from the computer memory. These styles of work are adapted to by officers.

Field-Message Distinction

Any incident handled by the controller is received in and intrudes on an ongoing field of behavioral events and a situation filled with social obligations, expectations, feelings, and ritual chains of interaction (Collins 1981). For the controller these include the present activities within the immediate ecological or physical setting (discussed in part under the signal-noise distinction). Also included are the controller's expectations with respect to speed of action, knowledge of appropriate alternatives, locations on the ground, and workload. They also include modes of accommodation to other work in the later afternoon or early evening, when shifts are changing, or when other station activities require the controller's advice. Each of these alters the meaning and "demand power" of the current message. The field intrudes. A third aspect of separating message from field is personal preferences, considered to be stylistic matters. These pattern the way in which the message is separated from the field: A message may be viewed as a part of the field or as a police-relevant message. Weather may also alter the definition of the field.

Ordering Frame

The ordering frame is the way in which the sequence of messages is defined with reference to message similarity. The dominant approach to messages among controllers is simple and sequential unless there is pressure on resources. Some controllers, on the other hand, depending on their style, argue that, unless one is setting priorities, one is not using the system properly and is misallocating resources. This requires metaphoric framing in broad terms, grouping calls into types based on urgency and source (police, nonpolice, alarm calls). Controllers, much more than officers or operators, can queue calls, holding several for attention at once and choosing among them. They have great flexibility in patterning the order of their work, given that they must process all messages directed to them. Recall also that officers do not have to respond to calls; they possess great freedom of choice with respect to work.

Internal Message Analysis

Calls received by the controller originate from several sources (walk-ins, telex, messages from the reserve desk clerk, radio calls, telephone calls, and face-to-face communications from other officers, either PCs or higher ranks). They are processed once and in that sense are all police sourced: clerks' messages (written), PCs in the field (radio), PCs or other officers (face-to-face interactions), VDU messages from the center, PNC messages (VDU), and radio and telephone messages from the center.

VDU messages are of the following kind: information requested, information provided, and action requested. These three types of message require internal analysis. They are all police sourced and are seen within the action paradigm.

Partitioning Messages into Units

The source and the network in which the call originates has an effect on the predictability and equivocality of the messages. The type of transaction, whether requesting or giving information, etc., alters the degree of order in the message. Information given to the controller is the least equivocal (PC taking a prisoner to the "nick"); information requested from the controller is the next most equivocal (PC requests a vehicle check from the PNC); the most equivocal is a request for police action. Information given is often feedback from officers in the field about their status, their investigative progress, or their location. Requests for police action require internal differentiation by the controllers: They must establish the bits or syntagms relevant to their action, order them, and later assess their salience.[15]

The relevant syntagms for controllers, each of which is a variable internal feature of the call as represented in the incident, are the following: time (before/after an event), source of the original call (public/organizational/police, channel (radio/VDU/telephone/in person), location of the event (address/place/site) (Psathas and Henslin 1967), caller's name (collar number of PC calling), caller's location (address/place/site/call box), person acting (one/few/many), actions of persons, direction of action, and descriptive term for the action. Note that the sytagms are partially items derived from the format of the VDU and partially analytic terms derived from interviews with controllers concerning the information they sought when trying to take an action decision. The caller's location, the persons acting, and the action taken refer to the call, not the event in the object world.

These ten items make up the unit system of the call-as-incident and are the items from the which meaning of the message is constructed. They are ordered within the action paradigm. I analyze nine messages from the Queen's Fields subdivision, listed in what follows and elaborated on in tables 4.2 and 4.3. Calls 1 and 5 are what I call collapsed incidents, in that they report actions that occurred before a report was made to the controller. Actions taken to resolve the incident were reported at the same time. These require little interpretation other than registering them as completed incidents on the VDU. They are both opened and closed at the same time, unlike other incidents.

1. PC radios to say he is taking a prisoner to a jail in the subdivision.

2. VDU message (999 call) is received from the center reporting that a Mini Metro parked in front of a house without number plates may be stolen.

3. VDU message (999 call) from the center saying a man has reported a stolen van.

4. VDU message (direct line) from Centre Bus Control reports a fight on a bus.

5. VDU message (direct line) from the center saying that Ambulance Control reports that a man has been taken to the hospital.

6. VDU message (999 call) from the center saying a woman has reported a disturbance outside a community center (and her house).

7. VDU message (999 call) from the center saying a man has reported youths fighting outside his house.

8. VDU message (seven-digit phone number) from center saying a woman has reported an attempted theft of her vehicle.

9. VDU message (direct line) from the center saying that Bus Control reported a wounding aboard a bus.

Table 4.2
Syntagms found in recorded incidents from nine calls at Queen's Fields (January 1980)[a]

Syntagm	Call 1	Call 2	Call 3	Call 4	Call 5	Call 6	Call 7	Call 8	Call 9
Time of call	After	During	After	During	After	During	During	After	After
Source	(PC) police	Public phone, 999	Public phone, 999	Direct phone line	Direct phone line	Public phone, 999	Public phone, 999	Public phone, 7 digit	Direct phone line
Channel	Radio	VDU	VDU	VDU	VDU	VDU	VDU	VDU	VDU
Location of event	Place (sub-division) cells	Caller's address	Caller's address	Bus	Hospital	Caller's address (near community center)	Near home address	Home address of caller	Bus
Caller's role	PC 107	Citizen observer)	Victim	Bus official	Ambulance official	Citizen observer)	Citizen observer)	Victim	Bus official
Caller's location	Police sub-division cells	Caller's home	Caller's home	Bus control	Ambulance control	Caller's home	Caller's home	Caller's home	Bus control
Persons acting	Police	Citizen	Citizen	Official	Ambulance	Citizen	Citizen	Victim	Official
Action reported	Made an arrest	Possible stolen vehicle	Stolen van	A fight in progress	Took man to hospital	Fight	Report	Report	Reported to police

Table 4.2 (continued)

Syntagm	Call 1	Call 2	Call 3	Call 4	Call 5	Call 6	Call 7	Call 8	Call 9
Direction of action: toward whom or what	Man (offender)	Thief(ves)? car	Thief(ves) van	Fighters, to each other	Information	Fighters, to each other	Fighters, to each other	Attempt to steal a car	Knifer, to victim
Descriptive term	Disorder[b]	Possible stolen vehicle	Stolen	Bus fight	Overdose of drugs	Large fight	Youths causing trouble	–[c]	Man wounded

a. Note that "caller's location" in the case of official calls is the ambulance, fire, or bus control and that "actions taken" and "persons acting" refer to the actions that the control center took, not the actions of the observer/participant in the event. These must, of course, be reconstructed by the controller on the basis of secondhand information relayed from the control center.

b. In this case, "Descriptive term" refers not to the incident (arrest) but to the basis for the arrest.

c. Data missing on records or no entry made.

Table 4.3

Paradigms and subparadigms for controllers, BPD

Paradigm	Subparadigm Reconstruction	Action or Prediction	Result (Classification)
Collapsed Incidents			
Call 1	Man caused disorder.	PC arrested man.	30 (miscellaneous)
Call 5	Man took charge. Call made to Ambulance	Ambulance took man to hospital.	21 (miscellaneous)
Ongoing events			
Call 2	Car abandoned, plates lost, stolen? Victim/owner called police	PNC check "stolen" list, PC required to investigate.	?
Call 3	Person(s) stole van. Owner called police	PC required to take statement from owner/ driver.	?
Call 4	Fight on bus. Driver (or citizen) reported incident to Bus Control. Bus control rings center on direct line.	Area car and panda required to sort out fight.	
Call 6	Boys came out of community center, began to fight. Citizen called police	PC(s) required.	Disorder 13
Calls 7 and 7a	Same as call 6 (different caller).	Same as call 6.	"Crimed"
Call 8	Person(s) attempted to break into car and steal it. Victim/owner called police	PC required to take statement.	Crime; 13
Call 9	Person beaten/cut on bus. Driver called	Area car needed. Others in reserve.	Crime; 6

These nine calls can be further analyzed to discern the way in which the syntagms are related and how they form the *structure* of a story used to reconstruct events and to predict requirements for police action. They can be formed into paradigms or associative contexts. The first paradigm is constituted by calls 1 and 5, collapsed incidents in the sense that the call is entered in the VDU for information or record keeping only. The second paradigm, *on-going events*, is composed of calls 2–4 and 6–9. They call for action from and recording by the controller. In order to act, as has been suggested in the previous discussion of imaging and prefiguring an event, the controller must cognitively form two paradigms and form and utilize three subparadigms (reconstruction, action, and result). He must reconstruct certain actions, situations, settings, and actors to understand how the reported event came to the attention of the police and/or to make a prediction about the nature of the event to which the police will be sent. For calls 1 and 5 the controller is required only to reconstruct the events leading to the reported action. In the other calls both reconstruction and prediction are required.

These reconstructions and predictions are mapped in table 4.3. On the right-hand side is a third subparadigm labeled "result," which contains the classification number given to the incident by the operator and received by the controller. The controller can add a number at the completion of the incident if he wishes but rarely does so. These results, the prediction, and the reported outcomes are not sensitively related but would appear to be loosely coupled. They cannot be predicted by the features of the call alone, and the first and second classifications often seem unrelated. Calls 1 and 5, requiring no action, are nevertheless classified. Another matter other than classification is ordering the calls, giving them meaning and priority.

These syntagms, when placed in a new array, constitute the basis for a narrative. They are the principal units necessary for the construction of a "police story" (Scholes and Kellogg 1966). The general action paradigm initially frames the syntagms, whereas subparadigms frame them as types of stories, provide an unfolding line of action, a set of characters, a plot, central and peripheral actions, and outcomes.

These incidents, or transformed calls as messages, possess an apparent structure, order, and coherence. They are *mininarratives* or stories. The narrative structure contains within it a host of richly contextualized meanings, imputed understandings, and expectations of reactions that are used to make sense of the incidents as read. The paradigm, the ongoing event, however, forms incidents as stories of a particular type. These stories can be rendered or reordered to produce simpler and yet more abstract relational patterns (Propp 1958; Rumelhart 1975).

Table 4.4

Coding of calls

Incident type	Actor in the event present (+) or absent (−)	Target in the event is property (+), public order (0), or person (−)	Call source is person (+) or agency or official (−)
1	+	+	+
2	+	+	−
3	+	0	+
4	+	0	−
5	+	−	−
6	+	−	+
7	−	−	−
8	−	0	+
9	−	+	+
10	−	−	+
11	−	0	−
12	−	+	−

In the analysis that follows I show that incident stories posses a narrative structure based on the actions of the central figures as seen from the modality of the police. There is a protagonist, a set of mutually affecting actions, and conditions on that action. The event or the central crucible transforms the hero and the others through interaction, and the police play something of an unfinished metahero role. Using the list of calls, I can further reduce some features of these stories.

Preliminarily I map the nine calls used as exemplars of the approach into a grid of types of incidents that are in turn transformed events reported by citizens or officials to police operators who then send them on. The callers' role may be indexed by an automatic alarm or the call of an official of a company. These represent surrogate victims. An individual victim or an observer of someone else's plight may call. The callers can be coded as victim (person or organization) or observer, as shown in table 4.4. The target of the action reported in the incident about the event can be a person, a social order, or a property. The source of the call can be either an official or a citizen. These three axes, when combined, describe types of incidents or associative contexts for assembling texts.

Each of the calls or incidents can thus be typed using the pattern of present or absent attributes given the information known and its construction by the controller. These types are shown in table 4.4. Further subtypes could be produced if a larger number of calls were analyzed. These incidents demonstrate a specialized body of knowledge and interpretation of

Type 3: Property event/reaction/police called (call # 2, 3, 8)

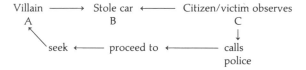

Type 5: Person/event/official reaction/police called (call # 4, 9)

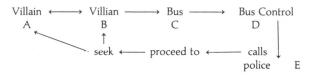

Type 8: Order event/observer initiated/police called (call # 6, 7)

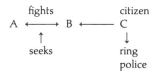

Figure 4.3
Seven police stories as narratives: three types.

human behavior. They contain a set of figures, motives, expected outcomes, and moral implications.

Figure 4.3 shows aspects of the cognitive substructuring of commonsense police knowledge in regard to these types of calls in this
subdivision.[16] Each type is a summated story. It captures the subject of the
event, the object of the event, the observer (victim), the villain, their
implicit action sequences (observed car was missing, checked memory for
where last parked, rang police, requested, they came), and the implicit
hero or metahero (the police). Figure 4.3 illustrates the narrative expansion of table 4.4 and the calls in table 4.2.

All the calls are mapped from the police perspective or modality; it can
be assumed that citizens may view the syntactic structure of events rather
differently. The combinations suggested in this preliminary analysis, such
as the relations among hero, villain(s), metahero, target, and subject within
a police story with an ongoing plot, story line, climax, and resolution, require a much more detailed analysis with additional data and an expanded
conceptual framework to illustrate it properly (Scholes and Kellogg 1966).

It would appear that the sequence of events is a partial rendition of
stages 1, 2 and 3 in an expanded narrative.[17] For example, an expanded

sequence of the following kind might be imagined: preliminaries (argument, plan, fight, car stolen); crime event (various sorts), event reported (to officials, police, etc.), investigation (uniformed branch, branch, CID, specialist squad), resolution (closed investigation, court, clearance of crime, etc.). Not all empirical events progress through all the stages listed; the order may not follow this precisely, and some of the stages may overlap.

The analysis of texts that draws on narrative structure of police stories also draws on general knowledge of plays, television, novels, fairy tales, and traditional folk tales. Police stories are a particular copy of everyday life; any copy risks being bogus, false, deceptive, and intrusive in social reality that is not so marked and framed. In one sense police stories represent a reversal of nature, or narratives of everyday life; they are a copy of nature, in this case defined as culture. Thus the modeling of everyday life in the text of a police incident and of police narratives should be examined not for veracity or irony but as a specially framed bit of culture (Barley 1983).

Determining the Salience of the Units

The controller receives predigested materials, but the channel and source filter his appreciation of the salience of the units. The interest of the controller is in the action taken (the event), the victim or the object involved, the location of the event, the time (in progress, terminated, or may happen), the persons acting (types, especially age, rather than names or descriptions), and the descriptive term used by the operator. The controller is rarely interested in whether a call arises from a seven-digit or 999 line once it arrives by the VDU. The caller's location and name is relevant only if the officer sent cannot find the location or requires information from the caller (if, for example, the victim is absent). The attention of the controller shifts from the call and the caller, the interest of the operators, to reconstruction of the event and anticipation or prediction about what will be required on arrival. The incident is a set of signifiers that now have a new set of signifieds. The new signifieds are those imagined by the controllers. By contrast, the signs entered by the operators indicate, redefine, and extract only those features they see as being the basis of future relevant action.

Surrounding Understanding

Surrounding understandings alter the salience of individual units into which the message has been partitioned. Two processes are at work here for the controllers. The first is that the focal point of a message can change. That is, if in the normal course of events the weather is irrelevant to a message and a storm develops that knocks down trees and power lines and floods drains, then the location of a call becomes important in understanding the pattern of demand that surrounds the particular job that might be sent forward to an officer. Thus the third most salient unit in the message system becomes the most salient, replacing the actions taken in the report. This is a function of the controller's understandings of the consequences of the storm. A second process that alters the salience of bits is the creation of a central theme of an incident as a result of events that make several features of the message newly dominant. The examples provided earlier on the impact of terrorists and bombers are relevant for the cognitive processes of controllers.

Officers: Codes

Assigning Codes

Codes and coding effects are context sensitive in the officer subsystem. The accomplished coding is by now reified by colleagues in subsystems 1 and 2. Messages come to officers "uncoded" in a formal sense. They are broadcast or given "requests," heard as orders ("Would you go around to see Mrs. Smith at 111 Cozy Close about a car parked out front?"). They are not given formatted VDU messages but a series of assignments or jobs. In the extreme, one could argue that there are few coding constraints on the officers as a result of format or classification because they must in sense "recode" the message using elements in the message. It could be said that recoding begins when officers hear a message. They must process information outside the context provided or even known to the operators and must do so with less information and high equivocality. What officers hear from controllers is critical: The bits of information provide focus and limit alternatives.

Coding Effect

The coding effects outlined for operators hold here with several additional elaborations. BPD officers are not constrained by formal priorities. They develop their own sense of priority for received assignments and then act.

The format itself has little constraining effect. The controller's reading of a shorthand version of the incident becomes a basis for the officers' initial understandings. Many matters are taken as understood between the officers and the controllers. Format constraints give way to informal standards, priorities, and practices of the officers in this subsystem, to interpretative work, and to the here and now of the event as constituted. Codes become transmogrified into questions, such as which format-given categories might require further paperwork.

A duplicity of meanings arises from the contradictions among the expectations of the controller, the formal priorities and classifications of the command and control system, and the informal standards, interpretative work, and here-and-now effects of the job. The incident becomes a job by means of the constitutive conventions arising in the occupational culture that define the nature of such things. What might be called secondary codes are developed; they embed the primary or official codes. This contradiction is fundamental in both organizations.

Officers: Technology

Source Effects

Officers are on call. They orient themselves to their work using the cues provided by the radio *when* the radio is on, and they are more likely to listen to it than to look, smell, hear, or touch what is happening around them. When they are talking with people, dealing with human problems, "in action" as it were, they are viewed by controllers as being "out of service," unavailable for the next call. When patrolling, driving randomly around an area, they are viewed as being "in service" (George Kelling, personal communication). A consequence of this is that the public rarely initiates direct contact with an officer but increasingly calls the police, often using the emergency number.

The primary source of messages and work and the dominant communications technology for the officer is the radio. There are two types of communications technology of importance for officers: the personal or VHF radio that connects the walkers and the pandas to the subdivision and the UHF radio that connects the area cars and specialized units with the center. Thus a radio call from the center, regardless of content, communicates urgency or importance when it arrives. These calls are sent directly because time is believed to be critical in choosing if and how to act. Emergency jobs of whatever kind are closely linked in subcultural logic to the self, the role, and notions of being of service to the public. These calls produce "call jumping" and "swarming" to incidents such as "burglar on premises," "possible breaking in progress," or a chase. Because all VHF calls are also received by the area cars, officers sometimes speed, using lights and siren, to arrive first to "assist" or, if possible, to make an arrest. Often a panda car, an area car, and a dog van will arrive at a scene where a "breaking" is possible (Holdaway 1983).

This conflation of communication channel and source obviates the concerns of others in the communication system with source credibility, fringe meanings, and format effects. The radio is the dominant template against which all contacts in environment II are seen. It is not only that it is the dominant channel but that it is virtually the *only* channel and link between officers and the police organization. Given the perception of officers of events in the world, the salience of individual experience in assessing an event, and the dynamic of calls-for-help processing, it is clear that a shifting frame of reference for handling events is produced by the conjunction of radio calls and commands and experience with the job as the officers see and know it. The resolution of this conjunction is an important dynamic in all police organizations (Cain 1973; Manning 1982a, forthcoming).

Consider the fact that, while the operators and controllers deal with an absent other, revealed only by voice or record, officers frequently confront both request as broadcast and the persons whom they contact on the scene about the event. In effect, they reverse the effects of the absence of presence and must mentally reintroduce the body to a disembodied message.

This leads to the effects of the transformation of the job into a record, what might be called channel-specific meanings. When a completed task is thought to require writing up, it is transformed in several ways at once. It changes format from an incident into another form of a record. It is changed from a verbal channel (in the citizen-police encounter) to a written record by the officer. The once verbal incident placed on the VDU is written in a new record. It changes textual form from the original text produced on the VDU-typewriter to a handwritten copy. The times it recreates are multiple and it changes in degree of permanency. In short, the incident simultaneously changes its symbolic meaning in several ways.

The patterns of feedback detailed in the vignette of the woman who believed there was someone sleeping in her loft, because they involve both the controller and the officers, serve to illustrate the role of feedback in the officer subsystem. The technological uncertainty explicated under the controller's section is the officers' problem in reverse.

Officers: Roles and Tasks

Receiving, sensing, and sorting out of the facts incorporated in the incident, when it arrives from the communications system, is the primary task for officers.[18]

The environment as enacted can be considered an image, partially unconscious and tacit or implicit and partially articulated and conscious, an explicit notion or conception based in part on the occupational culture or the commonsense reality of the organization members.

The police occupational culture, like all cultures, is viewed as a mode of adaptation to the uncertainties and vicissitudes of collective life (Swidler 1984). As such, it typically contains an image of the basic concerns of the group, the principal ethics and bodies of manners, rituals, ethics, and ideology, the strategies and tactics of the work, including notions of good and bad work, various bodies of folklore and legend, and a set of principles that organize the work (Hughes, n.d.; Manning 1979, forthcoming). However, such a "menu" does not explain actions and their meanings; it only provides options. As a result there is considerable debate over whether it is useful to refer the behavior of police or other occupational groups to some set of principles or rules, glossed with the term "occupational culture" [see Ericson and Shearing (1986) and compare with Manning (1982a and forthcoming)]. The idea or concept of an occupational culture is perhaps best seen as a set of symbols, verbal and otherwise, that are used to justify, refer to, rationalize, and organize police behavior when reflection occurs. It stands to groups as accounts do to individual behavior, a resource in problematic situations. As such, it shapes work and talk about work, especially the characteristic "war stories" told. Also contained in the symbolic repertoire called an occupational culture are examples of good practice used to represent the desired, or preferred, outcomes of policing. In some sense these tales and representative anecdotes, as Burke (1962) would call them, index a larger body of knowledge that is tacit, unspecified, known in the breach, and taken for granted by experienced officers. This knowledge is socially distributed and not equally shared among all officers. These ideas, notions, and rules of thumb are an example of knowledgeability (Giddens 1984). In what follows I describe an example of "good practice" and some of the general features of occupational knowledge. These are a reformulation of previous ideas (Manning 1977, 1980a, 1982a, forthcoming).

I have chosen to illustrate some of the dynamics of good practice by means of an example of ordering behavior by a police constable. This man had about five years of experience at the time I rode with him in England in the winter of 1979. The situation observed is of ordering and controlling and is probably a rather common one for officers in Queen's Fields. Such behaviors, I argue, are set in the context not only of occupational knowledge but of the rules and regulations of the department and laws known to the officers. The dynamic or dialectic that results from this contrast between formal constraints and action is explicated in other sections.

Constable E was showing a young "pro-con" (probationary constable) and me the ropes and giving us a general tour of the subdivisional ground. We received a call on the UHF (subdivisional) radio. We drove quickly to the address given. I asked him what he expected to find, and he refused to speculate. It was described as a "domestic," on the basis of a phone call made for a woman involved. The location was a council estate (low-cost state-owned high-rise apartment complex) known by the constable to be a place where there are many family problems. We parked the car, and Constable E and I quickly went up three flights of stairs. We wandered a bit looking for the flat and level within the estate. On arrival, we found three people waiting on the landing outside the flat, and a group of people watching them from inside their flat to the left off the same landing. Constable E glanced from left to right, assessing the "audience," an older man and woman on his left (I was between the constable and the man and woman) and a sobbing woman directly in front of him. The door to the flat was half-closed, but soon it opened and a man appeared. Constable E moved forward while asking what happened. The young girl sobbed that the man, Mr. McK. (her stepfather) had beaten the woman (her mother). As the man appeared in the doorway, Constable E stuck his foot in the door so that it could not be closed. He moved closer to the door and, looking down at the man from beneath his visored cap, told him that he wanted to talk with him inside. The constable's voice was low and controlling as he spoke to the man, but it was nonjudgmental in tone. He solicited the information from the two women and another man who had been apparently drinking with them. They had all been drinking, but Mr. McK., still inside the flat, was barely able to speak and stand. It was alleged by the two women that he had beaten the woman tonight and had caused her hospitalization earlier that month. Constable E persisted in asking the man to let him inside the flat so that they might have a talk. Mr. McK. refused. Mrs. McK. wanted to go inside to get her key so she wouldn't be locked out; Mr. McK. finally let her in after repeated requests by Constable E. She soon reappeared, holding the key proudly. The constable did not look at me or at the observers but focused on Mr. McK. After about five minutes, he turned to me and told me in a quiet voice so that others could not hear that I should leave and return with the young constable, A, who was presently waiting in the car. I ran downstairs, college scarf flying and raincoat flapping, to summon the tall, rather awkward 18-year-old curled in the backseat of the panda who would supply the "muscle" in case they decided to arrest Mr. McK. We returned, and shortly thereafter Mr. McK. slammed the door. Mrs. McK. decided to use her key to let herself and her daughter in. Once they were inside, silence surprisingly descended. We waited a few minutes outside on the landing, listening carefully for noises. There were none. We turned together and started walking down the stairs, telling the onlookers to return to their flats. I asked Constable E if he was worried that the man might be violent, fight, or try to resist him. Constable E said he wasn't worried because he was taller, stronger, heavier, and sober. "It wouldn't have been much of a fight," he said. While I was worried about a fight and the consequences of it, he was thinking, "Can I win it?" He had sized up the situation and decided he could easily win. His concern was what would happen if we had to try to arrest, handcuff, and drag the drunk Mr. McK. to the panda. We would then have had to call a van or use the small mini to take the four of us to the subdivisional lockup. That would have been another sort of struggle, with other practical problems associated with attaining the desired smooth and consensual outcomes.

Full analysis of this vignette is not possible given space limits. The focus here is on the practical, concrete, taken for granted aspects of this incident. Note that nuanced and orchestrated acts were involved in creating the desired outcomes from the flow of interaction. The constable asked what happened to each of the persons; he did not allow interruptions; he looked directly at each person when he or she talked; he did not turn his back on anyone there, taking a position to the right and against a wall by the door to the flat. His voice and manner were controlling. Once the door was opened, he placed his foot there and came as close as possible to Mr. McK. He looked down at him but did not threaten him physically, verbally, or symbolically (other than by his large presence, uniform, nightstick, and powers of arrest). He sensed that, if Mr. McK. refused once more to grant him entry, he would have to arrest him. However, when Mr. McK. closed and locked the door, Constable E allowed the two women and the man to return inside. He did not permit the two women to scream at Mr. McK. or let him threaten them. The work was done without great effort, paperwork, and legal involvements. There was therefore little chance of having something "come back on you." No interpersonal disruptions requiring other solutions emerged. Constable E worked through the incident successfully in commonsense police terms.

What has been called the occupational culture is probably best seen as a set of vague and tacit ideas, not firmly held, not well known, and given to frequent and acceptable violations or permissible exceptions. This is consistent with the general belief that the constable has original authority at law and must have widely ranging discretion. Because officers are also seen as the primary source of powerful ideas about the level and nature of their work effort, as is true in all work (Hughes 1971, pp. 301–303), the definition and redefinition of events on the ground is only under the control of officers. In this sense they take mostly unreviewed decisions. Officers believe that, regardless of their present spatial position, intrusive events provide warrant for avoiding, setting aside, ignoring, or offloading a current task. The nature of the new task can only be seen relative to the current task, rather than in absolute or algorithmic terms. These decisions are not, in short, transitive. There are important expectations about expectations, to use Luhmann's felicitious phrase (1985), of the public carried by the police. They believe that they are expected to intervene to control a situation with whatever force is required.

The work is seen as clinical and face to face, and dispatch in action is admired in others. Paperwork is disliked as a feature of work encounter, but if required by administrators' expectations, it will be written with that audience in mind. Officers admire immediate tactical closure rather than prolonged handling of situations, especially those that may be volatile or explosive or may threaten to escalate and spread. Events are not seen as predictable in their appearance, consequence, outcome, or scale. Nevertheless, they are viewed as controllable, once encountered. It is the expectation of uncertainty in the nature of the events with which police deal that

produces stress, anxiety, and disease. The variable appearance of long periods of boredom is punctuated by excitement. But the sequence and the
contrast between "boredom" and "excitment" is situational and contextual, and one is known from the other. No absolute program of objective orders patrol, although expectations concerning the number of calls
one may answer in a given turn of duty may be quite firm. The work is
teamwork when officers face the public (Goffman 1959, p. 104), but the
choices made by members of the team may not be well communicated to
other members of the team (Van Maanen 1974). The underlying themes
of secrecy, duplicity, and mistrust of the public and colleagues are quite
dominant in war stories and tales (Skolnick 1966). This distrust of people is
complemented by a distrust of general rules and procedures and what
might be called formal rationality in the form of plans, policies, administrative aims, and directives. When a rational facade is placed in front of
an event, for example, when an incident is written up by officers, other
officers tend to distrust it unless they were present or know the officer
who wrote up the incident. Such events are opaque, not transparent.
Events reported in official paperwork bear a problematic relationship to
the event on the ground. The incident record and the behavioral episode
are independent and seen as two parallel but slightly distorted versions of
each other.

Ideally, or normatively, police should be neutral and cool, skilled verbally and physically if necessary, able to adopt a shifting but flexible attitude to the public, and able to produce a set of expected outcomes. These
idealized expectations are constantly violated and redefined contextually.
This is done to maintain autonomy and power on the job, to avoid punish-
ment or guilt over errors and mistakes at work, to cover oneself (Hunt
1985), and to increase power with peers or the public. The ideals and
practices are further decoupled by the cynicism and guile that the work
rewards. Rather than a set of definitive guidelines, the practices represent the code for representing errors, conflicts, problematic scenes, and
disruptions of routine tacit expectations. It is this reserve status that "culture" or "subculture" holds in complex societies (Swidler 1984; Horowitz,
forthcoming).

The practices illustrated here are subtle. They involve such matters as
eye contact, constructing an order of speaking, positioning one's body in
the setting, controlling the movements of the participants, listening to
them without exchanges out of order, anticipating the need for backup,
sizing up the participants physically and psychologically, and knowing
when to exit. The incident went well and was a success in police terms, but
it could have been an occasion for culture, that is, rationalization and redefinition. Bayley (1980), Skolnick and Bayley (1986), and Bittner (1967) have described these tactics. Bittner has noted, in a detailed treatment of the police's

problem, the endless setting-specific nature of such practices. They are not easily amenable to listing, taxonomy, or cognitive eliciting. They are meant to be a set of setting-specific, reflexive, and recursive descriptions in a developmental sense. Some constraints, as noted, are organizational (Smith and Klein 1983).

The action outcomes of BPD officers must be reported so that the incident can be officially closed. The outcomes can be reported in person, through another officer, or over the radio. (The contingencies involved in this sort of feedback and the calculations it touches off have already been discussed.) This requires closure of the event by a statement of a new status in the BPD.

It should be noted that in the officer subsystem the occupational culture is most significant, with the collective aspects of decision making, roles, and task construction foremost. This contrasts sharply with the individualistic performances and standards of the operators and the controllers. Neither operators nor controllers, unlike officers, monitor each others' calls. The importance of the officers' collective definition of the situation cannot be too strongly emphasized. There are many reasons for this collective solidarity. However, ties created and maintained through the police communications system are at least one source of shared and collective identification. They are also a source of differentiation and individuation (Cain 1973).

Officers: Interpretative Practices

Message Handling
Noise-Message Distinction
There are three types of noise for the officer: technologically produced noise from the failure or malfunctioning of radios primarily; socially produced noise coming from the action of associates, other vehicle passengers, or citizens or from the timing of messages; and proximal environmental noise, such as traffic sounds, bad weather, or construction work.

Technologically produced noise is dealt with in the controllers' section. It is less worrisome for officers because they are at the interface of organization and environment. They do not have demand from other parts of the internal system. On the other hand, in the absence of ability to send messages, officers may be unable to summon help or to communicate results to the controller or to the center.

Socially produced noise varies with the role of the officer—whether primarily specialized and individual in work assignment (most beat officers drive pandas; dog vans) or collective, such as special patrol and area cars, which are double staffed. The partner's demands or chat may intrude in the message-receiving process. The timing of messages, as with the controller, may vary the salience of noise versus the message. When working an incident, officers treat other messages initially as noise, regardless of their content.

The primary marker of a message from the center or controller is the radio call for an officer, but this must be validated by the officer to establish this as a message, not noise. In a sense the ultimate acceptance of a call as a message lies with the officer.

Field-Message Distinctions

Officers value the present over the abstract, the distant, and the formal. Even the exterior events of environment I, as represented to officers by calls from the center, are less immediate than street-based events. They maintain, by means of a set of communicational rules, a priority of the present over later arriving messages. Sir Kenneth Newman, former commissioner of the Metropolitan Police, terms officers "demand led" or "tied to the radio." This is true only after they consider what is defined as the current field of activity.

A number of broad ideas organize what is viewed as a message by the police. In general, situational rationality is preferred; actions and decisions that give insight to the facts, forces, people, and contingencies in the current encounter are sought (Mannheim 1949).

In an almost existential fashion the current moment is the focal point of experience and attention and is more salient in determining future actions than past actions. Officers prefer action, especially direct action, to inaction and to thought, once a decision is made to alter the current routine or activity, but the purpose is to control the situation. Rules, legal precedents, and organizational policies and directives are a kind of background for decision. Ironically officers may use nonaction to permit the situation to evolve toward preferred outcome. Outcomes are problematic, so sometimes visible and dramatic action, especially to those who are viewed as team players, is preferred to private actions in public. At other times, actions that merely control, order, constrain, and diminish the potential of the encounter are preferred. Depending on the situation, officers prefer actions that reduce the length of an encounter. Once an event is closed and if paperwork is required, officers prefer brevity of communication, whether written or verbal, when framing the communication "officially." This means that jobs are open to renewal, and an eye is kept open to prevent jobs from "coming back on you" (being reviewed or questioned by other officers, especially supervisors), being written up, being reassigned, or reappearing. Action is not always sought; being "out of service" is preferred to being in service (or on call). When in service, officers seek to complete the job. This is done in order to be out of service again, but to be in service is to anticipate another focused encounter. Events that increase the likelihood of risk, chance, and contingency are sought. Actions will be taken to amplify those features of any event. This rule also holds for retellings (Holdaway 1979a). As I have shown, communications received are received in a demanding and intrusive field. The field is more salient than all but a few assignments. On the other hand, radio calls that fit these preferences are sought and made messages. Others are likely to be defined as field if the officer is engaged, on a call, on break or momentarily off duty.

Patterns of priority interact with these references in the BPD. It is thus impossible to create a formal algorithm of officers' responses to calls. In rough terms they follow an outline of priorities. Officers are able to construct a mental queue if they have more than one call. They adopt a three-level priority system. Low-priority calls, to which they would "take their own sweet time getting to" are such things as sudden death in a house, premises entered but intruder now gone, and report calls. Medium-priority calls are such things as domestics, pub disorders, and road traffic accidents without injury. High-priority calls are "punch ups" fights, fires where people are on the premises and may be injured, and officers requesting assistance ("Bobbie wants assistance.").[19] These issues always involve a consideration of the context in which the call is received by the officer.

Officers would rank as first priority, injury or possible injury; second, crime in progress; third, fights, especially ones involving a large number of people (for example, after a pub has closed); fourth live crimes (ones in which the suspect may still be nearby); and fifth, youths or vandals about. Calls after this blur and are not distinct. At the bottom of the list would be clerical matters, such as informing people of court dates and making an address check and any duty that involves.

Several important qualifications should be added to this list. Recall that at Queen's Fields the workload is so low that there is more frequently a problem with boredom than with excessive work except at rare times [Friday or Saturday night and evenings between 5 and 8 P.M.; for parallel days of workload, see Hough (1980a) and Ekblom and Heal (1982)]. Because it is rare for workload to require such "prioritizing," officers in fact rarely queue their assignments. They respond to jobs as they come, one at a time. If calls must be held in a mental queue, it is usually because the officer is already near the location or because the officer is known to be "good at handling such things." Furthermore, because the number of officers available in the subdivision on any one shift is fairly small (three to five) and at any given time one or two will be tied up with court, paperwork, or longer calls that involve inquiries, few officers are available to take a job.

It should be further emphasized that these are hypothetical lists, because of the essential discretion of officers in handling and responding to calls, the situational nature of the definitions of relevant police work, and the interaction of sequence effects (what has come before the present call and what is anticipated as coming later or after the present call), surrounding understandings, and the field-message distinction.

From a phenomenological perspective officer preferences shape the horizon within which a given call is placed. That is, the present location of the officer in the spatiotemporal world and the structure of practical relevances (Schutz 1964) determine the definition of the calls. The preferences move in and out of relevance. Thus, when driving back from a "domestic," an officer spotted a "drunk driver" (apparently by his weaving, shaky handling of the car on a turn, and slowing down when the police car came in sight) and decided to stop him and have him blow into a balloon to test his blood alcohol. He then brought the driver into the station to have a police surgeon draw blood for a conclusive test of alcohol level. I asked him how he spotted the driver and why he stopped him, and he replied, "It was obvious; didn't you see him? I had decided I'd get a few drunks on this shift." The impulse and interest in the event at hand, at the moment, determines largely what is done by BPD officers. Algorithms had priority lists are so highly contextual that they can be best seen as a sketch of features of the occupational culture rather than of actual behavior. If these abstract categories of events were made concrete, one could not use them to predict the order in which any set of officers would respond.

These priorities are modified further by officer's role definitions. If they are crime oriented, crime calls become high priority, with domestics, injury, and order calls moving down. Order-oriented officers, or "uniform carriers," and traffic officers tend to avoid calls or to "finesse" them whenever possible (Walsh 1972, 1977; Cain 1973). It should be appreciated that it is possible to avoid most work temporarily when one is not or cannot be reached by a controller, when one is occupied at the moment with a call, or when one lies about current location, duties, or availability. These can be considered stylistics of the role of the officer and represent both what the officer does and does not do, his or her "operational style" [see, for example, Muir (1977)].

It could be said further that the "pull" or excitement potential of a call, the memory or recall of past such calls, and the consequential call-centeredness of police activities all orient officers to messages rather than to the field.

The Ordering Frame

Officers define calls metaphorically in terms of associational similarities. They receive twice-mediated messages that are well framed and thematized as officially police relevant. Because the messages come in shorthand versions, the application of a frame is context or field dependent rather than information dependent.

Internal Message Analysis

Officer's internal message analysis is both more and less complicated than controllers'. It is more complicated because of the context-dependent nature of their interpretative practices and less complicated because the channel, source, and network dissolve in relevance. The message is immediately divisible into two paradigms: actionable calls and nonactionable or information-only calls. The partitioning of messages into units, the salience of the bits, and the effects of surrounding understandings are collapsed because the message-field axis is so permeable and the situated nature of the assessment of calls is so dominant as a cognitive style; most important, the units are lightly held because in due course they will become elided with the event in environment II.

The partitioning into units and the salience of units is contextual with respect to message-field distinction and priorities. They can be seen abstractly as a set of logical and formal categories that contrast with situated actions. The aim here is to sketch the formal outlines and to identify some of the recognized situated pressures shaping action choices.

Officers, once oriented to a message, orient themselves to the following characteristics of the message, or its syntagms:

1. Descriptive term for the event given by the controller (persons actions taken + actions toward),

2. Time of the event in environment I (before/during/after a job or call),

3. Location of the event (address, place, site),

4. Persons acting.

The descriptive term offered by the controller may be vague and unrevealing, such as "Could you go round to 45 Palsey Close and speak to Mrs. Gummer about dogs in her garden." In general, assignment is not done by the numbers, nor are the classifications used to discuss events or to write them up; officers are not given categories of events on the air that would constrain their subsequent decisions. No instructions are given concerning how to reach a location, what to expect, how to approach the situation, past history of the event, participants' characteristics, etc. (Heal and Ekblom 1982). Thus the officer must rely on memory of the area, the general location (for example, a block of council flats), local knowledge about the streets, the way there, and so on. The controller rarely supervises the content of the work and only modestly shapes its pace (Ekblom and Heal 1982). The controller does not guide the expectations of the officers concerning the event but merely presents it on the air as a preconstituted, tentatively held set of facts and expects the officer to place it in context.

The officer must impute, develop, or imagine the actions that might be relevant in the situation. The subterms (actions taken and actions toward) listed under "descriptive terms" are in fact constructions of officers based on their own experience, time on the job, local knowledge, time of the day, and other surrounding understandings rather than information received. This parallels the imaginative reconstruction of the controller but is based less on information provided by either written material or from another participant in the communications system.

The time of the event is relevant, as the potential for injury or actual injury is more important if the event has just happened or is in progress rather than if it is over. However, the actual elapsed time between the call (the incident) and the job being dispatched is itself variable and unknown to the officer unless the controller says on the radio, "In progress" or, conversely, "Happened half an hour ago." Location obviously is relevant for finding the event. It is assumed to be given more or less without exception. The relevant meaning of "location" is the significance it may have for characteristics of the event, the participants, or possible development potential. An officer's previous experience with such locations, events, or persons may be relevant but is not communicated. Portions of the ground have moral meanings attached. Certain parts of the ground, for example, are known as "good middle class areas" where the only relevant problems are a few burglaries, stolen cars, and calls to rescue a cat from a tree. Other areas are considered "rough," multi-ethnic, and rich with potential for crime, immorality, deceit, and vice. There are also several areas in which prostitutes normally work and where youths "hang out." Youth clubs and pubs (where heavy drinking during and after hours occurs) are also known. These provide a moral topography of the area, embedding calls for more experienced officers.

"Persons acting" is important because it alerts officers to events that may be exciting or fun, such as a fight outside a pub or a youth club or a "suspect on premises." Thus a descriptive term such as "fight outside a youth club" implies the promise of excitement as well as location cues (because all the youth clubs are known by name and place). It may also indicate whether a large number of officers will be needed or at least whether one should go "just in case." Even if more than one car is not called for, several may go—the "blue mice syndrome."

These matters of priority and the cognitive partitioning into bits are shaped in an important fashion by the use of the radio and the ways in which radio messages are both transmitted and received by officers. As noted in the discussion of channels, pandas and walkers are only on the VHF radio and receive calls only from the subdivisional controller. Therefore they hear calls sent to them, to other panda drivers, or to constables on foot. Because of limited mobility, walking officers rarely "swarm" or "queue jump" (take a call to which someone else was closer). Panda and area car drivers will take any call they believe they can reach, even if it takes them into another subdivision, and will also attend calls to which others have been assigned. Panda and area drivers like to race each other to locations. The area cars and the dog vans are on the UHF and receive calls from the force radio, the communications center (even if the calls are intended for officers in other divisions), and the controller. They also receive calls on their personal radios. They are roughly assigned to an area but cruise quite widely on and off the ground to which they are assigned [see Smith and Gray (1983, pp. 29–34) on the same behavior in London]. The controller does not know where they are at any given time, although he may have a record of what they have been asked to do and the time at which they accepted a call. The controller cannot read off the behavior, location, and priorities of given officers, unofficial or official, from their radio behavior. An implication of this, of course, is that it is difficult to anticipate the behavior of units for which one is searching.

Surrounding understandings is, like the matter of partitioning the message into units and the salience of these units, context dependent. The central theme of a message can change when external events, such as a string of robberies, change concern with items in the message that might connote robbery. The salience of a given bit can shift as external events "intrude" into message analysis and interpretation. Furthermore, it is clear that the matter of priorities and internal message analysis are closely related, for policing is a practical art. The aim of interpretation is to act.

Conclusion

In this chapter I outlined the effects on messages of coding, technology, roles and tasks, and interpretative practices within each of the three subsystems of the BDP. In effect, one has a series of snapshots of the perception of messages as a stream affected by these matters or variables as their internal features are recognized and used by the operators, controllers and officers. Although several of the effects are similar in the three subsystems, there are some salient differences in the social organization of the response to these messages. As the communicational unit moves, it is less affected by coding and technology and more affected by roles, tasks, and interpretation. In other words, subsystem-specific context effects become necessarily a part of the analysis. That is, the relevance of the information basis of the unit diminishes as it moves. Finally, formal cognitive matters, in part linked to formats and technology, are replaced by more situational judgments and assessments linked to the demand, ebb and flow of tasks, and the field in which the message is located.

The Midwest Police Department: Synchronic Analysis

The pattern of analysis employed in this chapter, each subsystem being examined for the effects of main variables, replicates that found in chapter 4 with the following exceptions. General points made in chapter 4 are not repeated here. Somewhat less attention is paid to the actions of dispatchers in this system because their duties are somewhat lighter than those of BPD controllers. If the reader holds lightly in mind a picture of the BPD, this chapter can be read through the experience of the BPD: Intertextuality results. Inevitably, one system is seen in terms of the other, and vice versa.

Operators: Codes

Assigning Codes

The click indicates a caller is on the line (operators in the MPD wear headsets). The operator answers, "Police, where is the problem?" This frames the call from the operator's perspectives as a police call. Callers, however, are often confused either because they are prepared to explain their personal dilemma, worry, anxiety, or need of assistance (all of which is irrelevant to the operator unless and until the address is given and the computer is thereby "accessed") or because they are seeking the emergency medical service (EMS) or the fire department. Before operators respond to the call, they insist on obtaining the address of the problem. This creates further confusion, for some callers give their home address or the address from which they are calling rather than the location to which the requested unit is to be sent. The answering procedure marks the call as a police call, but the call may have to be redefined as an EMS or fire department call. The operators think of themselves as employees of the police department rather than of the city, not of the fire or EMS services, so they view these calls as qualitatively different.

The channel is not marked reciprocally by caller and answer, and therefore turn-taking patterns are violated, many being attempts at clarification.

The operator does not automatically accept the call as being a police call, although once accepted as one of the three basic sorts of call (police, fire, EMS), specific data is requested (address, type of problem, whether still occurring, and sometimes caller's name). Persistence in repeated questioning and concern about current spelling of streets (essential for a "valid address" and name of the caller) affirm the wish of the police to actually respond to every call or to be seen as responding to every call.

There are strict, inviolate constraining format effects; those coming in the order in which items are to be obtained and the items that must be obtained. Operators do not listen randomly but tend to be brisk, terse, active, controlling, and affectively natural. They do not commiserate with callers, unless they think the person is suicidal, in which case they are under strict instructions to keep them talking and on the line. They do not comment in any fashion about the human situation described except to each other, usually in a tone that conveys irritation, incredulity or anger. They maintain the fiction of referential reality of the language and strip the emotive aspects of communication. Operators comment only on the phatic ("channel checks") aspect of the communication and do so by giving orders—"slow down; I *have* to have your address"—intended to control level of volume, speed, and accent ("I can't understand you").

Many calls are lost or callers dissuaded (about 60%) because the format effects lead to mutual frustration of the callers and the operators. This is marked when calls arise from children, those with foreign accents, or people who are perceived to be drunk or under the effects of other drugs.

The image-forming work that goes on in the operators subsystem is linked to short- and long-term memory and to the interpretative practices that link bits and pieces of information to the grammatical and syntactic rules governing English and the deep structure of meaning. The most important aspect of assigning codes is imaging the event in the object world, or environment I. Two sorts of observational data provide evidence of the process of image formation: asides, or comments made to other operators after a call has been sent to dispatchers or zone controllers, and marginal notes made on the side of the classification sheet used to code calls.

Folk concepts of crimes (Sudnow 1965) link the calls with the formal classification system that operators utilize to encode the calls as messages and format them as incidents.

The operators' call coding is not checked by any external supervision, and, as explained later, everything is viewed *as if* it were a burglary or *as if* it were extortion: It is not a mutually exclusive category but more like a family term having overlapping similarities with other categories.

As an example of the complexities of coding on the basis of imagery, consider the following: A call was received from a young woman who reported that her child had been "kidnapped" and that she wanted the police and the FBI alerted (she feared that the baby might have been taken out of the country as the Canadian border was not far). When asked what the problem was, she said that her ex-husband had taken the baby out to "show some friends" but had not been back for two hours. She feared that he had taken the baby.

This call presents problems because if the common sense term applied by the caller, "kidnapping," is used, then the call is classified as an assault. It can be classified as either

3452   1-3452 Kidnapping in progress

        2-3452 Kidnapping just happened

3453   3-3453 Kidnapping attempted, just happened

        3-3453 Kidnapping reported.

There are no rules given to determine selection among these options, other than formal description of the legal category "kidnapping" in the operator's procedure book. The book is virtually never used because it is huge (300 pages) and unwieldy and there is no room for it on or near the operators' small consoles. If, on the other hand, the call is not termed a "kidnapping," it could come under other categories, such as "missing person" or, more generally, "family trouble" or "disturbance." Family trouble is defined officially as a "civil matter." Police are urged to avoid contact with such matters as undertaking negotiations or advising persons. Callers are referred to legal aid, a family counseling clinic, or spiritual counseling. There are no rules for interpolating among these various categories, other than their formal definitions. The context within which such a story is to be cast is not and perhaps cannot be formalized or written. Note that this call would be a first priority call to another agency, or the caller may simply be told that an officer would be requested (knowing that if the call were classified as a missing person report that it might not even be undertaken by a unit); it would for all practical purposes be a way of refusing to attend to the expressed need of the caller.

The call was termed a kidnapping in progress (this was queried by the dispatcher, and the operator told him that she felt she had to classify it as such), but the operator explained to me that "that don't sound like no kidnapping to me; a man'll take a kid for a while to show his friends, bounce it around a little, and show it off, but when it needs changing or is hungry and starts to cry, that daddy'll bring the child home to its mama." In this case the personal preferences of the operator were placed in the background because the potential difference between the most serious and least serious categories she could have employed was so vast that she feared that it might "come back on her."

This call-handling process suggests that several possible images of events are produced by calls. These in turn become a basis for encoding. But any one of them may be used by any operator, and slight variations in cues (accent, speed, tone of voice) can change the operator's assessment of the credibility of the caller and thus of the category of the message. Certain rules for handling such ambiguity thus arise.

Another source of coding templates or images is the marginal notes made by operators on their classification sheets, comments they make to each other, and the history of the system itself. Particular calls such as automobile theft are listed as "UDAA in progress." One operator wrote out in longhand, "unlawful driving away—auto." This suggests that the legal template is being used for the classification of the incident and thus that the calls and legal categories are directly equivalent. The operators are taught these legal definitions in a required one-week training school. However, they call out to each other for clarification of calls (usually after they have named it and sent it forward), asking how one should differentiate "UDAA in progress" from "UDAA just happened" or "UDAA report." Concepts cover many ideas.

For example, people will often say that there has been an accident, but they do not say what sort of an accident. The operator woul ask, "Is it an automobile accident?" If the answer is yes, some comments would be made about the automobile accident. But it could be a shooting or some other sort of accident. Then the operators have to ask if anyone was injured. When a caller reports a stolen car, the first question asked is whether or not the theft has been previously reported and then whether or not the caller has been behind in the car payments. If the caller is behind in his payments, he is referred to the auto squad because the auto squad has repossession information. (The insurance companies or the finance companies have to notify the police department when they reposses an automobile.) Often people do not remember if they made their last payment or if they are behind, or they will not admit it. A lot of effort can be saved if the payment question is clarified early in the call. Also, people rarely give their names. They usually begin with an account of the incident. Callers have to switch from their own concern with the event to the priorities of the operator, which begins with the location. It would appear that, as people learn to use a 911 system, they will be more aware of the fact that location is the principal key to any further response by the police department.

Certain invisible cues seem to be used to determine whether or not a call is an emergency or whether an event is what the caller claims it to be. Two operators received calls about a bank robbery. One hung up when she heard that it was a child and did not enter any information on the call. Another operator (at another time) received a call from a child saying that there may be a bank robbery in progress, but he doubted the child. He asked the child for the bank's address, or location, and the child gave it. She entered it as a bank robbery in progress. Because there may be as many as twenty operators on duty at a given time, calls can come back to different people and be coded differently. Callers will lie when asked if they have called previously. Operators can check on this by flashing up on the screen all the calls from a certain address. The computer will scan and present all those within a four-block square area. Some callers ask, "Did I talk with you before about this?" Because the calls are automatically distributed, the chances of talking with the same operator are small. Sometimes there are complaints about the way a call was handled. Supervisors will come in the room and ask the operators, "Did you take this call?"

Because MPD operators have no police experience (recall that they are civilians) and are denied by union contract from riding in police cars, they cannot employ whatever specialized knowledge police might bring to imagine the event reported to them.

Once a call has been accepted and coded, the format constraints are rigidly adhered to: Operators interpret callers and probe for information ("Is he still there?" "What is the address where you are calling from?" "What freeway intersection?"), bring the caller into disciplined observation of the format, and then close the call (unless the person is suicidal or has attempted suicide).

Comments made to the caller about the content of the event index the image they are "filling in." Metalinguistic comments that alter the referential meaning of a word are made—"Breaking, you mean larceny?" "Have you made the payments on your car? It may not be stolen, but towed away by the finance company." This chunking and coding of items into clusters is first held in short-term memory. They are then shifted back into use and connected with long-term memory and previous experiences of such events. They are connected as the structure of the story unfolds (Cicourel 1973).

Some sort of filtering occurs as the stories are told. Some items are classified semantically as "irrelevant" ("I just came out of store and found ..."); Some are viewed as factually relevant ("My car is not in the parking place where I left it"), and some are merely registered, such as tone of voice, accent, and prosodic features of the caller's speech, unless the caller is viewed as not credible. This ability to draw out deep structure of messages from their surface features is difficult to describe fully. It is perhaps best illustrated by example.

The comments about imaging and the filtering effects of format and tacit knowledge are quite analogous to the observed procedures and perspectives of BPD operators. One important difference is that the hierarchy of filtration is more visible and verbal in the MPD. This difference is almost at the level of ontological rules governing the nature of the world and epistemological rules about the constitution of knowledge in and of that world (Castenada 1968, appendix).

The trust of the caller is the basis on which calls are entered. Operators are taught specifically to mistrust callers. The entire series of actions described here as coding is suffused with mistrust and a low-level disdain of callers and their problems. The sense that service is to be rationed, controlled, apportioned, and otherwise shaped at the source is shared among the MPD operators. Like the street-level bureaucrats described by Lipsky (1980), the operators act to control what they see as excessive demand for a scarce yet collective good.

Another important difference between the MPD and the BPD that affects coding is the level of demand. The MPD receives almost $2\frac{1}{4}$ times as many calls as the BPD (1.8 million compared with 800,000). Much stress is placed on reducing demand by reducing the number of incidents entered and at the zone controller level dispatched to cars. So far as I can estimate, some 60% of the calls are screened out or lost between the initial answering by the operators and dispatching. It is not clear how many are dispatched but lost because the car never arrives.

Once the call is accepted and entered into the computer by the operator, formatting effects take place. But operators receive an unknown number of calls that are terminated, the wrong number (611 is for telephone difficulties), refused because they are not true emergencies in the operator's mind, or buried for information only. Few calls are terminated unilaterally by the operators, but some calls are abusive, incomplete, incoherent, vague, rambling, or in a foreign language or dialect. The operators are skilled at hearing and rendering English in organizationally relevant terms. Termination is always problematic because it can lead to complaints from the public, the several well-known tragedies have resulted in the MPD from operator's errors. Terminated or lost calls are usually brief, probably less than thirty seconds. Most of the remaining calls are also brief, usually between thirty seconds and a minute. This means that the format effect on calls is severe in the MPD and that callers have been socialized to use the format. Recall that the computer requires a valid location before one can process the request for service. The algorithm (see figure 5.1) that results is counterintuitive, because from the caller's perspective the problem is primary, not the location of the problem. For the computer program and as a result of police organizational tactics, which assume a car will be sent to all trusted calls, location must be obtained. If the caller refuses to provide a location, it is "invalid"; if the call is terminated, it will not appear in the computer memory.

If a call is not brief, succinct, or clear—the information provided is rambling, sketchy, redundant, and inconsistent in character or the caller is unclear about what is happening, where, and why—the calls are termed "ambiguous." Translation of ambiguity into calls that can be sent forward to the zone controllers is not a linguistic skill; it is based on tacit knowledge and the ability to chunk and code information. Operators must then link the information to categories used, wait and see what is being said, and use long- and short-term memory to store and quickly recall information. Also useful are local knowledge of the city and its people and rough rules of thumb.

Several of these rules of thumb are used by operators to convert ambiguous calls into incidents. The first of these is the rule of social reality: Calls made are calls made about the here and now. They do not refer to events in the distant past, dreams, fantasies, wishes, plausible interpretations of events, guesses or hunches about events or persons or hypothetical extrapolations of events based on inference, abduction, deduction, or induction. The second rule of thumb is implied by the first: Tacit knowledge of events is used to make sense of them. The kidnapping example suggests the importance of tacit knowledge to operators coding activities. The third rule is closely linked to the first concerning the referential reality of calls. Just as operators assume that calls have referential reality, they must also assume that calls have a coherence and order and refer to an underlying social order or set of social relations of which calls are indexes, represetations, instances, or examples. How this reality is actually marked or framed such that it can be communicated is not explored by the operators (Garfinkel 1965; Castenada 1968, pt. 2; Leaf 1972). The order derived and coded is an ordering of natural types found in the differentially organized networks from which calls arise. These types are nominally and usefully translated into the police classification system. The calls index chaos in an ordered and orderly fashion. This is one of the paradoxes of operators' work.

Because for calls from high-information sources the operators' problem is conversion into actionable, partially ritualized call classification, operators maintain the notion that classification defines the object. The problem, so to speak, is the symbols used to encode it. The "as if" framing of the object is permanent within the subsystem, a permanent transitory reality, until the unit moves on. The power of this symbolic reality within the now formalized system takes precedence over the natural world of citizen's interpretations [Leaf (1972, p. 240) calls this the rule of definitional primacy]. This maintains the hegemony and power of the idea of assault, the idea of auto theft, and the idea of disturbance over the experience of such matters.

A fourth rule governing ambiguous calls is that they are seen as analogical, not as precise literal representations of previous calls or events, even those resulting in the same classification that day or previously. The precise character of the links connecting, for example, "disturbance, boys" (4-8200), "miscellaneous crime, gambling" (3-3860), and "traffic, hot rods" (5-8151) is unexplored. Their relations to each other, between the across categories, is nonproblematic. No formal rules, commonsense police wisdom, or specialized knowledge is brought to bear on the question. They stand linked in an invisible and assumed fashion.

A fifth rule is the timing of the call. For example, a call from a woman who claims her husband is abusing her will be viewed as a "typical wife calling about a drunken husband on payday night." It may be coded as a domestic or ignored. A call may be seen as a stage performance, such as the mother who called the police, spoke loudly, and kept saying to nearby child (it is assumed that there was a child who could hear), "I'm calling the police on you, hear me?" and reporting that the child had been abusive to her but divulged no further facts bearing on illegality. This type of call is ignored. A call made by a child is usually distrusted and the call terminated, regardless of the facts reported. It is highly distrusted from 3–5 P.M. when children come home from school before adults and play with the phone out of boredom. The facts are not heard as facts in these cases, because they are seen in another context—a kind of "as if" framing for police purposes that has no action potential for the police. The call is police business, but the police are being used for private purposes. Police operators think they can discern degree of credibility of any call by cues they read off from the call, caller, and other context-based features of the communication.

Yet another rule of epistemological importance is the rule of pragmatic interactional primacy (Leaf 1972, p. 236), which in formal terms is defined as follows: "The criteria for acceptability of a given formulation lies not in the way the putative object of the proposition behaves, but rather in the effect it has on the interactional relations between the users of the proposition and people of interest to him." Primacy involves manipulation of descriptions to fit the situation, as Leaf argues. The relevance of this rule to caller-operator interactions is that the stipulation of pragmatic relevance lies almost entirely with the operator. The operator, however, must gain the tacit compliance of the caller so that the caller will not continue talking, call back and repeat the request frequently, or become abusive. Operators retain control by reducing feedback to callers about what the incident is called or what classification it is given, by closing the conversation with a promise to request police attention, and by refusing to attend to the phatic or connotative aspects of communication.

It has already been suggested that hearing a call requires specific modes of listening and recording such that natural or everyday language can be translated and "back-translated." Nonverbal aspects of the communication are invisible, so that other features of the talk become more salient. Communication about the channel ("Do I have the right number?" "Is this police?" "I'm calling the police"), idiosyncratic particulars of the caller (hesitation, enunciation, stammer, or stutter), and irrelevant information (noise, depending on the timing of the information given and its relevance to the putative classification given by the operator) are also reduced in salience. It should be emphasized, however, that "normal form inclusions and exclusions" are used in imposing the classification (Bottomley and Coleman 1980; Ekblom and Heal 1982). What is included is based on the modes of listening and then made routine. This inclusion is informal. All operators omit their impressions of the person, for example, even though that may be seen as critical to understanding the nature of the incident and its potential for development and consequentiality. The result is that such impressions, although formally excluded at this point, are reflected in the classification of the call as incident. This classification is done without specific reference to these features of the caller's communication.

Once a call becomes an incident and is in the computer, rules of a more specific character govern processing. These are working rules that are of an operational sort and are to some degree police specific. They can be seen as a series of subrules based on the basic operational rule, "Send everything along to the dispatcher." One has nothing to lose by this action and it both "covers your ass" and meets the organization's stated purpose of responding to all emergencies. "Covering your ass" in this case means not refusing "to request a police vehicle," the technical language used by the operators to callers) if the call is trusted and formatted. If an operator does refuse, she must do so in a manner that precludes the call from coming back on her. Everything sent on is seen as tentative, potential, and subject to final legitimization by police officers on the scene. Operators also send all communications in a form that can be altered by officers when they arrive. Because dispatchers read out a shorthand description of the job on the air to officers, the operator's language is key only with respect to reproducing a conventionalized translation of the call.[1] In one sense this means that events are "upgraded" in seriousness to ensure that the officer is alerted to any potential danger or awkwardness on arrival. When encoding the talk into incident form, operators attempt to find and establish one and only one reading of what has been reported. It is assumed that it could have been otherwise. This is implicit in the written communication at every point in the system. An operator does not write in the remarks section, "I called it a rape but it might just be a "family fight," although this might be communicated by phone to the zone controller after the incident is sent to him.

Coding Effects

Coding has preconditioned general effects that can be further divided into format-supplied constraints, ordering constraints, and interactional constraints. There are also item power and informational constraints.

Format-supplied constraints are patterned by a number of facts in the MPD. The computer automatically enters a number for the phone call, the console at which it was received, the ID number of the operator, the date, and the time. However, it leaves open address, type of dwelling, classification of the incident, incident description, remarks, and unit requested (police, EMS, fire, or some combination thereof). Each action reduces the operator's next choice. Initially there are twelve bits of information to be supplied, six of them automatically produced once a valid address is entered, and subsequent items, taken one at a time. After the six are automatically added and given a valid address, the operator can add or subtract items in any orders, but the mechanics of the process make line-by-line, left-to-right progress easiest. The choices within each type of item are constraining. Address and remarks are binary, type of dwelling and unit requested have 3 options (apartment, single-family house, or multiple dwelling complex), and incident classification has 245 categories.

The classification system includes a digit to communicate the priority of the incident (1–5). Cars are dispatched notionally on the basis of an assessment of the "seriousness, urgency, growth rate [of the event] and availability of [police] resources." The next two digits indicate the crime. The next digit indicates a specific offense, and the last digit indicates a "seriousness" dimension. The codes themselves are a constraint in regard to the information and possible actions that result. The number of kinds of classification in this code is extreme. The constraint of assigning a message to a category is therefore less than it might be in a system with fewer categories [such as that reported by Lilly (1978)]. Few of the categories are in fact used, and those used are used repeatedly and do a wide range of service. These are seen as logical and referential categories intended to reflect the logic of things, not of persons as sentient beings. They order factual relations best used to describe physical time-space relationships.

Internal ordering constraints on the next action, given the first item of information, are produced by following the format but are also used to order an acceptable message form from the caller. It orders caller's talk and operator's talk and formats printout, record keeping, and retrieval possibilities. Calls and data gathering from calls are templated by this format.

Interactional constraints constantly shape interaction because the computer is keyed to an address opening of incident logs and proceeds from the correct address to the next item.

When a caller refuses to give an address, the call is terminated by the operator (or buried in the computer as incomplete "for the file"); it the caller gives the address and the address is not accepted by the computer, the operator must make a decision: Is the caller lying or is the caller just confused about the location? Is the caller unable to spell the street name correctly? (The computer requires correct, not phonetic spelling.) Is the caller confused, excited, or distracted because of the incident about which the call is being made? Are none of these true, but the street is not on the computer (because it is a new street, created since 1974, or because the name has been changed and the computer not updated? Is it lack of information or inability to tell east from west, left from right? The sequence of information required drives conversation rather than the problem the caller wishes to resolve. If the operator decides to investigate, street name books must be acquired, usually misplaced somewhere in the center, and the street verified, and the computer must be given instructions to "override" the computer's block on the next entry.

Like the BPD, there are several types of categories or constraint-producing codes.[2] The classification system, developed by computer engineers in consultation with the police, contains functional groupings keyed by the second digit (see figure 3.6). Thus these are commonsensical groups or families of calls referring to crime, medical services, order problems generally and alarm calls, and officer, vehicle, or internal maintenance calls.

It is obviously not a closed classification system but has the apparent aim of functioning in that fashion and includes catch-all categories, such as "noise/radio" (3-8290). The categories *within* any digital group are not mutually exclusive; for example, the listing under EMS contains three listings for burns, three for stroke, and three for sick. Nor are the digital groups mutually exclusive; for example, drunk, auto accident, and crowd gathering could all apply to a given incident but only one is accepted. Also, the digital groups within the larger family of classifications are not internally consistent. Across the several groups the consistency within and between categories is obviously a variable in the sense that there is an "obvious" linearity or dimensionally to the listing of homicide, attempted suicide, and dead person (in terms of the seriousness of threat to human life and the violence involved) but none at all to boys, crowd gathering, disorderly gang fight, and family trouble.

It is perfectly clear that, not only is the system not closed, but also the number and kinds of categories used are spuriously precise and too numerous. They are not mutually exclusive. Facets of situations might benefit from multiple coding rather than standing as a gloss of a type of problem. A classification is simultaneously synecdochic and far too broad to characterize many kinds of events. A violent family fight with several participants, weapons, neighbors, and children involved is not usefully glossed with the term "family trouble."

Because the multiple character of the event is not captured in the classification rules, which permit only one classification, it is not clear which aspect of the call is the determinant category into which a changing, shifting event seen within several perspectives should be classified. If classified, the incident cannot be arrayed vertically or horizontally in an order that would suggest a single dimension of classification. The logic of the system itself is elusive.

The classification is skewed to crime categories, 51% of the categories are considered crimes (by the first digit of the code). These have a great salience for coded incidences in phenomenological terms for several reasons. Crime is the central focus of American police rhetoric, the occupational culture, and the drama of policing seen in the mass media. The operators share this view. Furthermore, crime implies action or sets a future course of events to intervene, punish, gain retribution, set things right, restore the honor of the victim. This means that crime-labeled incidents imply a future orientation, action, and ameliorative intervention in everyday life. Other categories do not set this orientation. Let us then contrast the four broad category families.

Crime-probable categories, which obviously include such things as "bomb threat" (1-8330) and "prowler" (2-8450), set orientations to further future developments and information, have action-resolution potential (catch a disorderly youth, arrest a thief, prevent a rape), and key the high probability of dispatch. They also imply attendance at the scene, paperwork, and exclude other categories. These also tend to have the highest official priority ("1") assigned to them. Order-related categories, excluding alarms and including catch-all categories, set orientations to developments and information forthcoming and have a high action but low resolution potential. The content of these categories is highly variable, once confronted, as are the outcomes. These are the most frequently used categories. Medical/ambulance categories dispatched to EMS have "no action necessary" implications unless an additional category is used, for example, "meet EMS." (2-8500). Finally, internal business categories indicate a present status rather than a future state or command to action. The actions indicated are predictable, and the resolutions are already known, few, and relatively certain. These are system maintenance categories.

Finally, it should be recalled that about half the calls processed by the operators are information given, information requested, or internal police calls that have no action implications. The point is that, once the call has been seen as non—information related, there is a gradient of action potential ranging from information only to present status and system messages (another large percentage of calls coming through the message center) to EMS messages (all of which refer to present state, are resolved, and require no future action) to order-related categories (which refer to future actions to "correct" a present situation). These calls are problematic and in fact are likely to have a low resolution potential. They are equivocal in character. They are variable and dynamic as events with assorted outcomes and crime categories. Crime categories, like order categories, connote future action required to intervene (but not all do, as some calls are after the fact and are somewhat mini–action calls requiring only affirmation rather than solution or action) and are problematic but may be resolvable by arrest (a good piece of police work). They may also have a dynamic and exciting character and variegated outcomes.

These constraints suggests that there is greater power or action potential in the connotations of crime categories than others and therefore that they produce greater constraints on other members of the system than other kinds of categories.

The amount of information may be a relevant feature constraining whether a call is classified, whether it is defined as a call or a "good call" (one that the computer accepts), or whether it is buried or terminated. In this sense information is an important constraint on operators, and this is especially true because of the rigid format constraints in the MPD.

Operators: Technology

Operators in the MPD work in a harsh environment governed by arbitrary discipline and threatening rules and risks. The general working conditions are bad. In their cocoon above the city, guarded by closed circuit cameras, in the drone of computers, behind locked, electronically controlled doors, heated and cooled by the city, they are engaged in a semifatal and stressful dance with technology. Calls call the tune.

Operators are in many ways the epitome of the assembly line worker with little or no control over the quality, pacing, content, aims, or evaluation of their work. They are timed to the second on every break by computers; they are supplied work by an automatic computer that shifts calls their way as soon as they are "free"; the order of their task is technologically determined and demand driven. They are the servants of the public in name only, for although the city pays them, they work for the machines that lurk behind them, glow in front of them, click and buzz in their ears, and fill the air with dull electronic sounds. (Field notes)

The operators receive messages on three channels: the telephone (both internal and external lines), the microcomputer with a VDU, and the various officers, supervisors, and fellow operators and zone controllers. The room is dominated by the demand represented by incoming telephone calls. The primary work is the action of processing phone calls and entering or not entering them on the VDU. The effects of technology in the message are telephone and VDU specific and concern the credibility of the message, the form of messages received and sent the fringe meanings associated with the channel on which the message was received, patterns of feedback, the absence of presence of the caller, channel alternation effects, technologically produced uncertainty and ambiguity, single channel effects, and technological mediation.

The telephone is an intrusive democratic instrument (Ball 1968) and as a source is less credible than messages from the VDU (mainly feedback from dispatchers who have received a message directed to them) or from personal sources. Calls from internal police lines are more credible than calls from external (citizen-sourced) lines. The exaggerated power of calls from citizens, arising as they do at thirteen or fourteen per hour per operator, makes the question of work control salient because the more the message is distrusted, the less work it produces. This implies further that, as supervision of these calls increases, distrust of operators increases and the zone of tolerance decreases. In the event of a crisis, the focus is immediately on why the apparently trustworthy message (seen retrospectively) was not sent on as usual.[3] Conversely, police-sourced messages on internal lines are treated as routine and are not referred or queried but passed on automatically.

The form of the message is created by the channel on which it arrives and, if it is sent on, the channel on which it is sent. Phone messages dominate, thus aural, nonvisual, temporally developed messages without other meanings set the tasks and the response of operators. Telephone messages are transformed and formatted on the VDU, thus taking two forms in a matter of some 10–15 seconds.

The channel on which a message is sent in the MPD provides a set of fringe meanings, or a degree of permanence (written) or impermanence (aural) for messages. The tendency is to freeze messages into the VDU quickly at this point to avoid chat, context-filling conversation, or remarks in order to squeeze the message into the form and receptacle (the VDU).

Feedback takes four forms: (1) operator to caller, (2) dispatcher to operator, (3) caller to operator, and (4) EMS and fire. The forms of feedback between operators and callers are (1) format-constraining feedback, in which operators continue to repeat "Where is the problem?" to obtain a valid address, ignoring the event description; (2) denial, referral, or negotiating the request when it is seen as not police business; (3) reassurance when a call has been previously made and a "unit requested" (repeat calls can be rescreened by calling for either the address, the incident, or name of the caller); and (4) intercommunicative feedback during the course of the processing of the message ("uh-huh," "um," "I see"). Callers can initiate feedback also by asking if a car will be sent, how long it will take, calling again, having another person call for the same incident, calling for information about where the police will arrive if sent, and redefining their role in an incident. They call, refusing to give a name or information, to request an officer or to ask for additional service (an ambulance and a police vehicle).

Dispatchers can query the operators by calling them on the internal phone lines to check on a fact or one of the remarks added to the incident form. These relate to such matters as the degree of danger implied by a caller, the possible presence of a weapon, or the degree of trust of the operator in the caller's description. These are fairly rare, happening perhaps once a day per operator.

Transfer feedback occurs when a call has been sent by an operator by electrowriter to the EMS and it is shown as being received or when the EMS rings to check a dispatch. Another form of transfer feedback occurs when a call has been received by the EMS or by the fire department. Once an operator answers the caller, she coms back on the line and thanks the police operator.

Because the MPD, like most other American police departments, "generally respond[s] to the calls for police assistance as if they were isolated events without any prior history ... police are essentially restricted to reactive response strategies, and must decide how to respond only after the event takes place" (Pierce et al. 1981). There is neither prospective feedback nor responsive or retrospective feedback because each event is seen as sui generis and fluidly patterned. Observations made to me concerning ongoing or just completed events were anecdotal, sporadic, and casual. Operators sought a diachronic ordering of calls in sequence from their person, their neighborhood, or area of the city. The calls were incident centered, about the current family trouble, child's call, or domestic, unless they were recognized repeat calls.

The absence of presence of the caller varies in importance with the technology involved. Telephone calls increase the salience of the prosodic features of language style. They are focused on how to determine trust in the MPD. VDU and electrowriter transmissions produce stylistic particulars. The handwriting of the sender goes on the electrowriter to be read by the EMS clerk. Verbal and nonverbal messages, such as making faces through the glass, are self-referential and expressive, giving context to information-bearing messages. One operator would provide feedback or forewarning by a wave to the dispatcher when another call involving a "crazie" was sent, as if to negate and apologize for the sent information.

Operators chunk and code information from listeners to produce an encoded message, producing channel alternation effects. They translate between aural data and written text production by assembling an image of the event in the world about which the call is made. They also "clean up" and make grammatical Midwestern American speech from caller's talk. They move messages from one channel to another, laminating it with their own knowledge about what is left out or included. Remarks may be added. What is left unexplicated is the salience of various sign systems in the decoding done in the other subsystems.

There are three sources of technologically produced ambiguity for the MPD operators. The first is the ambiguity introduced by reliance on a single channel, the telephone, for receiving incoming calls and by the inability to verify or validate information received from a citizen. Operators can certify that the address given is valid or "good" within the city limits (this does not, of course, mean that the caller is there or that the event is at that address). The nonverifiable and acontextual nature of the information is amplified by the fact that the operators have been neither dispatchers nor officers. When the positions of operator and dispatcher were combined (before 1967), the dispatchers in the precincts answered the phones and could rely on multiple sources of information to verify and validate the data given. These included personal experience, the radio for feedback, and other operators who were also officers. Specialization and single-channel input *increases* rather than decreases uncertainty in meanings.

A second source of technological ambiguity is the absence of feedback among the various members of the three subsystems: 911 operators are not meant to call dispatchers (but do), receive no feedback informally from the EMS, fire department, or scout car officers, and receive only rare formal feedback on calls that go through 911. 911 operators are shown on their screens a confirmation that a message has been received by the dispatcher but do not receive any further information on the call—whether it was assigned to a car, whether a car went, what was done, what the resolution of the event was. If they check informally with dispatchers, they may be told, but there is no required formal feedback on the disposition of the call. Dispatchers do not, on the other hand, know whether a call sent to them was received fifty times or once by 911 operators, because all calls are received only once by dispatchers. Callers will sometimes call back in five or ten minutes to inquire why a unit has not arrived. Previous calls can be retrieved by address and shown on the screen by operators to determine when the last call was made, other problems in the area, and the nature of the five most recent runs. These operators are physically, symbolically, and technologically at one end of a large funnel.

A third source of technological ambiguity derives from the electrowriter. When the computer is down or on low power, messages can be transmitted only by electrowriter. When the computer is down, operators begin to hurry and are frustrated because messages take longer to be transmitted and received. If a heavy load of calls results under these conditions, they begin to write faster, and the messages often become illegible. This adds to confusion, the rush, and the ambiguity.

Unlike the operators in the BPD, MPD operators receive calls from the public only over the 911 lines and a few direct internal phone calls. They do not receive telex messages, written messages, internal memos, alarm calls, or radio calls; they are locked into a segment single-channel input from the outside. They send out messages on the VDU. The connection they recognize is one incoming channel and one outgoing channel. This marks these channels as links with the outside world and escalates the importance of clear communication, the loss of power on the VDU computer, and the tension associated with sending and receiving messages from the public.

Messages to operators are always technologically mediated. Few verbal face-to-face messages are given to operators, other than supervisory ones or second-level messages (communication about communication). The operators are extremely isolated, and virtually all the information they receive is through technologically mediated channels. This makes their own personal knowledge and asides spoken during message processing secondary. All technologically mediated messages are thought to be less credible than face-to-face ones, so operators perceive themselves to be processing material suffused with distrust at the same time they are to assess it, discover valid calls, discount ambiguous calls, and the like. The processing of messages in a given subsystem can thus increase the average doubt about it. Technology thus increases equivocality.

Operators: Roles and Tasks

The structure of items coming to the attention of operators are assembled mentally and reflect a latent structure of meaning. The physical actions or behaviors described in chapter 3 are surface manifestations of forms of life of which they are indexes.

Coding, credibility, and relevance cohere to permit an algorithm of calls received (see figure 5.1). The aim is to mark the intent of the calls. The focus is on the location of the problem in order to send it forward: Effort is initially made to locate the place to which the officer should go to respond to trouble. This omits who is calling about the trouble, who is distressed about it, from where they are calling, their relationship to the call, the event, and the possible victim. Speculation about intent is secondary. Why someone calls is not an issue unless the call is subject to termination or is distrusted for other reasons. This obviates the usual police concern for motive, intent, opportunity, relationship, consequence, and legal concerns. The pass-through function of such systems is negatively related to contextual, richly detailed information gathering and is aimed at response only. It is only when attention shifts to internal message analysis that distinctions about callers' motives, the nature of the call-object relationship, and the action consequences of the call become salient.

The sensitivity to "covering one's ass" or to avoiding a charge that nothing was done means an orientation to prospective understandings of

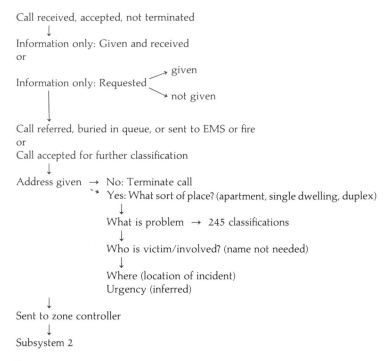

Figure 5.1
MPD operators: algorithm of calls.

the occupational culture. Police assumptions about the object world and the disciplinary rules guiding procedures for operators also pattern roles.

Encoding is transformed into an inwardly oriented practical action in touch with the operative rules of the communications center. When the VDU is activated, it is a basis for a conflated imagery of the call, objective world, and procedural regulations.

There is no discretion or choice in the sequence in which calls are taken. They are automatically shunted to one terminal after the other; they must be seen as a mechanical sequence. All calls sent on are sent by VDU to the dispatchers. The operators are oriented to the call as a signal: Their head-sets are their eyes, ears, nose, and fingers. They are individually oriented and do not interact around calls except to comment about their stupidity, excesses, or banality after the fact. Their personal views are depressed in salience. They have little group support for their decisions, low morale, and high alienation, leading to considerable employee turnover.[4]

Once a call is sent forward, if there is no crisis, it is not heard about again. The tendency is to send everything on and close one's eyes. It is like dropping a pebble down a well. The individualistic nature of the work means that few decisions are affected by group interactions or effects. Thus, although discretion is least and supervision highest in this sub-system, it is also the group for which stress is highest and worries about "errors" most profound.

Operators: Interpretive Work

Message processing illuminates the movement and meanings attributed to the message regardless of content. To be processed, a message must be delineated from noise, the field, and nonmessage activities. The ordering sequence within which messages are viewed must also be marked. When attention shifts to the "internal" meaning of a message, operators must examine the differentiation of the message into units or bits (connotative and denotative meanings of signs), arrayed by salience and significance.

Message-Handling Processes
Noise-Message-Distinctions

Some calls are noise. Several types of calls can be viewed as noise and not messages. The first are misdirected calls [calls intended for information (411) and telephone repair (611)]. The second are repeat calls for the same event that have been previously received at the center; the third are calls made as nuisance calls to operators. The fourth set of noise calls are "phony runs" and other calls where the caller is seen as categorically untrustworthy. The fifth are untrustworthy calls generally, and the final group are personal calls received by operators that they refuse to answer on tape (rare).

Sometimes it is not clear to or for whom the call is being made, and it is heard as noise. For example, callers will call the operator, refuse to give an address, or give an address and then begin to ramble about the situation in which they are involved. A child called to tell the operator that his father was beating his mother, the details were given, but no address would be given over the phone, suggesting that this was a way of controlling the father by requesting police assistance. In another call, the woman gave an address and described that her husband was going to beat her, but did not want the police to come to the scene. These types of call are refused. No unit was requested, and the caller was informed of this and that the event was not a police matter.

Once these message types are eliminated, technological noise and the noise of the proximal environment remain. Smoke, the constant sounds of the operators' talking, the movement of people in and out of the office, and the conversations between operators and operators and supervisors all constitute proximal noise.

Noise can also be a function of the timing of a call (in the midst of a rush of other calls), the stylistic aspects of the speech of the caller, or the language spoken (some callers will break into another language from time to time or speak one language to the operator and another to someone else in the room in which the call is being made), or a function of speed, tone, or quality.

Field-Message Distinction

Any call received by the operator intrudes into a field of personal involvements (side conversations with others, thoughts, and feelings), social interactions, current behaviors (reaching for a purse, chewing gum, sending a call by electrowriter), and events going on in the room (laughter, conversations, jokes, and banter). This field, it should be emphasized, is restricted in effect to operators. Their primary discretion lies in the placement of the call data into classification categories and the priorities produced thereby.

The pull of the message is strong among the operators in the MPD. The surrounding noise, activities, and field are far less compelling than the messages coming in. There is little opportunity to develop a personal style because supervision and the computer counting the number of calls processed in an hour and the number of seconds off duty are quite constraining. The message in this subsystem is less field dependent than it is for zone controllers and officers. The answering of the call as police business—"Police, where is the problem?"—continuously locks the operators into a question and answer sequence and reaffirms message over noise and field.

The Ordering Frame

The ordering frame refers to the definition of the relevant connections between the calls as messages. The most common orientation for operators is to the actual sequence as given, but this is a variable. Generally, operators are oriented to the metonymic aspects of the sequence. A computer automatically shunts the next call to an operator who has completed a call.

The metonymic orientation of the operators is the only sensible one because there is no practical reason for them to orient to the metaphoric similarities in the messages. From an analytic point of view, metaphoric thinking requires the operator to shift orientation from message processing to internal message analysis. In order to combine calls into types, content becomes a relevant basis for ordering the calls. The following hypothetical sequence of calls perhaps suggests the variety of calls received and classified by an MPD operator:

1. 1–3511, Breaking and entering, in progress
2. 1–3941, Family trouble, fight
3. 3–8270, Disturbance/trouble

4. 4–8469, Missing report

5. 1–3101, Robbery in progress

6. Wrong number (wanted 411, information)

7. Nuisance call—Obscene harrassment of the operator by a caller

8. Repeat call—refer to computer memory

9. 3–3740, Investigate auto

10. 1–9000, Officer in trouble

For these operators all but calls 6, 7, and 8 must be entered on the VDU and sent. A priority is automatically given as a result of the selection of a classification. The content of the calls has little bearing on operators' workload, does not alter their priorities, and does not change the significance of the next call. Meaning is almost entirely given by the temporal sequence of calls.

As was noted in the discussion on the effects of a metonymic classification of messages, syntactic regularity is produced by such automatic call ordering for operators. All the signifiers are treated as equal and their signifieds are frozen or made nonproblematic. It means that the referents of the signifiers remains unclear or subject to repeated redefinition within subsequent subsystems. Furthermore, the sequencing of calls in this subsystem shows how limited power constrains discretion and choice, because no alternatives to the linear arrangement are permitted. The fact that alternative groupings and clusterings of types of calls (crime versus noncrime or internal communication versus information-given calls) can be created only highlights the irrelevance of such clusterings for operators.

Internal Message Analysis

When the orientation of the operator changes from message handling or processing to message analysis, message content assumes greater importance. The messages arise in variously organized networks in the social world and thus come with varying degrees of coherence and predictability. When operators consider the metaphoric combination of messages, they are rendering the texts of the messages as a kind of moral topology, which is in turn the surface of a deeper substructure. Only those with action implications require further internal message analysis. Messages seen to contain a prospective action significance are of most interest. The question that motivates attention to such calls is, What do I do with or about this call? This places the call into the action paradigm, a call to be classified for the purpose of someone acting on it. Other calls are seen within the metacommunicational paradigm (information given or received) and are viewed as of secondary importance.

Partitioning the Message into Units

Six types of valid calls arrive at operators' consoles in the MPD center. They arise from two sources: the police and the public.

1. Public Source
   a. Information given
   b. Information requested
   c. Referral requested
   d. Action requested
2. Police source
   a. Information given
   b. Information requested

Types 1c, 2a, and 2b are nonclassified; that is, internal calls and referrals, once a label (classification) is given to them, are irrelevant for action other than referring, giving, or receiving information. Types 1a and 1b are also relatively unimportant even as valid calls because they require no consequential action and may not even be logged into the VDU if they are opened and closed with the same act of answering and giving or receiving information. In practical terms action requests dominate operators' concerns, even though they represent less than one-half of the calls processed.

Let us take action requests (type 1d) as an example to show how format constraints provide a clue to the facts required and the syntagms used. From table 5.1 it is clear that formal records do not contain enough information to reconstruct what was said to the operator (other than the classification employed), the precise nature of the problem, or the event's dynamics. Only from data (not shown here) on the time lapsed between accepting a call and calling in clear can one infer what might have been done. Many incidents are sent forward with only the most minimal information [address, description of the problem, and potential (contained in the classification number)]. This is essentially sending incidents out "by the numbers." There is no requirement on officers to report to the zone controller or operator what actions, if any, were taken. Outcomes are impossible to reconstruct from this data.

This pattern, in turn, affects the behavior of the operators who do not probe for detail of the event, other than whether it is life threatening or for any particular information that officers going to the scene should know. Operators simply tell caller, "A unit has been requested." When asked whether a scout car has been sent, is on the way, or when it might arrive, operators simply slowly repeat that a unit has been requested. (This is done, I was told, to "cover one's ass," so that no citizen can claim to have been told that a car is en route when in fact none was sent.)

Table 5.1
Syntagms for five calls to the MPD: Operators (January 1979)[a]

Syntagms	Call 1	Call 2	Call 3	Call 4	Call 5
Location	17 Charles Rd.	20015 Benson	W. 7 Mile Road	1503 Bon Jour	21100 Ford Freeway
Character of location	Street	?	Street	House	?
Description of the problem	Person w/weapon	FT-fight	UDAA report	Narc in progress	B & E (dwelling) report
Potential for development	1-3431	1-3941	4-3709	2-3881	4-3519
Actions taken	Stealing?	Fight	Stealing	Narcotics	Broken into
To whom/what	Car?		Car	?	House
Persons acting	One	?	?	?	?
Incident number[b]	0747	7571	8326	9001	9920

a. Selected from a two-hour period; calls directed to 16th precinct. A question mark indicates data imagined or not included in printout of calls.
b. Actual incident numbers have been disguised.

Although some reconstruction and imagination of the nature of the event is involved in creating a classification, operators send everything that is defined as a message to zone controllers. There is little need to try to interpret or understand what the officer might see or encounter because this is either the job of the zone controller or will be requested by officers of the operators if it is needed. Operators thus disconnect themselves from the events and truncate their obligations toward guiding future actions.

The Salience of the Units

MPD operators are constrained to an extent that is not characteristic of the BPD operators. Greater information is automatically entered in the VDU as a result of opening an incident file. The primary interest of the operator is filling in the incident format or characterizing the call rather than the event. The units of interest in order are the location of the problem (address, intersection, place), the caller's location, when the event happened, the descriptive term for the event (classification number), the persons acting, the actions taken, toward whom/what, and remarks.

In routine activities this ordering of units of information is fairly stable, maintains the idea that referential activity dominates the work of the operators, and makes coherent what they do. But because the meanings of these units change, this is a misleading assumption.

Surrounding Understandings

Surrounding understandings are the proximal influences on the meaning of information. As such, they are fluid and changing. Several sources can be mentioned for MPD operators.

Remarks can change the significance of a bit of information. The remarks typed below the message sent by operators to dispatchers indicate the priority-related meanings listed in the classifications. These remarks could, of course, be used at any point in message processing to change the meaning, priority, and event classification of any given communicational unit, no matter what the original code or demand of the caller. These meanings change over time and from subsystem to subsystem. The codes and priorities can change and the negative feedback capacity and activity is limited.

The particular bit of information that is seen as salient, if message content is the orientation of the receiver, changes the nature of the incident. There are no rules for choosing between the items focused on or within the categories, except as a result of the way in which the operator construes the message given by the caller. Stored facts (kept in the computer memory and easily retrieved and shown on the VDU) that only the operator possesses, for example, the last five calls nearest the address or location given in the previous twenty-four hours, may also function as priority-meaning data. For example, if the call is third in the last few minutes from an address, it is referred ("buried"), not forwarded to the dispatcher. Thus each message has not only a fact and context aspect but also a temporal or sequential aspect that patterns its significance and meaning.

Various semihistorical or biographical contexts can feed into the meaning of the incident. These can include the previous history of events in that neighborhood or that block or even events happening near the caller's location. Certain areas have a reputation for being violent. The time of the day can be seen as relevant for some types of calls, such as domestics, family trouble, breaking and entering, fights in bars, and gangs. The time of the day, for example, means that in the late afternoon fights are less likely to be drunken (and dangerous) than in the early evening or late evening in the city (especially on a Friday or Saturday night). This will change the significance of certain bits within the message. The time of shift change may be crucial in obtaining an officer to respond to certain calls, such as "take a report," making some kinds of calls less important and some information more important. Day of the week is also a consideration of the potential for some development of incidents. These matters of timing of course have an interactive effect because the heavy load of calls and service demands on Friday and Saturday evenings means that calls change in their significance anyway. More calls means that fewer less serious calls are sent forward and may not be forwarded by zone controllers.

Dispatchers: Codes

The dispatchers receive once-processed data that has been converted from a call about an event in the world into a message processed as an incident. The text that the zone controller receives as a printout. Although there are occasional calls from the operators to the zone controllers and from the officers as feedback questions and some face-to-face interactions with operators, the primary form of communication from environment I is the printout the dispatchers receive from the printer by their desks. The complexity of the message received by the operators is compressed into a single-channel source.[5]

In many ways the dispatcher has a focal position that receives highly compressed and reified messages or incidents and transforms them into rather subtle jobs whose connotative meanings must be expanded by imagination of the possibilities that await the officer.

Assigning Codes

All the problems of coding in the initial instance are reproduced at this level, with fewer data bits (they may not be information). The phenomenological and interpretative work is not constrained by formal classification coding. To some degree the formal fiction of the existence of the event as a police matter, as an object and event in environment I, is reified when it appears as dispatcher's work. The dispatchers are constrained, however, in that, according to procedure, they must deal with the incident by requesting a scout car or choosing not to. Approximately 53% of all calls resulted in dispatching a unit (no data are kept in dispatching records on the actions taken by the officers, if any, on the scene, nor whether they in fact ever went to the scene).[6]

The dispatcher does not have to act as if the classification is real for the present purposes. He can ignore the classification priority (officially), act as if the event has another priority informally without making any written change on the hard copy, and can add comments in his transmission to officers that are not written on the copy.

Officially there are no multiple classifications or reclassifications of an incident. The dispatcher's next actions are constrained by the appearance of the incident; he must either reject or accept it.

Informal priorities are contrasted with or are complementary to formal priorities. A pad is kept next to the desk on which the dispatchers may write notes about the whereabouts of certain cars. Notes are also written on the cards in the slots when assignments are made. The operator's preferences interact with the classifications and priorities.

Coding Effects

Constraints arise for dispatchers from five sources: format, ordering of the data, priority, reclassification, and the classification given. Once the message is received by VDU printout, it is both format frozen and format constrained: No official format changes are required and all are forbidden. When the dispatcher receives an incident card, he places it in a machine that stamps on the time. Data are not recorded, nor are priority classification numbers changed. No feedback is used to reclassify in writing any informal reclassification. There are two action domains or paradigms: action taken or assignment (written on the card before the card is placed in the slot) and time cleared.

Dispatchers: Technology

One in-channel dominates (the VDU printout), and one out-channel dominates (the radio). Radio messages tend to be feedback rather then initiatory calls. The effects of technology are focused on two channels, one in and one out: telephone and computer [National Crime Intelligence Computer (NCIC) and Department of Motor Vehicles (DMV)]. Face-to-face communications present slight variations in that all computer-based information is explicitly trusted, whereas telephone calls are internally driven; they invoke personal "business" or are metacommunicative. Personal communications are related to shift and break changeovers, gossip and other personal business, or discipline or supervision issues. They are viewed as essential but external to work tasks.

There is little value in comparisons across channels with respect to message credibility, except that the radio as a police-sourced channel is more credible than the VDU printout that indirectly reflects citizens' calls mediated by civilian operators. The inputs are thus in once-mediated form, whereas radio communications are in an immediate form of "raw communication" between officers and dispatchers. The immediacy effect attaches to verbal messages, making them more demanding of attention than written or once-mediated messages. Dominant channel effects are nonexistent because the radio-VDU pair excludes other messages from practical reference.

Radio feedback is constant for MPD dispatchers. The radio fills the dispatchers' area with cracks, booms, whistles, and blasts. All feedback is focused on telephone calls to and from operators concerning messages. Sometimes feedback forms a double loop. Messages vary in the potential for required feedback because certain messages are for information only (sent or received); for example, "I'm clear," "Nobody home," or "Going on break" require only dispatcher acknowledgment. Many brief and common messages are immediately answered—"What street follows x going north?"—and require only a single action, for example, giving a street name. Some messages, however, require a series of articulated interchanges between dispatcher and officer.

Even a dyadic response pattern is likely to be embedded in other call responses so that they take the character of multiply-nested or embedded sequences. Perhaps this can be shown diagrammatically. Each scout car is a letter A, B, C, and each transmission to the controller from a car is a superscript number; the controller's reply is in parentheses. If scout car A transmits and the controller answers, it would appear: $A^1(A^1)$ meaning that, immediately after the first message was received, it was answered. However, the sequences are rarely so clear and are often nested so that responses to one car are deferred while other messages are being received or transmitted by the controller.

A sequence might read as follows:

$$A^1(A^1) \ A^2(A^2) \ B^1(B^1) \ C^1(C^1) \ A^3 \ B^2(B^2) \ C^2 \ A^4 \ (C^2) \ A^5(A^5).$$

This depicts a sequence of messages in which A transmits and is answered immediately, as is the second transmission. B transmits and is answered, as does C. Then A transmits again, followed by a second transmission by B and a response from the controller to B's second transmission. Then C transmits, again followed by a fourth transmission from A and a response by the controller to C's second response. A makes a fifth call, which is answered by the controller. In other words, the ongoing stream of events in which the various cars are involved does not present itself as a preconstituted whole but as an intervention from a stream of discourse that must be mentally integrated by the controller for each of the assignments being monitored. Note further that this is but one channel of the VHF radio and that other (force-wide) channels may also be active and require monitoring and/or response. The nested character of communication is further exaggerated by the officer's interjection of comments (say by car D) into $A(A^1)$ dyads so that it becomes $A\ D\ (A^1)\ (D^1)$, etc. Calls may not be closed, so that vehicles will continue to call $A\ A\ A\ A$ while dispatchers are on another channel, or cars may not respond to an initial call or a "pull."

The fewest contingencies are introduced by the telephone. The radio, on the other hand, given the size of the city, the atmospheric conditions, and the centrality of that single channel, produces a great many contingencies and technologically related ambiguities.

At the dispatcher level technological ambiguity is somewhat less pronounced than at the operator level, and discretionary actions are greater in any case. The reasons why technology exercises less control and produces less ambiguity are past experience of dispatchers with street work; visual, voice, and radio-controlled monitoring by a chief dispatcher of all zone dispatchers; and the two-way radio communication with cars.

A degree of technologically produced ambiguity is created by the radio system.

In Metro City there are a number of points at which the radio signal is caught, amplified, and directed back to the communications center. Sometimes these signals "bounce." Lighted boards with gauges monitoring signal strength for the various amplification points show cars assigned in one precinct sending signals from the other end of town. It is impossible to know whether the signal is being amplified from a car in the proper area or from one fifteen miles out of place. Officers in cars can answer for each other; officers can call for other officers because they are not required to preface a call using their badge number or vehicle number when transmitting to the dispatcher. Cars sometimes do not respond to "pulls" or inquiries from dispatchers. There are no rules requiring officers in the MPD to report when or even if they arrive on the scene of a job. No response time is measured. Dispatchers are required to, but seldom do, transmit a pull or inquiry every fifteen minutes to cars assigned a call. This is intended to check on the location of the vehicle, to monitor the progress of event, to maintain the safety of the officer, to sustain command and control, and, finally, to ensure completion of assigned tasks.

The time at which an officer calls in "clear" is not tightly tied to termination of the action of the event to which the officer is assigned. Other observers (Van Maanen, personal communication; Rubinstein 1973) have pointed out that officers rarely clear a call when they are in fact clear (with the exception of rookies and some marginal officers) but instead are guided by the sanctioned practices of the officer subculture. These practices increase officer autonomy and are amplified by the dispatcher's almost total dependence on the aural channel. Officers do a reading on the type of call and make some judgments about how long they can stay "out of service." For example, anything involving report writing would result in a "credit" of half an hour or more, depending on the workload and the expectations of others in the precinct.[7]

Perhaps the most confusing situations are those in which radio-emitted data and personal knowledge contradict. The dispatcher must rely on or trust the world of the officers. He is limited to only two channels. The dispatcher does not know at that point what the car's occupants have done about any of the previous calls unless he directly asks. He inquires only when he needs them for another job or when another car has asked the controller what has been done about a call they heard go out on the air. It is impossible to verify precisely the actions of officers, even with the tapes of dispatch, the computer printout of the calls (they do not contain disposition data), and the activity logs of the cars (they do not contain all that officers did, only what they wrote down as having been done). Direct questioning is required. This suggests that the impact on the environment is of little actual interest in the organization. Processing messages takes on a power of its own.

Dispatchers: Roles and Tasks

Although dispatchers carry out both physical and mental operations, mental tasks are of most importance. The stimuli received are of four types: the printout, the electrowriter, internal calls (largely irrelevant), and alarm calls that are handled exclusively by the officer on the city-wide desk. The actions of the dispatchers are controlled by message source, channel, and format.

The dispatchers must select and sort calls that are police relevant and require police presence. They give them a priority. Dispatchers receive a previously coded and classified incident and must reconstruct an image of the event signified by the contained facts. These facts are only partially given by the incident code because the dispatchers must reflect in their actions what they think the caller "had in mind" and the transformation made by the operators and must predict the expectations that officers will have. The dispatcher considers how he should communicate to officers his understandings of what they might expect about the incident or job. These are associative contexts or paradigms sequentially and simultaneously considered for clustering incidents and jobs.

The process produces a taxonomy of calls sanctioned by officers as requiring police assistance (see figure 4.2). The salient facts that order the taxonomy are officer threat, crime potential (apprehension possibility), action/intervention potential, danger to others, noncrime. The zone controllers' informal taxonomy reflects the degree to which they share the occupational culture of policing. The informal priorities do not reflect the formal classification system of the MPD in a number of important respects.

"Crime" is a gloss that omits interest in crimes that have already occurred. Although the MPD schedule has an ordering based on the seriousness of the call, the internal differentiation is so great that it is useless with respect to either formal or informal priorities; for example, an accidental death is second priority, as is a suicide report, a missing person, a flat tire, and "move the auto." Furthermore, mutually contradictory qualities of formal priorities are not explored, and the commonsense wisdom of dispatchers, based on the occupational culture, must suffice. Distinctions among categories are not given either, for example, among "cutting, just happened," "meet EMS," "suicide report," "attempted suicide in progress," "FT cutting," and "accidental cutting." The base for the operator is classification of the event as reported in the call as an incident of this kind. Factual differences *between* the classifications or the actual implications for officers once there and priorities are based on knowledge that may or may not be provided by the dispatcher.

The selecting and sorting of facts is constrained by the perceived credibility of the caller, the facts provided by the incident sent, and the imagery of the event. As in the BPD, the dispatcher must try to recreate mentally what is happening on the ground and image the actions of the caller, the operator, and the participants in the event. This image is placed within the context of the reconstructive imagery so that the dispatcher can then attempt to assign the incident as a job. He must attempt to assess the event, to image the location, and to assess priority. And he must consider an informal reclassification and whether to add remarks to the verbal transmission required to assign the job. He may check with NCIC or DMV.

The dispatcher must then check for an available unit. If there is an option in assigning the call, he may consider the skills of the officers, their present location, age, and sex. He may evaluate the number of available units, their mobility (given weather conditions, for example), how many officers might be needed for the assignment, the present workload of the precinct, and what he has previously assigned that is presently being dealt with.

The incident will remain on the counter in front of the dispatcher until he is able to assign it. If the job is assigned, this is scribbled on the edge of the card and the card is placed in the slot with the unit number. Units do not always answer inquiries. When officers arrive, they broadcast this. They are not obligated to report when they finish a job, only when they are clear to accept another assignment.

It is not possible to operate as a zone controller on the basis of facts alone. Assumptions must be made about the nature of a person's motives, about the formation and change of the natural and social world, about the limits and intentions of police action, and the nature of social events in environments I and II.[8]

Rules of thumb are used, as in the BPD. These include assuming that limited information is contained in the printout and chunking and coding using normal form inclusions about the call as incident (Bottomley and Coleman 1980). The remaining information must be filled in by the controller and the officer. Such matters as the dangerousness of the person, who did what to whom first, the past history of relations between persons, and the credibility of the caller are seen as outside the concern of the controller. These must be imagined or assumed to be of a character that requires no action. The dispatchers assume that each incident must be processed as a single item in a series.

Finally, construction and reconstruction of the action and inactions of officers is required. The dispatcher assumes that the officers will inform him of whatever is done that must be registered on the formal record of the incident, that is, anything that is defined as a message. Other tacit rules are observed in interactions with the controller. Officers do not tell the controller "more than he needs to know," and they define what that is. Officers communicate using silences when they choose not to reply to a potential job, when they do not report the outcome of a job, or when they ask the controller to ask another car to call them at the station on the telephone. These are silences that maintain the autonomy of the officers. Requests for alteration in status are carried out on the basis of trust of the officer's transmissions. Calling in "clear" means that the car wants to be shown as clear; conversely, accepting a call means a car wants to be shown as out of service. The classification takes in a reality insofar as all formal classifications are nominal, and informal agreements serve as fundamental bases for action. Incidents or jobs need not be relabeled so long as something is done. These known matters embedding the handling of incidents create an independent symbolic reality surrounding and patterning the flow of messages, regardless of their content.

Attempts to assign an incident as a job are not entered in the computer and printed out. Only the time the car received the dispatch and when the car called in clear are entered and printed. Any attempts to reach unit must be retrieved from the tapes of the radio transmissions between the zone controllers and the cars, a difficult and time-consuming job. There are no automatic time limits on an assignment or automatic checks on the actions

of the dispatchers. The dispatcher is responsible only to immediate supervisors and officers.

Assignment of jobs to cars must take into account the occupational culture, rules, and practices. The assignment pattern that results is a man-
nered compromise between metonymic and metaphoric ordering. The
orientation of the dispatcher to aspects of the communication is relevant
here because the format is standardized and the text is written. This de-
presses the salience of idiosyncratic particulars of communication and
makes orientation to factual aspects of messages more likely.

Dispatchers' styles vary. Some are more formal in their delivery and use
more official language in their transmissions; others are more informal and
casual. Some prefer to dispatch in batches; others do not like to have more
than one unassigned incident before them.

Dispatchers: Interpretative Practices

Dispatchers have the least complex task of interpretation if this conclusion
is based on the number of channels they operate, the message sources
with which they must deal, and the level of information processed. On the
other hand, message interpretation is dispatchers' main function. They
mediate several codes, two subsystems, two microcultures, several types
of records, and several sorts of time. Dispatchers are meanings brokers.

Message-Handling Processes
Noise-Message Distinctions

Dispatchers encounter four types of noise: technological noise and ambiguity; socially defined noise having to do with the timing, present load,
and nature of the message; contextual noise of social interaction and ban-
tering (which is relatively rare in the center); and proximal noise in the
environment produced by telephones, the talk of other dispatchers, the
chatter of the computers, and the rumble of officers' radio transmissions
heard in each zone. Radio transmissions may be switched to an amplifier
and broadcast in the room (used for the controlling of incidents that cross
zones or are defined as city-wide incidents). Because noise is primarily
technologically produced, issuing from the radio and computer, social
noise is relatively unimportant. Messages do not create the layers of complexity that they do in the BPD.

Field-Message Distinctions

Field-message distinctions for dispatchers are behavioral events occurring
in the room, personal preferences and tolerances of the dispatchers, expectations of the dispatchers of themselves and of the units, the timing of
events the activities of units in the field (those that infringe on the assignment of calls to them), and invisible or unstated contingencies in the use of

time by the officers (delivery of prisoners to jail, cars for personal duties, taking people to vote). The isolation of the zone controllers in the MPD means that the external intrusions are limited and likely to be self-created. The environment as seen in the room is constraining because the invisible activities of cars alter the field-message relationship, which in turn alters the dispatcher's view. The demands on the controllers arising in the proximal environment are rather limited and are such things as informal chat in the room, organizing for breaks, changes of shift, and events that demand attention across all the zones (such as a high-speed chase or a hostage or kidnapping situation).

Ordering Frame

Unlike the operators, dispatchers can queue jobs they are handling and alter the order in which they assign them, grouping and clustering them if necessary. The dispatchers have great flexibility in the ordering of their work, although the workload can create pressure to act quickly.

Internal Message Analysis

All messages that arrive at the desk of the dispatcher arrive from the computer and all are police sourced. The cognitive structuring of messages arriving from operators and being sent to officers is virtually the sole intellectual task of zone controllers. All have an action implication.[9]

The source and network within which the original information arises patterns the response of dispatchers. If the call arises within the police, then the messages are information-only messages restricted to police business and precoded by the operators. If the call originates in the loosely organized (high-information) network, it is more likely to have decision-action implications. These are all first-level decisions. The second-level calls, that is, messages or requests received from operators over the telephone or from officers by radio, are properly conceived of as feedback rather than as messages requiring internal cognitive analysis.

Partitioning the Message into Bits

Requests for police action received by the zone controllers require internal differentiation or cognitive substructuring and a determination of the action implication. The relevant syntagms for the zone controllers are shown in table 5.2. Other data are printed out for the dispatcher and later printed for use by the precinct: Automatically assigned are the incident number, time the call was received by the 911 operator, console at which the call was received and sent on, and the personal ID number of the 911 operator.

The dispatcher examines the eight sytagms organizing the incident as reflected in the call. The dispatcher, unlike the controller in the BPD, does not have to reconstruct the call about the event because the data are not forwarded to him. The four calls shown in table 5.3 do not represent the

Table 5.2
Several calls within the MPD format

Syntagms	Call 1	Call 2	Call 3	Call 4
Location	12900 W. Outer Drive	08863 Plain View	Fenkell and W. Outer Drive	16591 Harlow
Descriptive term	B and E DWL in progress	F.T.—Fight[a]	One over wheel	Mental run
Incident code number	1-3511	1-3941	3-3750	2-8510
Unit/system	1610	1602	1604	1604
Person acting	Burglars	Fighters ("family")	Driver	Mental
To whom/what	Dwelling	Each other	Self	Self
Character of actions	Broke in	Fight	None	None
Time frame	Now, in progress	Not known, now?[b]	Now, in progress	Now

a. 3900 is family trouble (F.T.); 3941 is "F.T.—Fight."
b. Because other codes contain "in progress" it is not clear what "F.T.—Fight" is, as opposed to "A and B in progress," "F.A. in progress," etc.

Table 5.3

Reconstruction and prediction work for ongoing events

Call	Reconstruction	Prediction
Call 1	People/person broke into house; victim/other discovers it (property taken?), calls police; now in progress	Probably not in progress by time unit arrives; report to be taken by scout car; swarming to site by other cars hoping to be in on action
Call 2	Either one of the fighters (most likely, wife or female) called police; did not mention weapon or fear for life; heat of the fight unknown	Domestic trouble, unpredictable, messy, could be dangerous and time consuming; car to be sent

range of messages. Information-only calls are omitted. The absence of information is notable in these calls. The details in particular about the persons involved in the event are almost totally missing and must be surmised. The specifics of the call, such as whether something is now in progress, just over, or disintegrating or improving, are not included. The burglary (call 1) may be months old or a matter of minutes, but this is not included in the message. No information about the burglars is included (whether the caller mentioned this or not). The FT-fight (family-trouble–fight) is quite limited and truncated. Furthermore, one does not know if the category was used advisedly or whether the other categories were not considered or considered and rejected, or how it relates to legal categories. By implication, the other categories were not deemed relevant —just happened, person with weapon, spouse abuse law injunction/peace bond. The potential of the fight is omitted. The last two calls are especially mysterious because the content is of widely varying potential—mental run and one over the wheel. These are basically wait-and-see types of calls.

The information-only calls or the EMS calls are collapsed incidents because the action and the message are one. There is little need to construct the meaning of the messages. The one over the wheel and mental run are something of that sort as well. The construction and prediction work is limited in these four calls to calls 1 and 2, in which dispatchers must reconstruct the event and make a prediction before sending a unit to respond to the job. These reconstructions are shown in table 5.3.

The dispatcher's predictions may or may not be affirmed by officers; he may not be informed of the outcome or result. Issues of reclassification, adjustment of predictions, and the like do not arise in the MPD with much frequency. The salience of trying to work out what is involved and how long it will take and what the narrative structure of these events is relatively low in the MPD.

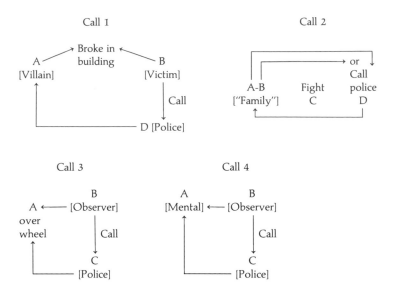

Event/observer/calls police/ongoing
Event/victim/calls police/done
Police anticipate event/call police/create

Figure 5.2
Calls as stories in the MPD.

In figure 5.2 the structure of the four calls in table 5.2 is shown. Because the dispatcher in the MPD encounters fewer types of calls and does not encounter once- or twice-mediated calls, as do the controller and operator in the BPD, the structure of the incidents is simpler and fewer diagrams capture the relevant dimensions in the calls as incidents. Unlike the BPD, there is a simpler structure that does not entail mediation of the calls; only the two prime axes are needed: whether the caller was the victim or the observer and whether the job involves persons, property, or social order. These structures are not shown, for they are a reduced version of figure 5.2; the only addition is that the officer must call the center to reach other officers and precincts must call the center to reach officers (or to have them call the station, meet another officer, or come in). These calls are prospective or action-creating calls in which the police anticipate the job, call the center, and ask the officer to call in, thereby creating a job by internal means.

Salience of the Units

The zone controller has a limited scope of interest in the incidents received. He is interested in actions taken (to whom and by whom), temporal aspects of the event (now, in progress, finished, "cold"), location of the event, and operators' descriptive term and character of the actions listed. From a dispatching perspective location is a necessity, but from logical or cognitive perspective the structure of the event has equal salience.

The zone controller is in an axial position because he must transform the event-call-incident formulation into a prediction of the character of the job and record the event in environment II. Yet there are no rules by which this is to be accomplished. The signifiers in the communicational unit (the incident) come in referring in part to the call and in part to the event and must be shifted to a new set of signifieds in environment II.

Surrounding Understandings

As is the case in the BPD, two kinds of events change the internal structure of salience. The first is the salience of such matters as weather and time of day, which alter the salience of items in the message; the second is the relevance of the political climate for changing the significance of certain kinds of events. In the MPD a series of rapes of children on their way to and from school in February 1984 became a public scandal, and special patrols were developed. Utilities company employees were trained to watch for suspicious circumstances. Rape or possible rape then became a more salient kind of message and made the descriptive term "rape" more salient within the message-unit system. A rape scare tends to lead supervisors to tighten procedures for questioning callers about possible rapes and to overcoding of events in that category to avoid the claim that nothing was done. It also means that zone controllers ensure that calls containing potential rapes are handled more carefully and that as much information as possible is provided to officers. Procedures for referral are also questioned. At one point in the February 1984 scare, all rapes were referred to a city social services office for preliminary investigation. Subsequent changes in the law requiring arrests under certain conditions in domestic disturbances or spouse abuse made police presence required. The result of such a crisis is also to make decisions about cases defined as rape cases qualitatively different from those that are otherwise classified (Manning and Hawkins, forthcoming).

Officers: Codes

Assigning Codes and Coding Effects

For officers a message received is always informally recorded. This is true for four reasons. First, it is likely that communication between dispatchers and officers is subtle and that the context tacitly communicates more directly than the actual classification if transmitted. Second, officers develop their own priorities concerning the salience of events in the absence of competition for their attention.[10] Third, incident classifications are not binding on the subsequent actions of officers. No effort is made within the department to see what relationship exists, if any, between the initial classification and the classification into which the officer places the job after it has been attended to. Fourth, the informal priorities and practices of the officers and the official paper and records often contradict. The salience of secondary codes relative to primary or official codes requires further discussion. That is, formal coding cannot be reconstructed as it can be for operators and dispatchers. It should be borne in mind, however, that this is so despite the formal classification made by operators, received by dispatchers, and used as a basis on which to aggregate daily incident patterns.[11]

All calls heard by the police, it has been argued, are embedded in the officers' understandings of such calls. The meaning of calls is thus context dependent. This is in part communicated by the fact that calls are broadcast by dispatchers as interrogatives rather than as commands. Despite naive observations to the contrary that suggest that "dispatchers generally act with the voice of the chief, and their instructions are so recognized" [Scott and Percy (1983), with reference to Wilson and McLaren (1972, p. 120)], they most decidedly are not.

There is an elaborate etiquette of communication between dispatchers and officers that involves several basic principles [see also Rubenstein (1973, ch. 3)]. The first is that all calls are heard as requests; all calls may be refused by officers (implicitly or explicitly) so long as standard "accounts" are provided; dispatchers can talk to officers, but officers do not talk to each other on the air (the dispatcher patterns the flow of talk); talk is accepted on face value (although tone of voice, speed of talk, and nonverbal indications of consternation, anger, or fear may be queried); officers assume that the dispatcher has told all that is known (or that one needs to know) and rarely query jobs assigned (although additional information about location may be requested). Furthermore, officers assume that there will be "errors" known after the fact when they arrive on a scene: Participants may not be at the address; callers may not be present; and the event found in environment II may not be as described by the dispatcher using the operator's classification. For example, the office will not be told over the radio who has called, whether the address is that of the caller's, or whether the victim, potential victim, or the site of the incident should be investigated further. Thus the source effects, the algorithm that distinguishes caller as victim from caller for victim are not operative for officers. Source effects frame calls merely as an index to what officers might encounter. Thus an officer's response to a call cannot be taken as a measure of his belief in its truth but rather as a measure of what he sees as being necessary to do his work successfully if the call is correct (Rubinstein 1973, p. 101).

The implicit meanings of calls indicate the multitudinous consequences of coding. Any view of policing based on a presumptive notion of the authoritative nature of police communications is misleading and can become a basis for false theories of police organizational structure and policies. Code effects, as noted in the previous paragraphs, are fictive, a tentative rendering of the world for action purposes. The event as described in the call and incoded as a message-incident job may capture some features of the situation in environment II that can become actionable.

Additional effects can be best understood as providing the preconditions for other actions, unanticipated by the dispatchers and officers. These might be labeled as secondary calls because the first call or arrival at the job makes it possible for other encounters and calls to transpire (Rubinstein 1973, p. 91; Davis 1983). Perhaps the most obvious of these is the "domestic" or "family trouble" call that indicates little or nothing about the nature of the anticipated problem. It would appear that the officer's aim is to control and order such situations. This may lead to her ordering one person to leave the scene. If this request is refused, the officer may threaten to arrest the person. If at that time the person does not leave, the officer will arrest him or her for assault (for example). This arrest, in turn, can lead to the intervention of the other partner. The emergent and nonpredictable quality of certain types of police encounters (such as family calls or rape calls) is well known (Black 1980, ch. 1). What is not appreciated is that the features of the situation may not have been indicated by the call or that the actions have to do with the officers' being at that scene rather than with the originating call. It is the vague uncertainty of the event, not the call, that is most stressful.

Duality of meanings arises in this system for several reasons. That is, there is a consistent understanding of calls on two simultaneous levels or tracks: the formal track arising from the associations among calls of this sort (those classified in this fashion in the past), formal legal consequences to be anticipated before attendance at such calls, and variations on themes of such calls; and informal associations of such calls within the metaphoric system of the occupational culture.

The formal track cues associations with other similarly classified calls and determines whether they are within or outside the action paradigm, given that classification. The formal legal consequences arise only when there is a formal legal component to the call; for example, many order calls have little if any identifiable legal content. "Domestics," for example, have been described by many observers as calls in which the legal constraints are known. The power of the police in private places in essentially civil disputes is quite limited (Stinchcombe 1964; Parnas 1967). On the other hand, domestic calls are quite problematic. The event can change in its demand features. What I have termed "variations on the themes of calls" has to do with the alternatives in openings, strategies, and outcomes for such encounters (Bayley and Bittner 1982; Davis 1983). These tend to take the form of "if *a*, then *b*." For example, the sympathy of male officers is generally with the male in a dispute, and the preference is to handle such calls "informally." Given these preferences, most calls will be handled to produce a "semblance of order" (Davis 1983). This may involve tactics such as sending one partner off, trying to separate the partners, extracting promises of good behavior, and leaving before the dynamics change. If, however, the partners turn against the officers, then the officers will respond legalistically against both. If the husband has beaten the wife, then the likelihood of legal action increases. This occurs because male officers are sexist and feel that this is taking advantage of women and because the laws in the MPD's state require arrest in "wife abuse" situations. These variations on the theme of a call cannot be read from the message, but they embed the hearing of them because they fold back on the call and are implicit potentials. The metaphoric associations in the culture arise from the connotative meanings of a term such as "rape." The connotative meanings of the sign "rape" are derived from the occupational culture, and they form a kind of secondary code composed of the denotative meanings of the first or primary code. The question of which is in fact the primary code and which is the secondary code arises. This matter is addressed further in chapters 6 through 8.

Officers: Technology

The source effects of officer's work are several; officers both create and respond to jobs. Some of these sources are technologically mediated; others are not. Studies suggest that some 10–15% of patrol officers' time is spent on self-initiated jobs or officer-produced work (see chapter 3). These may or may not involve legal matters or result in any paperwork but are the result of decisions officers make in response to their own sense of work. A second type of work is citizen initiated, the result of a stop on the street. This is quite rare, perhaps because officers are so rarely accessible to citizens when driving in cars and responding to radio calls. Studies of police workload in both England and the United States show that the patrol officer is engaged about half the time in work resulting from radio calls arising from citizen calls. For the rest of the time, the officer is "driving around." (Cordner 1979). It must be recalled that, because most of the time officers are free to do anything they wish, the artifactual nature of dividing police time in attending incidents into percentage of time devoted to types of incidents and the like is obvious. Nevertheless, considerable work done by officers results from the responses officers make to technologically mediated or produced demand. This third type is the radio-sourced job transformed from an incident forwarded to the zone controller as a result of a call converted into a message by an operator.

The police are in this sense responsible for and responsive to calls or are propelled by situated demand over which they have little control. When such stimuli for work arrives, in this sense officers are controlled, not with respect to whether they choose to respond to the stimuli but when, how, and in what style they choose to respond. They are more likely to respond to the radio than to events in which they are involved. This is repeatedly shown by field observations of calls, and it is a reflection of officers' priorities. That is, if officers are engaged in a low-priority call, such as an order call, a domestic, or an administrative task, they will respond to a radio call that suggests a higher-priority matter.[12] This suggests the pull and paradox of the radio: When the radio is on, officers orient themselves to its sounds and ignore smells, sounds, events, and sights around them. They cut themselves off from the immediate environment. In summer, when the weather is hot and car air conditioning is on, little outside the car can be heard, nothing can be smelled, and the radio fills the air.

Officers in the MPD are tied to the radio, a fact that distances them from the public, people's distress, and direct supervision (Rubinstein 1973, pp. 112–123).[13] The restriction of communication to the radio means that officers do not have to concern themselves with matters central to members of other subsystems: credibility of the source, fringe meanings (by comparison with other channels), and technological effects (because there is no other technology against which to compare). As noted previously, the officer must add features of the event, call, and caller that were "out-coded" by operators. Officers are constantly confronted with discrepancies between the broadcast message and the realities they encounter in environment II. They reverse the absence of presence effects. When and if they write up the job as a police-produced record, they selectively act to create or enact features of the encounter relevant to the reconstruction of the transformation of messages thus far documented.

Feedback between the officers and the dispatchers is of three types: incident or job communication, routine reporting of status, refreshment breaks, or meals, and reports of being out of service for some other reason (seeking repairs to the car, going out of radio range, or traveling out of the zone). These are secondary effects of feedback. Officers are able to monitor the actions of other officers by listening to the radio and dispatchers' messages and by attending certain calls. This means that much of the imaging of the work of others must be done through a crude, technologically shaped mirror.

Officers read off cues about where others are located, what they are doing, how long they might be occupied, and the level of their work by listening to their radios. As a result, several qualifications arise. The first is that conventions of talking and listening are indicative of activities and meanings. If officers do not answer calls repeatedly, it is cause for concern. If officers are constantly answering calls that might be taken by others, they are seen as "rate busters" or "call jumpers." Additional information about their patrolling habits may also be relevant, for example, the fact that some officers seek out drunk drivers when they have free time. Officers are also aware that a report about a unit's present location may be inaccurate or a lie calculated to avoid a call or have it assigned. In addition, because in the MPD no outcome or incident report is required, units may call in clear and there is no reasonable way to gauge what they have done, how long it should have taken, or whether there were difficulties in the assignment that were not reported to the zone controller. The job hangs in social space. Whether officers report outcomes even incidentally or in passing is discretionary. The connections between the job and the record are pieced together by understandings of the officers' styles and interests rather than by official rules and regulations and/or the nature of the dispatched job. Given that officers are the only participants in the communications system who actually encounter the event in environment II, the only source of feedback on the validity or veridicality of the event is severed unless a crisis arises during or after the disposal of the job. This means that in yet another fashion content of the message is phenomenologically and operationally defined as irrelevant to the actual practice within the communications system. In this sense the message jumps from one environment to the other in non-content-relevant terms.

Ambiguity and uncertainty with respect to dispatcher-officer interaction have already been discussed. The previous discussion captures the relational and interactive features of uncertainty and equivocality. These are elevated by the single channel, radio, from which virtually all messages are received and sent.

Officers: Roles and Tasks

The operations and tasks of the officers in a fundamental fashion involve some kind of dance between environment I, a reported environment of abjects and events as processed by the communications center, and environment II, in which the officers are physically located. This cannot be captured in any formal sense by rules or principles, although they provide a beginning.

The images that officers possess of the events they attend are some sort of amalgam of their past experience with such events, what others have told them in the form of stories and tales, and a reconstruction of the images that might have been possessed by others as they processed the message through the communications system. In some sense this involves the lamination of images to create a perspective on the event. One might think of the analogy of a deck of cards. If one draws one card from the deck, it is one of fifty-two possibilities and the other cards are assumed to be of a certain character. If the card is a heart, for example, then there are twelve remaining hearts. However, the reconstructive work of officers is based on an assumed deck that is never checked for completeness, comparability, and the like. A call is like a card drawn from an unknown or partially known deck.

Insofar as officers draw inferences from their assumptions about the meaning of the call, or first-order inferences, they create a metaworld of understandings only partially shared, yet determinant of, their expectations of the event in environment II. This secondary or informal set of understandings cannot be captured in "occupational culture" because it is of a fairly low level of generality. Perhaps the loosely coupled nature of the knowledge and the events in the world may itself be indicative of the lines of analysis required.

Officers: Interpretative Practices

Message Handling
Noise-Message Distinctions

Noise-Message distinctions must be made when officers are attending to the radio. Noise can be seen in three broad types. The first is technologically produced noise that results from the malfunctioning of the radio, the "dead spots" in the city where transmissions are blocked by clouds or buildings, interference from other channels that occasionally intrude into police transmissions, or failure of the radio. These are relatively easy to identify in the car itself, but because they are problematic and situational as the car moves through the city, they require repeated adjustment and coping. Although the MPD system has a digital warning system that allows an officer to push a button which generates a signal ("officer in trouble") and shows the number on a screen in the communications center, it is not used and is said to be useless. Thus technologically produced noise concerns officers primarily with respect to their ability to send messages (and receive confirmation that it has been received) rather than to routinely receive them.

Socially produced noise is that arising from colleagues in the car, from the timing of messages, and from the pull of a message when one is already out of service (involved in a call) but wants to respond to the message rather than to the present job. These conflicts may be understood by zone controllers silently and provide a basis on which to understand why cars may swarm to an incident or be out of service for a period of time inconsistent with past expectations of handling such a call. However, zone controllers are not normally informed of conflict in calls except when they call and the officers are currently occupied. During high-demand periods several jobs may be mentally queued by a car, and each new one has the potential for being construed as noise rather than as another job. The validation of a radio call or job as a message to the officer occurs when the officer responds and accepts it, not when the message is transmitted. Dispatching is of dubious and negotiated authority, and thus the mutual trust and collusion of the officers with dispatchers is important.

It should be emphasized that this is rarely as tightly articulated as Rubinstein describes (1973, pp. 101–123). The zone controllers I interviewed did not claim to know the officers with whom they communicated. Although they would work a given zone, they did not know who was in a given car on a given shift or day of the week. Furthermore, officers do not identify themselves on the air by badge number and may not answer with the car number when communicating routine information.

Environmental noise is a variable, given the weather, traffic sounds, and precinct location (the center of the city is much noisier during the day than any other part of the city but quiet as a tomb after about 6 P.M.).

Field-Message Distinctions

Field-message distinctions must be seen in the context of the situationally oriented nature of police work. As Bittner (1967) has perhaps best described, police operate in terms of three types of *horizons*, or sets of conditions in which any given call is viewed and seen as an organization of the perceptual field. The first horizon is temporal, the perceived relationship between the present problem and past and future events. The second horizon is scenic, the stable features of the background employed as a basis by which to handle the problem. The third horizon is manipulative, a consideration of the practicalities of the situation [see also Manning (1984)].

In an ironic fashion, of course, the orientation of officers to the present maintains their sense of control of the work. This is so because officers hold the present and the near future as the most important domains of activity and minimize the more distant implications of their action for social order. They define their aim as control of the current situation sufficient to leave with apparent grace. The imposition of other, more complex or diffuse sorts of duties, such as crime prevention, community relations, or investigative work, are avoided by an orientation to the here and now and the view that holding oneself ready to respond to the next call is the duty of a patrol officer. Like narcotics officers who argue that anything can happen and that one always has to be ready to exploit an opportunity (for an arrest, for initiating an investigation, for making a buy, or creating an informant), this obviates longer-term planning and foreseen lines of action. A related feature of the police perspective on the present is the view that, if something goes wrong, people will call or inform the police. If the police are not informed, then the consequences are the public's responsibility. As in many other ways, this maintains the officers' view of the job as reactive, individualistic in character, and crime focused.

The consequences of this perspective for queuing and setting priorities on calls are not clear. On the one hand, queuing is rarely necessary. Officers occasionally have more than one call and do not set inflexible priorities. Unlike their colleagues in the BPD, MPD officers consider coming to the aid of another officer as their first priority at all times. On the other hand, even this is situational in nature. It depends on how far one is from the scene, what one is currently doing, how confident one is of other officers' responses, one's current assignment, etc.

Ordering Frame

The ordering frame of the MPD officers is not easily discernable. If officers are oriented to the message as referential (and not as noise) and there is a fairly heavy burden of work typically between 4 and 8 P.M., on Friday and Saturday evenings, and in difficult weather, officers will organize their responses to calls in terms of their sense of their priorities. This would appear to be a function of officer style in answering calls, their personal preference for types of calls, and their willingness to accept general calls ("Anyone near the intersection of x and y street?"). They respond to calls in metaphoric terms or according to their association within the action paradigm, not in metonymic terms. Metonymic response occurs only when there is low workload in a precinct.

All the messages officers receive are twice mediated and well framed as police calls, so message credibility is unquestioned, but the content may be viewed as dubious. In another sense the officers are field dependent; their present activities shape their priorities. Officers, more than any other group in police communications systems have great discretion, freedom from supervision, and substantial autonomy.

Internal Message Analysis

Internal message analysis would appear to be based rather importantly on the context in which calls arrive. Because the primary division into actionable and nonactionable calls is made on the basis of a few facts in the message and outside, once the message is seen as actionable, the officer sets off to see what is happening. To a marked degree internal features of the message are less important to the officers than to any of the other participants in the communications system. This is because messages are seen as so context dependent. The officers, unlike anyone else in the system, expect to arrive and view the predicated scene in environment II. Meaning and action collapse.

Partitioning the Message into Units and Salience of Given Units

Officers orient themselves to the message if they are called on the air or if the call is for any unit in the area or any unit. The last two are more compelling calls, regardless of content, although calls for any unit tend to be used for high-priority calls that require immediate action. If a call is directed to a particular unit and the officers accept the call, they listen for the following items in order: the descriptive term for the event, actions taken (and toward what or whom), the location of the event, the time of the event in environment I (before or during or after a job call), and persons acting.

The zone controller may not mention the operator's classification of the job, and radio codes are not used on the air. Some verbal framing is done, such as "Say again?" Units simply come on the air and answer: "We'll take that" and then give their number. The descriptive term used may be general and vague. The concern for content is allusive and elusive. The zone controller acts to control work in the MPD by pacing calls and selecting units. Whether requested or not, officers may choose to attend the scene. The stylistics discussed under message handling also affect salience of jobs.

It cannot be overemphasized, however, that most of the time officers are merely driving along the streets, looking for something to intrude on the boredom. Repeatedly observers have noted a kind of bored urbane tolerance of the surrounding world by police and an indifference to most of what passes before them (Pepinsky 1976; Van Maanen 1974). Rubinstein's (1973) heroic cop is seldom found outside his pages or those of Whittemore (1968).

The time of the event signals the likelihood that it will be ongoing when the unit arrives. The standard approach to complainants who are not available, events that are over, or no evidence of the event is found in key words. Terms such as "no sign on arrival," or "all quiet" or "police not required" are used (Meyer 1974). All are ways of closing events in environment II. The other extreme, the rare "on site" or "in progress" event is attended by a large number of cars who hear the call on the radio.

Because the computer contains geocoded addresses created more than fifteen years ago, many addresses may not be on maps and location may be problematic for officers. It is considered an indication of incompetence to query the zone controller on location or directions to a scene. The location may provide clues to the degree of dangerousness or potential seriousness of the crime or may be an area that the officers know. They have a crude moral topography into which the city or at least their precinct is fitted.

One of the most perplexing aspects of the relationship between job assignment and location of the cars, from the perspective of both the officers and the dispatchers, is that so little information, except in chases, is volunteered about vehicle location. Zone controllers may be kept ignorant by officers. They often do not know how many cars are available. Although this number is called in at the beginning of each shift, precincts lie about the number of cars available when they assign them to other duties within the precinct, especially transporting prisoners to jail.

Surrounding Understandings

Surrounding understandings alter the salience of given bits in the message and may change the dominant bit. The same themes are found here that are found in the BPD with the exception that the MPD is subject to periodic scares resulting from political pressure to respond to moral panics.

Conclusion

As in the BPD, the dominant role is played by officers. Technology, roles, and interpretations also shape messages and their disposal. Because of the more centralized communications system, technology has more salient role here than in the BPD and is especially powerful in shaping operators' behavior. The outlines of police behavior on the ground are quite similar in both departments, and surrounding understandings therefore are a powerful but unpredictable force altering messages.[14] The consequences of message movement, or temporal effects, are explored in the next chapter.

III

Ironies and Practicalities

6

Diachronic Analysis

In this chapter I provide a perspective on organizations as frames for change in meaning. Change is of course elusive and ever present. In previous chapters messages have been seen as communicational units in subsystems and treated as phenomenologically equivalent. They were in a way aggregated and seen in cross section or in one subsystem at a time as affected by identified structural features of the police communications system. Content, with the exception of the analysis of interpretative practices, was viewed as irrelevant, except as marking the difference between the units of analysis.

The stability of the message-producing system has been assumed also in this analysis. Perhaps it is more fruitful to bracket this assumption and to seek to identify the sources of stability and the sources of disruption in message processing.

A set of disruptive influences arise from fitting together complex factual elements associated with moving messages through time and space. Disruptions also arise from structurally induced transformations and cumulative transformations associated with coding, technology, roles and tasks, and interpretative work. Changes are associated with modifications in connotative and denotative meanings in subsystems 1, 2, and 3. A fourth source of change is syntactic; the ordering of signs differs in each of the subsystem. Each contains a conception of time, text, and rules for their interpretation. These four sources are glossed by the term "organizational context" or "comparisons" insofar as they differ in the BPD and MPD.

There are also three sources of stability. The first is mechanisms of transferral or commonsense meanings that embed the messages. Imagery facilitates the suspension of disbelief in the idea that messages are really fundamentally different, virtually reconstituted in each subsystem. How are communicational units seen as "the same" while there is much evidence that they are viewed and constituted (reconstituted) in each subsystem? Second, stability in message transmission arises from tacit rules for enactment. By organizing the response to messages in the subsystems, they bring form and order to rather disparate communicational units. Finally, there are some cognitive bases for stability.

Separating instability from stability perhaps implies that these sources are independent and act in a differentiated fashion. The factors exist simultaneously in organizations and are thus in dialectic rather than static relationships to each other. The presentational order suggests more difference than exists and a more independent existence than is possible. It is important to bear in mind that the posited certainty and obvious nature of the passage of messages through the police communications system is a conceptual fiction and a reification of "messages" that is useful for the analysis of theoretically salient things other than the message. These sources of change are a part of a diachronic analysis of the structure of difference within and between organizations with respect to communicational units.[1]

Sources of Instability

Shifting Facts

In the face of the ebb and flow of transient and sentient experience, one might ask, What penetrates or disrupts flow? What punctuates everyday experience? There are obvious reasons why people consider everyday life as a constant flow of unrecognized experience, not without meaning but with a kind of fluidity.

Meaning tacked to one set of cues transforms itself. One person gets one pattern and another quite different one from the same events; seen a year later, they take a different aspect again. The main problem of social life is to pin down meanings so that they still for a little time. Without some conventional ways of selecting and fixing agreed meanings, the minimal consensual basis for society is missing. (Douglas and Isherwood 1979, p. 65)

An examination of the movement of messages across subsystems and from the environment to the organization suggests that there is a remarkable number of sources of disruption of continuity in messages. Previously I suggested that "drift" is both produced by organizations and reduced by organizational stipulative marking actions. Are there some clear points at which drift is produced?

The factual content of calls, with the possible exception of alarm calls and internal calls, is often unclear. They are ambiguous. This results from the source, distorted communications, organizational effects (coding, roles and tasks, and interpretative practices), the social reality of the event, the elusive nature of everyday conversation (with its uncertain orientation of speaker and hearer to the message), absence of presence effects, and the often concrete codes used to communicate (Bernstein 1971). The differentiation of meaning also occurs; as calls move through the communications system, they become culturally differentiated. The relaying of demand creates partially shared denotative meanings ("burglary") and partially shared enunciable or connotative meanings ("good police work," "danger"). Only part of this is captured in codes, myths, and police classifications. The facts, often sparse in the first place, that are used to classsify messages are merely "circumstantially cogent," as Needham has argued (at a lecture in Oxford in November 1982). Their facticity is never fixed when regarded as a feature of a classified message. The analogic or polythetic modes of classification of calls do not establish a unitary relationship between fact and category or between one category and another within the scheme.

That is, the categories do not have a natural order based on severity of offense, promise of good police work, or time that might be required to fulfill the task. Facts can be placed in any of several categories and often are; the categories are not naturally exclusive. Thus facts are always subject to redefinition; order and sense is made by frames, provided by observers, that are only sometimes shared. Exceptional cases have a disconcerting role—when police do not appear when called or refuse to intervene in a domestic dispute or insult the citizens on arrival. The facts provide *markers* used by all participants to affirm the uncertainty of message results. Uncertainty in meaning increases the penchant to "send everything down" in an undifferentiated fashion, thus putting more pressure on the officers and giving them greater discretion. Thus marking underscores the uncertainty of messages until an outcome is declared to have been achieved. It ramifies to other participants who combine the just-in-case and the wait-and-see rules. This means that individual cases are always fraught with uncertainty on the one hand and made routine on the other.

Information given is often garbled or unclear and is condensed into a category, summarily adding to the sense of unpredictability in reading events from incidents or jobs from incidents, for example.

The commonsense theory of objects used to order discrete calls reinforces the changing and unpredictable nature of the relevance of the social world that touches the police communications system. It is a view of the mercurial nature of human perplexities brought to police attention. Police theory thus rationalizes complexity and unpredictability. There is a constant tension between the past as reified in positions, responsibilities, and obligations of, in this case, bureaucratic functioning and the dispositions and feelings of the individuals. This is a field of struggle from which meaning arises (Bourdieu 1977, p. 305).

Such broad characterizations of fluidity in fact is a general feature of all message-processing systems. In addition, the research reported in chapters 4 and 5 provides ethnographic evidence of the further importance of differences within and across the MPD and the BPD. When messages move from one subsystem to the next, the variables affect meaning within the subsystem. Changes in meaning produced by variables within are also problematic when messages move within the organization. The analysis here focuses on the specific and discernable changes identified in the synchronic analyses that are relevant to a diachronic analysis. I begin with the controllers as recipients of once-processed messages and by inference ask what changes are noted by controllers in messages sent by operators. I then ask the same of officers' response to messages sent by controllers.

Clearly transformations differ for each of the four sources from which messages are received by controllers. Differences arise, however, for messages that are sent and received between subsystems 1 and 2, that is, those involving the radio or telephone and the VDU. No messages are received by the controller personally from the public (unless by accident); thus the elaborate features of assigning codes for verbal stimuli, calls, are reproduced only for internal messages that originate outside the center. All calls are framed by the technology and channel and viewed as police relevant; thus the appearance of the stimuli and the cognitive frame are isomorphic. Messages from the center are either visual or aural, but the assumption is that the language used is referential. The words are believed to refer to actual events in the real world, and the linear written text symbolically represents that reality.

The experience reported to operators is understandable to them because they are able to recall or imagine such experiences themselves, even when they are given limited and elliptical summaries of events. Controllers must engage in some of this image work, but they must carry out additional "mental operations." Controllers imagine the event that is summarized in the incident sent on, and they also project forward the nature of the event in environment II that officers may encounter. They hold both of these images. Both operators and controllers assemble and hold images; images are experienced at both points in the system.

The relationship between the operator's image and the controller's image is nowhere articulated so that one can view the articulation of these code-produced images as loosely coupled and based on implicit assumptions about continuity. The links established among the operator's image, the controller's image, and the event are further problems. The encoding at the operator level contrasts with that at the dispatcher level because dispatchers are given precoded messages on the VDU. They accept the code but reconstruct the event and project it into environment II. In informational terms the communicational units become less informationally loaded and more redundant if each message is seen as independent of the event that it indexes and as conveying digital yes/no unit bits of information. However, this view decontextualizes the signifier-signified relationship. The semantic connections made between signifiers and signifieds and those between messages are not based on changes in the information level of the messages. These general points can now be seen in reference to the four sets of variables as they affect message transmissions between subsystems. I compare the BPD and MPD along these lines.

Coding and Assigning Codes

There are six distinctions made when differences in processing in the BPD are compared with differences in processing the MPD. First, there is a sense shift when the aural to visual or visual to aural change in the communicational unit occurs. This means that cognitive organization is changed from assembling heard data to assembling seen data, and this calls out different contexts of recall and retention, or links between short-term and long-term memory. Second, the actual links made by operators between these sensory sources can be understood only in terms of other knowledge they possess. In the MPD the shift is made more complex by a third change: from text to spoken word. Fourth, the links produced are stabilized by the cognitive frame around the message that in the BPD is double framed (by the GPO and police operators) before being sent by VDU, which mechanically frames it for controllers. The radio output amplifies the redundancy of the message to the officer. The message in the MPD is single framed, forwarded by machine source, and sent by radio. The condensation of the first aural message into the written text and/or VDU in both systems means a focus on key words (the fifth distinction) around which the message is organized, but these key words need not be the same because an explication of the message is not always supplied verbally when it is dispatched. On the other hand, the expansion of the message that occurs parallels the process of encoding and decoding of messages across the subsystems. This is the case because the coding is based on different principles or constitutive conventions (Culler 1975, p. 30). The assumptive links made between key words and action implications vary.

The orientation of the actors across subsystems changes structurally so that, although operators in both systems are variously oriented to phatic, emotive, connotive, and referential aspects of the message, dispatchers and controllers are exclusively oriented to the referential mode. There is a collapsed variation in orientation, which is retrospectively organized from call to caller in environments I and II; officers organize [to use Weick's (1979) term referring to cognitive processing] from a referential orientation toward the event in environment II. They derive prospective cognitive organization or prefigurations, that is, what they can expect to find or do, given the set of real events in the constituted world.

There are effects of transformation from spoken to written text, which invoke in both organizations a degree of elision of complex facts into a few formatted messages and expansion from this by other participants. The transition made between subsystems based on text rather than sound have been explored by Derrida (1976). In particular, Derrida contests the notion that writing is equivalent to text and makes the interpretation of writing one of the meanings of contrasts and differences whenever they may appear (Norris 1982, p. 47). This is relevant to the question of internal textual analysis. What sort of high-level cognitive organization provides a kind of social glue that stabilizes meanings over time and through organizational segments and even through formal transformations? Is it possible to call the resulting stabilized unit the same communicational unit as it moves?

The clustering and chunking of information to create an image has two features of importance. First, the process differs in the BPD and the MPD insofar as one relates the call to the event by interpretation of the loose links between talk and the world and between talk and the event reported. [The links could have been made in a dream, a fantasy wish, in the past; it could represent, in Goffman's terms (1974), a fabrication, a misrepresentation, or a rekeying of a natural event.] The process in the MPD involves linking a formatted, encoded message to the world (environment II), a realistic, operational, or objectivist action rather than a constructive action based on a person-based psychology, as advocated by Harré (Oxford lecture, October 29, 1982). Second, the first operation is retention of ideas in the here and now; the second is representation or rerepresentation of the past projected forward.

Coding or Classification Effects

Coding effects can be noted in five areas: technology, roles and tasks, interpretative practices, stylistics, and internal message analysis. The consequence of squeezing a message into a format reduces options for subsequent readers if the format is credited. The principal effects are not, however, found in the mere reduction of informational bits provided but in the modification of the formatted items by feedback, adding data or knowledge, forming of "informal queues" and priorities, and analogical association of the items to other similar events or images.

Classification effects are less pronounced in the MPD than in the BPD because the number of classes is so large in the first instance and has so little constraint on the next action. Furthermore, adding, changing, or redefining a classification permits the imagination of options in the BPD. The particular classification is priority linked in the MPD, but the difference between the two organizations lies in the domain constraints connoted by the classification, that is, by the near-clusters of incidents of given types in semantic space. This is implied in the priorities of officers, the types of calls used by operators, and the algorithm of calls used in both forces. The particular class assigned is significant analogically, not literally.

The informational content of a message varies, and in both the MPD and the BPD it is extracted from the message by hearer-readers, but information is often contravened by meaning.

The duality of lines of action, produced by the formal-informal distinction, is critical in discipline, accountability and supervision, and planning. In both systems the referents of a message are known by the conditions under which it will be thought to be officially relevant (Smith and Gray 1983; Ekblom and Heal 1982; McCabe and Sutcliffe 1978; Bottomley and Coleman 1980).

Technology produces other disruptions in message flow across systems and can also be seen comparatively in the two systems. Mechanically the number of sources of messages varies, as do the channels on which they are received. This alters their credibility, power or authority, degree of information conveyed, action implications, and fringe meanings in both systems. Alternation in channel or source alters the interpretations of the message. Technology produces meaning in this fashion. The dominant channel in a subsystem becomes relevant as a demand source in the sense that the phone, the VDU, or the radio becomes ceteris paribus the most important source of work, whatever else is unfolding. It becomes definitive of work tasks literally and symbolically.

Feedback, with its erstwhile, unpredictable, occasional, and weak nature across all systems and both organizations, means quite simply that the social organization of cognition and meaning flows along, guided by rules ordering the social world rooted in subsystem conventions, occupational cultures, organizational microcultures, and enacted links across systems based on belief. These are beliefs and axioms such as those discussed under "rules." The extant sorts of ambiguity depend on technology. In an obvious sense, the greater the dominance of technology in a given subsystem, the greater the ambiguity produced by it. Uncertainty is amplified by technological failure. This is continuous across both organizations, but greater in the MPD than in the BPD.

Roles and tasks are mental and operational; tasks are of little interest; it is argued here that the image of action is outlined by language and is a function of the embodied perspective of the observer. The concern with establishment of credibility and relevance in both systems is high. It plays an important role in the transition from operators to dispatchers in the BPD more than in the MPD. Among officers, the caller's intent is a concern in shaping the expectations of officers once they arrive on the scene [see Ekblom and Heal (1982) for counterarguments to this]. In both systems the salience of the occupational culture for message transformation increases from operators to officers, whereas the effects of supervision, accountability, written records of performance, and workload decrease. The context of decision making is "situated individual" for operators and "situated collective" for dispatchers. Monitoring of the mutual effect of lines of action is greatest among officers in both systems. This permits strategic manipulation of the forms of communication by officers, but it is quite restrictive on dispatchers and controllers and operators.

Assignments are made mechanically and undifferentiatedly in both organizations. In the transition between operators and dispatchers, the negotiated nature of assignments predominates. The conflict of idea or image as a purpose, a practically accomplished action, submerges all three subsystems, increasing as a theme from the front to the back of the system. Thus what is termed workload (Hough 1980b; Cordner 1979) is a dialectically relational matter based on the ratio of one's style, image, and aims and the actual task level. Ekblom and Heal (1982) make a convincing argument for the relevance of workload on adjustments made by controllers, for example, on priorities and assignments. This tension between officers and controllers is discussed later with reference to the level of disruption in transmission vis-à-vis the mechanisms of transferral.

Interpretative practices integrate thought and action within what Bourdieu (1977) calls a habitus. Message handling in both systems is ecologically and technologically patterned. The level of interpretative work required *increases* broadly from subsystem 1 to subsystem 3, and the type of noise changes from technological to social. Social noise is highest in the BPD controllers' offices. This interplays with the demand features of the radio for the BPD controllers and officers. The field-message distinction is most salient in subsystem 2 and 3, and activities, behaviors, and expectations most influence controllers vis-à-vis messages. The workload effect is plainly seen here (Ekblom and Heal 1982). Stylistics of controllers and dispatchers are crucial because they affect the ordering of calls, their definition, their position relative to other work (for example, clerical tasks), whether they are answered at all, by whom, when, and to what end.

The stylistics of the role are interdigitated with the microcultures or traditions of given subdivisions. They are further perpetuated through apprenticelike socialization (Van Maanen and Schein 1979; Ekblom and Heal 1982, p. 35). The fine balance played out between external public and internal public is most significant in subsystem 2. Officers manage on average so few calls that there is little conflict between public demand and internally generated work (paperwork or jobs to attend).

The ordering of calls does not differ in the MPD and BPD: In subsystem 1 metonymic ordering is used; in subsystem 2 a mix of metonymic and metaphoric ordering is used; in subsystem 3 all calls are ordered metaphorically. The priorities vary, but the form does not. These conceptual distinctions are relevant to internal message analysis: The capacity to order is based on epistemological assumptions about the nature of the message, bits, or units of information.

Internal message analysis hinges on several assumptions of structuralist analysis. The factual nature of bits seems to be confused with meaning in information theory (orientation), or, in literary terms, perspective (Burke 1962) or narrative voice (Fowler 1977). In any case, it stands in synecdochic relationship to the message once one establishes the key words it stands for, the underlying order and contingent coherence that is, in turn, the basis for extracting a bit as representative (Garfinkel 1965; Cicourel 1976). Bits are context bound and temporally shift in their reference; that is, the communicative aspect of the signifier-signified relationship shifts from subsystem to subsystem. A bit is analogically similar to a phoneme in speech because the message is made static and is not autoreferential. Furthermore, a shift in the salience of a bit is subsystem defined, because only officers must attend to the consequences of it, and all other messages are sent on or down if they are credible or not refused, deferred, or referred. As sign combinations or bits (communicational units) move in both organizations, their epistemological status changes.

The referent of surrounding understandings changes as it refers to completing the sequence in a format, completing a job, and considering *how* the incident is to be closed and written up. Although the concern initially is with rapidly sending a message and keeping the radio and phone clear, the concern later becomes the just-in-case rule described by Ekblom and Heal (1982, p. 37). This is complemented by the or "cover yourself" rule of officers on the ground. The transformation in the practical consequence of an act orients the organization inward rather than outward.

These structural transformations are produced by changes in the message or unit across the subsystems when viewed from the perspective of coding, roles, technology, and interpretation. It is argued that movement across subsystems is patterned, as is movement within, by coding, technology, roles and tasks, and interpretative practices. By comparing these processes in the two organizations, another level of inference about process is possible. There is a basic similarity, or grammar, in both, a grammar of change. Semantic shifts allow one to look at the meaning of changes in meaning.

Chains of Signification
The semiotician Umberto Eco (1976, p. 71) has suggested that, when the denotative meanings or direct expressions of a sign are recorded at another level, they take on connotative potential. That is, the relationship between the expression and the content of the sign are seen at another level of analysis above the first level at which they are understood. The calls to the police have, of course, a first level associated with the connections between the expression and the content of a sign, each of which is designated in terms of a unit and a system. The associations mapped for

the relationships between the various units and systems of a given sign expression may be either metonymic or metaphoric, or, of course, both. This is perhaps best illustrated with an example from the MPD, using a call whose defining feature is the term "rape."

Figure 6.1 shows that the two domains "rape" and "persons" contrast and that "persons" has two subdomains, nonmedical and medical. The two subdomains contrast as do "rape" and "persons" (noted by the word "opposition" situated between them in the figure). Looking at the bottom of the figure, classification refers to the MPD classification of calls. The expression is divided into units (the numbers given to calls from the classification scheme) and the system (priorities, given the call classification number), and the content is divided into system (priorities) and units (names of the alleged character of the event).

Expression and content are linked semantically in metaphoric terms; there is an associative meaning attached to the one expression that is arbitrarily connected with given content labels. The vertical relations within expression and content are metonymic, or a sequence determined by spatial proximity. These are denotative meanings derived from the connection between elements of classification as a sign. If classification is now taken as the expression for another content, in this case "priority," and priority is taken as the expression for crime and crime for work, the connotative associations move upward. They in turn contrast with the same sorts of connotative meanings in the "persons" domain.

In this figure and in the analysis that follows, my aim is to illustrate Eco's notion that a message is nothing more than a sign correspondence between a sign vehicle and a meaning realized during the course of a transmission or communicational process [to paraphrase Eco (1979, p. 54)]. That is, the aim is to show that one source of disruption of meaning is the semantic drift that occurs as changes in sign function occur in the course of message transmission. It is this invisible change in the interpretant that establishes connections between the signifier and the signified. As Lacan has written, the message is something like the "purloined letter"; it is constructed as imaginary object, a migratory signifier, by those who possess it (Lacan 1977). There are in this analysis three loci for pinning down semantic drift: the operators (shown in figure 6.1), the dispatchers (shown in figure 6.2), and the officers (shown in figure 6.3). The illustrations are taken from the MPD, but analogous processes occur in the BPD as well.

Turning again to the analysis in figure 6.1, classification is composed of two analogous codes, or system and units of rape categories, so that a change in one signals or denotes a change in the other. Both expression and content (1) are related both vertically/metonymically by proximity and horizontally/metaphorically. The other denotative meanings within the domain move from classification to priority and from priority to crime;

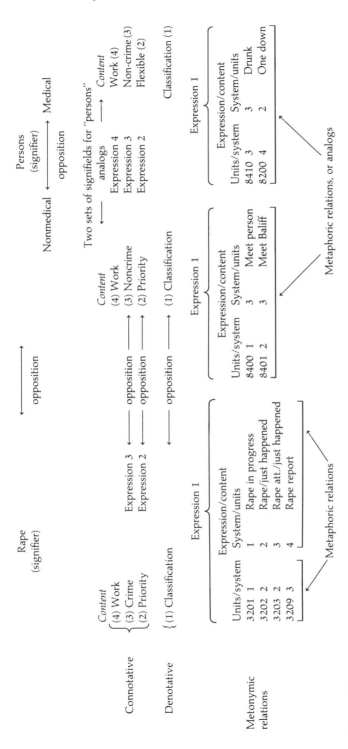

Figure 6.1
MPD subsystem 1 (operators). Each side of the expression/content is equivalent to the other: a list that can be read as "3201-1" or "1—rape in progress." A unit plus a system equals an expression or a content. An expression (signifier) and a content (signified) equal a sign.

connotative meanings are restricted to work. In the "persons" domain the subcoding is more complex, because two of the units in the expression system require the operators to inform EMS and two do not. The two groups of categories are related metaphorically. The relations between content and expression in the two domains are related by opposition, except at the highest level, where "work" refers to both.

The cognitive map of the dispatchers for the same two domains is shown in figure 6.2. A similar expansion to that shown in figure 6.1 for the relations between expression and content for classification (1) are shown for both the "persons" and the "rape" domains. The relations within expression (1) in both domains are metonymic. Two denotative and two connotative levels order each domain for dispatchers. The relations between the contents and expressions in the two domains are related by opposition.

Figure 6.3, showing the cognitive mapping of the domains "rape" and "persons" for officers, replicates the contents of the first three denotative meanings (classification, priority, and crime) and their oppositions. It should be noted that, because the dispatchers call officers and provide brief descriptions of the job they are requesting the officers to undertake, content (the unit, "rape in progress") is actually the expression, for the formal/classifications (3201, 3202, . . .) are not used on the air.

Several general points can be made about the three figures. The two domains exist for all three subsystems, but their internal structure and complexity vary. They are related by oppositional relations, except among operators who view their work in terms of the cognitive shaping of the call and sending it on in contrast to the dispatchers who must "translate" across subsystems. The number of denotations differ. In figure 6.2 classification, priority, and crime are all denotative, and only work is connotative. For dispatchers, however, there are two levels of connotative meanings, and for officers there are three. All the chains are produced by hyperelevation of the codes from denotative meanings of the terms within the two domains. This pattern indicates that there are different numbers or levels of layered meanings for the three subsystems. Although there are four, four, or five levels, respectively, for the three subsystems, there is one connotative level for operators, two for dispatchers, and three for officers. This means that the complexity of the cognitive mapping is greater for officers, that the degree of structural replication across the three subsystems is moderate (that is, they differ in the ways pointed out in this paragraph), and, most important from a semantic point of view, that the dominant or head term for the two domains for officers is the degree to which the sign ("rape" or "persons") is likely to provide honorable materials (Manning 1984). The extent to which this dominates the occupational culture of the officers and, to a lesser degree, dispatchers who are

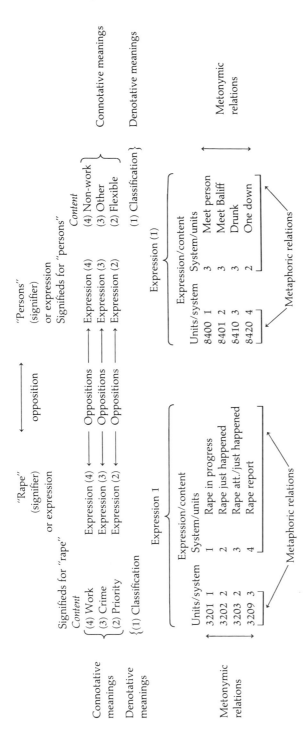

Figure 6.2
MPD subsystem 2 (dispatchers).

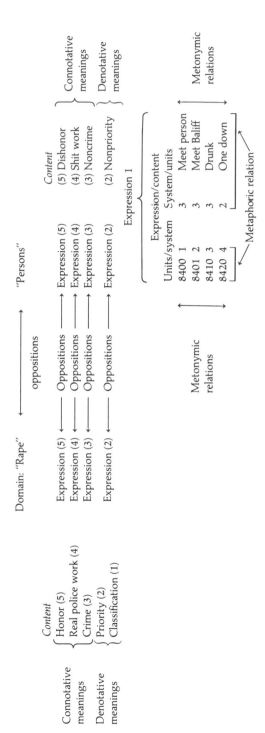

Figure 6.3
MPD subsystem 3 (officers). The content is actually the expression here because dispatchers read out descriptions on the air: "possible rape in progress."

also officers is considerable. It shapes the meaning of calls in ways unknown to the public and to the operators who initially place the calls
within the police classification system.

The piling up of meanings and their layering within the communications system is done through connections within and across domains.
These meanings are given coherence by the binding force of the occupational culture. This envelope itself is only occasionally examined. Nevertheless, it orders transmission of messages through the subsystems. The
extent of compatibility between and among other domains that might
have been chosen is not known.

If one focuses on the semantic consequences of the processing of messages, it is probably not fruitful to view message processing as transformation, because that would perhaps connote something more formal than is
in fact taking place. It has been argued that one consequence of message
processing is the production of drama. In one fashion the messages can be
said to become more poetic, for they are more self-referential and reflexive in character, overlaid with connotative meanings not derived from the
nature of the call or from the caller's intentions, and selectively highlight
certain features of the call as it becomes revealed as a job. Alterations in the
semantics of messages, regardless of their content, are loosely articulated
from subsystem. Those processing in one subsystem do not know that
previous connotative meanings have changed because there is no significant feedback.

The character of the change is specific: alteration in meaning, which, it
is argued, results from change in the interpretant. This changes denotative
meaning to connotative meaning. This is a kind of semantic change, or
semiosis. The change has four identifiable features. First, there is a demonstrated shift in the number of levels of meaning (from three to five).
Second, there is a difference in the character of the contrasts at the first
level. Third, there is an observed change in the degree of differentiation of
meaning. Three levels of connotative meaning exist for officers, whereas
only one was found for operators. Fourth, there is a change in the content
of the expressions within the two domains. There are no changes observed, on the other hand, in the coding rules themselves or in the classification system. The semantic change produces what might be called a drift
associated with the elaboration of connotative or implicit meanings. There
is also syntactic change from signs ordered by an encoding process in
response to cues provided by callers and heard by operators to signs
ordered by encoding and decoding based on data that are linked organizationally and occupationally derived meanings.

The two processes of syntactic progression and semantic elaboration
need not work in a consistent fashion. Although growth or increasing
complexity captured by formal axioms and rules of deduction, induction,

abduction, and even recursivity (Hofstadter 1979, p. 152) can be mapped or programmed, implicit meanings are more difficult to model. The links between expression and content are often feelings, intuitions, values, or vague, semiconscious understandings and have powerful but less discernable features (Grimaud 1983). They have a way of spiraling, but the pathways are less well understood. The two processes, syntactic progression and semantic elaboration, furthermore depend on each other in complex ways for their separate effects. Stability in meaning and syntactic chain is supplied by the assumed semantic links between expression and content. On the other hand, semantic elaboration requires syntactic stability. It is the background of assumptions in both cases that permits the more apparent transformations to occur.

Organizations and Time

Organizations are sedimentations of time. They transmit information by reifying its component parts into sanctioned encoded messages. Time is represented by structure and embedded within it. In the MPD and the BPD time and information come into contest.

There is a critical truth resting in the notion that organizations are information-processing systems. One aspect of the structuring of organization is the types of experience coded as information, recorded by formal means, collected, processed, and reduced in a stylized and semipermanent manner (as, for example, the computer printouts that clog the shelves of police communications centers). This is one modality of a text and has been seized on to characterize the essential nature of organizations (Weber 1958).

Organizations produce texts that contain a conception of time. The linguist Halliday (1978), for example, sees the notion of text as a foundation for discourse analysis. Text can be adapted for organizational analysis. In Halliday's scheme the mode (symbolic rules that organize discourse) must be seen in concert with the tenor (rules that dominate the interpersonal relationships of the persons involved) and the field or the activities of the persons. In short, symbolization, organizations, and behavior are seen as underlying dimensions of discourse. These are collectively termed "text" by Halliday (1978, pp. 142–145). This vertical (temporal) organization of discourse can be read off against the horizontal (synchronic) organization of police processing of calls to reveal the multiplicity of times within the organization (table 6.1).

Table 6.1 represents an autonomous semiotic system and isolates those aspects of the MPD and BPD communications systems that can be captured in formal terms. The codes into which a call to the police can be placed are also forms of collective time and collective memory. The call in code 1 is encoded in "my time," personal time, immediate and face-to-face

Table 6.1

Codes, rules, and text in police communications systems

			Text	
Code	Rule	Field	Tenor	Mode and channel
1. "My time"	Vernacular	Event/ Call	Caller, dispatcher/ operator, or operator	Commonsense logic Oral
2. "Routine" time	Operating rules	Incident	Caller-operator or operator-dispatcher	Police classificatory system. VDU script
3. Metaphoric time	Police rules	Job	Operator-dispatcher or dispatcher (controller)-officer	Subcultural logic Oral. Radio
4. "Paper" time	Administra- tive rules	Records	Officer-records- administrator	Administrative rationality. Visual- linear-spatial. Written-text-record

time. Code 2 is time within the organizational boundary or routine time and is indicated as clock time. Code 3 is metaphoric time ordered by the crime-noncrime distinction within policing and is closely tied to the immediate demands and pressures of the craft. Code 4 contains another conception of time, what might be called paper time or administrative time, time governed by rules, orders, policies, and officially stated formulations of proper practices.

These codes are also reflected in the style of communication or rules underlying talk. In code 1 the style is the vernacular; in code 2 it is a form of operating-dispatching talk that contains elements of the legal system and the classification system of the organization. The rules that, in turn, govern the assemblage of speech objects transform common talk or the vernacular into organizational talk and permit a segue into police talk governed by police rules. Just as various codes can variously organize a text (Barthes 1974), various codes are found in speech (Bernstein 1971). The question is how the units of discourse, the unit systems in which signs find their capacity to signify, can be organized by such codes.

A set of rules, or ordering premises, can be seen to guide the organization of talk, which governs operating and dispatching activity. However, they function primarily as subsystem-specific rules for the interpretation of ambiguous calls. The term "system integration" is a paradox because these same rules are not consistently used throughout the police communications systems. The alteration of the communicational unit is done unconsciously and quite routinely. The creation of a message is rule guided marks the unit as a noncasual feature of everyday life, and permits symbolic manipulation of it as an organized and organizational commodity. Precise rules for enactment serve more than this syntactic function, for they are stabilizing and unifying. The aim here is to designate a domain of discourse primarily by coding and associated effects. Paper and event are problematic, as are call and event, call and incident, incident and job, and any observable actions on the scene and the written or oral reports of such.

Note that each of the times is captured by a code and that as one moves from the top to the bottom of each of the columns in table 6.1, the degree of formalization, distance, abstraction, and elaboration increases.

The last three columns of table 6.1 are drawn from Halliday (1978). The field refers to the activities described in the occurrence and relate initially to an imaged event in the mind of the caller. (The question of the epistemological nature of this event—whether it actually happened, is happening, is thought to be happening, or will happen—is irrelevant if the received signal is seen as codable.) Recall that, when an event is reported in a call, it is transmitted across the boundaries from environment I and is received or encoded as a message and, once written up by an operator, an incident. An incident, then, is the event as reported in the call as classified within the operating-dispatching code according to the operative rules obtaining within this segment. Its analytic character arises because it is a reproducible, permanent, linear, written representation of the event as call as classified. An incident becomes an assignment for dispatchers and becomes a job when it passes from subsystem 2 to subsystem 3. The record is organized by code 4 (administrative rules) and placed in the files. The field is represented by the transitivity of the relations between the codes. The tenor, however, can be seen in the relationships between members of the segments and between segments. The caller-operator-dispatcher interaction dominates the first stage; operator-dispatcher-caller or dispatcher-operator interaction the second, and dispatcher-officer the third. The record provides the constitutive basis for the final tenor. Triadic interaction involves the officer, the administrator, and the record. The record indexes the incident in the sense that it has some "natural" connection with the matter described, and the record symbolizes or represents in some culturally arbitrary fashion the event and the call (Leach 1976).

The last column in table 6.1 arrays the mode and channel that dominate the text based on each of the four codes. Commonsense logic and reasoning dominate in the first instance, and the oral channel is the symbolic vehicle for conveying signs. In code 2 the classification system of the police dominates and the VDU, on which the calls are written up, is the mode in which the code is represented. In code 3 the dispatcher-operator dispatches the officer by radio. The subcultural rules of the police dominate the meaning system, and the channel is the radio (oral). Records index this flow retrospectively.

This analysis suggests that time has space and a location indicated by codes. The times of structures are seen metaphorically vertically and horizontally. "My time" becomes encoded as clock time, is then recorded in metaphoric time, and then in paper time. These times are incompatible with respect to locale, logic, commonsense typifications of events, field, tenor, and mode. The unification work accomplished by the organization's formal system of control constrains variations of the negotiation of the time code. As one moves outward to the community or external world, the initial coding remains relatively intact because of the absence of feedback on the message and the actions of the police on citizens, whether callers, participants, or observers. The effects also create perturbations insofar as members of subsystems must negotiate and renegotiate messages in their mutable coded form. They exist in this fashion in the organization's structures.

Sources of Stability

The several sources of instability (transmission of communicational units, factual disruptions, structurally induced transformations and effects, chains of signification, and time) all act as demonstrations of the discrete unitary nature of communication and support the case for a semiunique set of processes linking the message chain through time and space. On the other hand, communications are seen as enduring units only superficially modified by having been sent through a police organization. There is a kind of black box assumption that reifies continuity and isomorphism. There are sources of stability that reinforce the view of similarity and certainty in management; in a way, the uncertainty-reduction notion of organizations is a gloss for highly predictable transmissions. How does stability arise in the routine processing of messages? What principles underlie the observed patterns in the MPD and the BPD? How is the fiction of continuous calls' flow unity socially constructed and maintained? Call groupings are metaphoric and are based on subtle cognitive knowledge.

Stable meaning arises and is maintained within semiotic systems embedded in organizations by a set of factors not inherent in any sign system. The system cannot explain or reveal its own legitimacy or coherence. Thus reproducing a set of flowcharts or diagrams of the movement of messages may explain how messages move from one subsystem to another, but it does not explain why. Stability certainly arises from the ecological location and proximity of the various subsystems, various symbolic markers (such as uniforms, badges, technology, shared language, and role signs), the physical form of the message as it is finally located in the paperwork of the officers, the category in which the call is initially placed in the MPD (which is carried through the system without change, regardless of implicit changes or connotative layering of meanings), and formal record-keeping practices that are based on the assumption of continuity of the event-call-incident-job-record stream. These would be found in any formal bureaucratic organization of this kind.

There are three sources of stability in the movement as seen from the perspective of the phenomenological field of the two organizations: (1) mechanisms of transferral, which are cognitive and experiential and refer to the assumptive or tacit basis of everyday reasoning and the importance of imagery in message transmission, the grounding of much organizational understanding; (2) rules for enactment, or metarules for ordering ambiguous calls and reducing operational uncertainty (used primarily by operators and dispatchers); and (3) cognitive and phenomenological characteristics of organizationally organized perceptions. These might be labeled the cognitive biases of organizational participants.

Mechanisms of Transferral
Tacit Knowledge
The variety of modes of thinking required to order, sort, name, classify, and delineate denotative or cognitive information and the variety required to separate, group, chunk, and assemble connotative meanings seem distinctive (Eco 1984; Langer 1951; Needham 1981). Tacit knowledge integrates ideas at several levels but does not obviate the role of material, ecological, and organizational structures. On factual and material grounds there are several arguments for continuity of messages: physical form, ecological boundaries, code integrity, and formal record-keeping practices. One characteristic difference between cognitive and tacit knowledge can be glossed in a number of ways but is a background-foreground distinction featured in gestalt psychology and phenomenological analysis. Simply put, this orients the analyst to what is in the foreground of a perceived scene and what is not in focus, the background. Both are recognizable forms, so that they can shift.

Logically, any framed matter in social life will possess a background-foreground dimension, and knowledge of the content can never reduce which is the focal point, foreground, or theme around which a pattern forms and which is the background. Such knowledge is working knowledge that grows from recognized effects and has a practical character. Consider this tale.

When driving west late one winter night bound for Boston, I stopped, exhausted, at a motel off a four-lane highway in upstate New York. It was reasonable in price, I stayed only a few hours, and I ate at the fast food restaurant next door to it. About seven months later, in the same car, now driving east, late on a winter's night, I again decided to stop for the night.

I was near the same city and took an exit. Following that, a second exit appeared, which I took. Signs for lodging, gas, and food appeared, and I turned left following my feelings. As I drove west toward the light, I felt a sense of recall—something about the place, the lights, and the road struck me. Could this be the same exit road? Had I intuitively retraced my steps? A red stoplight loomed ahead. On the left loomed the same motel. I turned left and left again into its parking lot.

This vignette is a tale of intuition. The same place was found by a vague association of road signs, topography, internal sensations, and personal memory. This is a class of knowledge, which contrasts with denotative cognitive knowledge. It is, as much as anything, representative of the logic of everyday life. I focused on the facts of the road but was aware of the general character of the experience and responded to both. I was using such knowledge to organize my choices and actions, but not in an "intellectualized" self-consciously rational fashion.

When one focuses on an item, a fact, a bit of information, or even a cluster of information, other information, although recognized, retained, and available, is secondary. Nevertheless the two taken together create an emergent meaning. One may be aware of both but speaks of or focuses on only one of the two events, facts, or parts of a representation. We know the first term (foreground) only by relying on awareness of it for attending to the second (Polyani 1967, p. 10). Tacit knowing is composed of semantic and ontological aspects, both of which are important in examining message continuity in police communications systems. The semantic aspects of tacit knowledge are seen in the effects it has on what it is applied to: "Meaning tends to be displaced *away from ourselves*" (Polyani 1967, p. 13). The ontological aspect results because tacit marking establishes a meaningful relationship between two terms and an understanding of the entity that these two terms jointly constitute, the particular (foreground) and the background.

These effects can be seen as governed by two separate sets of ordering rules, one for each level of reality. "Operations of a higher level cannot be accounted for by the laws governing its particular forming at the lower level" (Polyani 1967, p. 34). More important, understanding by concrete logical operations does not allow one to understand secondary levels and vice versa. Focus on particulars can in fact be destructive of understanding, and cognitive knowledge is not a substitute for tacit comprehension [see also Hofstadter (1979)].

Tacit knowledge integrates message transferral because, although the units, bits, and message are the proximal focus (the analogy works for bits and the message as well as for messages and the "flow"), the continuous flow across subsystems is a distal focus. Tacit knowledge can be thought of in another fashion, that of integration of discourse (linear sequential information) and presentational or holistic or comprehensive knowledge (Langer 1951, pp. 75—94). Semanticists have seen discourse as denotative and referential in character and presentational knowledge as connotative, self-referential, associative, and thematic (Leech 1983, p. 23). In the event, they are not separable but simultaneous in operating. Thus, as the exercise in internal message analysis suggested, meaning is a function of a presumed pattern in which a term holds an identified position (Langer 1951, pp. 56—57). Seeing meaning, as we have seen among operators, controller-dispatchers, and officers, is simultaneously holding on to particulars (one set of bits in a message) while seeing it as a whole and as a point in an ongoing flow of messages of a given type or in a given paradigm.

Discursive reasoning, according to Langer, works for language in its referential or denotative mode; but, as many have said, not all that is worth saying can be spoken, not everything can be said, and language is not our only articulate product (Langer 1951, p. 83). Or, as Needham has written: "Men do not reason often; they do not reason for long at a time; and when they do reason they are not very good at it" (1978, p. 69). That is, all that is reasonable is not captured by formal, obvious syllogisms or even language, for music, art, and myth and tacit knowledge may not be "captured" in the written or spoken word. This is one of the dilemmas of artificial intelligence.

Computer simulation of work processes is based on putting into the computer those facts that can be programmed and then seeing how close the computer output resembles what humans do (parallel to teaching a machine to play chess). All matters that are not on the machine—externals, emotions, interaction effects, confusion, and anxiety—cannot be programmed and can neither be a cause of failure nor a source of success. Thus human emulation of the machine leads to the simulation of machines that think.[2]

In trying to unravel the human understanding of messages, one cannot omit from consideration the factors that make the notion of a message powerful, evocative, important, and police relevant. If information is only a part of the power of the message, then an analysis based exclusively on cognitive and formal problem-solving models will be quite misleading. The importance of what is called presentational knowledge by Langer, for example, and treated in more detail by Goffman (1959), cannot be overlooked. Presentational knowledge is the background knowledge that permits the fiction of message processing to live metaphorically. This is, like art, music, and myth, background knowledge that works tacitly and is not a language in the same sense in which it is usually understood (Langer 1951, p. 89).

Tacit knowledge is some mixture of the explicit facts of messages *and* the implicit meaning of the message stream, which is in turn connected to the occupational culture and conceptions of the object world. Some remarks on the role of tacit knowledge on change link the general philosophical arguments here with the particulars of the diachronic analysis of the MPD and the BPD.

The logical and material formulation does not address several issues revealed in analysis of message movement across subsystems. It does not account for the tacit knowledge used to connect talk to events and persons in the world, nor does it put this talk in the context (assumptions made about the message) in which it is heard.[3] Tacit knowledge is non-systematized, shared and taken for granted, affectively laden, resistent to formulation yet predictable in form and underlying structure. Such tacit knowledge is often contained in epigrams, tales, and anecdotal materials. It is a form of connection between islands of logic. Much of what is understood is analogical in form rather than digital (present or absent). Belief embeds facts such that the belief entails the facts produced, but the reverse does not obtain. Belief runs ahead of knowledge. Meaning and information interact and confound each other in a kind of reflexive configuration. As a result the message is not seen as a purely cognitive construction or as a mere physical thing but as a set of signifiers with ambiguous signifieds.

These points suggest that the connection of the message to the model is done in part by content and referential meaning and in part by tacit knowledge, analogy (familarity with events "like" these), beliefs about events and about the message stream, and wholistic assessment of the entire set of transformations.[4] Perhaps imagery is the most obvious form in which the experience is transformed into knowledge and back into the experiential realm. The image is the second mechanism of transferral that stabilizes message transmission.

The Nature of Eidetic Transmissions

Gregory Bateson has underscored imagery in this way: "Speculation suggests that image formation is perhaps a convenient or economical method of passing information across some sort of an interface. Notably, when a person must act in a context between two machines, it is convenient to have the machines feed their information to him or her in image form. . . . At these interfaces [between two systems] images are economical or efficient" (Bateson 1980, pp. 40–41).

That images are both necessary and efficient for moving messages across the several subsystems and channels (aural to visual, visual to aural) and man-machine interfaces is incontrovertible. It can be seen as the necessary visual equipment that permits the *idea* of a message to be transmitted when the facts or information are partial, seen as inadequate, wrong, or misleading. Conversely, of course, the wrong image will suffice even when facts are present.[5]

I have argued that an image shapes and precedes classification, that encoding is an operation of reified imagining. What if images are transferral mechanisms? They serve initially several functions that stabilize perception and pattern, order, and organize experience. Consider several examples of these functions.

Apparently underlying the sorts of imagining that produce change and stability in message transmission are some primary factors of perception that pattern, organize, and order experience. They work in what Needham has called the "comparative interpretation of human experience" (1981, p. 1). These preeminently social facts are set in context by "factors of experience which form the elementary constituents of culture. Among these relatively steady agents are synthetic complexes recognizable as archetypes" (Needham 1981, p. 1).

It could be argued that the facts to be construed, the data presented concerning operators' assemblage procedures, is to varying degrees context sensitive and that these relational ties are in large part a function of that context sensitivity.

The concrete manifestations of these facts in messages is perhaps elusive, but one can alter the focus and seek ordering from the ways people order sensory experience to see how these factors operate in message movement. Primary factors are defined by Needham, from whom the agenda is drawn, with characteristic elegance:

The "primary factors" which are described as forming the elementary constituents of culture correspond to aspects of thought and imagination, as exhibited in cultural traditions, which appear to have a universal distribution in world ethnography. These factors of experience are heterogeneous; they include sensory perceptions such as texture or color, and abstractions such as number or binary opposition. Also, they vary greatly in the meanings that they are made to carry; and there are no necessary connections among them such as would compose them into systems. In regarding these factors as primary, the idea is that they may play in forms of consciousness a part similar to that of ultimate predicates in epistemology. (Needham 1981, p. 3)

In message analysis that takes place within an institutional framework (policing and police organizations), it can be seen that generalized variation in communication units becomes shaped. Primary factors differ from each other and are not generally clustered into systems [there are exceptions; see Needham (1978)]. They are neither randomly arrayed nor created or altered deliberately. They are elementary and symbolic and do not have a rational or even primarily cognitive institutionalized locale. They are implicit and tacit and generate "secret sympathies." If we extend this further, we see that aspects of these primary factors are relevant precisely because they cohere within policing as organizational images. This means that the comparative epistemology of corporate life (indexed by images) can also be seen as a format for analysis of transmitting and transforming images across and within institutional structures.

Tacit organization or institutional images also function to set constraints on the pictures of reality possessed (and projected) by the police of themselves and those they ostensibly serve. In truth, as Langer writes, "pictures are the mind's stock-in-trade" (1951, p. 128). The question of the nature of the link between an individual mind's images and institutional or collective pictures continues to challenge sociological analysis (Halbwachs 1980).

In the Renaissance sharply drawn figures from biblical literature, well-known paintings of the past, and a coherent and shared culture among the professionals gave a fund of experience for the interpretation of images (Baxandall 1973). In modern times in Anglo-American society, no such fund exists; it must be dragged together from films, novels, plays, literature, and art. They are no modern equivalents to the Renaissance "code." Needham (1981, pp. 1ff) suggests, however, that affecting representations are unifying exemplary scenes. These constitute the implicit bases for organizing emotive experience that are absorbed, not taught but felt and known, and transmitted repeatedly. These vary in intensity across time and culture and social organization, but they are a means of achieving economy of expression, of condensing contingencies, or mobilizing emotions. Needham provides several quite moving and well-known examples: Peter betraying Jesus three times before the cock crows, a scene from Tolstoy's *Anna Karenina,* and a scene from Kurwasawa's *Seven Samurai* (1981, pp. 89–90). These are drawn from the little and great traditions of films and literature and present a set of fairly conventionalized indexes or icons. That is, they draw on and resonate within known literary traditions. These images are indexes of the great traditions, such as the collective representatives drawn on by Durkheim for the analysis of religion, kinship, and collective life. The opposite of these is the individualized images that are used to organize personal experience.

It is likely that scenes of a basic sort orient coding and interpretation across the subsystems, but they are not traditional, formal, and firmly set in well-articulated institutional imagery. They probably derive, as was suggested in the discussions of the narrative structure of police tales, from fundamental notions of hero and villain, victim and victimizer, loss and gain of property, categories of age, sex, and gender, relational categories, and basic transitions such as aging, reproduction, death, birth, moral transgressions and their display, and the like. The absence of a closed system of mapping, such as a moral geography, onto police categories means that a variety of semiloose events stand for them as overcoded examples.

Affecting depictions, drawings, or written texts share the institutional locus of policing but do not possess the generally available power of paradigmatic scenes. In the following summarized policing vignettes, generalizable human experiences are rendered. It is these basic shared and common experiences captured awkwardly in language that are the actual bases for collective ties and the subtle signs about signs, or ethnosemiotics (MacCannell and MacCannell 1982). Thus the focus of each scene is not the call to the police but the fact that it can evoke general properties of experience that bind even those sharing a brief and perhaps even fleeting communicational encounter.

1. A blind woman called the BPD, nearly sobbing on the telephone as she reported that her house had been broken into. "I'm a poor blind lady, luv," she told the police operator, and "I'm frightened and alone here. Why would anyone break into me house?" She was listened to, reassured by the operator, and told "not to worry, my love, someone will come 'round and see you." (The terms, "my luv," and "luv" are generally used in this part of England by both men and women to each other in a variety of semi-public transactions in shops and on the telephone and are generally used by adults to children and older people. They are not taken as offensive or sexist.)

2. In another BPD call a man rang to ask if the police could notify the motorway police that there was an "old sheep just lying there in the road.... Must have fallen off a truck." There was concern and worry in his voice when he asked if someone could be notified and if they could come quickly.

3. The English, it must be said, are by American standards extremely kind and gentle with their pets and with all animals; pets are treated as family members, and the breadth of reference includes horses as domestic beasts. In a one-hour tape of calls, no less than five of them were concerned about animals: one sheep story, one a plea for police to come and collect a dog from an old woman's back garden, one a request that the police render assistance to a dog that had been the victim of a hit and run accident in front of the caller's house, one about a horse running free down the road in front of a house in a residential neighborhood, and one about a dog that had been apparently abandoned in a van parked beside the motorway. These calls do not take on the nagging, irritated, or annoyed tone that they might in America; they are exchanges about matters of mutual concern.

4. In another long and somewhat tediously rambling call, a mother reported that a week previously her daughter had been extorted out of ten pence by a black youth on the top level of a bus while on a journey to visit her grandmother. As her daughter was to take the journey again in a few days, the mother wanted the police to know about this and asked them if there was anything they could do about it. The mother rang the police just before she was to leave for work and her child was to leave for school. The operator listened, did not interrupt or prompt, and reassured the woman that she had done the right thing to ring the police. He asked if the woman would wait at home and keep her child home with her until a PC could come and speak to them.

There was little by way of crime solving involved here, but the purpose appeared to be general comfort and social support.[6] These calls display a variety of emotional states that are themselves paradigms for the classification of police calls. Furthermore, the paradigms suggest that these both produce and reproduce scenes or images that in turn form the tacit basis for communicational unit continuity across the subsystems of the police organization.

If one now considers the embedded or condensed nature of the images derived from the written record at whatever point in the MPD and BPD, the inference is that they are emblematic or graphic moots. They are encoded, encapsulated, and otherwise collapsed versions of basic human experiences. The discussion of filling-in and filling-out captures a considerable aspect of this condensation and expansion, but perhaps it can be further clarified. The various operations of filling-in and expanding are evidence of some invisible image or paradigm, suggested in internal message analysis, that anchors particulars of any communicational unit. Various aspects of "ad hocing" in coding, factum valet, and errors all refer to an underlying order presumed to remain while items come under its control (Garfinkel 1967, ch. 1). In other words, errors and anxiety elucidate order and continuity.

The following points might be considered. When controllers or dispatchers become overloaded, they tend to cope informally with the work by burying items in the queue, assigning them to units that have not actually accepted them, and focusing on a few items in order to characterize a message (Hulbert 1981b). They create informal queues and do things briefly and officially. This behavior also suggests that there appears to be a contradiction between thinking and doing, producing stress, error in notes when compared to previous information given to the operators or dispatchers and controllers, and elision of phrases. Perhaps more generally stress is produced when one is forced to write or type and listen simultaneously. Furthermore, anxiety is reported by operators and controllers and dispatchers when message and field tend to "flow together." This happens when there are many calls arriving and when noise increases. Information loss in transfer results (Hulbert 1981a). Reported anxiety also produces "jumbled concatenations" in that high-stress messages, for example, a near-violent incident with a weapon, a catastrophe, or a shooting, have consequences: failing to maintain communication between dispatcher and officer(s), swarming, altering the chain of command, and increasing interest of the zone dispatchers in the event. They stroll over to see what's happening. The written records from these collapsed messages resemble graphic moots because they suppress the emotive field and noise within which the "facts" were initially considered.

The sorts of error generally encountered are notable in the sense that they are indicia of both the distribution of attentional energy and stress. It is likely that the allocation of importance to an incident is based on the mental image constructed, and "blends and spoonerisms," "strong habit intrusions," and "place-lapsing errors" reflect a distorted sense of factual assemblage (Reason, 1982).

The images used both expand and contract with the words used to describe the event. The tendency for BPD controllers in particular to jot down notes, or aide memoire (Ekblom and Heal 1982, p. 26), means that they omit some facts when sending out messages, that operators always omit facts given to them from callers, and that controllers omit facts given to them by operators. A large amount of information given by callers is omitted from the incident (the coding effect), and inaccurate and misleading statements are sent on. Operators focus on facts (caller's name, address, location, etc.), not details of the reported event. The more urgent the call, according to Hulbert (1981a, p. 17), the shorter the time spent in taking details on it. Actions can be taken on brief and rather elliptical phrases such as "man with a gun" or "holding a prisoner at Littlewoods" (a large departmental store). These inferences are consistent with my observations.

These points suggest that quasi-institutional images function in message transmission in several quite significant ways. They can supply the connection between short-term and long-term memory and between task-action and mental function (Cicourel 1973, ch. 4; 1975, 1976). Anxiety may produce effects that are bound together by a tacit sense of the event rather than the incident. On the other hand, the jumbled facts seem to produce an orientation to the message itself, or the poetic function.[7]

Controllers and operators in particular make coherent the communication they hear by chunking and clustering information and by organizing it into a semblance package: Meaning, not facts, is used to form a précis or abstract core for all practical purposes. This chunking may lead to either filling-in facts or leaving them out, depending on the situation.

The image organizes the facts to be used to show it or make it visible. Officers report "embarrassment" in arriving at a job and being given wrong or insufficient facts, meaning they imagined something different to be there; this is also a problem with younger officers who do not know what to expect (Ekblom and Heal 1982, p. 30). The information sent, rarely plentiful, is conveyed in a way that leaves much to the imagination. The wish to produce similitude among the code of experience, working rules and principles, the police classification, and the event produce pressures in the direction of collapsing the code and the event into the working rules and classification.

Image work is relevant to understanding not only how a communication is "seen" but also how communicational units are viewed as being part of a continuous unitary and meaningful flow across the subsystems. Images are something like schemata, or protassemblages of ideas that cohere. They serve to transform or to shape experience into units, a "blueprint."

It has been suggested by Rosch and co-workers (1975, 1976) that people organize cognitions around some representative image or prot-image which centers or produces a kind of phenotype for a number of genotypes. Thus the word "fish" may suggest an image that is closer to or more like a "trout" than say a piranha, eel, shark, or sturgeon. "Trout" serves as something like a prototype. Of course, other meanings of "fish" (to drop a line, to seek something, etc.) may have other, alternative prototypical images. The previous discussion of crime suggests that some prototypical images arise that elicit ideas associated with categories, such as robbery, burglary, murder, stealing, and rape.[8]

These prototypes are produced in the first instance by framing and, by the index of these, a "cognitive lock." Note that when one names a thing ("crime" or "domestic" or "alarm call"), one is noting a *point* in a field, an x, but one is also doing another thing, locating x in a field of unnamed "not x's":

Naming and characterizing an x only implies what not-x is or represents, such as when "crime" implies "noncrime." This is a difference that does not specify the dimensions along which x varies from not-x. The not-

x or negative field is not equivalent epistemologically to x, marked as significant. Any focus contains a focal point plus a field or periphery, but the
focal point is guided by values, choices, organizational routines, and
names. These become the unspecified background for a focal perception.
The "meaning of a term is likewise, a function; it rests on a pattern, in
which the term itself holds the key position" (Langer 1951, p. 56). The key
position held by a term, in this case a named crime category, is known by
tacit knowledge and the association of images with the particular message.
Thus a bit that provides the basis for a cognitive lock is something like
the flash that occurs when two ideas come into juxtaposition as in an
aphorism, poem, or epigram. It resembles in this sense the punctum or
focal point of interest in a photograph (Barthes 1981, p. 41). It will pass on
or convey a particular segment of experience, which is fragmentary but
raises in this fragment all the alternative ways in which such an experience
might be conveyed. That is, the cognitive lock works to highlight both
the arbitrary nature of conventional assumptions and a particular, perhaps
illuminating interpretation of a general and known experience. The shift
between the background, which makes the item general, and the foreground, which conveys the particular, produces a fruitful opposition (Stern
1959, pp. 164–165).

The cognitive lock, as seen in internal message analysis, is not revealed
by any given communicational unit or information bit. Each message is
framed, it is argued, or given order and coherence, by a set of rules (unspecified) for the organization of experience as seen by participants in the
activity being so defined (Goffman 1974, p. 11). This framing is a way of
putting a cognitive lock on activity, given its unity and objectivity, separating it from nonframed activity and negative experiences that threaten
the frame and following "operations" (transformations) to be performed
on it. If a central or core activity, say, an event in the world such as a
report of a stolen car, is then keyed as a message, it is transformed from
one sort of experience to another. All this has been discussed. A key is
required for the movement of a message across subsystems (even if it is
being rekeyed as again being the same sort of experience). Whenever a
key occurs, it "performs a crucial role in determining what it is we think
is really going on" (Goffman 1974, p. 45). A key is the signaling of a
convention within which voices are heard. It functions as a basis for
transformations, the logic for converting one thing or social object into
another. It is clear that keying and framing play a role in the movement of
messages, but it is perhaps rather more complicated than viewing them as
a means of merely accomplishing transformations.

Transformations produce changes from "this" to "that" and are worked
in language by paradigmatic and syntagmatic associations. They are also

worked in more general ways by a variety of gestures and actions (a raised hand and a whistle begin a soccer match, a whistle blown four times ends it), speech acts (a welcoming speech opens a meeting, an introduction begins a conversation), even physical markings (the entrance to a holy place is marked by a vaulted arch or liminal stones).

In the case of messages, as argued in chapter 2 (figure 2.1), an event becomes a message when it is keyed through police and/or operator response and framed physically by being entered on a VDU and written through coding practices. This is a first-level transformation [an event (the copied) is now found in the form of an incident (a copy or product of the first transformation)]. Associated with such transformations are images, so one now has a set of signs (the communication about the event) mapped onto another set of signs (the incident report) embodied by the VDU. This is an isomorphism; the parts of the one can be mapped onto the parts of the other (Hofstadter 1979, p. 159). The keying of incident into record is done mechanically at the time the incident is entered into the VDU, but the keying of the second transformation, from incident to job, is done by formulaic contacting of officers by members of subsystem 2. The third transformation is from job to record, keyed by the act of writing—transforming activity seen in environment II and the job into one.

The transformations are complex, the feedback rare, the rules for organizing the messages variable, and the images produced quite varied and tacitly communicated. The analogical aspects of the several images produce uneven relations within the signs of a given form (for example, a call, an incident, a job) as a format locus. The reflexivities, or the backward- and forward-looking aspects of encoding, make the transformations context sensitive and not independent of the subsystem which they are read off. Although "rape" suggests a subsystem-based reading, as does internal message analysis, the mapping of one set of signs onto another is not rule guided in any formal sense. All texts must be scanned for their *intertextuality*: "the transposition of one or more systems of signs into another accompanied by a new articulation of the enuciative and denotative position" (Kristeva 1980, p. 15). Any sign must be seen as part of a triad of signifier and signified viewed by an observer who is spatially, temporally, and culturally situated as a "reader" (MacCannell and MacCannell 1982).

Visual displays, such as those produced by VDUs, represent in eidectic terms a stimulus to the rehearsal of images of events and the sending of intentions; visual displays provide a set of surface features of messages accompanied by a set of deep features, such as the primary factors "bridged" by interpretative practices. The interpretative practices, in turn, are ordered by a set of tacit rules for message processing and interpretation.

Rules for Organizing Ambiguous Calls: Enactment

The previous arguments underscore how important assumptions and patterns of reading off processed messages are to producing a stable communications system. The focus here is on the ways in which messages are made internally coherent and seen as instances of a reigning pattern.

Previous research on calls to the police (Manning 1980a, pp. 200ff), suggests that the fundamental question asked by answerers was, Do I trust this caller? This can be considered the basic rule of interaction, but the absence of other cues in telephone calls hyperelevates the need for careful assessment of trust cues. The rules discussed with reference to operators' responses to ambiguous calls are developments and elaborations of the basic trust rule. In what follows it is to be understood that, unless the caller is trusted, additional rules do not apply. Untrustworthy calls are seen as undermining and eroding the relevance of other rules to the point that operators may call dispatchers to tell them that they distrust a caller, providing a problematic within which the incident is subsequently handled and an informal system of meaning paralleling the formal and written text. Calls are thus formatted, classified, and sent on if credible, but the degree of credibility of a given call once formatted, classified, and sent is unstated and variable and thus remains implicit in any transmission.

Credibility nevertheless is seen by participants as varying from call to call. The rules for organizing a response to ambiguous calls are the means by which operators enact an environment and encode data for organizational purposes (Weick 1979). They are also a means of organizing a response to calls that constrains the range of possibilities to those and only those actions that police carry out. They link formal codes with the diverse data brought to the organization by callers. They are a representation of the invisible link connecting the caller, the code, and the coder (Descombes 1980, pp. 92–106). The practice of organizing a response complements and extends semiotics to explanations of encoding and processing.

Although the rules discussed in chapters 4 and 5 have been shown to be relevant to the actions of operators in the BPD and the MPD in slightly modified form, the relevance of their place as sources of cognitive stability is that they provide one aspect of the formal scheme into which communicational units are placed. As Garfinkel and Bittner have emphasized in their work, the schema provides the basis for the organization of the objects coming under its control; the objects do not possess an essence that exists independently of intentional and human cognition. One has to reverse the conventional wisdom to see that the calls, the incidents, and the like do not create meaning by virtue of their appearance in the sense world of the operators. Their meaning is created by the perspective of the operators, dispatchers, and officers and by the paradigms and subparadigms they use to sort, order, classify, transform, and store and recall the units. Furthermore, although this generalization refers to the ordering function of such rules on the message stream, regardless of the content of the individual communicational units, such perspectives or interpretative practices also function at the message-processing level of analysis of meaning.

Cognitive Bases of Stability

Semantic drift and elaboration is countered by other phenomena that anchor meanings. This anchoring occurs in concrete ways but also occurs as a result of the pattern of social relations and social interaction revealed in the examination of formal features of natural decisions made in the MPD and the BPD and by rules that guide the enactment of calls.[9] These grow up around the codes and make possible the formal operations. They locate meaning in a place and time and reflect the observer's interests in social organization. They mediate or connect the symbolic constructions and syntactic and semantic processes.

The isolation of the code from the coder and from the situation in which encoding and decoding take place omits the fundamental interpretative rules that make them possible. A formal theory of organizations as systems of codes and signs must incorporate interpretative rules guiding the application and understanding of the relevance of the identified codes. What is required is a phenomenology of organizational experience as exhibited by organizational cultures. Some clues to this lie in the examination of perception as it sustains the background reality of culture, for surely the perception of any visible cue is seen against some sort of field or ground. It is argued that the route to understanding the context within which coding in organizations is made sensible follows from a deeper analysis of perception. The links connecting the perception of social reality, its differentiation and refined categorization, and the resultant sentiments and behavioral sequelae are a powerful source or grounding for order.

We experience senses, sensations, and ideas in the event, but we can never know those facts because "what is known can never exactly correspond to the immediate occasion. At best, their relationship can be by similarity or analogy. The degree of this similarity may vary, but we can never know the inherent nature of objects and their relationships as such" (Ames 1960, p. 4). We do not know the true nature of things, only their relation to our position in space and time. "We fail to realize that we can know nothing of things beyond their significance to us" (Ames 1960, p. 4). The experience of a series of items of what we localize as an object becomes a background for other experiences of subsequent events. Experience, according to Ames, provides prehension, awareness of what one expects the nature of a subsequent event to (consequence) after having experienced the preceding event or sequence of events. The initial experience is based on stimuli, but subsequent experiences are organized against the previous stimuli, now organized into patterns or ultrastimuli based on their relevance to immediate purposes. The form in which experience is placed differs with the concrete experience of sequential significance (for stimuli) and the focus of attention and purpose at hand (for ultrastimuli) (Ames 1960, p. 100).

A series of associations arises from these perceptual distinctions, which bear on the unpacking of the meaning of "underlying sense of order" from which specific encoding emerges. Cognitive psychologists and Ames suggest that the contrasts between digital and analogical coding, metonomy and metaphor, and foreground and background bear on the contrast between two modes of perception or experience captured by formal codes (Ardener 1971). They contrast unity, flow, association, and assumptive context with discrete items, sequences, proximity, or serial order, an occasional event. One encodes concrete objects that become the basis for anticipating, prefiguring, and working out in advance one's possible actions in future situations with similar features. The encoding and retrieval of these similar features of past organizing is not well understood, but perhaps it is better understood in organizational context than in everyday life. Experimental evidence is limited in its generalizability to the contingencies and vagaries of everyday life. The bases for prehending objects arises in patterns of signs discerned in situations that resemble those within which the prior pattern is repeated. It is the codification of experience in patterns that makes the work of confronting the everyday environment invisible. This perceptual structure is consistent with ethnomethodological analyses of the nature of everyday life (which is in turn informed by the work of Heidegger, Husserl, and Schutz).

Phenomenologists influenced by German formalism and structuralism have approached the problem of the patterning of experience by attending to the shared, collective, known-in-common-and-there feature of a presuppositional world. A certain type of event (the event about which one calls the police) in the commonsense environment (an organizing frame by which persons prehend events) has been of interest here. Events such as the objects in the natural world that are the proximal stimulus for a call to the police have features that, if the actor views them as present, will be reproducible as a basis for ordering events in the everyday/anyday world.

A series of characteristics, if the witness uses them to order the world, is the basis for the definition of an event in the commonsense environment [Garfinkel (1963, pp. 214–215); see Cicourel (1964) for the methodological implications of this position]. Garfinkel has specified eleven such features, and three are of critical importance. The first is that the event has as its context of interpretation, "a commonly entertained scheme of communication consisting of a standardized system of signals and coding rules and what anyone knows, i.e., a pre-established corpus of socially warranted knowledge" (Garfinkel 1963, p. 215).

The second is that the present determination of the events, whatever they may be, are determinations that were intended on previous occasions and that may be intended again in identical fashion on an indefinite number of future occasions. The third is that from the user's point of view the intended event is retained as the temporally identical event throughout the stream of experience (Garfinkel 1963, p. 215). Taken together, these three features of events in everyday life complement Ames's view of the role of perception in ordering stimuli. Both mark the importance of background features as a stabilizing ground against which individual events are seen. The phenomenological base is stabilized by institutional practices that in turn structure the taken for granted background.

Such attributed features inform the user about any particular appearances of an interpersonal environment but without these necessarily being recognized in a conscious or deliberate fashion. Instead, these attributions are characteristically seen without being noticed features of socially structured environments. Although they are demonstrably relevant to the recognizable character of environing events for the person and, from his point of view, for others around him, they are rarely attended by him. As Schutz points out, a special motive is required to bring them under review. The more the setting is institutionally regulated and routinized, the more does the user take for granted their features "known in common with other." ... A perennial task of sociological inquiries is to locate and define the features of their situations that persons, while unaware of, are nevertheless responsive to as *required features*. (Garfinkel 1963, pp. 216–217)

Institutions and social organizations provide the means for marking events in the context of assumptions about such events never explained but there as part of the recognition of such events in the first instance. The marking, routinization, and structuring of background-foreground relationships is the symbolic work of organizations. Within such work, the specific processes take life.

Conclusion

Semiotic structuralism cannot explain system change. Structuralism illuminates diachronic change within a system by examination of syntactic progression and semantic elaboration. These processes in turn are embedded in a social context of reading and reading off meanings. From a sociological view the issue is one of identifying the sources of stability within the organization that facilitate the freezing of signifiers and the conventionalization of signs that thus occurs (Weick 1983b). Thus explication of such matters as the routinization of meanings and the interpretative practices characteristic of given settings, subsystems, and situations are required. There are no rules that explain how rules are to be applied, how codes are to be used, or how discrepancies between various organizational rules and regulations are to be resolved. This requires one to examine coder-code and message-code relations. In this way the irony of structuralism is rediscovered in yet another form: Once the role of the code-coder-message triad is well understood, structuralism dissolves into the phenomenology supporting the observed encoding of events.

Does this analysis speak to more general questions of the relations between organizations and codes? An organization can be thought of as a bounded, named, rationally organized field of activities with a characteristic set of sign systems with institutionalized or conventionalized functions, contexts, and over- and undercoding. The sign functions are relatively fixed because stabilizing influences are at work. These are structures of rules, norms, values, and information acted out and acted on that constrain choice. Information in the form of communicational units transformed in various ways is reduced within the organization. The location of this coding is in real time and space. There is in fact no tight link between the event in the object world and any subsequent unit form (call, message, incident, assignment, job, record), even given knowledge of the semiotic system at work and the organizational dictionary. Each text at each point is reflexive, a set of several signifiers with various codes to which it is referred, conveying information at several levels (a signified becomes a signifier at another level) and always in variable relationship to unstated knowledge [for example, deictic knowledge (Levinson 1983, ch. 2)], noise and field(s) of activities to which attention is periodically drawn.

The message is a misleading focus because it is always to some degree a function of background features unaccounted for by the sign functions assembled in the message.

Organization is not a precisely delimited concept. It is often a stipulative or hypostatized concept. It might be better imagined as a large room or a sounding board with a limited range and familiar resonance in which sounds play, echo, and are only partially captured. Organizations never speak literally but render their communications metaphorically. The way in which organizations are like speakers, using a linguistic model, or indeed whether organizations are anything is worthy of consideration. Text is yet another concept that directs attention or points, and a change in aspect produces a change in meaning (Needham 1983). Texts, records, documents, and the like are always synecdochically related to structures (Garfinkel 1967; Lemert 1979a; Cicourel 1981) in exceedingly complex ways. Some of these complex ways are suggested by Eco (1984, pp. 177–

188) and will serve as a concluding comment on textual and organizational analysis.

Codes in the formal sense of rules for constructing statements of the "*p* not *q*" or "all men are human" type can generate propositions that can be shown to be either true or false. Eco has suggested the utility of S-codes or institutional codes. These formal dictionaries of usage provide a kind of outline of potential meanings, but they are nontautological, open to failure, deontic, and choice based. S codes are used by organizations and organizational members to maximize control and increase autonomy. They serve to produce room to maneuver within the rules and codes of an organization. The choice of interpretation is not simply a matter of meeting various functional aims of the organization. It also serves members to preserve semantic looseness and syntactic flexibility. If the series 2, 4, 6 is listed, then 8, 10, and 12 will be anticipated by the listener if the series is heard as a simple progression, but a series of calls could be misinterpreted if the signs heard as a message are coded into the wrong category. If an encounter produces a "rape," one cannot reason back to the call as expression because "rape" refers to the content of the encounter, not of the call. They are not, in other words, reversible. Institutional codes are deontic systems, or choice based. The choices produces the echoes. Such choices make pure textual analysis a misleading source of organizational inference. The operator's initial choices are fundamental in constructing the social meaning of the call in the first instance: the choice to use or employ the system of police overcoding of events rather than alternative codes (law, fire, etiquette), to use the code to lie (to tell someone the police can do nothing about a family argument because it is a civil matter), to pretend to use the code to lie (to talk to callers as if information were being taken down when it is being ignored), to use the code improperly when dispatchers enter false information about the status of an officer to allow her to carry out other informal tasks such as finishing paperwork), to act as if the S-code allowed no choice (act as if it were a code such as mathematics or chemistry, with formed rules determining a correct decision or denying choice or discretion in a decision to arrest or charge), to shift in and out of an institutional code (when taking a complaint, discrediting the message while entering it on the computer, producing a devolved meaning, or a contradictory encodation).

The coding that produces texts may be organizational, but it is in part a structure or a set of rules and resources existing outside time and space and is in a part a system, or a constantly reproduced set of relations between actors or collectives situated in time and space (Giddens 1981, p. 172). The actual coding of a call, message, or encounter is contextual and situated. It also reflects culturally stabilized sign functions.

To explore institutional codes one must see through texts to underlying rules and practices. As a result, one may grasp the potential of gathering richly textured field data on the basis of which further, perhaps formal, analysis can be performed. Only once this fieldwork has been undertaken successfully can an adequate formal or semiotic analysis be formulated (Manning 1987).

7

The Logics of Administration

The logic of administration is based on presumptions about the nature of the environment, the internal communications system and how it conveys information, and the relevance of information as a basis for decisions and resource allocation within the police. This logic is flawed because it is based on false assumptions. I have attempted to establish through much of the material in this book the various metaphors by which police organizations can be constituted. I have also challenged the basic ideas surrounding the concept of information. Policing is a loosely coupled sort of organization whose links with an enacted environment are varying, occasional, uneven, and even sporadic. The relationships between the environment and the organization are seen through the concept of demand, but even that is shaped by the same forces that shape the organization's concept of its environments.

Police decisions are affected, of course, by many factors, but I have argued here that the technology, codes, roles and tasks, and interpretative work within the subsystems are constraining. Because information itself is not a thing but an idea, it fades into the context supplied by these shaping forces. The messages that travel through the organization are thus not merely transmitted but transformed by several forms, texts, and channels and by socially derived understandings of their content. I have argued elsewhere (Manning 1977, 1980a) that understanding such ideas requires a contextually sensitive approach to planning, policy, and administration. In this chapter I summarize the case for the relevance of loose coupling to administration and the role of drama in administration and challenge the false hope that technology represents with respect to police administration.

At the center of any organization is the communications system. Some assert that a communications system is the basis for a definition of a formal organization (Barnard 1938). The communications system not only refines, constrains, controls, and limits discretion by control of the range of signs available to interpret messages and the codes used to encode and decode messages but also introduces equivocality and ambiguity. These issue from the inherent problematic relationship between concept and sound and from the structural features of the subsystems. Discretion and ambiguity are amplified in loosely coupled systems, in part because supervision in an aspect of a ritual structure rather than closely tied to everyday events. Supervision is ritualistic partly because people-processing organizations contain or are characterized by complex, variable tasks, vague theories of causation, and unclear standards for judging achievement (Thompson 1967; Wilson 1978). They tend to be based on the "logic of confidence" that results from the implicit trust between supervisors and subordinates (Meyer and Rowan 1977).

Loose Coupling, Semiotics, and Drama

Several general points can be made about the police communications systems and their relation to the organizations' external transactions. Organizations such as the police seek to attain an organizational mandate in terms of an enacted or perceived environment that they construct, maintain, and reify. This reified conception of the environment is maintained in large part by the commonsense knowledge of members of the three subsystems that transform citizen demand into manageable, meaningful units of action. Their encoding and decoding produce an organizational filtration that affirms the organizational reality entailing what is assumed by members about the nature of the outside world. Loose coupling and myth making maintain the independence and autonomy of these beliefs.

The police organization produces quite limited measurable effects in the environment; it has few means to do so and largely operates with efficient measures relating to the allocation of resources rather than environment impacts. It avoids effects as bases for evaluation. Instead, it "decouples" from the environment: Activities are not open to supervision; goals are made vacuous and ambiguous; data on technical performance are eliminated or made invisible; evaluation is ceremonial; and program evaluation is neglected (Meyer and Rowan 1977, p. 357).

From the perspective of semiotic analysis the technological system of communication provides a set of channels or forms of contact. The channels through which messages flow in each of the three subsystems are different: Computers and phones in subsystems 1 and 2; electrowriters between subsystems 1 and 2; two-way radios between subsystems 2 and 3; and face-to-face communication in subsystem 3 only. These channels not only produce the possibility of varying levels of information and information overload but also contain their own associated features as contacts and tacit features of language: voice tone, speed, and level. This means that the potential for differential information levels is maintained in each subsystem. The logical (and semiological) independence of the three subsystems means that from a structural point of view the events processed through them are not uniform: The ways in which information is encoded, decoded, chunked, and processed fundamentally alters (the nature of) the message received in each subsystem.

From the point of view of meaning the events are types of tokens found within the subsystems. The logical contradictions between type and token are resolved by interpretative work done within the subsystem. Because the constraints provided by technology and information vary from subsystem to subsystem, with greater freedom as one gets closer to the streets, technology and information become weaker ties between the subsystems.

The nature of the informational units used also varies so that differentiation of meaning occurs in each subsystem [compare Kitsuse and Cicourel (1963)]. The supervision and control of decisions decreases from subsystem 1 to subsystem 3, increasing the expressive aspects of communication. Communication channels that differ, technological ambiguity, supervision, and discretion also serve to differentiate the system of signs used in each of the three subsystems and to produce what Bateson (1972) terms schismogenesis: the differentiation of values. This value differentiation further produces and maintains decoupling from the environment and internal loose coupling. These value premises, or shared assumptions that are taken for granted, are rooted in reflexive subsystems that depend on two sources of outside information: the citizen and the patrol officer. But neither of these sensors is isomorphic; each is different. There no set styles, theories, and criteria that can be easily applied to all police officers; there are individual differences in practice that cannot be known independently of their message transmissions. Each patrol officer senses a different aspect of the environment and is seldom monitored such that the organization might have independent knowledge of the event observed.

Although all systems are to some degree closed in that they maintain preestablished sets of codes, channels, and systems of signs, in the police preexisting structures of information processing are open to observation and transmit multiple and variable pictures of the environment. There is unity in processing, but there is even less unity in what is termed "observed variability." Each kind of unity is of the special sort described here. Each of these features of the organization produces drama. The dramaturgic effects are not produced by the structure of intentions of the actors but by the differentiation of meanings and the nature of the communicative links among the subsystems (Manning 1982a; Cooper 1985, 1986).

The extant differentiation of meaning, taking on the differences, exists despite the belief, widely held in police circles, that technology will resolve primary difficulties in crime control, community policing, and supervision.

Technological Conceit

The police depend heavily on communications systems but not necessarily on information. Thus some themes from *Police Work* and *Narc's Game* resurface (Manning 1977, 1980a): What is the relative importance of information and ritual in organizational communication? The efficacy of technological solutions to crime control must be evaluated in light of the role of information in crime control generally, the organizational capacity to process information, the relative importance of information in operational decisions, and the role of occupational and organizational culture in routinizing and controlling messages.

Technology means most generically all the means by which things are accomplished, or a "technical means for achieving a practical purpose," and is closely linked with the notion that it is the "totality of means employed to provide objects necessary for human sustanance and comfort"(Webster's *New Collegiate Dictionary*). The technology of the police is something of a means to the end of crime control (one of several ends one might identify), whereas the accomplishment of that end requires an understanding of the relationships between ends and means (one definition of social rationality). The aim of this analysis is to connect the substantive aspects of police work—the daily rounds, the tasks, the records, and the concretely defined systems of work flow—and communications systems in particular with uses and definitions of technology. The natural system of communication, the technology, the channels, the messages sent, and the codes used must be seen within the context of human social definitions, actions, and subjectively intended meanings.

Some Observations

There are at least four types of situation in which the technology of police communications and the everyday work of the police interact; they fit together in a somewhat awkward fashion. By focusing on how the police define and use the technology, I saw not only what it meant to them but also how these meanings shape their intentions and wishes to utilize it.

The first observation emerged as I sat watching police operators answering calls from the public. They implicitly asked themselves while recognizing the need to obtain the necessary information from a caller, Do I trust this caller? Is what he or she is saying credible? If it is credible, is all or part of the call credible, and, if so, what is to be done about it? Even if the operator distrusts the call but sends it on, it is redefined as a nuisance, a trouble call, a lie, a prank, or something other than what it was represented to be. There is a list of "no goes" (in the MPD) or "phony runs," addresses to which units will not officially be sent: Some are known dope pads not to be disturbed; some are addresses from which "paranoids" or "crazies" call; some are addresses that have been harrassed previously as a result of false calls.

Operators also terminate calls if they view them as noncredible. For example, a child reported a robbery in progress and was told by the operator, "Tell your mommy to call us back with the truth." The operator then hung up. In another call an operator told a child who was mumbling into the phone and would not give the address from which he was calling to "go play in the freeway." Operators are sometimes wrong in terminating calls. In one case a woman called, claiming that she was going to be robbed and raped and that the people were trying then to break into the house. The operator told her that the crashing knocks on the door were just someone's attempt to get her attention. (They did break in, murdered her husband, and raped her, the newspaper reported later. The operator was fired.) This suggests that, if a call or caller is distrusted, the call becomes not a request for police help but something else, regardless of what is entered in the computer, recorded on the tapes, or sent on to the dispatcher.

The second observation is that the computer message is used for play by operators, controllers, and officers. For instance, BPD controllers sent around soccer scores on Saturday afternoon and sent themselves reminders to make tea, run errands, or call their spouses. They also used the computer to simulate a massive train crash. MPD operators sent messages to each other on the internal message system. They would ask how dates were, whether they could borrow money, made puns, and sent messages meant to embarrass a third party who they knew to be watching.

By playing with the machinery, the police create an alternative world of fun and games embedded within the everyday world of policing in which the machinery stands in a part-whole relationship.

Third, the police communications system provides a *partial rendition* of events on the ground. Calls are selectively recorded. Duties and functions required for the internal management of the station (for example, errands to pick up supplies outside the subdivision, paperwork on previous arrests or charges, running researchers to the train station, picking up lunch for the controller) are not entered on the machine. This creates an *official version* of what people are doing at the present time, their locations, their obligations and future obligations, their accomplishments for a given period of the day, their co-workers, their required equipment and materials, and the current official workload of the subdivision. An *unofficial version* of these same things is also created. The first is carried in the VDUs, the official paper and records, and the second is carried in the "heads" of the officers involved. Two parallel worlds of thought and action exist coterminously. The implications of this for control, management, and discipline, and the allocation of units and personnel to duties are explored in what follows.

Fourth, all the observed instances signal something about what the police trust and what they consider useful to tell the computer. As one officer said, "They're [computers] are only as useful as what you put on 'em, aren't they?" Conversely, the police consider some types of data in the computer and what they receive from it as "true," incontrovertible, and actionable in legal terms. These are messages that they consider to be the basis of "good police work," that help them "get on with the job": PNC record checks on criminal records, stolen cars based on registration, and/or license plate numbers. These are viewed as valid uses of the computer that save time and are handy when one is holding a person in a car and as crime relevant. Information so received is viewed as reliable and trustworthy. It produces the expected or "necessary"number of arrests, drunken driving citations, and signs of activity. If one objects to "producing," one can be criticized by supervisors. One young WPC tried to "get her stats up" by arresting people for failure to sign their driver's license; another officer in the same subdivision refused to engage in this and was not pressured. When the second WPC's supervisor objected and threatened to send her to speak with an assistant chief constable, she voluntarily went. The assistant chief constable agreed with her and said that she should not feel pressured to produce.

Some Products of These Encounters

These instances represents four types of encounter or use of the police communications system: trust, play and playfulness, the partial rendition of events and the dualism of police life, and outputs viewed as crime relevant. But these encounters reveal something more profound about the police system and its relationship to crime control than simply telling us that the police are lazy, frivolous, silly, or crime oriented. They may be on occasion, but they are also diligent, eager, and quite earnest and concerned with maintaining community relations and enhancing crime prevention.

There are three principal products of these police actions and the meanings they project on them. First, these definitions produce a sociotechnical system. Technology, however, can obscure ends by reifying work in terms of technology. The tradition of organizational analysis predicated on the dominance of technology [the work of Cyert and March (1963), Trist and Bamforth (1951), Emery and Trist (1965), Lawrence and Lorsch (1969), Woodward (1965), and others] construes technology in such a vague and general fashion that it is difficult to disentangle social organization from technology (Zey-Ferrell 1979). They have been defined as isomorphic: Technology is seen as the structure of the organization.

However, it is *not* the structure of organization; it is a means by which work is accomplished that interacts with other structures.

The structure of policing is only partially determined by technology. The occupational culture, the norms and values that define "good police work" or a "good copper," the commonsense assumptions about that work, and the working rules and practices that have emerged to handle its vicissitudes shape work more than technology does. One sees this in the ways memory, controller's assumptions and knowledge, call refusal, and the continued use of the incident book in the station *as if* the VDU were *not* in service occur.

The participants in the law enforcement "game" do not view their experience equally. There are contrasting versions of reality in policing, and they are directly related to the observer's position in the organization. From their perspective officers have developed quite different strategies for coping with the contingencies of their work, whether it emerges from a computer, the voice of a sergeant, or written orders. These strategies, which have only been suggested here, allow officers to set their own priorities, to queue calls, to "jump" and "swarm" to certain incidents, to draw and maintain a separation between the incident and the event, to ignore or distrust certain messages, and to interpret others in multilayered detail.

There are some general consequences of the encoding of events into police logic. In both the MPD and the BPD the occupational culture of the police is the relevant context within which to view the incident. In other words, the police connect or draw pragmatic connections between the signs contained in the heard or seen incidents and the event. They see events, regardless of their position within the communications system, as problematic. They view the communication of events as having been done on the basis of the interests and perceptions of the caller, the incident as having been received, abstracted, and coded by civilians (at two levels—by the caller and by the operators), and passed on by decision processes they may not understand [for example, the ways in which operators and/or dispatchers (controllers) queue and send incidents for attention]. They view events and incidents as changeable (temporally, spatially, and interpersonally) and uncertain (in appearance, in sequence or order, in frequency in consequences, and in content). These generalizations hold within their frame of reference, regardless of the ostensively nominal character of the event. Incidents as reported, transmitted, and recorded stand in a problematic relationship to the initial called-about event. The record and the behavioral stream accompanying it are two independent, interacting matters. Phenomenologically the effect is something like watching a film in which the sound is not synchronized with the picture. All formal systems of dispatching are necessarily based on recorded facts. They are in that sense based on necessarily partial renditions of actual events. The difficulty is that what is shared and uniform and what is variable and context bound is not known by any member of the system.

Although administrative rationality has the character of a formal public gloss on the codes, it is in a constantly changing position with respect to other modes. Its formal dominance is not sufficient to reshape and transform the coding that is done at other points in the system. This is one of the principal contradictions between authority and power in police and other organizations. There is a constant dialectic between the times found in different vertically arrayed aspects of administrative control and between the semiotics of time of indicated horizontally codes and the composite elements of the text.

Invisible rules of the game develop through a silent dialogue with the command and control system. The problems of analysis lie in discovering the rules of the game. It has been said that technology constrains the options of participants; so it does. On the other hand, the constraints on technology are perhaps less visible but no less real. Some of these constraints are attempts by officers to maintain a sense of autonomy. Crozier has written that the confrontation of the emotions and sentiments of participants with the technology, law, and formal organizational structure should play a central part in the dynamic aspects of organizational analysis:

This confrontation [between emotions and the constraints of technology] makes it possible to show that the technical, historical and environmental determinants only partially govern the rules of the game. The development of these rules also relates to the organizational capacity of its members expressed in a sequence of free decisions from managers and other members of the organization (Crozier 1972, p. 243)

If the rules of the game of policing are one of the sources of freedom and autonomy and if they play against technology, law, and informational constraints, then an analysis of the interplay of the rules of the game and the technological system must be further explored.

A second product of these encounters, the police recordings from which researchers are inclined to work, represent a selective sort of secondary social reality. The recordings are a result of the elision of aspects of information and police work that are not found in the records and official on-line status listings but are nevertheless known to have happened and to have been taken into account. This secondary reality contrasts with and exists side by side with the primary reality of immediate on the ground actions and decisions of the police, only some of which are organizationally known and logged in the files. Furthermore, knowledge that is known at another level officially is thought not to be shared fully.

Perhaps this requires further explication. Information that arises within the officer-sergeant segment of the organization is differentially shared with the "middle management" (inspectors, superintendents, and chief superintendents). For example, messages are only created when certain tacitly known conditions other than the content of the message exist: when something might "come back on you," when it is thought that something should be done or was done about the call or event, when there is an upsurge of events or calls of a particular sort, when doubt exists about whether the message will require further information to make it complete, and when a specific policy about recording calls is invoked. This means that selective and situationally known filters operate to transform calls into messages. Whatever information is officially known and said to be officially known is understood by all concerned to be a partial and selectively rendered version of the primary reality.

The existence of the official or secondary reality in concert with the primary reality has several consequences. Sometimes official versions of events are constraining and politically powerful. They can be used to investigate and assess blame and responsibility (for example, when officers do not arrive quickly at an address, further escalation of the event occurs and it becomes a public event). They can be used by outside investigators, such as inspectors, looking into a complaint to construct a version of events that does not take into account "mitigating circumstances." Unless this context of circumstances is provided, actions can be taken on the basis of information that virtually all view as false and misleading. Thus it is assumed that good police administration ignores these official records and proceeds by informal inquiries to establish the truth. For example, a chief superintendent asked a sergeant whether a certain detective could manage his job at the moment because he was having personal problems. It was decided that the detective could do the job or, conversely, that the superintendent would not enter the problems on the detective's personnel file but that he would not be given any responsibilities. He was at risk and did not know it. Another example illustrates that a certain "ticket" must be realized to create a formal record. A police view is that there must be a valid excuse to create a formal record, an "excuse" that is based on criminal law and/or on police procedures rather than on a definition that resides in community life. Many problems that demand police time and attention are not written out because the title for the event is not an officially acceptable one.

The vague and amorphous nature of expectations of police means that they are resistent to writing out or creating a record for anything that cannot be easily formulated as police business. This has the effect of making records more a representation of matters of management of the organization rather than a matter of what has been done with respect to the problem (McCabe and Sutcliffe 1978). The police record station business if it can be recorded with official language, forms, and procedures. The claims that the police have encountered everything is an accurate representation only of the primary reality. Much consultation surrounds finding the proper format for describing what was done, and the problems faced by the police are seen only if and insofar as they meet these format and procedural requirements. The records are not literal renditions of events but always bear an indexical or synecdochical relationship to what "actually happened." They are formulations of what happened for all practical purposes. Records are not kept on a large number of discretionary decisions, phone calls, inquiries to the station, and incidents dealt with but showing "no trace" on arrival. Many records of individual police officers are "idiosyncratic," and no comprehensive rules govern (in the BPD) what is shown in the vehicle logbook, incident log, occurrence book, officer's diaries, and collators' records. This is also true of the crime book itself, which is always written with the advice and assistance of the station sergeant or the inspector if he or she is available.

Just as there is a distinction made by officers between events on the ground and what is captured in the official records, there is also a distinction between what is told to other officers at the same level and to administrators. This arises from the view that all events are problematic on the ground and cannot be captured fully in records. It makes events as received subject to endless reinterpretation or gives them accountable features subject to retrospective-prospective recontextualization. An event as rendered by an observer is always seen in a context of distrust unless otherwise indicated. Controllers and others exercise discretion in their descriptions (as does the office in forwarding their messages by radio or in writing). The changeable nature of events means that, even as they are being described, processed, sent forward for attention, and dispatched, they are being shaped and reshaped. Formal systems such as computer dispatch, resource monitoring, incident controls, and headquarters command capacities for major incident controls are all based on necessarily partial reditions of actual events.

The difficulty is that what is omitted and what is included are an unknown and invisible constraint. Any command based on such a system is patterned by information and can control only those aspects of the event that are known by participants in the classification exercise and in turn by selective depictions provided by officers on the ground (who are themselves not observed by those who must later reconsider the event). The written story, or scenario, no matter how detailed, precise, full, extensive, and comprehensive, is always contextual; it is a written version of a complex event. It must omit much meaningful nonverbal material—what was seen, felt, experienced, and heard in situ by the participants. Furthermore, such a picture is in fact a linear, temporally limited description of an experience that is nonlinear, aural/oral, contextual, visual, and spatiotemporally extended.

A third product of these encounters is ignorance and error. It would appear that many of the basic assumptions of the managerial strata when viewed from the officers' perspective are inaccurate. They do not capture the meaningful dimensions of the ways in which information is defined by those on the ground; it does not capture their perspective of the work, and it does not adequately capture the intentionality of the participants. As such, the relationships between the system of control and the process of work come into radical, repeated, continuous, and occasionally disruptive contradiction. Thus there is an ongoing negotiation process within an organization to fit the formal rules of the organization to the ongoing tasks, work processes, and constraints.

Implications

There are at least two reasons why these observations and products of these observations characterize the settings in the MPD and the BPD. The first is that the occupational culture of policing provides a coping system for making the work reasonable, practical, and possible. The second is that, within the various levels of the police organization, indicated by the primary segments of constables and sergeants and other officers, fundamental drives to maintain autonomy and work control exist.

The occupational culture defines events in a way that can be managed by the police so that they are not overwhelmed with work, so that the administrative view of the work does not take the fun out of day-to-day activities, and so that the potential danger and uncertainty of the environment does not stress them to a degree that might render their collective lives impossible. Occupational culture, it might be argued from the examples of police communications systems, is something of a tertiary reality integrating the primary world of events and the secondary or official world of records. It stands in some dialectic relationship to each.

Basic assumptions of organizational analysis suggest that segments of any organization will attempt to maintain power and increase their autonomy from other segments of the same organization (Crozier 1964). This is done, according to Crozier, by means of producing, maintaining, and utilizing uncertainty, or unpredictability, in response to organizationally typical situations. The realities of primary and secondary renditions of lines of action produce an uncertainty about what is generally or specifically known, what is said to be publicly known, and what is unknown. This is turn produces contradictions mediated by the praxis of the officers. Displaying playful attitudes, distrusting certain messages, making all renditions partial of events on the ground, and trusting only a few select messages originating in the constables' segments and returned to them (PNC records, license and automobile registration checks) all maintain symbolic distance from the organization and produce further uncertainty in social relations. They also act to reduce the authority of the managerial segment in relation to lower participants. Crime control is secondary to organizational autonomy. It would thus seem that the means by which crime is controlled is always defined initially by officers on the ground. These definitions and meanings embed technology. It can be converted to the uses of the constables rather than to the end of crime control, and, if it can be so easily transformed, then its guises and its function require analysis.

8

Organizations

I have considered the imagery of organizations based on the linguistic metaphor as embodied in structuralism and provided some rather general overviews of police organizations and the intentions of police to control crime through the use of high-technology command and control systems. I have concentrated on ethnographic materials on the workings of two police control systems. A number of issues have surfaced as a result, including the limits on the informationally based structuralism arising from noninformational matters of coding, technology, roles and tasks, and interpretative work. I addressed questions arising from the linguistic metaphor, such as the limits of the language paradigm for social organization generally, the independence of message, code and coder, the tensions between diachronic and synchronic analyses, and the difficulties associated with explanations of change. Some of these questions result from the application of a formal theory of communication to an ethnographically situated account of communicational practices, but more general questions arise as well.

Findings

Semiotics has provided the metaphoric framework within which I have conceptualized organizations. With the framework in hand, I analyzed two organizations. Messages were seen in cross-sectional and in process perspective: The messages focus is informed on the one hand by information theory and structuralism and on the other by organizational analysis. It is a severely limited perspective.

In characterizing the structure of message processing, I argued that at each stage in the production of messages (event, call, message, incident, assignment, job, record) a set of *cues* or stimuli or bits of information are socially defined, given a status as phenomena, and organized as semi-coherent amalgams of meaning. The fiction of the analysis, drawn from structuralism, has been that a message exists as a set of facts transmitted by a sender to an intended receiver over a given channel. The message is encoded or decoded in accordance with rules or conventions governing accepted meaning. This fiction permits one to identify social factors that shape, constrain, guide, or are associated with a given message.

I have shown that the BPD and the MPD encode messages by supplying format-producing constraints on message choice, coding in a given category, and transforming communication from aural to visual to aural, from spoken to written to spoken, and from everyday talk to police talk. Both organizations focus and sharpen everyday images and constructions, set priorities, array the talk as "spontaneous demand," and maintain a binocular view of the message as both a formal entity and a construction of informal consensus, situated actions, and subcultural logic.

Technology gives the message a source, provides a channel, potentially a dominant channel, a means for producing feedback and ambiguity, and a mechanical form. Both organizations view technology as a cause of message production, a source of control over work, and a symbol of formal authority and supervision and indirectly of citizen control. In both the MPD and the BPD the social organization of message production is based on delegated, legitimate, and named roles with which tasks and duties are associated. As the message moves from one subsystem to the next, the aim changes from defining, organizing, filtering, classifying, and judging the credibility of the call and the caller to ordering the message as a police message governed by subcultural principles to an occasion for individual independent enterpeneurial action and the performance of variable physical, clerical, and interpersonal tasks. The matter at hand becomes organized and organizational rather than human and personal.

Interpretative work is the intersection of the cultural (meaning), the technological, and the organizational (as a structure of coercive authority). Messages *qua* messages or as a stream of unbroken communications are handled as forms without regard to content at this level. They are distinguished from diverse noise and from activities, or a field. Noise and messages interact, as do activities and messages, and the field-dependent character of the message varies temporally. As a stream, messages are clustered into types or groups of associated messages, but these type are more salient in subsystems 2 and 3 than in subsystem 1. Metaphorically grouped calls are mostly found in subsystem 3 (officers). Conversely, when messages are seen as having internally relevant features (units of information), they are attended to as well as read or merely handled. Internal message analysis requires the operation of identifying units of information, determining the salience of that bit, and placing the message in a context of other matters demanding attention (or what has been termed "surrounding understandings").

What distinguishes the MPD from the BPD with respect to the police communications system or mode of message production? Symbolically

Table 8.1
Number of syntagms used to characterize a communicational unit

Subsystem	BPD	MPD
Operators	8	7
Controllers	10	8
Officers	4	4

(encoding and interpretative work), the focusing and sharpening of communicational units in the MPD is more extreme and condensation more severe; the mechanical means of control, discipline, and supervision ensure a tighter system of coding and categorization. The effects of coding are to reduce options, to place the call in a general domain, and to separate formal from informal procedures; these are more easily seen to operate in the MPD.

The syntagms differ but tend to diminish in number as the unit moves toward environment II, even though in both organizations "everything" is sent down (little interpretation in the interest of exclusion is done). The degree of overlap in syntagms is striking (table 8.1), suggesting some general properties of police interpretations across organizations and the salience of given units. Consensus within organizations (between environments I and II) and across organizations on the relevance and salience of an item is low (about 50% or less). But these rankings are based on an acontextual notion that obviates the interpretation of the "call" as heard in each subsystem: It is not, in short, prediction of salience but of the features likely to be assessed in a given situation.

It is clear that the technological impact is greater in the MPD than in the BPD in terms of constraint on choice, supervision (autonomy), lack of feedback, dominance of a single channel (radio), technologically based ambiguity and uncertainty, and source effects more generally.

The sociobehavioral pattern (roles and tasks) in the MPD is likely to increase the caller-specific effects of processing, the tenacity of the occupational culture, and individualistic and entrepreneurial behavior, decrease reported actions, and generally center police dependency on itself rather than on technology (and the public). The BPD by contrast is less organizationally centered and technology dependent; it remains more publicly oriented, more field dependent, and noise sensitive. Stylistics seen in the execution of the roles of controller and officer and collective representations of police-public transactions are decisive differences between the two organizations. This, I assume, extends into police-public interaction in environment II.

The feature missing in a static analysis is brought out vividly in the diachronic analysis in chapter 6. The importance of chains of signification and shifts in the position of the signifier suggest that organizational analysis can examine cross-sectional data only at the risk of excluding those dynamics of change or shifts in connotative meaning that constitute social structure. The role of everyday understanding and eidetic transmissions challenge the decision tree view of a single message being examined sequentially. The codes by which time is captured are varied; the principles ordering the transformation of the event as an object change. The structuralist view is blind to the sources of stability that I have shown to be cognitive and habitual rather than organizational, informational, and technological. The differences dissolve into the social grounds for envisioning continuity.

An information systems approach is also flawed when seen as a perspective for analyzing the police communications systems. Society is seen as a set of information-meaning systems, differentially organized and hierarchically arrayed. These systems periodically emit signals that can in turn be interpreted within contexts and encoded in various ways according to rules of interpretation. Systems are linked to each other in ways that allow processes, moving and changing environments, to emit signals that cross boundaries and are subsequently converted from qualitative to quantitative indicators. Changes in ecological processes are signaled by a single act. The link between signal and act can be in terms of either informational signals (as in dances or smoke) or symbols that convey meaning (as in rituals). Changes in information across systems can be variously made credible or trustworthy. In simple societies this is done by visible, concrete means, such as when ritual actions summate ecological change and regulate system interchange. Rappaport (1971) implies that in complex societies this sanctification occurs by means of technological dominance or political authority (stripped of sanctity but legitimate). Analogously, perhaps, transactions between the civilian and the police mean that police organizations act as transducers, producing ceremonies that regulate the internal system of police organization, in belief or "nonhuman" aspects of the external system, and the operational system in Rappaport's terms. This action produces adaptation of the police as a system to short- and long-term variation in the external environment. If the communications system is a "sensor" or "homeostat" that maintains, regulates, and controls flow, there must be sensors in the environment, continuous comparisons made between the actual state of affairs and the ideal, and negative feedback (Rappaport 1971).

However, the possibility arises that (1) there are only fuzzy sensors that tend to overload and receive considerable noise and that meaning in setting is vague and information is used as a symbol internally and externally

(Feldman and March 1981); (2) the standards are unclear and there is considerable slack and loose coupling within the system and between the system and the environment; (3) the negative feedback is weak and various. The difference between simple and complex society inheres not only in this absent mechanism but also in the political context within which the ritual of communication takes place. Sanctity is problematic—the message (as information) may or may not include the social purpose of communication with "the other world." Orderliness and credibility must be maintained. When uncertainty is high, rational myths are used to justify activity on the basis of community values generally rather than on the basis of evaluation with sharp criteria and "products." Loose coupling prevails (Meyer and Rowan 1977).

What might be revealing is examples of the way in which *context* enfolds the thinly orchestrated police communications system and how context markers partition the meaningful units by which moral meanings are communicated and exchanged. Moral meanings exchanged in places and times are in every way ritually articulated and established and affirm and reaffirm the nature of the parts of the moral systems in which they occur. Underlying all such exchanges are trust and credibility. The trustworthiness of the communicant, the communication, and the recipient are reflexively linked and are inseparable. The tools by which people encode what others say, do, and believe are secondary. The code-coder-coded linkage cannot be depressed into a mechanical chain; rather, it is a loose, fragile crocheted net. This linkage is moral and tenuous, and its fabric is worthy of examining. Imagery, as I have suggested, is essential in everyday life and serves a variety of functions. When exchanges take place between absent others, imagery and reality merge and become unitary. How could it be otherwise? (Is it ever otherwise?) This needs to be explored further.

For the police, signals communicated to communications centers are in themselves mere physical stimuli and meaningless in the abstract: *All social communication is encoded meaning.* In order to understand the complexities of the encoding of calls, three general issues should be reviewed: interpretation of the signal as a sign, connection among signs of the same sign system, and relative power of categories of messages.

The first issue is the interpretation of a signal as a type of sign, an instantiation of a sign type as a sign event. Doing this requires an understanding of three interpretative bits of conduct. The link between the sign and the referent(s) is a process that can be syntactic (governed by some rules of grammar), semantic (based on similarity of meaning), or pragmatic (Peirce 1931). The relationship realized by the operators in receiving the calls cannot be resolved with reference to a table of sign-referent links. Once it is taken to be complex, the particular way in which this instance of communication (taken at the moment only at the sentence level) is linked and is interpretative in character. As Garfinkel has argued, the assumed constitutive order of events defines the "correct correspondence" between sign and referent:

What holds for sign-referent relationships holds for relationships of term and word, term and concept, phoneme and lexeme, word and meaning, behavior and action, sentence and proposition, appearance and object. All of these pairs are formally equivalent. A behavior signifies an action in terms of an assumed normative order. (Garfinkel 1963, p. 195)

The sort of "transcendence" (or context location) that can be attributed to a sign as an actual behavioral stimuli involves more than code-specific knowledge or the sign-referent pattern possibilities. The problematic nature of the correspondence is clear only when it is *not* a relationship of signification that is always mediated:

The problematic nature of this correspondence consists in providing the rules whereby it may be decided for the two, standing as they do in a relationship of signification, i.e., a sign relationship, what this relationship of signification consists of. For example, is the sign relationship one of mark, sign, symbol, index, icon, document, trope, gloss, analogy, or evidence? Or is the actual observation not an event "in the game" in the first place? (Garfinkel 1963, p. 194)

The *form* of the sign-signifier relationship has to be understood in some way by the speaker and hearer.

Actions of encoding involve ordering a series of signs in some patterned relationship, not simply as a single sign event. The construction of the message moves to higher levels of abstraction because neither the "word focus" of Saussure nor the "sentence focus" of Chomsky can provide answers to the making-sense activities of speaker and hearers over a period of time in complex discourse. That is, the actual pattern of speech is not predictable or grammatical; nor does it easily accede to organization into algorithmic structures *even after the fact*. Even question and answer sequences that are formulated as these calls are reflect both their context sensitivity and their emergent character. Cicourel has brilliantly summarized this:

The exchanges can be described as loosely coupled sets of schemata or islands of informational content or knowledge that seem to possess internal organization based on topical questions and answers. The clusters of information have a sequential appearance, but the clusters can be disjunctive at times. The schemata can be orthogonal despite their juxtaposition in serial position.

The non-algorithmic quality of the clusters in interviews and conversational exchanges can be attributed to the constraints of attention, memory searches, semantic problems associated with linking internal schemata with external representation, differences in participants' possession and attribution of knowledge, issues the participants want to pursue, and issues triggered by the exchange. Hence emergent topics may occur that are not related to the ... motivation to seek ... help. (Cicourel 1975, p. 55)

The process described involves chunking and coding bits of information, searching memory files for related schemata, sorting out irrelevant items, and working out a kind of syntactic structure of the reported event while making a series of assumptions about the communicant. These matters are summarized by Garfinkel as the "assumed-normative character of events which must be assumed by speaker-hearers if such phenomena are to be construed as perceivedly normal events"; the character of their being "normal" in this sense is a contrast with a conception of events as criminal, deviant, or otherwise naughty (Garfinkel 1963, pp. 214–215). These issues touch on sign-referent patterning and its relationship to events in the normalized world.

A second general issue is that of the connection between signs within a sign system. We have noted that signifier and signified can be constituted within an open or closed system of interpretation. For example, a highway traffic sign system is a closed interpretative system, whereas literary criticism is an open or hermeneutic system. Messages to police departments, despite the format effect, require an elaborate hermeneutics or interpretative exercise. Once placed within a given system of interpretation, such as the police format for classification of messages, two interpretative questions arise. The first is the nature of the relationship between signs in the system: Is it analogical or homological in structure? It is argued by Guiraud (1973) that scientific classification systems are homological, mutually exclusive, cumulative, consistent, and organized in a binary (or zero-sum fashion) and that the relationships between the categories do not change with time, context, coders, or the content of the item being classified. *None of these assumptions holds for complex everyday life systems.* Nor do they hold internally for police classification systems.

The third issue, given a system of classification, is the relative *power* of available categories to frame messages as instances of objects in the social world. This might be called the strength of the items within a classification system rather than the hegemony or authority of a given system. Categories are obviously not of equivalent power or authority and thus possess an unequal potential to drive the message as it moves through the system.

Classification schemata are made problematic by the perceptive subtleties of Needham (1972, 1978, 1979). Any classification or ordering is based on difference and context, but the notion of difference depends on two entities connected in the same way, and this connection varies not only by context but also by the tacit connections, the noninformational aspects of the discourse, that are made in the dialectics difference. The connections between categories vary, even when they are defined as oppositions, transformations, inversions, negations, and the like. The episteme itself (the set of rules for organizing discourse) cannot produce an algorithmic set of syntactic structures as a representation of the sequence of the telling. Certain forms of similitude remain in the coding of human experience.

Interpretation can be seen as poetic. In organizations messages may possess a poetic imagery such that tacit and implicit meanings are made salient or highlighted; on the other hand, "obvious" meaning can be "suppressed" or elided. The eidetic mediation of experience is unexplicated in formal theories. The question of meaning and intention is fundamental to the reading of signals as messages. The place of affective involvements and affective depictions is not addressed in this formulation. The relationships between the selecting and sorting of signals into messages is based on an agreed on set of signs. The signs are mapped onto the formal classification system, leaving the sign-referent relationship unexplicated.

The practices by which coding occurs are not well known. Clearly, when operators hear calls, they engage in the interpretative practices described by Cicourel. The keying of the event is critical to its transformation into an object of scientific or practical investigation. Given the centrality of the oral telephone channel, this keying can only be done on a limited range of dimensions of the speech act by means of limited channels and primarily with the voice and silence. The ordering of the question and answer sequence is not given in informational relations (or the algorithms discussed) because the link between the questions and the answers is not given in the temporal positioning of a sequence of utterances (Cicourel 1976; Goffman 1981). Thus sorting and classification involve (such) recognized communicative work and encoding into police logic.

Information, Messages, Rules

Message analysis, which is derived from communication and information theory, is based on the notion that there is one message exchanged between two parties (the "sender" and the "receiver") and that there is a consensus about the nature of the exchange, the roles, the message, the units, and the "secondary matters" referred to by MacKay [see also Cooper (1983b, 1985, 1986)]. There are some further assumptions of message analysis that bear the initial burden of my argument in the first chapters of this book:

1. Each message is an independent unit or vehicle that can be defined unproblematically, selected easily from other messages, encoded validly and reliably, and is trustworthy.

2. Each message arises in and represents a segment of the social world that is differentially organized with respect to the information available and presented or transmitted.

3. Each message is holistic and unitary in a given subsystem and in each of the other subsystems in precisely the same fashion.

4. Each message signifies or stands for an object and event in the primary empirical social world and is not a dream, fabrication, lie, or systematic distortion. The content of messages is unaffected by such organizational matters as workload, technology, classification or coding system, discretionary practices, organizational differences in structure, technology, and role-task organization, or interpretative work. Information and meaning are equivalent.

5. The system of message transmittal is a closed informational system; that is, information is neither gained nor lost in the process of transmission through a police communications system.

6. The unit message is the basic term for the analysis of organizational processing of calls to the police. Code, classification system, and message are assumed to be independent of the coder and the encoding process.

7. All aspects of language structure, grammar, syntax, and phonemics are viewed independent of context. Context markers are clear, shared, unchanging, and located in stipulated ecological settings or subsystems of organizations.

8. The message-processing system is recursive, iterative, and nonreflective.

9. All categories within a classification system are equal in the strength of their framing. Information, as passed on through messages, is the basis for police decisions, allocation of resources, strategies and planning, and responses to calls for service.

The message focus of such a view obviates a concern with the fundamentals of organization (a means for ordering choice) and complexities associated with the embeddedness of messages in socially meaningful interactions and structures. Some problems are associated directly with the complexity of social structures.

The isolated nature of the message has been discredited. I now argue that what is or is not a message is operationally and phenomenologically defined. It is an "interpretant" (Eco 1976, pp. 68–72) or something from which something else can be read. The message disappears into a set of signs, each with varying salience, and into noise and the field at other times. It changes form, location, channel, genre, surface features, and key defining words. It can be framed within metonically or metaphorically organized clusters. Depending on the subsystem and organization, it takes on different levels and a number of connotative meanings.

A message is a dialectical concept, by which I mean that it contrasts with and is wedded to what it is *not* at any given moment: It extends backward and forward in time because its meaning must be "predicted" at some point as well as accepted. It is a bit from an undefined whole of experience. (It is missing from a whole at some point, and abstracted from it now.) It is selected from among other (potential) messages at any point in time and plays off and on this sequential relevance. It is produced by forces out of sight to the sender and receiver but doubly represents both, one to the other (Cooper 1985).

Messages change in character whether one is oriented to message handling or internal message analysis. Messages shift between being objects of mechanical rules to being objects of cultural rules. Messages are bound like the fibers of a rope or, as Wittgenstein wrote, "by a vast number of overlapping similarities" (1969, p. 87).

Messages are not things but ideas or collective representation. Thus no "essence" or a truth beneath "elaborations" exists for them; nor is a single instance pointed to as one of a concrete type or sort. It is always something *and* something else.

I have shown several times how these changes in meaning of messages are found in the two organizations, but consider:

A "domestic" can be a crime, an order, or an information-only job, depending on the connotative association of the key words in a subsystem.

Information-only messages become "dead" messages as defined at that point.

A communication unit changes from a forward-looking call about an event to a backward-looking incident and becomes again forward-looking as it moves from environment I to environment II.

The tighter the mechanical guidance of the message, the more cultural definitions intrude.

The similarities within and across messages are produced by various forms of analogical thinking, ostensive definitions, and training (Wittgenstein 1969).

Of course, all this sees the message as a single bounded text. However, once it becomes a focus for internal scrutiny, it can be variously constructed or selected for. That is, as a cluster of signifiers, the message dissolves into a field pointing away from itself. For example, when a message is classified as a "domestic" in the MPD, it refers to itself as a police message having certain internal practical and aesthetic features and as a lock to an event in environment I and a fluid situation in a social world (environment II). This generates ambiguities for messages as wholes and as constituted parts. If these points remain, then it is more than abundantly clear that a message is a selectively constituted organizational product, as much a reflection of perspective or aspects as elements said (or seen) to constitute it.

I have also argued that a message is a function of rules for processing and rules guiding the handling of ambiguous messages (metarules). The rules are in some ways a means for defining facts, or relevant facts in a message, rather than a means for handling facts that have been preconstituted. They are in effect a closed system of reasoning supported by the primary rule for organizing data: "whenever there is an apparent contradiction or disjunction between observable phenomena which can be taken as the referent of an idea and the implications of the idea itself, the interpretation of the phenomenon, not the idea, is modified" (Leaf 1972, p. 240). This sort of rule is a "director" or metarule and sensitizes the reader to the issue of rules in general as a feature of communication.

The notion of rules is itself problematic (Winch 1958; Hart 1961; Wittgenstein 1969). Rules are generalized statements that stand for options in problematic situations. They are administratively supported procedural guidelines having nominal authority within an organizational context or boundary. They signal authority when invoked. They may also stabilize and order situations that have diverse character as ostensive empirical events. In these senses of the word, rules are objective statements or norms. Rules also index and are indexed by feelings, diffuse cognitive thoughts, or a sense of social structure (Cicourel 1968). These features of rules suggest their indexical power. Rules both order and disorder situations because their invocation can arise from either sense of the unfolding lines of action. Rules stand in and stand for situations and cannot be seen except as "in action."

Work in semantic information processing (Minsky 1968) suggests a further consideration about the hierarchical nature of rules. The core meaning of a rule, that which is reputedly seen as a relevant cognitive domain situationally, can be the basis for constructing a hierarchy of relevance of rules. The most general rules may assume the position of metarules, which order the relevance of other rules. In the behavior of operators and dispatchers, I could discern rules that governed their behavior in situations involving ambiguous calls. These first-level rules, such as the use of analogical reasoning, belief, tacit knowledge, and nonexclusive classification, are operationally submerged and fairly nonreflexive. Rules for organizing ambiguous calls are reflexive in that they are called on once the operator recognized features of the call. The calls must first be trusted, and as such this is a guiding or preference rule constraining or bringing into play the following rules for organizing ambiguity: the believing-is-seeing rule, the referential primacy of words rule, the normal rule, the just-in-case rule, and the minimal data coding rule.

Rules are self-validating once the "director" or preference rule is mentally invoked. They follow from the presumption. This means that the texture of a rule-governed situation is "thick" in Geertz's terms (1973) because director-validated subroutines are guided by rules whose only reality lies in their being framed as relevant by the director rule(s). The director rule is available for all practical purposes when the operation of first-level rules has been questioned. The question is answered by other rules producing a set of subprograms. Thus:

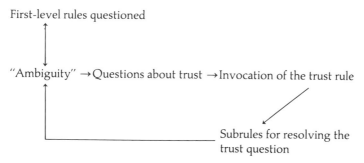

First-level rules questioned

"Ambiguity" → Questions about trust → Invocation of the trust rule

Subrules for resolving the trust question

Each rule, when invoked, connotes its opposite even as it denotes a situation. The consequences are dialectically generated by merged opposition. As Needham (1971) writes about "belief," context is supreme, not the word, rule, or procedure that it generates for resolution. Rules are effects as well as causes of action.

Thus all communication is mediated in some way, or in other words, all communication is symbolic, referencing the sender, the receiver, and itself simultaneously. It is encoded, but the precise nature of this can never be fully resolved because messages always leave more to be said or thought; they cannot "stand alone." Messages exist as stable entities in part because they partake of familial resemblances unrevealed by language.

Let us ask the question: Suppose I had explained to someone the word "red" (or the meaning of the word "red") by having pointed to various red objects and given the ostensive explanation.—What does it mean to say, "Now if he has understood the meaning, he will bring me a red object if I ask him to"? This seems to say: If he has really got hold of what is in common between all the objects I have shown him, he will be in the position to follow my order. But what is it that is in common to these objects? (Wittgenstein 1969, p. 130)

An implication I have only alluded to is that, insofar as organizations create or *enact* the resemblances or similarities among incidents (for example, "crime," "order," "information only"), created incidents produce responses based on their tacitly known clusterings based on unexplored cognitive processes. The framing of messages, seen in the algorithms in chapters 4 and 5 (figures 4.2 and 5.2) and the paradigms of action versus nonaction are frames for a language game. They are metaphors for action seeing, a set of signs in a text seen as having police-relevant meaning.

This formulation also assumes that messages and information are non-problematic. This is an equally false and misleading belief. Information has been defined as a difference that makes a difference, a unit, or "a measure of one's freedom of choice when he selects a message" (Shannon and Weaver 1964, p. 9). It is thus, in information theory, a unitary, sharply defined, bounded unit subject to quantification and formalization (Cherry 1978). The message is seen as a function of the sender (who sets the limits by transmissions) and "envisions the message source as a fixed set of possible communications" (Leaf 1972, p. 7). But "source" is a structure of socially defined, normatively integrated networks giving rise to a message carried through an established channel. Because I have shown that a message is a social construction that cannot be separated from the act of defining the facts contained in such a text, the process of communicating messages is always only a *part* of a whole pointing to many features of a social situation and setting. Thus use of a source, production of a message, symbolic communication "becomes a part of, or reinforces, the structure and contributes to the organization and content of the message source for the next communication in that set of users of the source" (Leaf 1972, p. 7). Communications articulate reality in that a source in police operations is also a destination; it shares with language the capacity to communicate about the world and to be self-referential and to symbolize or stand for the attachments between ostensive senders and receivers.

Thus we encounter the question of the role of information in social structure, especially corporately organized, coercively articulated structures. Information presumes a difference and a prior extensive undifferentiated *whole*. "It is a binary structure based on division" (Cooper 1983a, p. 3), and "a division both separates and joins because the act of separation creates the perception of something that is also whole or unitary." One can focus on information as on two forces juxtaposed, the rim of a glass, or the division between frame and message; on message and field or message and noise; on the overlap or "shared wholeness" of the points that a message must be seen as not-noise and noise as not-message; or on the separate parts—signs within the message, a single message, or a set of them—or a type of noise (for example, technogically produced noise). Following Cooper, I assert that the primary structure (overlap) and secondary structure (individual parts) are in tension and can be dynamically related. "Information or structure [is] a dynamic relationship between primary and secondary structures" (Cooper 1985, p. 6). It is this sort of structure that constitutes organization or the differences that are institutionalized and sanctioned by power and authority.

This formulation suggests, as Cooper does, that organized communication always has a "double reference" to primary and secondary structures, which are themselves in a reversible and reflexive position. They stand in theoretic terms as zero, having value only as the focus on alterations or as these indicate structure or organization.

Unlike single exchanges, stimuli, or messages in information theory terms, information in this view is reflexive, or, more simply, depends on reciprocity of exchange between whole and parts, or, more concretely, between individuals or between an individual (an organizational actor) and the organization. Because this is true, the essential "otherness" of communication must be reaffirmed. That is, a sign is incomplete without its interpretant, and a message is incomplete unless it is validated or seen to be received. By the same reasoning, individuals do not experience a feeling of loss or difference except as part of a whole. One desires to be both alone and apart, a desiring person who shares experience with others, including a potential loss of self.

> It is precisely this sense of loss that defines the human condition.... Social organization is a system of information exchange whose function ... is to defer loss of itself. The actors in the social structure thus represent themselves to each other as lacks of a larger whole. Desire is the presence of a lack or loss that is represented to us by another, whose desire is the reflection of in our own lack. It underlines the ontological, as opposed to the instrumental, basis of knowledge, that is, lack is information that is missing to being....
>
> The other, or organization, shares out "an essentially indivisible and permanent whole." (Cooper 1983b, pp. 215–216)

Organizations strive to mediate differences and in a sense provide unity. That is, of course, a paradox shared with language more generally, for it, too, transmits meaning by contrast and distinction in a whole or context. Rationality is a formal way of sharing a lost whole (Cooper 1983a). It is linked then with control of desires (individuals and their needs) and their "repression" or producing order from entropy—hence the need for sanctity and legitimacy organizationally and institutionally discussed in *Police Work*.

Knowledge, as a systematic extension of this idea, is not always fully understood, as Wittgenstein reminds us (1969) in his series of examples of doing, comparing, knowing, and surprise. Thus intrinsic knowledge stands midway between primary structures of desire, need, and idiosyncratic feelings and secondary structures of rationality, control, and distribution. Intuitive knowledge is that which cannot be systematized, cannot be easily written out yet is a part of the very opposition of "seeing," the expectation of behavior accepted as a part of being a normally competent member of society. It is this knowledge and experience that should guide wisdom and judgment, not "rationality" seen in artificially drawn decisions and inferred after the fact from an observed capacity to accomplish some practical end.

Structuralism As a Metaphor and Organizational Meaning

Structuralism was behind our search for a theory of the production of organizational meaning. It suggested a way to creep into communication and integrate various forms, channels, and modalities of sense stimuli to try, as Cicourel wrote (1976), to map meaning onto syntactic and grammatical categories and to integrate, as humans do, modalities of sense intake, short- and long-term memory, selective memory and attention, the differential distribution of knowledge, and various forms of communication (speech, writing, visual nonverbal sequences, pictures on television and on VDUs). In a specific way structuralism has guided the search for underlying structure in calls to the police, police subculture, priorities and algorithms, and call-message processing and the assumption of an underlying code. Although cognitive anthropology had produced taxonomies (Tyler 1969), it had no general theory of communication that could confirm shared domains of, for example, color, disease, firewood, weddings, and illness. If there is a deep similarity, it is not clear how it articulates various codes in a society or indeed in an organization. Although codes can produce several formally similar types of calls, they have different similarities in different subsystems. This cannot be explained merely as an elaboration of a code.

The approach advocated by semanticists is to identify key signs, points of stability, that freeze the signifier-signified relation. Researchers have used legal categories and the police classification system as frozen signifiers. From this police communication has been elevated to a single form of rational transaction between two reified parties, the "citizen" and "police," who serve or "request" or "demand" or provide. Meaning in police communication cannot be captured in a single set of signifiers, texts, codes, or words because signifiers shift by context, codes require interpretation, and organized understanding and not action can be verbalized. This is in part due to the projected otherness of meaning.

All meanings are rooted and reflected in language, which existed before a person's existence, outside his or her experience, and which provides the structure of choice for individual expression. It is a condition for meaning. Meaning is found in world of others' interpretations; it is not imposed by authoritative structures but is limited. Neither is it constructed by individuals because they can only do so with materials, behavior, symbols, and ceremonies available in the culture. "Structure" is best described as a metaphor with slippage, or a cluster of connotative meanings. As Eco writes (1984): "No algorithm exists for the metaphor, nor can a metaphor be produced by means of a computer's precise instructions, no matter what the volume of organized information to be fed *in*" (p. 127). A metaphor's success is due to a sociocultural format that organizes a "network of interpretants" and "the identities and differences of the properties" (p. 127).

Several points about the relationship of metaphor to organizational communication can be made. Cognitive scientists have defined metaphor as an association among metonymically analyzable items. It retains a kind of frame character in which the freeze frames are sought once a perspective or theme is established. This does not recognize the sloppy everyday nature of metaphor or the embeddedness of much talk in anaphoric and deictic (implicit) references. Who is talking for whom? in the name of what? by what means can the metaphor be understood formally or even purely cognitively? Such understanding draws on the studied nature of each sentence and "rhetorical comprehension [which is] dependent upon general world and situational knowledge" (Grimaud 1983, p. 152). Thus metaphor is always to some degree representational and has its origins in rebuslike allusions to shared (presumed) knowledge experience. Form or discourse frames many metaphors, setting the stage for literal and/or "exceptional" types of metaphors. This is a characteristic of organizations. That is, typical or routine metaphors and metonymic patterns are produced in police communication, and these contrast with patterns that suggest linguistic anomalies.

The cognitive semantics presented in chapters 4 through 6 were influenced by Eco and do not resolve the word focus or even the sense focus of that sort of work. That is, using "rape" as a sign only makes a synecdochical expansion from a word to a seme (Culler 1975, pp. 77–81) to a message to a subsystem context. Seeing "rape" as a signifier does not solve the question, What is a sign? [which is unanswerable with respect to level of abstraction according to Peirce; see Eco (1984, pp. 2–3)].[1] But linguistics is best dissolved into rhetoric in that it might be better to see speech as being only a point in a field of meaning. Not only does a message change in connotative reference, it also changes its field and noise surrounding, which in turn changes its embeddedness (Goffman 1983a).

The police metaphor is a form of talking about behavior as conduct or readily constituted actions. It closes off non-action-relevant categories and claims on police time by either "killing" a message, not making it a message at all, or refusing to act (at the operator level). Once it is a message, it must be decontextualized or deconstructed to retrieve its "original" meaning. Conversely, messages are ritualized and converted into metaphoric speech.

Structuralism relies on metaphors, as does all scientific theory (Orotony 1979); however, structuralists assert that one code, structure, or narrative is represented by a text. Poststructuralism has questioned whether structures of meaning correspond to "some deep-laid mental 'set' or pattern of mind which determines the limits of intelligibility" (Norris 1982, p. 3). Deconstruction simply means the eschewal of a single determinant range of surface meanings of a text read from an identified or single code (Culler 1982). Some of the connotative meanings derivable from a code are overcoded or ritualized (Eco 1976, p. 14; 1979, p. 19).

This latter point in any search for a metaphor for organizational communication is critical. MacCannell (1981) has argued that "ritual" refers to a basically political act of seizing on discrepancy between one code and another in a given situation in which the *difference* is sanctioned as appropriate; "ritual is an act of signification which does not so dependably establish a particular interpretation as it establishes a *difference* between itself and practical behaviour" (MacCannell 1981).

The gap between behavior (which, it must be emphasized, is an interpretant, not an actual physical action of some sort) and ritual, another encoded interpretant, is a difference, itself encoded in some fashion. So, for example, when somebody twice calls the BPD for another person to report that "dogs are in her garden" and is told to provide the required information, the caller is being subjected to a framing, a prefatory opening that signals a ritualized power exchange. The caller reports behavior and says, "I'm phoning for my neighbor; she'd like somebody to come," a request that puts a narrative voice or modality (phoning for someone else) speaking on her behalf (synecdoche), saying she'd like "somebody" (police metonymy) "to come" (ellipsis: to her house to deal with the dogs, find the culprits, calm her). This exchange is predicated on the paradox of all human communication: It is a lie, because to use signs is to present a version of one's situated life. It can always be otherwise.

> It is obvious that when someone creates metaphors, he is, literally speaking, *lying*, as everybody knows. But someone who utters metaphors does not speak "literally": He *pretends* to make assertions and yet wants to assert *seriously* something that is beyond literal truth. How may one "signal" such an ambiguous intention? (Eco 1984, p. 89)

Eco suggests a way out by stipulating an encyclopedia of listings, or a range of possibilities from which dictionary meanings are drawn. Encyclopedias provide rules for interpretation, whereas dictionaries stipulate them (Eco 1984, pp. 46–86). I have briefly explored the notions of context markers, thematization, frames, and framing as means for limiting lexical choice and semantic extension. I have claimed that calls are transformed into messages by organizationally determined roles, tasks, codes, technology, and interpretation, that the working of transformation is symbolic and indicates a liminal condition, that such working is a way of seeing one thing in terms of another, and that these workings are described in the police subculture. These units are cast in Eco's terms in an institutional code, which follows *deontic logic*, or the logic of preferences (Eco 1984, p. 179). The communicational unit is seen in terms of a set of categories into which it is coded, metaphorized as a police-relevant symbolically marked incident. Consider the following example:

BPD: What's the address?

Caller: [Gives address; operator enters address on VDU.]

BPD: What district is that?

Caller: [Gives district.]

BPD: Yeah, what's your name, just for the record?

Caller: My name is Mrs. Canny I live next door, but one . . .

BPD: Yeah, what's your number then?

Caller: [Gives number and then relates that dogs are in the neighbor's garden. Operator types in information.]

BPD: Yeah. All right, we'll get someone down to see you.

Caller: OK. Thank you, luv. Bye-bye.

BPD: . . . Bye-bye.

The operator has made all the important choices. Precisely, the gap signaled by questions in order after the initial interchange about address, name, caller's address, and relation to the called-about district, the non-verbal clicks of the word processor keys signaling a concern with the technology of transformation, the implicit authority in granting the request, and the closing of the exchange, marking the end of what Goffman (1981) terms a "memorable event." The absence of any expressed concern about the persons, property, or relations by the operator also signals neutral authority. What is omitted from reference signals ritual, as does what is included.

The work of interpretation sets out a difference that can itself be deconstructed in two fashions. The first is that each rendition of a behavior, in this case the police "rewriting" a human problem, ritually undermines some aspect of it and overvalues some other features—an invisible proportion is struck. The second is that social life establishes situated conventions. If one interrupts another's speech or act or paper, this calls for an account or excuse. If it is absent, the silence speaks for the interrupter. The negative or absent matter negates the negation or signals awareness of an unwillingness to accept a ritual order. It comments on silence, a gap between action and ritual. In the example police undervalue emotion, feeling, or life situation in the call but postpone response to later (sending an officer), a sign of authority and of a "referential" orientation to the call. It also represents an overvaluing of format-derived information. Police also value institutional preference over personal preference with respect to interpretation. The act of ritualization, an awkward word for the selective rendition of features of life, is a kind of mini–myth production that stabilizes message meaning and the institution of policing. It is the process of overcoding and difference that produces laminated meanings from texts. So, as I have argued, the first set of signs in the "dogs in the garden" call were in the primary world of experience and were selectively coded (as seen in sections on coding, especially format effects), which in turn produces a difference between reported (lay) behavior and code *ritualized* by operators, later by dispatchers, and finally by officers.

Each transition across a discourse domain produces liminal states that are marked by ritualized transformations ["taking on the difference" as Cooper would argue (1983b)] and counterfactually stabilized (Luhmann 1981). There is, as Eco shows, also the hyperelevation of codes, which might be called mythological in character in that, by overcoding or by the difference between two codes (for example, practical everyday life and police) as authoritative and sanctioned, great ideational realities are reified. This is a political act.

This was broadly explored in *Police Work* and with respect to drugs, in *Narc's Game* (Manning 1977, 1980a). The invisible repression of certain political acts, such as controlling the powerless and poor, beating prisoners, lying on television about police aims and objectives, and refusing service to callers is done through myth. What myth does by working on contrasts between codes, not conduct, is to disconnect action from accountability, discussion, and scrutiny. It disconnects itself from a referent other than those it creates (MacCannell 1981, p. 20).

Ritual is always about someone and directed to and from someone, as MacCannell reminds us, so it depersonalizes meanings and sets out a reality of lies, for if one communicates symbolically, one must inevitably be seen to lie. Myths are formalized lies and are at the heart of social order.

The Limits of Structuralist Organization Theory

An organization is not a thing, does not occupy a single place or time (although density of interaction in a space is a signified of the signifier organization), and cannot be identified except as *not* an environment on which it depends for existence. As a semiotic construction an organization is best seen as a system of codes for signs. The task of organizational analysis is to define "organization" and distinguish it from other social forms, to assert a set of metaphors and concepts within which organizational analysis can proceed, to place organization" in societal (institutional legal, interactional, etc.) context, and to establish correlations or conditions under which other causes, effects, or correlations occur, given an alternative definition of "organization."

This delimitation requires further limitation. All ideas contain inherently contradictory metaphysical ideas and language; even stipulative language cannot escape connotative meanings or be contained by speakers' intentions. Explanations are never adequate to explain assertions because tacit knowledge is far too broad and complex to be fully captured in any given set of specific explanations. Furthermore, theory and method are means of disclosing objects, giving them a reality—language is a construct that itself outlines social worlds within which one sees or grasps features of the world.

The Linguistic Metaphor

The working assumption, almost the fundamental assumption, of this analysis has been that language models the social world. It has been appreciated, of course, that the implied division is nonexistent: How could one establish the existence of a social world without linguistic signs? Method produces its fruits. Is social life a model, perhaps a tacit, cognitive but not systematic model on which language is based? Are all types of social order ordered, encoded, and decoded by means of the same deep structure? The analogue seems at this point stretched because, although formal rules or principles may be identified as abstractions (such as number, color, and assertions of a propositional sort), the formal notation merely aggregates diverse connotative meanings and does not dissolve them (Wittgenstein 1969). For example, organizational rules, especially procedural and regulatory rules, have an open context and can be endlessly extended and elaborated (Hart 1961; Wittgenstein 1969; Manning 1982a).

A number of works, especially the tour de force of Jonathan Culler (*Structuralist Poetics*), raise serious questions about the applicability of the linguistic model to the study of meaning, especially to text-bound meaning. It has been noted that the application of linguistic metaphor to social life perhaps places undue weight on the assumption that language *is* reality. Colin Sumner writes: "There is an absence of argument as to why these concepts are appropriate: the metaphor becomes the reality" (1978, p. 78). The mechanical language of nineteenth-century physics is used in modern structuralism as in information theory, but it is unclear that discourse can be easily disaggregated into informational bits that take their meaning from an ordering system of relationships governing their significance. This assumes, as Sumner points out, that the system is static and unchanging, that each bit, although it may vary in strength, has its strength provided by context, that the code used (not multiple codes) is universal and shared, that the communications system is autonomous and not embedded in other "external" systems of constraints, that the relationship between the sender and the receiver is based on agreement, and that information is equivalent to meaning, noise to misunderstanding, and feedback to learning. The extension of physicalistic language, when combined with the superordinate status of the linguistic model more generally, has created difficulties for social science [if not for communications theory more generally; compare the changes in the three editions of Cherry's *On Human Communication* (1957, 1966, 1978)].

The work of the poststructuralists contains an attempt to broaden the basis of analogies and the substrate of quasi-linguistic models: Neologisms, puns, and even stylistic barbarisms are treated as "imaginative." The apparent aim is, as much as anything, to produce in literary or "academic" texts the sort of shocks of awareness, shifts in mood, and interpenetrations of logic with poetics that are considered aspects of the stylistics of poetry. Regardless of the several sources of this wordplay and play words (cultural, social, personal-biographical, logical), wordplay contributes to the sense in which the fringe meanings and aims of poststructuralism are nonlogical. Playfulness subtly attacks the linear zero-sum binary logic of structuralism as originally conceived and even prose and the bourgeois model of the novel as a narrative form.

Can the linguistic analogy, the "linguicity" in Said's terms (1973), of life be properly extended to all sorts of settings, from literary texts to organizational texts, records, files, interview data, the spatiotemporal patterning of activities, the structure of roles and tasks in organizations? Drawn from these sources, can inferences be made about higher-level abstractions, such as myths, political mandates, and domains? What additional knowledge is gained by this approach in reference to understanding the relational constants within an organization and environment-organization transactions? This issue is related to the issue concerning the place of change, history, and process and thus to the more substantive relevant question here of the evolution and development of organizations as systems of signs, as bounded activity systems and spheres of discourse (Weick 1979).

Language, no more than any system of signs, can adequately define, model, or completely capture social relations, for what is aimed for is an analysis of representations in all their affecting, imaginary, rich contextualized facets. "Messages," "information," "organization," and "technology" are dialectic situational concepts; they arise from differences and are not isolated, single, locatable present phenomena.

Likewise, "organizational culture" cannot by analogy replace "organization," "occupation," or technological-strategic models that preoccupy the contributors to *Administrative Science Quarterly.* The fashionable rejection of such concepts as efficiency for situated action or contextual rationality, stories and tales for rules and regulations, symbols for material culture, or ideas for technology (as signs, they should be in quotes) (see the December 1983 culture issue of *Administrative Science Quarterly*) does not draw on semiotics or on linguistics as master models. It simply treats past organizational analysis as ironic. It is passing an ironic touch over past research, and conventional wisdom, the dead hand of positivism, is ever so slightly animated. The assumption is still made, as Pinder and Bourgeois (1983) show, that language and reality stand in some kind of opposition in which the language of science is one of precision drifting to literalism, whereas poetry, fiction, novels, and art are metaphoric or figurative in nature. Of course, the cage of organizational discourse preempts open revelation of the chaos and poetry of life, its self-reflexive, creative, and spontaneous nature. Only glimpses are given (Broms and Gahmberg 1983).

How does the change seen in chapter 6 arise? The cognitive stability that permits messages to flourish, flow, and to be seen as bounded entities is in opposition to the factors producing differentiation in the two police organizations. They are two parts of a whole, a differentiating metonymic series within an organizational metaphor. The need is for a context-bound logic and a situated rationality that encompasses organizational communication (Putnam and Pacanowsky 1983; Weick 1979, p. 83).

Situated Rationality

Previous studies have established the limited utility of the concept of long-term rationality and have suggested the relevance of a "bounded rationality" (Simon 1976), "situated rationality" (Mannheim 1949; Manning 1980a), or "enactment" (Weick 1979). Weick (1983a) has previously outlined views of information, message organization, and environment that are based on logical analysis of knowledge in action, or praxis, or on doing and then discovering what has been done and labeling it.

The analysis of organizational behavior that has precluded the final section has been based on presumptions about language, thought, and experience, drawing on the fertile writings of Karl Weick, Rodney Needham, and Erving Goffman. They outline a program for further research and a focal limitation. Perhaps a final résumé of these ideas will serve as a kind of conclusion to this volume. It has been argued that language is not a mirror for nature (Rorty 1979) but is a crude system of signs from which one can analogically capture segments of a social world. This permits a kind of "sizing up," a sort of heuristic for uncertainty. In a tentative fashion I have shown (for example, in the case of surrounding understandings and salience of bits) that all categories of calls, bits with a format, or messages are understood as contextualized oppositions, the relations between which are unstated but understood within each subsystem, as "as if" guesses about a matter at hand, a predicted but unknown and fluid future and a past (an event) that are conflated in the message, and as symbolic forms related by interpretative work to formal decision rules, discourse formulas, syntax and grammar, various sense modalities, formal rules and technologies, and, in particular, words.

All forms of formal logic for capturing such equivocality and ambiguity are couched in or demonstrate a conventionalized notation or logic but do not reveal the constitutive conventions, what has been termed here the "occupational culture" by which the information takes on centrality and meaning with respect to organizational plans, agendas, or aims. Any notation will contain convenient room into which all sorts of abstractions can be fitted rather than a single abstraction fitted neatly by a notation (Needham's 1982 lectures). Thus messages are like Wittgenstein's arrows (1969, pp. 33–34, 95–98), or signs such as those I have noted over the years:

"Help wanted" on a theater marquee.

"Way in" and "Use other door" on the same door.

"Grand opening" (large sign over smaller "Closed" sign in window).

"Opening hours 8–12, 1–5" (on a closed door at 1:15 P.M.; door is closed all summer to contain the air conditioning).

"Not an entrance" (on a door).

In each of these examples a change in aspect is a change in meaning, but the ways in which such logical contradictions or others [such as between thought and action (Needham 1972)] "work" cannot be formally demonstrated or written out in rules (Needham's 1982 lectures). Variety in coding context is never specified, so organizational language is an attempt to reduce perceived variety ("information") in the environment to simplify and routinize work and social relations, to signal events of a certain type as relevant, to constrain type-token relationships to "a manageable range," and to signal ritualization. This "bounds" rationality according to Weick (1983a) but maintains the loose coupling explained here [see also Manning (1977)].

Even framing or some attempt at discerning the rules guiding experience or formulating it can never provide the rules for applying the frame to a given event; speech is always partial, and all that is worth knowing cannot be said or reproduced in words. As Needham has argued, the aim of comparative sociology is to understand representations in their various settings, organizations, cultures and societies.

When one speaks of framing or recalling a memorable event, the implication is a focus on remembering a set of facts, an address, a particular name or crime or arrest. But these are seen in an aspect or context, which might be seen as a situation having objective or material facets, phenomenological facets, boundaries, and placement in space and time. These constitute the facts and make the differences, which are all that matter. They also create the "trace" of Derrida, the remnants of what is *not* the focus in a situation but that make the basis from which a difference is masked. A formal language of "domestic" or "burglary" allows one to refer to a range of concrete cases or situations lacking essential similarity (Malcolm, speech at Michigan State University on October 11, 1968). Whatever is a common response is the case, the messages, the events: Meaning is indicated in the response to them.

An agenda for comparison would recognize that images or talk about images is enduring and the basis on which people indicate or point to commonality. This book is an encyclopedia of pointers, no more. Pointing is a game that is itself a basis for feelings. These may be talked about using conventional genres, vocabularies, or constitutive conventions (such as those that frame art schools or architectual styles), or they may be commercialized emblems. The basic markings of experience, sounds, rituals, smells, colors, and spatial arrangements are the product of language and the cause of linguistically described experience.

By isolating facts, seeing rationality as standing outside a situation of apparent conjuction, one can separate persons from the resonances of life. By stripping back one layer of sporadic resemblances (or of laminated experience, a layer of connotative meaning), one does not come closer to a "truth" or a firm basis for rationality. One just finds another layer. The revelatory conceit, attacked by Wittgenstein, Lacan, and Derrida, cannot be the basis for organized rationality. One seeks the knowledge of the situation, the tacit, intuitive knowledge that is the basis for conducting human affairs, the knowledge of analogy, of practice, of aesthetic comprehension of the wanderer along paths strewn with bits of knowledge, the juxtaposition of moments, dreams, fantasies, poetry, and mathematical calculation, the work of Borges, the aphorisms of Lichtenberg in which two opposites are fused in a single phrase, story, or epigram, oxymoronic excursions.

Conclusion

When one sees through experience, words follow. Words cannot lead where experience does not lie. If one finds such experience, it was there (Needham 1982 lecture). Sociology is language search, not a language game (Brown 1977). As such, it is not poetic or aesthetic but merely a language for expressing and elevating contradictions. In the end, when the sun shifts, splays against the carpet, and radiates in the room, words fail to capture its warmth and logic cannot "restore" human attachment, which, like the sun, regularly fades, dips, and perhaps rises again. At times and between the gaps and gasps of communication, we are alone. Does it help to have written it?

Notes

Introduction

1. The communicational model of human life, spawned by engineering and mathematics, founded by linguistics, and given life by anthropology and literary criticism, is an Anglo-French invention. Like a Bach fugue, it taken many forms and exhibits canonical variations: Aspects of the scope of the model have been examined. The simple model in which there is a message sender at one end linked by a channel through which the message passes to a pipe with a receiver at the other end is an almost iconic figure, a mental hieroglyph. It assumes that speakers are oriented always and continuously to a known message, the units of which are standard and conventional, and that the intention to communicate mutually understood messages is indicated by the recognition of that intention. Organizationally embedded communication in which many actors communicate through many channels with organizational members and those outside the organization is often assumed to be accounted for by the communications model.

2. Pragmatics (Levinson 1983; Lyons 1977) stands between microsociological analysis of talk and social structure (Goffman 1981, 1983a, 1983b; Cicourel 1973, 1981, 1985; Atkinson and Drew 1979) and is a fruitful field for semiological analysis (Eco 1976, 1979, 1984).

3. It could be argued that variation, evasion, fantasy, imagination, and ratiocination in its logic, linear, and denotative forms capture portions of experience, but experiences are never simply one or the other (Langer 1951; Needham 1978, 1980, 1983). Variation in modes of thinking is cross-culturally validated (Needham 1972). From such data it is not indefensible to assert that rationality is an exceptional feature of thought over time and across societies and cultures. Needham reminds us of this on page v of this volume.

4. The linguistic model omits questions of the orientation of the speaker-hearer dyad, whether to the context, the speaker, the hearer, the channel, the code, or the message content (Jakobson 1960). Although important for the study of organizational communication, the linguistic model omits the questions of how general knowledge of language, issues of context, and the metalinguistic marking of communicational units, what Goffman (1974) calls framing, operate within linguistically defined settings. The limitations of the linguistic model, in short, are severe when analysis of organizational functioning is combined with analysis of the process by which communication is accomplished (Jameson 1972). The analysis of the communication (and understanding) of transmission of units larger than the sentence, communicational units seen as messages, texts, records and the like, requires an ethnography of speaking (Hymes 1974).

Chapter 1

1. See Banton (1964), Wilson (1968), Westley (1970), Bittner (1970), Reiss (1971), Rubinstein (1973), Kelling et al. (1974), Greenwood et al. (1977), Black, (1980), Manning (1977, 1979, 1980a), and, more recently, Ericson (1981, 1982).

2. Figures concerning the volume of incoming calls are variable because the definition of a call varies from department to department and is in part a function of technological capacity to store and retrieve such data. Some departments only count externally sourced calls, although it is clear that more than half of the calls processed in any police department are *internal* calls on police lines (Shearing 1984, p. 14).

These calls, which are passed on for serious consideration, are a sample of those received (omitting lost, terminated, incomplete, incorrect, and information-only calls). Of these, most come to the central number if there is one, for example, 999 or 911, but some departments maintain an emergency number and several seven-digit nonemergency numbers or have tiers of call processing that permit the collection of calls at both central communications centers and peripheral precincts. The peripheral calls are neither stored nor counted.

Once the calls are received and become, in terms used here, incidents, the coding or classification is a step that varies widely from department to department. Conclusions about the percentage of calls that are crime related or "real emergencies" are a function of the social organization of call processing (number of filtering points before the point at which data are gathered), the coding (or recoding, as most studies reclassify the original police classifications), nominal decisions about what is to be construed as crime related, regardless of the classification used to aggregate the data, to some lesser degree the sampling frame itself, including where and at what times the data are gathered, and such obvious matters as the number of police lines coming into the communications centers, the number of operators, and equipment used to store, queue, and retrieve calls.

It is also extremely difficult to ascertain the impact of political decisions on call processing. For example, the usual and assumed pattern to describe demand is a slowly rising use of central police numbers and an upwardly rising curve in overall demand. It would be naive indeed to conclude that public demand for police assistance varies as widely as some data suggest. Yet no study has systematically studied the pattern of exclusion, screening, reduction in seriousness, or relevance of calls to the police. There are exceptions, such as McCabe and Sutcliffe's brilliant and innovative study (1978) and the efforts in Detroit to study and reduce demand (Impact Detroit; Adams 1972). Perhaps the most thorough study is Shearing's meticulous examination of problems of sampling, generalization, and inference in a study of calls made to the Metropolitan Toronto Police (1984).

Not all calls received are answered; not all answered are entered in official records; and not all that is entered in official records becomes a job or assignment; not all assignments are actually accepted [for example, in Detroit in 1982, more than 8,000 calls were either not dispatched or, if dispatched, were not accepted by cars (*Detroit Free Press*, November 7, 1983)]. Many calls are multiple, referring to the same event, or are recalls from the same number.

3. This is implicit in the writing of Bordua and Reiss (1967), Reiss (1971), Larson (1972), and Black (1980) and is explicitly rejected by critics such as Rubinstein (1973), Kelling (1978), Manning (1977, 1982a, and Hough (1980a) and implicitly rejected by Hall et al. (1978), Brogden (1982), Holdaway (1983), and Jefferson and Grimshaw (1984).

4. Studies examining the potential of technological systems from an engineering standpoint (Colton 1978; Larson 1977; Tien and Colton 1979) have found that social organization constrains and patterns technology such that promise is not realized. Studies that focus on the command and control potential of technology have shown equally disappointing results (Hough 1980a, 1980b; Ekblom and Heal 1982). Studies that examine the potential of such systems to increase the quality and quantity of police service also reveal a mixed set of results, suggesting that the social organization of policing and the political, ecological, and cultural organization of cities (Black 1976) are more powerful patterning forces than technology [see Lineberry, (1977), Mladenka and Hill (1978), Manning (1980b, Anthunes and Scott (1981), Spelman and Brown (1981), Cordner et al. (1983), Scott and Percy (1983), Percy and Scott (1985), and Shearing (1984)].

Chapter 2

1. The social organization of networks of callers is differential in various cities. In other words, the probability of a call to the police, given the same event, is not equal across all cities. At the least, one would have to consider such matters as the number and location affecting the probability of a call. In England, for example, two important social facts affect the rate of calls to the police: the number of telephones per thousand and the propensity to use the phone to call the police. The consequence of these factors is that the determination of workload is virtually impossible without making a number of dubious assumptions. Thus only rough comparisons based on volume and workload can be made in this study.

2. Although some formal sign systems contain analogical and homological links between signifiers and signifieds, for example, chemical formulas, mathematic equations, flow charts, and logical syllogisms, informal systems, such as etiquette in America, are subject to extensive elaboration and situational accommodation. The information necessary to understand and interpret such sign systems also varies [see Guiraud (1973, ch. 2) and compare Barthes (1972) and White (1982)]. Anthropologists have attempted to provide analyses of one system in terms of another, for example, illnesses and moral conceptions, one form of kinship with another, or spatial location and social status.

3. Leaf (1972) argues convincingly for classifying sources of communication by their degree of organization and information.

4. In some departments, for example, each organization with a direct line has a special button on the console. When it is lit, the call is processed using a preestablished routine, producing a set procedure and response.

5. The association between transition among special statuses, places, and roles and "danger" perhaps arises from a sense of being out of place or socially dislocated, but it also inheres in transitions between systems of discourse [compare Douglas (1965) with Needham (1979, pp. 43—47)]. These transitions are generally marked in social life at the group level by rituals and ceremonies (Rappaport 1968, 1971) and in communicational interaction at the face-to-face level by linguistic, iconic, grammatical, or diacritical markings [compare Goffman (1974, pp. 16—20) with Derrida (1976, esp. p. 1 but also pp. 5, 6—26)].

6. As Culler has suggested, form is debated in literary circles: At what level does unity or "isotophy" reside? (1975, p. 95). Does coherence reside in the words, using the model of the sentence (subject, predicate, verbs, modifiers), utterances, phrases, sentences, chunks of

text (such as chapters, sections, and volumes), or genres? What basis can be systematically used to examine meaning or to build up meanings from an assemblage of units? Griemas has suggested the concept of a seme as a unit of analysis (in Culler (1975, pp. 77ff)]. Inevitably, however, the text in which a seme is located, according to structural dogma, is the basis of its meaning.

7. The derived deep structure is based on the analysis of the discourse and content of police messages. It should be understood that this kind of linguistic structuralism leads to a series of problems that have been dramatized by poststructuralist critiques of structuralism, such as Derrida (1976), Kristeva (1980), Barthes (1974), and Culler (1982). The reader should refer to the technical materials on this subject (Chomsky 1957, 1965; Lyons 1977; Fowler 1971, 1974). It is fruitful to look for structure, but not a single one; to seek cognitive encoding processes, but to enjoy and employ the several that are found in organizational locations; to eschew a single reading while holding the notion that there are some apparently universal similarities among formal systems of communication. Thus message analysis in this book engages in deconstruction as well as construction, being sensitive to the postponement of meaning that results from the juxtaposition of nonexclusive contraries, multiply coded oppositions, laminated sets of meanings residing in the reading-off of messages, and the changing referent of the signifiers in the message.

8. Literary critics have an unexamined advantage shared with historians: They know what a sonnet (a battle, a struggle for the throne, etc.) means because a long tradition of interpretation within established conventions exists and/or because the outcome is well known. The "facts" are rarely at issue.

9. See also Kurzweil (1980), Sturrock (1979), and Robey (1980). Structuralism assumes that binary distinctions between units [the basis for the difference and contrast noted by Hawkes (1977)] govern a pattern and that one set of rules governs relationships. This assumes also that there is a single system into which the elements are broken or from which they are derived and one regulative matrix that governs the perception of meaning. It assumes further that code operation is sustaining so that a text is bearer of a set of stable meanings that can be ascertained by careful and objective analysis (Norris 1982; Descombes 1980; Culler 1982). These assumptions are to be questioned in part because such a strategy of textual analysis appeals to the static and frozen view of singular causality, meaning, and method rather than opening the question of interpretation to include situational and contextual matters.

10. This is indicated by Bourdieu's concept of *habitus*, or the concatenation of a perspective and action constrained by material factors (1977, pp. 72ff).

Chapter 3

1. More comprehensive reviews of police communications, such as those by Leonard (1938) and Tobias (1974), note the rapid growth of police technology since the first license for a radio station granted to a police department was issued to the New York City Police Department in 1920 (Leonard 1938, p. 22). In his review, for example, Leonard notes the growth of telecommunications from the use of the telegraph for fire prevention to the adaptation of the telephone, the wireless radio, and two-way-radio-equipped patrol cars for police work and maintains the rather uncritical view that each was a major step forward in policing. On the basis of anecdotal evidence, Leonard claims: "So spectacular have been the

achievements of radio in the police field that one is tempted to abandon plain statement of fact and describe them in the language of the sensational press" (Leonard 1938, p. 38). In such a fashion was the technological conceit given credence.

2. Kelling (1978) has noted that improved technology, such as radios, computers, and even helicopters, has been viewed by every American commission on the police—from the *Wickersham Report* (National Commission on Law Observance and Enforcement, 1931) to the President's Crime Commission (1967) and the National Advisory Commission on Criminal Justice Standards and Goals (1973)—as a solution to police problems.

3. Access to the study site came as a result of an adventitious challenge thrown out to me by a senior police officer at a conference on police research held in Great Britain. Gesturing to me from the rear of an auditorium, he said, "What you have said is so *horrendou* that I find it certainly could not happen in this country. I would challenge you to come to our force headquarters and observe the command and control system that we have developed." Secretly I was delighted. His perceptive and accurate interpretation of the chaos described in the preliminary paper on the communications center in the Midwestern department I had presented to the conference pleased me. Receiving his semirhetorical invitation was most welcome. At a suitable moment over sherry on the Fellows' lawn, I inquired about when I might be able to visit. He then produced his telephone number, suggesting I ring him the following week. I did so and arranged to visit.

4. It had also been studied previously by two sociologists who had published well-known monographs.

5. The four incidents were a road closure (10 pages), a strike (22 pages over 9 days), a murder (4 pages), and a tunnel collapse (24 pages over 3 days).

6. In an attempt to gain some broader understanding of police communications systems and command and control variations, I made visits to communications centers in London (the Metropolitan Police), Rotterdam, and St. Petersburg (Florida).

7. Because of the aggressive policies of the Conservative government elected in 1979 and still in power, governmental support for policing budgets and salaries have risen despite economic distress. Between 1979 and 1980 another 648 officers were hired in the BPD. The force nearly reached its established limits for the first time in many years. The major pressures on the local police, partially as a result of the riots in the area and in London, in 1981, has been for hiring more women and minority officers and increased community policing or crudely, "putting more officers on the street." The constabulary has operated a major community policing project in the region since 1978 and continues to emphasize this aspect of its public relations.

8. In practice, because of time off, leave days, sickness, seconding, and vehicles under repair, the strength may be half this figure.

9. The system's capacities, such as the strength of the radio signals, number of characters accommodated on the VDU screen, and the speed of transmission of teleprinter messages, in a formal sense are known. The technological details of the system are described in other documents available to the interested observer (see the pamphlets issued by the British Police Department on command and control systems, radio systems, and post office telecommunication).

10. Incidents defined as "major incidents" by the chief inspector on duty in the center can be controlled exclusively from the center. It was explained that in theory only 2% of all calls are deemed "major incidents," whereas the remainder of the calls are sent on.

11. The central switchboard number is a seven-digit number with a three-digit STD (standard telephone dialing) code, or area code in America, which must be used by callers outside Centreshire. The numbers in addition to 999 coming into the center may be six or seven digits if callers dial for police in one of the independent cities served by the BPD. Codes vary from two to six digits in Great Britain and are finely divided; for example, each village has a separate code. In America a three-digit code covers a large area and an even larger number of telephones including the standard code number. A call to the police may involve dialing as many as eleven numbers in Great Britain.

12. The national policy, unlike that in the United States, is that silent alarms are not directly received by the police but must be filtered through silent alarm companies who relay the message after checking for its validity. Some 90% of alarm calls to American police departments are false. This fact causes a great deal of wasted energy responding to them and reduces their credibility in the eyes of the officers. See Webster (1973, pp. 36–38).

13. Midwestern Police Department is a pseudonym that refers to an American force policing Metro City, with a headquarters there.

14. These totals have changed since 1979; as of 1986, 14% were female, but the total force is now 4,800.

15. In late spring 1987, another EMS scandal emerged in Metro City precipitated by failure of responses of units to several life-threatening incidents. The heavy workload, crude coordination by the electrowriter, and the interpretative problems discussed here were overlooked, and more units were organized by contracting with private ambulance companies.

16. The nostalgic yearning for this past overemphasizes community service and familiarity and deemphasizes the violence, brutality, and corruption of police in the early twentieth century (Walker 1984; and Wilson and Kelling 1982).

17. A "valid" or "good" address is one that the computer accepts. The operator must type out on the terminal either a valid address or street combination (two streets that cross) before the computer will allow the operator to enter further information. The streets were "geocoded" and entered in the computer in 1974, but many streets have been destroyed or extended since that time; new streets have been added, and street names have been changed. When a person continues to repeat what they claim is a valid address, or when the computer is down, operators have to refer to handbooks of streets to ascertain if the address is valid. If it is valid, they must decide whether to override the computer and send the request to the dispatchers. This causes some difficulty from time to time for the operators, dispatchers, and officers who cannot find an address or street.

Chapter 4

1. That an image of the event being reported is constructed by the hearer is suggested by research on the chunking and coding of information done by Simon and Barenfield (1969). They found that, with visual information, scanning and abstracting produce a pattern (a set of positions on a chess board). This pattern is then transformed into a verbal description.

Presumably a verbal description is visualized as well when scanty data reporting an event are given, and a classification system (police categories) can be used as a template. Bateson (1980, p. 40) notes: "Image formation is unconscious ... an efficient method for passing information across an interface, especially when a person must act in context between two machines." This changes the channel carrying capacity of operators, serves to link long- and short-term memory, and indicates the sort of cognitive operations that link the two memory files (Simon 1982, ch. 3).

2. Numbers in parentheses refer to the number of calls analyzed and range from 1 to 47.

3. This list summarizes a complex relationship between the message set at the time of the hearing and sending of the message, and the operators' project (intentional reading of the world in which the message is to be received). It is not possible to sort out the level of effects of the various influences in message processing because it is so context dependent (the context being other messages that are also being processed by the operators and the controllers). They are in effect simultaneous, in the same sense that speakers and hearers are oriented to content, channel, effect of speaker and the hearer, the expressive aspects of the message, and so on (Jakobson 1960). As is noted later, the factor of credibility is paramount; without that, the remainder of the named influences are markedly reduced.

4. Cicourel (1973) outlines some links between what is heard and ideas of social structure. Some that are specified in sections of this chapter are discussed as interpretative procedures.

5. See the work of Psathas and Henslin (1967), Psathas and Kozloff (1976), and Psathas (1979).

6. The clustering of a sequence of calls is not addressed here but is taken up in chapter 6. A series as a set is the unit of analysis there rather than the one-at-a-time synchronic perspective of this chapter.

7. Although this is explained further later, the varying degree to which time and space deconstruct the signifier-signified relationship (semantic component) and the relationship between the signs (the syntactic component as seen in this case as the syntagmatic arrangement and processing of calls) is crucial in cross-subsystem comparisons and in organizational comparisons. It is a fruitful source of empirical materials bearing more generally on the expansion of structuralist analysis.

8. There are rotas, but during the day surgeons carrying out their normal practice may be moving from place to place.

9. One controller said he looked forward to the computer failure because he could then take his personal radio into a nearby park and "run the subdivision from a sunny park bench." He did not say whether he had done this in fact.

10. These are summarized by Garfinkel's notion of the etc.-clause (1967, p. 74): Any communication is always partial and could be clarified or expanded to include further details and more depth or could exclude detail, including additional omission.

11. The controller sorts the message from noise in the situation and the field (conversations, requests such as the duty roster for the curry party, etc.). These also affect shifts in salience during the time the incident is being handled in the controller's office.

12. This message was not communicated to the officer while I was in the room, nor did the controller leave the room before the officers returned to the area car. The official paper was not printed out for the PBO by the controller. The abbreviation PBO stands for permanent beat officer. A PBO is assigned to an area rather than to a shift or turn, polices on a schedule negotiated with a supervising sergeant, and is responsible for investigating incidents and minor crimes on his or her ground, or area. Originally PBOs were called HBOs (home beat officers). HBOs were expected to live or have a home on the ground and be available as was the old "village copper."

13. These include, it should be recalled, failures in the radios, telephones, computers, and VDUs, erstwhile functioning of this machinery, shutdowns and uneven power supply, especially for the computer, and variable performance produced by individual radio sets, location of the radio on the subdivisional ground, weather, and even time of day.

14. In one subdivision the superintendent had the controllers' room locked for several weeks and excluded everyone except those with a key and permission to enter (the controllers, the superintendent, the subdivisional clerks, the sergeants, and the inspectors). This was not well received, and the order was soon rescinded.

15. It might be noted that, like the idea of "text" or "syntagm," what is believed to be known about such events in the object world is always surrounded by a set of understood but not stated premises. Barthes (1977) terms these indexes or characteristics assumed or repressed, not a part of the encoding of the text. The role of elevating of these meanings while suppressing others is played by organizational coding and interpretation.

16. These narrative substructures are extractions from a large set of influences. Analysis of additional calls might produce a set of subtypes of villain, for example, or callers by motive, or more complex action sequences. But it is likely that screening at this point is quite general and gross, and such nuances are merely incidental to the work, not essential.

17. This is a minimalist version of a formal model of the resolution of a police story. Even the absence of a stage is of course significant, and truncated stories, collapsed sequences, and "failed" or incomplete stories may be important for elaborating the model and explicating the possible connections linking narrative structure, catharsis, and shaping the experience of everyday life.

18. Neither officers' self-produced demand nor the encounter created by citizen-initiated contact is considered here except as a feature of the field and, more broadly, the context, for officers rely entirely on radio communication. A radio call must be imagined as an event about which a call was made and processed through the communications system by an operator and a controller. The officer recreated this process: This eidetic imagery of the event is based in turn on the police officers' conception of the object-event world, or environment I. The imagined environment is the basis for the enactment of the officers' roles and tasks. The actions of encoding, constructing, and reconstructing an image, mentally reclassifying it, and seeing it as a transformed event-call-incident-job-assignment-process-flow are rooted in a fundamental fashion in this concept of the environment.

19. There is little doubt that such a call would be highest priority, but it is sufficiently rare not to be mentioned without probing.

Chapter 5

1. Calls are tape recorded, and the full call can be reproduced to compare with the record made and subsequent action. This is rarely done and usually comes only after a complaint or potential scandal.

2. Within the scheme particular categories have more "power" than others. Some categories within the classification scheme have the capacity to suffuse the incident with power so that further information is more or less likely to be a result of action taken to encode the incident in that category.

3. Horrendous consequences of operator error are widely reported and add to the stress of operators who fear dismissal, suits, or criminal action against them. Two notorious events are retold in each story on the 911 system in the *Metro City News* (over the last seven years that I have gathered clippings). The first was in 1974 when a 66-year-old woman and her 58-year-old husband were slain while talking to a 911 operator. The operator later claimed that she mistook the twenty-four shots fired at them for sounds of hammering. The second was a father of six who was shot and killed on a freeway. A car did not arrive for ninety minutes because the operator had sent the incident to the wrong precinct. Other tales are reported in the national news from time to time; for example, operators mishandled calls in the 911 center in New York City, causing a series of incidents, including the death of a young nurse. Scott and Percy report a mishandled call as an example of operator's discretion: "There are instances in which discretionary decision making in *response selection* by call takers can have severe consequences for citizens and police. In a recent case in Indianapolis, a man called the police to report that his father had been severely beaten and was in serious condition in a hospital. When told that the victim could not speak following surgery, the operator directed the caller to contact the homicide branch when his father's condition had improved. Since the incident occurred on the first day of the long Christmas weekend, the son was told to contact homicide in four days. By the time homicide was notified, the victim had died and the police investigation was severly hampered because it lacked information only the victim could provide. 'The four day delay in beginning the investigation points to a problem in the communications branch in deciding which calls police should respond to,' the police chief admitted. 'We probably have a policy problem there' (*Indianapolis Star*, December 31, 1981, p. 16). Even with a clear-cut policy, however, the operator's discretion in determining the mode of response remains a significant factor" (Scott and Percy 1983, p. 139).

A final example may suffice. In Dallas an operator in the Fire Department, a trained nurse, refused to send units to homes of two women who subsequently died. Another nurse was shown on television in Dallas arguing with a man who wanted an ambulance for his dying mother. On the same day, an ambulance was denied to a dying woman whose son had to drive her himself to the hospital (*State News MSU*, March 9, 1984).

The point of these systems is to place responsibility on the people at the interface with the public, to supervise them, and to deny them all but the most minimal discretion, that is, yes or no. The errors, denial of service, violence and brutality, and insensitivity to human pathos and tragedy is vastly and incomparably higher among officers. This is a classic kind of scapegoating of the weakest member of the system. When experts and supervisors, especially those with the militaristic police mentality, deny responsibility and support to decision making yet claim that "60% of the calls to 911 number are not really emergencies, or should not be directed to the communication center" (*Metro News*, May 12, 1986) they produce a double bind that is bound to create stress. Furthermore, the rationing policy of the public bureaus described insightfully by Lipsky (1980) is in operation here: A collective good, police service, is promised to all but in fact is selectively, secretly, and informally controlled and limited. From a public policy perspective the implications are many, but the most central one from the data here is that the system is designed at every point to increase police power and to reduce the power of the citizen. As the call moves, the power of the citizen decreases, and less and less can be done to alter the police's decision making, which is unreviewed, uncontrolled and invisible [Manning (1982a); Lipsky (1980); for a general overview, see Goldstein (1960)].

4. The MPD has been plagued with periodic crises in its communications center. Three employees were fired and twenty-two transferred between 1977 and 1979. In 1979 operators were dressed in snappy blazers and skirts. Five supervisors were created to monitor calls, visually monitor performance, and handle complaints from zone controllers and the public. Starting pay was raised to $17,200. The number of substantiated errors was said to have dropped, but no definition of "error" or "substantiated" was given. The aim of the inspector in charge during the period of the study was to install military discipline, a loyalty to the department, and "the ability to follow rules" (*Metro News*, February 1979). It is not surprising that stress results: There is an absence of feedback, little training, close supervision without substantive reward for performance, and total lack of discretion in fact (other than refusing to accept a call) because everything is sent down that is accepted, and the actual decision is left to the zone controllers and the officers.

5. Recall that the controller in the BPD receives messages from several channels, each with separate degrees of credibility, representational form, action implication, and format.

6. Bercal (1970), in studies of calls to police departments in Detroit, St. Louis, and New York, estimates that 60% of calls were the basis for a dispatch.

7. Van Maanen (person communication) has pointed out that in his fieldwork he discovered that "there is a strong implicit link among patrol units stemming from the fact that they know what each other unit is up to at any given moment. The dispatcher works with far too many units to keep track, but the region of interest to the patrolman (is) about five or six other relevant units.... Plus [they are concerned about whether] the sergeant is on the air. The patrol squad develops some very fine-grained ideas of what is going on and who should be doing what. These squad-based understandings are very important.... There are lots of little games going on 'out there,' wherein units answer for one another and let others know what's up in very subtle ways." These ideas are consistent with my observations.

8. See assumptions of the occupational culture (discussed later) and the nature of the object world (chapter 2). There are other assumptions, something of the nature of informal rules, that order the actions of zone controllers. They provide a structure for the ambiguous task of ordering incidents received.

9. Messages that arise at the city-wide desk, such as alarms, inquiries to the PNC and the state department of motor vehicles, requests for helicopters, and chases are coordinated from the city-wide desk and are not the focus of this analysis.

10. Savitz (1971, 1982), for example, derived priorities for certain kinds of calls if officers were forced to rank them (a situation which of course never happens).

11. Davis, for example, in a recent study of police management of "family trouble" in a medium-size western city, neatly summarizes a key methodological point: Officers were interviewed across all shifts about their beliefs concerning domestic disturbance calls in general and about the details of particular calls they had recently been assigned. The log of radio calls and assignments was scanned daily for "318: Family" calls. "318: Family" is a dispatchers' and officers' classification of a radio assignment covering domestic quarrels and disturbances. "318" (a pseudonumeral) is the section of the state penal code that covers disturbances of all sorts. Officers may be assigned, for example, a radio assignment coded "318: Party," "318: Barking dog," or "318: Loud motorcycle." The initial coding of the call is a matter of dispatcher discretion, and the call may later prove in reality to be another type of situation. Throughout the study the "318: Family" was approached nominally, that is, according to the classifications of the police. Officers might note, for example, that even though they had been assigned a "318: Family" according to the log, the call was "not really a 318: Family." Perhaps it was a neighborhood dispute or "just a woman screaming at someone." Conversely officers would come forward with information about particular calls they had handled that were "really family fights" even though they had not been coded as such (Davis 1983, p. 262).

12. See, for example, Davis (1983), who described officers running off in response to a call while they were in the middle of sorting out a family dispute.

13. Call stimuli come almost exclusively from the VHF radio. The radio is also the almost exclusive channel on which messages are sent to the center. The minicomputer in some cars produces messages to which officers are expected to respond. There were few mini computers in service at the time of this writing and they are not considered here.

14. This is not to say that the occupational culture of policing is identical in both organizations [see Holdaway's (1980) critique of Manning (1977) and Manning (forthcoming)]. Rather, at the level of operational priorities, they resemble each other in the surface aims of maintaining autonomy and control over the work.

Chapter 6

1. Traditionally linguistics has adopted Saussure's distinction between synchronic and diachronic analysis in part to reassert the salience of studying systems as composed of parts in which change can only be indicated within a given system characterized by sets of relations in a synchronic state (Culler 1977, p. 41). This is the argument made in functionalist analysis of change (Parsons 1951).

2. Bittner (1983) finds this irony useful. He has suggested that the degree of standardization of knowledge in the society, the widespread use of techniques of objective knowledge, produces greater consistency between computer logic and everyday logic. Computers, according to Bittner, can best simulate the process of human problem solving using preestablished criteria for success. Because of this convergence, Bittner argues, computer intelligence increasingly resembles natural intelligence. The computer may become the standard of adequacy. We may come to judge the adequacy of a human response by its similarity to that of a computer model. Ironically, as computers gain the ability to learn, they may exceed humans in creativity. This is a primary irony. If we delegate creativity to the computer and take up only the technical aspects of computing, then humans may lose the intuitive and the playful.

3. The extent to which this tacit knowledge is essential in a culture can be seen in knowing when to communicate and when to remain silent, how to read off nonverbal messages and cues, and the extent to which directness is culturally warranted, for example. These are all matters that are prior to language. See Levinson (1983, ch. 2) and Morley's *Pictures from the Water Trade* (1985), a lovely ethnography masquerading as a novel.

4. From the viewpoint of semiotics the message is a bit in a string coded at a general level. It is never seen as a single unique event but always as a type or as representative of an instance of a broader code. It is, in Eco's terms (1979, pp. 135–136), undercoded: "The operation by means of which in the absence of reliable pre-established rules, certain macroscopic portions of certain texts are provisionally assumed to be pertinent units of a code in formation, even though the combinational rules governing the more basic compositional items of the expressions along with the corresponding content-units, remain unknown." This undercoding, or perhaps one should say the tacit bases for this undercoding, is not a matter of explicit or discursive logic but of the logic of presentation and expression.

5. Recall also that the evasion of the constraints of everyday life is also served by fantasies, dreams, myths, etc. They are, as it were, part of the "iconographical or imaginative resources that constitute culture in general" (Needham 1978, p. 75). Furthermore, the ambiguity in all imaginative acts, that is, their fundamentally "free" character, is that they set inner feelings and "inner dialogues," but they also can, by their power and currency, be the occasion for violation and evasion: "a preponderational characteristic of men, namely, the vagrancy, the inconsequentiality, and the fantasy of their imagination" (Needham 1978, p. 70).

   The tendency of dispatchers to increase the urgency of a call by including a weapon when one is not present, of officers to "swarm" at the report of an "in progress burglary," of controllers to introduce a "fear" of a weapon is both a filling-in of facts and a product of imagination consistent with drama and with the ritual of police presence punctuating ambiguity (even for themselves!).

6. Earlier analyses of calls to the police and their work have suggested that the police provide a social service or have emphasized the pragmatic and functional aspects of their role (Punch and Naylor 1973; Cumming et al. 1962). The symbolic and expressive aspects of policing are mentioned at the macrolevel of ritualistic reassurance, but it is certain that calling the police has more than a little ritual and expressiveness. Perhaps calls have not been sufficiently understood as a base for continuity, stability, and community integration.

7. Eco (1979) developed the implications of these negotiations on texts, noting that there are rules for dealing with ambiguity, equivocality, and errors within any code. Thus time is coded and recoded especially when shunting back and forth between segments. From the point of view of textual analysis the moving dialectic between the mistakes and rules for dealing with them and the transformation of the text produces an "aesthetic idiolect" (Eco 1979, p. 270). Tacit implicit meanings are highlighted, even while "obvious" meanings remain a focus. Thus the connections made between signs (such as a "domestic") and an event and within a message are tacit rather than logical and referential. The internal links between signs are analogic rather than homologic.

8. Langer suggests the way a word can freeze an event: "Language, our most faithful and indispensable picture of human experience of the world and its events, of thought and life

and all the march of time, contains a law of projection of which philosophers are sometimes unaware, so that their reading of the presented facts is obvious and yet wrong, as a child's visual experience is obvious yet deceptive when his judgment is ensnared by the trick of the flattened map. The transformation which facts undergo when they are rendered as propositions is that the relations in them are turned into something like objects. Thus, 'A killed B' tells of a way in which A and B were unfortunately combined; but our only means of expressing this way is to name it, and presto!—a new entity, 'killing,' seems to have added itself to the complex of A and B. The event which is 'pictured' in the proposition undoubtedly involved a succession of acts by A and B, but not the succession which the proposition seems to exhibit—first A, then 'killing,' then B. Surely, A and B were simultaneous with each other and with the killing. But words have a linear, discrete, successive order, they are strung one after another like beads on a rosary; beyond the very limited meanings of inflections, which can indeed be incorporated in the words themselves, we cannot talk in simultaneous bunches of names" (Langer 1951, p. 76).

9. From a semiotic perspective organizations frame semiosis, the constant shifting and reinterpretation of the interpretant. As meanings change, any sign without a context is incomplete. Organizations are machines for producing an enhanced degree of clarity by reducing uncertainty and equivocality in messages; they convert flux and process into messages encoded within organizational systems of communication. They punctuate equivocality (Weick 1979, ch. 6), mark the edges of meaning, and formulate a symbolic universe of discourse. The semantic amplification and dispersal of meaning, once the coding has been produced, is one kind of change that semiotic structuralism *can* illuminate.

Chapter 8

1. Yet one is not prepared to accept the "rhizome" or "net" formulation of metaphor either. The best image of a net is provided by the vegetable metaphor of the rhizome suggested by Deleuze and Guattari (1976) and quoted by Eco: "A *rhizome* is a tangle of bulbs and tubers appearing like 'rats squirming one on top of the other.' The characteristics of a rhizomatic structure are the following: (a) Every point of the rhizome can and must be connected with every other point. (b) There are no points or positions in a rhizome; there are only lines (this feature is doubtful: interesting lines make points). (c) A rhizome can be broken off at any point and reconnected following one of its own lines. (d) The rhizome is antigenealogical. (e) The rhizome has its own outside with which it makes another rhizome; therefore, a rhizomatic whole has neither outside nor inside. (f) A rhizome is not a calque but an open chart which can be connected with something else in all of its dimensions; it is dismountable, reversible, and susceptible to continual modifications. (g) A network of trees which open in every direction can create a rhizome (which seems to us equivalent to saying that a network of partial trees can be cut out artificially in every rhizome). (h) No one can provide a global description of the whole rhizome; not only because the rhizome is multidimensionally complicated, but also because its structure changes through the time; moreover, in a structure in which every node can be connected with every other node, there is also the possibility of contradictory inferences: if *p*, then any possible consequence of *p* is possible, including the one that, instead of leading to new consequences, leads again to *p*, so that it is true at the same time both that *if p, then q* and that *if p, then non q*. (i) A structure that cannot be described *globally* can only be described as a potential sum of *local* de-

scriptions. (j) In a structure without outside, the describers can look at it only by the inside; ... a labyrinth of this kind is a *myopic algorithm*; at every node of it no one can have the global vision of all its possibilities but only the local vision of the closest ones: every local description of the net is a *hypothesis*, subject to falsification, about its further course; in a rhizome blindness is the only way of seeing [locally], and thinking means to *grope one's way*. This is the type of labyrinth we are interested in" (Eco 1984, pp. 81–82).

References

Adams, T. 1972. "Impact-Detroit (Debroit Police Department)," in *Criminal Justice: Readings*, T. Adams, ed. Pacific Palisades: Goodyear, 322–329.

Ames, A. 1960. *The Morning Notes of Adelbert Ames*, Hadley Cantril, ed. New Brunswick, N. J.: Rutgers University Press,

Anthunes, G., and E. J. Scott. 1981. "Calling the cops: Police telephone operators and citizens' calls for service." *Journal of Criminal Justice* 9 : 165–179.

Ardener, E. 1971. "Introductory essay: Social anthropology and language," in *Social Anthropology and Language*, E. Ardener, ed. London: Tavistock, vol. 10, ix–cii.

Ashton, P. 1981. "Race, class and Black politics: Implications of the election of a Black mayor for the police and policing in Metro City." Research proposal. Michigan State University, Department of Sociology.

Atkinson, J. M., and P. Drew. 1979. *Order in Court*. London: Macmillan.

Baker, M. H., B. Nienstadt, R. S. Everett, R. McCleary. 1983. "The impact of a crime wave: Perceptions, fear and confidence in the police." *Law and Society Review* 17 : 319–335.

Ball, D. 1968. "Toward a sociology of telephones and telephoners," in *The Sociology of Everyday Life*, M. Truzzi, ed. Englewood Cliffs, N.J.: Prentice-Hall, 59–75.

Banton, M. 1964. *The Policeman in the Community*. New York: Basic Books.

Barley, S. 1983. "Semiotics and the study of occupational and organizational cultures." *Administrative Science Quarterly* 28 : 393–413.

Barnard. C. 1938. *The Functions of the Executive*. Cambridge, Mass.: Harvard University Press.

Barnett, P. 1978. "Investigation into the computerised police management information systems in Sweden, Hamburg, Kiel, Amsterdam and Rotterdam." Bramshill, England: Police Staff College.

Barthes, R. 1972. *Mythologies*, selected and translated by Annette Lavers. New York: Hill and Wang.

Barthes, R. 1974. *S/Z*. New York: Hill and Wang.

Barthes, R. 1975. *The Pleasure of the Text*, Richard Miller, trans. New York: Hill and Wang.

Barthes, R. 1977. *Image/Music/Text*. New York: Hill and Wang.

Barthes, R. 1981. *Camera Lucida*. New York: Hill and Wang.

Bateson, G. 1972. *Toward an Ecology of Mind*. San Francisco, Cal.: Ballantine.

Bateson, G. 1980. *Mind and Nature*. New York: Bantam.

Baxandall, M. 1973. *Painting and Experience in Fifteenth Century Italy*. Oxford: Oxford University Press.

Bayley, D. 1986. "The tactical choices of police patrol officers." *Journal of Criminal Justice* 14:329–348.

Bayley, D., and E. Bittner. 1982. "Learning the skills of policing." Washington, D.C.: Police Foundation.

Becker, H. S. 1970. *Sociological Work*. Chicago, Ill.: Aldine.

Bell, D. 1973. *The Coming of Post-Industrial Society*. New York: Basic Books.

Bennett, W. L., and M. S. Feldman. 1981. *Reconstructing Reality in the Courtroom*. New Brunswick, N.J.: Rutgers University Press.

Bercal, T. 1970. "Calls for police assistance." *American Behavioral Scientist* 13:681–691.

Bernstein, B. 1971. *Class, Codes and Control*, Vol. 1. London: Routledge & Kegan Paul.

Bittner, E. 1965. "The concept of organization." *Social Research* 32:230–255.

Bittner, E. 1967. "The police on skid row." *American Sociological Review* 32:699–715.

Bittner, E. 1970. *The Functions of Police in Urban Society*. Bethesda, Md.: National Institute of Mental Health.

Bittner, E. 1974. "A theory of police: Florence Nightingale in pursuit of Willie Sutton," in *The Potential for Reform of Criminal Justice*, H. Jacob, ed. Beverly Hills, Cal. Sage, 17–44.

Bittner, E. 1978. "The rise and fall of the thin blue line. Review of R. Fogelson, *Big City Police*." *Reviews in American History* (September), 422–428.

Bittner, E. 1983. "Technique and the conduct of life." *Social Problems* 30:249–261.

Black, D. J. 1976. *The Behavior of Law*. New York: Academic Press.

Black, D. J. 1980. *Manners and Customs of the Police*. New York: Academic Press.

Bordua, D., ed. 1967. *The Police: Six Sociological Essays*. New York: Wiley.

Bordua, D., and A. J. Reiss, Jr. 1967. "Law enforcement," in *The Uses of Sociology*, P. Lazarsfeld, W. Sewell, and H. Wilensky, eds. New York: Basic Books, 275–303.

Bottomley, K., and C. Coleman. 1980. *Understanding Crime Rates*. Farnsworth: Gower.

Boulding, K. 1956. *The Image*. Ann Arbor, Mich.: University of Michigan Press.

Bourdieu, P. 1977. *Outline of a Theory of Practice*. Cambridge: Cambridge University Press.

Bracken, P. 1983. *The Command and Control of Nuclear Forces*. New Haven, Conn.: Yale University Press.

Braslavsky, N. 1982. *Policing the West Midlands*. Ph.D. dissertation, University of Birmingham, Department of Law.

Brogden, M. 1982. *The Police: Autonomy and Consent.* New York: Academic Press.

Broms, H., and H. Gahmberg. 1983. "Communications to self." *Organizations and Cultures* 28:482–495.

Broome, R., and R. Wanklin. 1980. "The Centreshire Police Communications System." *Police Research Bulletin* (Spring), 34:32–37.

Brown, M. 1981. *Working the Street.* New York: Russell Sage.

Brown, R. H. 1977. *A Poetic for Sociology.* New York and Cambridge: Cambridge University Press.

Burke, K. 1962. *A Grammar of Motives and a Rhetoric of Motives.* New York: Meridian Books.

Buzawa, E. 1979. *The Role of Selected Factors upon Patrol Officer Job Satisfaction in Two Urban Police Departments.* Ph.D. dissertation. College of Social Science, Michigan State University.

Cain, M. 1973. *Society and the Policeman's Role.* London: Routledge & Kegan Paul.

Canetti, E. 1962. *Crowds and Power,* C. Stewart, trans. London: Victor Gollance, Ltd.

Castenada, C. 1968. *The Teachings of Don Juan.* New York: Ballantine Books

Chatterton, M. 1975. *Organisational Relationships and Processes in Police Work: A Case Study of Urban Policing.* Ph.D. dissertation, University of Manchester, Department of Sociology and Anthropology.

Chatterton, M. 1979. "The supervision of patrol work under the fixed points system." in *The British Police,* S. Holdaway, ed. London: Edward Arnold, 83–101.

Cherry, C. 1978. *On Human Communication,* third edition. Cambridge, Mass. MIT Press.

Chief Constable. 1979. *Annual Report.* Centreshire: British Police Force.

Chief Constable. 1980. *Annual Report.* Centreshire: British Police Force.

Chomsky, N. 1957. *Syntactic Structures.* The Hague: Martinus Nijhoff.

Chomsky, N. 1965. *Aspects of a Theory of Syntax.* Cambridge, Mass.: MIT Press.

Cicourel, A. 1964. *Method and Measurement in Sociology.* New York: Free Press.

Cicourel, A. 1968. *The Social Organization of Juvenile Justice.* New York: Wiley.

Cicourel, A. 1973. *Cognitive Sociology.* New York: Free Press.

Cicourel, A. 1975. "Discourse and text: Cognitive and linguistic process in studies of social structure." *Versus* 12:33–84.

Cicourel, A. 1976. "Discourse, autonomous grammars and contextualized processing of information." Paper presented at The Impact of Scientific Knowledge on Social Structure Conference, Technical University, Darmstadt, West Germany.

Cicourel, A. 1981. "Language and belief in a medical setting," in *Contemporary Perceptions of Language: Interdisciplinary Dimensions,* H. Brynes, ed. Washington, D.C.: Georgetown University Press, 48–78.

Cicourel, A. 1985. "Text and discourse," in *Annual Review of Anthropology 14,* B. Siegal, A. R. Beals, and S. Tyler, eds. Palo Alto, Ca.: Annual Reviews Press, 159–185.

Clark, J. P. 1968. "The isolation of the police: A comparison of the British and the American situations." *Journal of Criminal Law, Criminology and Police Science* 56:307–319.

Clark, J. P., and R. Sykes. 1974. "Some determinants of police organization and practice in a modern industrial democracy," in *Handbook of Criminology*, D. Glaser, ed. Chicago, Ill.: Rand-McNally, 455–494.

Clark, R., and M. Hough. 1984. *The Effectiveness of the Police*. Home Office Research Unit. London: Her Majesty's Stationary Office.

Collins, R. 1981. "On the micro-foundations of macro-sociology." *American Journal of Sociology* 86:984–1014.

Colton, K. W., ed. 1978. *Police Computer Technology*. Lexington, Mass.: D. C. Heath.

Colton, K. W., and S. Herbert. 1978. "Police use and acceptance of advanced development techniques: Findings from three case studies," in *Police Computer Technology*, K. Colton, ed. Lexington, Mass.: D. C. Heath, 139–151.

Cooper, R. 1983a. "Canetti's sting." Department of Behaviour in Organisations, University of Lancaster, England.

Cooper, R. 1983b. "The other: A model of human structuring," in *Beyond Method*, G. Morgan, ed. Beverly Hills, Cal.: Sage, 202–218.

Cooper, R. 1985. "Information, communication and organisation." Department of Behavior in Organisations, University of Lancaster, England.

Cooper, R. 1986. "Organization/disorganization." *Social Science Information* 25(2):1–15.

Cordner, G. 1979. "Police workloads." School of Criminal Justice, Michigan State University, East Lansing, Michigan.

Cordner, G., J. Greene, and T. Bynum. 1983. "The sooner the better: Some effects of police response time." in *Police at Work*, R. R. Bennett, ed. Beverly Hills, Cal.: Sage, 145–164.

Crozier, M. 1964. *The Bureaucratic Phenomenon*. Chicago, Ill.: University of Chicago Press.

Crozier, M. 1972. "The relationship between micro- and macrosociology: A study of organizational systems as an empirical approach to problems of macrosociology." *Human Relations* 25(3):239–251.

Culler, J. 1975. *Structuralist Poetics*. Ithaca, N.Y.: Cornell University Press.

Culler, J. 1977. *Ferdinand de Saussure*. London: Fontana/Collins.

Culler, J. 1982. *On Deconstruction*. Ithaca, N.Y.: Cornell University Press.

Cumming, E., I. Cumming, and L. Edell. 1965. "Policeman as philosopher, guide and friend." *Social Problems* 12:276–286.

Cyert, R., and J. March. 1963. *A Behavioral Theory of The Firm*. Englewood Cliffs, N.J.: Prentice-Hall.

Davis, S. 1983. "Restoring the semblance of order: Police strategies in the domestic dispute." *Symbolic Interaction* 6(2):261–278.

Deleuze, F., and F. Guattari. 1976. *Rhizome*. Paris: Minuit.

Denzin, N. 1983. *On Understanding Emotion*. San Francisco, Cal.: Jossey-Bass.

Denzin, N. 1984a. "Toward a phenomenology of domestic family violence." *American Journal of Sociology* 90:483–513.

Denzin, N. 1984b. "Towards an interpretation of semiotics and history." *Semiotica* 54(3/4): 335–350.

Denzin, N. 1987. "On the symbolic in symbolic interactionism." *Symbolic Interaction* 9: 1–19.

Derrida, J. 1976. *On Grammatology,* Gayatri Chakravorty Spivak, trans. Baltimore, Md.: Johns Hopkins University Press.

Descombes, V. 1980. *Modern French Philosophy.* Cambridge: Cambridge University Press.

Douglas, M. 1965. *Purity and Danger.* Harmondsworth: Penguin.

Douglas, M. 1986. *How Institutions Think.* Syracuse, N.Y.: Syracuse University Press.

Douglas, M., and B. Isherwood. 1979. *The World of Goods.* New York: Basic Books.

Durkheim, E. 1961. *The Elementary Forms of the Religious Life,* J. W. Swain, trans. New York: Collier-Macmillan.

Eco, U. 1976. *A Theory of Semiotics.* Bloomington, Ind.: University of Indiana Press.

Eco, U. 1979. *The Role of the Reader.* Bloomington, Ind.: University of Indiana Press.

Eco, U. 1984. *Semiotics and The Philosophy of Language.* London: Macmillan.

Edel, L. 1982. *The Stuff of Sleep and Dreams.* New York: Avon.

Edelman, M. 1964. *The Symbolic Uses of Politics.* Urbana, Ill.: University of Illinois Press.

Edelman, M. 1971. *Politics as Symbolic Action.* Chicago, Ill.: Markham.

Eglin, P., and D. Wideman. 1979. "Calling the police: Some aspects of the interactional organization of complaints in crime reporting." Department of Sociology, Wilfred Laurier University, Ottawa, Canada.

Eglin, P., and D. Wideman. 1985. "Inequality in service encounters: Professional power versus interactional organization in calls to the police." Department of Sociology, Wilfred Laurier University, Ottawa, Canada.

Ekblom, P., and K. Heal. 1982. *The Police Response to Calls from the Public.* Home Office Research and Planning Unit Report 9. London: Her Majesty's Stationery Office.

Eldridge, A. 1979. *Images of Conflict.* New York: St. Martin's.

Emerson, R. 1983. "Holistic effects in social control decision-making." *Law and Society Review* 17:425–455.

Emery, F. E., and E. L. Trist. 1965. "The causal texture of organizational environments." *Human Relations* 18:21–32.

Epstein, E. 1978. *Language and Style.* London: Methuen.

Epstein, E. J. 1977. *Agency of Fear.* New York: Putnam.

Ericson, R. V. 1981. *Making Crime.* Toronto: Butterworths.

Ericson, R. V. 1982. *Reproducing Order.* Toronto: University of Toronto Press.

Ericson, R. V., and C. D. Shearing. 1986. "The scientification of police work." *in The Knowledge Society*, G. Bohme and N. Stehr, eds. Dordrecht: Reidel, 129–159.

Feeley, M. M., and A. Sarat. 1980. *LEAA: Crime Control the Futile Myth*. Minneapolis, Minn.: University of Minnesota Press.

Feldman, M. Forthcoming. *The Role of Interpretation in Policy Making: A Study of Information Production*. Stanford, Cal.: Stanford University Press.

Feldman, M. S., and J. March. 1981. "Information in organizations as symbol and signal." *Administrative Science Quarterly* 26 : 171–186.

Fielding, N. 1984. "Police socialisation and police competence." *British Journal of Sociology* 35 : 568–590.

Fielding, N. Forthcoming. *Becoming a Constable*. London: Tavistock.

Fogelson, R. 1977. *Big City Police*. Cambridge, Mass.: Harvard University Press.

Ford, D. 1985. *The Button*. New York: Dutton.

Foucault, M. 1972. *The Order of Things*. New York: Vintage.

Foucault, M. 1973. *The Archaeology of Knowledge*. London: Tavistock.

Foucault, M. 1977. *Discipline and Punish*, A. M. Smith, trans. New York: Pantheon.

Fowler, R. 1971. *An Introduction to Transformational Syntax*. London: Routledge & Kegan Paul.

Fowler, R. 1974. *Understanding Language: An Introduction to Linguistics*. London: Routledge & Kegan Paul.

Fromm, E. 1941. *Escape from Freedom*. New York: Rinehart.

Fuld, L. 1971. *Police Administration*. Montclair, N.J.: Patterson Smith.

Garfinkel, H. 1963. "A conception of, experiments with, 'trust' as a condition of stable concerted actions," in *Motivation and Social Interaction*, O. J. Harvey, ed. New York: Ronald Press, 187–238.

Garfinkel, H. 1964. "The routine grounds of everyday activities." *Social Problems* (Winter), 11 : 225–250.

Garfinkel, H. 1967. *Studies in Ethnomethodology*. Englewood Cliffs, N.J.: Prentice-Hall.

Geertz, C. 1973. *The Interpretation of Cultures*. New York: Basic Books.

Giddens, A. 1976. *New Rules of Sociological Method*. London: Hutchinson.

Giddens, A. 1981. "Agency, institution and space-time analysis," in *Advances in Social Theory and Methodology*, K. Knorr-Cetina and A. Cicourel, eds. London: Routledge & Kegan Paul, 161–174.

Giddens, A. 1984. *The Constitution of Society*. Berkeley, Cal.: University of California Press.

Goffman, E. 1959. *The Presentation of Self in Everyday Life*. New York: Doubleday Anchor Books.

Goffman, E. 1974. *Frame Analysis*. Cambridge, Mass.: Harvard University Press.

Goffman, E. 1981. *Forms of Talk*. Oxford: Basil Blackwell.

Goffman, E. 1983a. "Felicity's condition." *American Journal of Sociology* (July), 89:1–53

Goffman, E. 1983b. "The Interaction Order." *American Sociological Review* (February), 48: 1–17.

Goldstein, H. 1979. "Improving policing: A problem-oriented approach." *Crime and Delinquency* (April), 25:236–258.

Goldstein, J. 1960. "Police discretion not to invoke the criminal process: Low visibility decisions in the administration of justice." *Yale Law Journal* 69:543–594.

Goody, J. 1977. *The Domestication of the Savage Mind.* Cambridge: Cambridge University Press.

Goody, J., and I. Watt. 1963. "The consequences of literacy." *Comparative Studies in Society and History* 5:304–345.

Granovetter, M. 1973. "The strength of weak ties." *American Journal of Sociology* 78: 1360–1380.

Granovetter, M. 1985. "Economic action and social structure: the problem of embeddedness." *American Journal of Sociology* 91:481–510.

Greene, G. 1980. *Ways of Escape.* London: The Bodley Head.

Greenwood, P., J. Chaiken, and J. Petersilia. 1977. *The Criminal Investigation Process.* Lexington, Mass.: D. C. Heath.

Grimaud, M. 1983. "Mindful and mindfree rhetorics: Method and metatheory in discourse analysis." *Semiotica* 45(1/2):115–179.

Guiraud, P. 1975. *Semiology.* London: Routledge & Kegan Paul.

Halbwachs. M. 1980. *The Collective Memory.* New York: Harper Colophon Books.

Hall, S., C. Critcher, T. Jefferson, J. Clarks, and B. Roberts. 1978. *Policing the Crisis.* London: Macmillan.

Halliday, M. A. K. 1978. *Language As Social Semiotic.* London: Edward Arnold.

Harris, R. 1970. *Justice.* New York: Avon.

Hart, H. L. A. 1961. *The Concept of Law.* Oxford: Oxford University Press.

Hawkes, T. 1977. *Structuralism and Semiotics.* Berkeley, Cal.: University of California Press.

Heritage. J. 1985. "Analyzing news interviews." *Handbook of Discourse Analysis,* J. von Dyk, ed. London: Academic Press, 95–117.

Hofstadter, R. 1979. *Gödel, Escher and Bach.* New York: Basic Books.

Holdaway, S. 1979a. "Changes in urban policing." *British Journal of Sociology* 28:119–137.

Holdaway, S., ed. 1979b. *British Police.* London: Edward Arnold.

Holdaway, S. 1980. *The Occupational Culture of Urban Policing: An Ethnographic Study.* Ph.D. dissertation, University of Sheffield, Department of Social Studies.

Holdaway, S. 1983. *Inside the British Police.* Oxford: Basil Blackwell.

Horowitz, R. Forthcoming. "Identity and organization."

Hough, J. M. 1980a. "Managing with less technology." *British Journal of Criminology* 20: 344–357.

Hough, J. M. 1980b. *Uniformed Police Work and Management Technology* Home Office Research and Planning Unit paper 1. London: Her Majesty's Stationery Office.

Hughes, E. C. 1971. *The Sociological Eye*. Chicago, Ill.: Aldine.

Hughes, E. C. n.d. "An outline of occupations and professions." University of Chicago, Department of Sociology.

Hulbert, J. 1981a. "Handling emergency calls: Implications of procedure for policing the community." Paper presented to the American Society of Criminologists, Washington, D.C.

Hulbert, J. 1981b. "Human factors in message acquisition for a computer-based police command and control system." Ph.D. dissertation, University of Aston, Birmingham.

Hunt, J. C. 1985. "Police accounts of normal force." *Urban Life* 13:315–341.

Hymes, D. 1974. *Foundations in Sociolinguistics*. Philadelphia, Pa.: University of Pennsylvania Press.

Ianni, E., and F. Ianni. 1983. "Street cops and management cops: Two cultures of policing," in *Control in the Police Organization*, M. Punch, ed. Cambridge, Mass.: MIT Press, 251–274.

Jakobson, R. 1960. "Closing statement," in *The Uses of Language*, T. Sebeok, ed. Cambridge, Mass. MIT Press, 350–377.

James, D. 1979. "Race relations: The professional solution," in *The British Police*, S. Holdaway, ed. London: Edward Arnold, 66–82.

Jameson, F. 1972. *The Prison-House of Language*. Princeton, N.J.: Princeton University Press.

Jefferson, T., and R. Grimshaw. 1984. *Controlling the Constable: Police Accountability in England and Wales*. London: Cobden Trust.

Jermier, J., and L. Berkes. 1979. "Leader behavior in a police command bureaucracy: A closer look at the quasi-military model." *Administrative Science Quarterly* (March), 24:1–23.

Johnstone, E. St. 1978. *One Policeman's Story*. London: B. Rose.

Jorgensen, B. 1981. Transferring trouble: The initiation of reactive policing." *Canadian Journal of Criminology* 23(3):257–278.

Kelling, G. 1978. "Police field services and crime: The presumed effect of a capacity." *Crime and Delinquency* 2(April), 2:173–184.

Kelling, G. L., T. Pate, D. Dieckman, and C. E. Brown. 1974. *The Kansas City preventive Patrol Experiment*. Washington, D.C.: Police Foundation.

Kitsuse, J., and A. Cicourel. 1963. "A note on the uses of official statistics." *Social Problems* (Fall), 11:132–139.

Klapp, O. 1978. *Opening and Closing*. Cambridge: Cambridge University Press.

Klapp, O. 1986. *Overload and Boredom*. Westport, Conn.: Greenwood.

Kristeva, J. 1980. *Desire in Language*. New York: Columbia University Press.

Kurzweil, E. 1980. *The Age of Structuralism*. New York: Columbia University Press.

Lacan, J. 1977. *Écrits*. London: Tavistock.

Lane, R. 1967. *Policing the City*. Cambridge, Mass: Harvard University Press.

Langer, S. 1951. *Philosophy in a New Key*. New York: Mentor Books.

Larson, R. 1972. *Urban Patrol Analysis*. Cambridge, Mass.: MIT Press.

Larson, R. 1977. *Police Deployment*. Lexington, Mass.: D. C. Heath.

Lawrence, P. R., and J. W. Lorsch. 1969. *Organization and Environment*. Homewood, Ill.: Richard Irwin.

Leach, E. 1976. *Culture and Communication*. Cambridge: Cambridge University Press.

Leaf, M. 1972. *Information and Behavior in a Sikh Village*. Berkeley, Cal.: University of California Press.

Leech, G. 1983. *Semantics*, second edition. Harmonsworth: Penguin.

Lemert, C. 1979a. "Language, structure and measurement." *American Journal of Sociology* (January), 84:929–957.

Lemert, C. 1979b. "Structuralist semiotics," in *Theoretical Perspectives in Sociology*, S. McNall, ed. New York: St. Martins, 96–111.

Lemert, C. 1979c. *The Twilight of Man*. Carbondale, Ill.: Southern Illinois University Press.

Leonard, V. A. 1938. *Police Communication Systems*. Berkeley, Cal.: University of California Press.

Levinson, S. 1983. *Pragmatics*. Cambridge: Cambridge University Press.

Lévi-Strauss, C. 1963. *Structural Anthropology*. New York: Basic Books.

Lévi-Strauss, C. 1966. *The Savage Mind*. Chicago, Ill.: University of Chicago Press.

Lilly, J. R. 1978. "What are the police now doing?" *Journal of Police Science and Administration* 6:51–60.

Lineberry, K. 1977. *Equality and Urban Policy*. Beverly Hills, Cal.: Sage.

Lipsky, M. 1980. *Street-Level Bureaucracies*. New York: Russell Sage.

Luhmann, N. 1980. "Semiotics and rationality." Paper presented to the American Sociological Association, New York.

Luhmann, N. 1981. "Communication about law in interaction systems," in *Advances in Social Theory and Methodology: Toward an Integration of micro- and Macro-Sociologies*, K. Knorr-Cetina and A. Cicourel, eds. London: Routledge & Kegan Paul, 234–256.

Luhmann, N. 1985. *A Sociological Theory of Law*, E. King-Utz and M. Albrow, trans. London: Routledge & Kegan Paul.

Lyons, J. 1977. *Introduction to Theoretical Linguistics*, revised edition. Cambridge: Cambridge University Press. Originally published in 1968.

McCabe, S., and F. Sutcliffe. 1978. *Defining Crime*. Oxford: Penal Research Unit.

MacCannell, D. 1981. "Deconstructing ritual." Baker Alumni Lecture presented to Cornell University.

MacCannell, D., and J. F. MacCannell. 1982. *The Time of the Sign*. Bloomington, Ind.: Indiana University Press.

McCleary, R., B. Nienstedt, and J. M. Erven. 1982. "Uniform crime reports as organizational outcomes." *Social Problems* (April), 29:361–372.

MacKay, J. 1969. *Information, Mechanism and Meaning*. Cambridge, Mass.: MIT Press.

Mannheim, K. 1949. *Man and Society in an Age of Reconstruction*. New York: Harcourt Brace.

Manning, P. K. 1977. *Police Work*. Cambridge, Mass.: MIT Press.

Manning, P. K. 1979. "The social control of police work," in *The British Police*, S. Holdaway, ed. London: Edward Arnold, 41–65.

Manning, P. K. 1980a. *Narcs' Game*. Cambridge, Mass.: MIT Press.

Manning, P. K. 1980b. "Crime and technology: The role of scientific research and technology in crime control," in *Five Year Outlook for Science and Technology in the United States*. National Academy of Sciences, ed. Washington, D.C.: National Science Foundation, vol. 2, 607–623.

Manning, P. K. 1981. "The police and collective goods," Department of Sociology, Michigan State University, East Lansing, Michigan.

Manning, P. K. 1982a. "Organisational work: Enstructuration of the environment." *British Journal of Sociology* (March), 33:118–139.

Manning, P. K. 1982b. "Producing drama: Symbolic communication and the police." *Symbolic Interaction* (Fall), 5:223–241.

Manning, P. K. 1982c. "Structuralism and the sociology of knowledge." *Knowledge-Creation-Diffusion* (September) 4:51–72.

Manning, P. K. 1984. "Police classifications of the mentally ill," in *Mental Health and Criminal Justice*, L. Teplin, ed. Beverly Hills, Cal.: Sage, 177–198.

Manning, P. K. 1985. "Limits upon the semiotic structuralist perspective on organizational analysis," in *Studies in Symbolic Interaction*, N. Denzin, ed. Greenwich, Conn.: JAI Press, vol. 6, 79–111.

Manning, P. K. 1986a. "Signwork," *Human Relations* 39(4):283–308.

Manning, P. K. 1986b. "Texts as organizational echoes." *Human Studies* 9:287–302.

Manning, P. K. 1987. *Fieldwork and Semiotics*. Beverly Hills, Cal.: Sage.

Manning, P. K. Forthcoming. "The occupational culture of the police," in *The Encyclopedia of Police Science*, V. Strecher, L. Hoover, and J. Dowling, eds. Dallas, Tex.: Garland Press.

Manning, P. K., and K. Hawkins. 1987. "Police decision-making," in *Policing: Now Where?* M. Weatheritt, ed. London: Gower.

Manning, P. K., and K. Hawkins. Forthcoming. "Legal decision-making."

Margalit, A. 1982. "Review of Fred Dretske, *Knowledge and the Flow of Information*." *London Times Literary Supplement* (October 22), 1170.

Marshall, G. 1965. *Police and Government*. London: Methuen.

Meyer, J., and B. Rowan. 1977. "Institutionalized organizations: Formal structure as myth and ceremony." *American Journal of Sociology* (September), 83:340–363.

Meyer, J. C., Jr. 1974. "Patterns of reporting non-criminal behavior to the police." *Criminology* (May), 12:70–83.

Miller, W. R. 1977. *Cops and Bobbies*. Chicago, Ill.: University of Chicago Press.

Minsky, M., ed. 1968. *Semantic Information Processing*. Cambridge, Mass.: MIT Press.

Minsky, M. 1977. "Frame-system theory," in *Thinking: Readings in Cognitive Science*, P. N. Johnson-Laird and P. C. Wason, eds. Cambridge: Cambridge University Press, 355–376.

Mladenka, K. R., and K. Q. Hill. 1978. "The distribution of urban police services," *The Journal of Politics* (February), 40:112–133.

Morley, J. D. 1985. *Pictures from the Water Trade*. New York: Harper Torchbooks.

Muir, W. K., Jr. 1977. *The Police: Street Corner Politicians*. Chicago, Ill.: University of Chicago Press.

National Advisory Commission on Criminal Justice Standards and Goals. 1973. *National Strategy for Standards and Goals in Criminal Justice*. Washington, D.C.: Government Printing Office.

National Advisory Commission on Criminal Justice Standards and Goals. 1975. *Report*. Washington, D.C.: Government Printing Office.

National Advisory Commission on Criminal Justice Standards and Goals. 1977. *The Police*. Washington, D.C.: Government Printing Office.

National Commission on Law Observance and Enforcement, 1931. *Wickersham Report*. Report 14 on the Police. Washington, D.C.: Government Printing Office.

Needham, R. 1972. *Language, Belief and Experience*. Oxford: Basil Blackwell.

Needham, R. 1978. *Primordial Characters*. Charlottesville, Vir.: University of Virginia Press.

Needham, R. 1979. *Symbolic Classification*. Santa Monica, Cal.: Goodyear.

Needham, R. 1980. *Reconnaissances*. Toronto: University of Toronto Press.

Needham, R. 1981. *Circumstantial Deliveries*. Berkeley, Cal.: University of California Press.

Needham, R. 1983. *Against the Tranquility of Axioms*. Berkeley, Cal.: University of California Press.

Needham, R. 1985. *Exemplars*. Berkeley, Cal.: University of California Press.

Nora, S., and A. Minc. 1981. *The Computerization of Society*. Cambridge, Mass.: MIT Press.

Norris, C. 1982. *Deconstruction*. London: Methuen.

Orotony, A., ed. 1979. *Metaphor and Thought*. Cambridge: Cambridge University Press.

Ortega y Gasset, J. 1932. *The Revolt of the Masses*. New York: Norton.

Park, R., and E. Burgess. 1921. *Introduction to the Science of Sociology*. Chicago, Ill.: University of Chicago Press.

Parnas, V. 1967. "The police response to domestic disturbance." *University of Wisconsin Law Review* (Fall), 2:914–960.

Parsons, T. 1951. *The Social System*. Glencoe, Ill.: Free Press.

Peirce, C. S. 1931–1958. *Collected Papers*, 8 vols., C. Kartshorn and P. Weiss, eds. Cambridge, Mass.: Harvard University Press.

Pepinsky, H. 1976. "Police patrolmen's offense-reporting behavior." *Journal of Research in Crime and Delinquency* (January), 13:33–47.

Percy, S., and E. J. Scott. 1985. *Demand Processing and Performance in Public Service Agencies*. University, Ala.: University of Alabama Press.

Pettit, P. 1977. *The Concept of Structuralism: A Critical Analysis*. Berkeley, Cal.: University of California Press.

Pierce, G., W. J. Bowers, and C. Spaar. 1981. "High-rate users of police service: Implications for the management of police community resources." Proposal to National Institute of Justice.

Pinder, C., and V. W. Bourgeois. 1983. "Contrasting philosophical perspectives in administrative science." *Administrative Science Quarterly* 28:608–613.

Polyani, M. 1967. *Personal Knowledge*. New York: Doubleday Anchor Books.

President's Crime Commission. 1967. *Task Force Report on Science and Technology*. Washington, D.C.: Government Printing Office.

"Profiles: AI" (on Marvin Minsky). 1981. *New Yorker* (December 14), 50–126.

Propp, V. 1958. *The Morphology of the Folktale*. Austin, Tex.: University of Texas Press.

Psathas, G. 1979. "Organizational features of direction maps," in *Everyday Language: Studies in Ethnomethodology*, G. Psathas, ed. New York: Irvington, 203–225.

Psathas, G., and J. Henslin. 1967. "Dispatched orders and the cab driver." *Social Problems* (Spring), 14:424–443.

Psathas, G., and M. Kozloff. 1976. "The structure of directions." *Semiotica* 17:111–130.

Punch, M., and T. Naylor. 1973. "The police: A social service." *New Society* 24:358–361.

Putnam, L., and M. Pacanowsky, eds. 1983. *Communication and Organizations*. Beverly Hills, Cal.: Sage.

Radzinowicz, L. 1968. *The History of English Criminal Law*. Vol. 4, *The Reform of the Police*. London: Stevens.

Rappaport, R. 1967. "Ritual regulation of environmental relations among a New Guinea people." *Ethnology* (January), 6:17–30.

Rappaport, R. 1968. *Pigs for the Ancestors*. New Haven, Conn.: Yale University Press.

Rappaport, R. 1971. "Ritual, sanctity and cybernetics." *American Anthropologist* (February), 73:59–76.

Rappaport, R. 1973. "Ritual as communication and state." Paper presented to the Symposium, Ritual: Reconciliation in Change, sponsored by Wenner-Gren Foundation, Burg Wartenstein.

Reason, J. 1982. "Learning from absent-minded mistakes." *SSRC Newsletter* (June), 46:21–23.

Reiss, A. J., Jr. 1971. *The Police and the Public.* New Haven, Conn.: Yale University Press.

Reiss, A. J., Jr., and D. J. Bordua. 1967. "Environment and organization: A perspective on the police," in *The Police: Six Sociological Essays,* D. Bordua, ed. New York: Wiley, 25–55.

Reith, C. 1956. *The Blind Eye of History.* London: Oliver & Boyd.

Reppetto, T. 1978. *The Blue Parade.* New York: Macmillan.

Robey, D., ed. 1980. *Structuralism.* Oxford: Oxford University Press.

Rorty, R. 1979. *Philosophy and the Mirror of Nature.* Princeton, N.J.: Princeton University Press.

Rosch, E., and C. B. Mervis. 1975. "Family resemblances: Studies in the internal structure of categories." *Cognitive Psychology* 7:573–605.

Rosch, E., C. B. Mervis, W. D. Gray, D. M. Johnson, and P. Boyes-Braem. 1976. "Basic objects in natural categories." *Cognitive Psychology* 8:382–439.

Ross, R. S. 1977. *Speech Communication,* fourth edition. Englewood Cliffs, N.J.: Prentice-Hall.

Rubinstein, J. 1973. *City Police.* New York: Farrar, Straus & Giroux.

Rumelhart, W. 1975. "Notes for a schema for stories," in *Representation and Understanding: Studies in Cognitive Science,* D. Borow and A. Collins, eds. New York: Academic Press, 211–236.

Said, E. 1973. *Beginnings.* Baltimore, Md.: Johns Hopkins University Press.

de Saussure, F. 1966. *Course in General Linguistics,* C. Bally and A. Sechehaye, eds; W. Baskin, trans. New York: McGraw-Hill. Originally published in 1915.

Savitz, L. 1971. "Dimensions of police loyalty," in *Police in Urban Society,* H. Hahn, ed. Beverly Hills: Sage, 213–224.

Savitz, L. 1982. "An officer requires assistance," in *Legal Process and Corrections,* N. Johnston and L. Savitz, eds. New York: Wiley, 19–25.

Scarman, Lord 1981. *The Scarman Report.* Harmondsworth: Penguin.

Schneiderman, S. 1983. *Lacan: The Death of a Hero.* Cambridge, Mass.: Harvard University Press.

Scholes, R., and R. Kellogg. 1966. *The Nature of Narrative.* New York: Oxford University Press.

Schutz, A. 1962. *Collected Papers. Vol. 1, The Problem of Social Reality,* M. Natanson, ed. The Hague: Martinus Nijhoff.

Schutz, A. 1964. *Collected Papers. Vol. 2, Studies in Social Theory,* M. Natanson, ed. The Hague: Martinus Nijhoff.

Scott, E. 1981. *Police Referral in Metropolitan Areas.* Report to the National Institute of Justice. Bloomington, Ind.: University of Indiana, Workshop in Political Theory and Policy Analysis.

Scott, E., and S. Percy. 1983. "Gatekeeping police services," in *Police at Work,* R. Bennett, ed. Beverly Hills, Cal.: Sage, 127–144.

Seidman, D., and M. Couzens. 1973. "Getting the crime rate down: Political pressure and crime reporting." *Law and Society Review* (Spring), 8:457–493.

Shannon, C. E., and W. Weaver. 1964. *The Mathematical Theory of Communication.* Urbana, Ill.: University of Illinois Press. Originally published in 1949.

Shearing, C. 1984. *Dial-a-Cop: A Study in Police Mobilisation.* Toronto: Centre of Criminology, University of Toronto.

Short, J. ed. 1971. *The Social Fabric.* Chicago, Ill.: University of Chicago Press.

Simon, H. 1976. *Administrative Behavior,* third edition. New York: Free Press.

Simon, H. 1982. *Sciences of the Artificial,* second edition. Cambridge, Mass.: MIT Press.

Simon, H., and M. Barenfield. 1969. "Information-processing analysis of perceptual processes in problem-solving." *Psychological Review* 76:473–483.

Skolnick, J. 1966. *Justice without Trial.* New York: Wiley.

Skolnick, J., and D. Bayley. 1986. *The New Blue Line: Police Innovations in Six Cities.* New York: The Free Press.

Smith, D., and J. Gray. 1983. *Police and People in London. Vol. 4, The Police in Action.* London: Policy Studies Institute.

Smith, D., and J. Klein. 1983. "Police agency characteristics and arrest decisions," in *Evaluating Performance in Criminal Justice Agencies,* G. Whitaker, ed. Beverly Hills, Cal.: Sage, 63–97.

Spelman, W., and D. K. Brown. 1981. *Calling the Police: Citizen Reporting of Serious Crime.* Washington, D.C.: Police Executive Research Forum.

Stead, J., ed. 1977. *Pioneers in Policing.* Mountclair, New Jersey: Patterson Smith.

Stern, J. 1959. *Lichtenberg: A Doctrine of Scattered Occasions.* Bloomington, Ind.: Indiana University Press.

Stinchcombe, A. 1964. "Institutions of privacy in the determination of police administrative practice." *American Journal of Sociology* (September), 69:150–160.

Sturrock, J. ed. 1979. *Structuralism.* Oxford: Oxford University Press.

Sudnow, D. 1965. "Normal crimes." *Social Problems* (Winter), 12:255–276.

Sumner, C. 1978. *On Ideology.* New York: Academic Press.

Swidler, A. 1984. "Culture in action: Symbols and strategems." *American Sociological Review* (April), 51:273–286.

Sykes, R. E., and E. E. Brent. 1983. *Policing: A Social Behaviorist Perspective.* New Brunswick, N.J.: Rutgers University Press.

Thompson, J. 1967. *Organizations in Action.* New York: McGraw-Hill.

Tien, J. and K. Colton. 1979. "Police command, control, and communications," in *What Works?* Law Enforcement Assistance Administration, ed. Washington, D.C.: Government Printing Office, 293–336.

Tobias, M. W. 1974. *Police Communications.* Springfield, Ill.: Charles C. Thomas.

Todorov, T. 1981. *Introduction to Poetics*, R. Howard, trans. Brighton: Wheatsheaf.

Trist, E. L., and K. W. Bamforth. 1951. "Some social and psychological consequences of the longwall method of coal-getting." *Human Relations* 4:3–38.

Tyler, S., ed. 1969. *Cognitive Anthropology*. New York: Holt, Rinehart & Winston.

Uspensky, B. 1973. *A Poetics of Composition*, V. Zavarin and S. Wittig, trans. Berkeley, Cal.: University of California Press.

Van Maanen, J. 1974. "Working the street," in *Prospects for Reform in Criminal Justice*, H. Jacob, ed. Beverly Hills, Cal.: Sage, 83–130.

Van Maanen, J. 1983. "The boss: First line supervision in an American police agency," in *Control in the Police Organization*, M. Punch, ed. Cambridge, Mass.: MIT Press, 227–250.

Van Maanen, J. 1988. *Tales of the Field*. Chicago, Ill.: University of Chicago Press.

Van Maanen, J., and E. Schein. 1979. "Toward a theory of organizational socialization," in *Researching Organizational Behavior*, B. Staw, ed. Greenwich, Conn.: JAI Press, 209–269.

Waegel, W. 1981. "Case routinization in investigative police work." *Social Problems* (February), 28:263–275.

Walker, S. 1984. "'Broken windows' and fractured history: The use and misuse of history in recent police patrol analysis." *Justice Quarterly* 1(1):75–89.

Walsh, J. 1972. "Cops and 'stool pidgeons': Professional striving and discretionary justice in European police work." *Law and Society Review* (Winter), 7:299–306.

Walsh, J. 1977. "Career styles and police behavior," in *Police and Society*, D. Bayley, ed. Beverly Hills, Cal.: Sage, 149–167.

Weber, M. 1958. *From Max Weber: Essays in Sociology*, H. H. Gerth and C. W. Mills, trans. and eds. New York: Oxford University Press.

Webster, J. 1973. *The Realities of Police Work*. Dubuque, Iowa: W. C. Brown.

Weick, K. 1979. *The Social Psychology of Organizing*, second edition. Reading, Mass. Addison-Wesley.

Weick, K. 1983a. "Loose couplings and relaxed meanings." Johnson School of Management, Cornell University, Ithaca, New York.

Weick, K. 1983b. "Organizational communication: Toward a research agenda," in *Communication and Organizations*, L. Putnam and M. Pacanowsky, eds. Beverly Hills, Cal.: Sage, 13–29.

Weizenbaum, J. 1976. *Computer Power and Human Reason: From Judgment to Calculation*. San Francisco, Cal.: Freeman.

Wells, J. 1979. "911: Concepts, constraints and implications." Department of Sociology, Michigan State University, East Lansing, Michigan.

Westley, W. 1970. *Violence and the Police*. Cambridge, Mass.: MIT Press.

White, H. 1982. *Tropics of Discourse*. Baltimore, Md.: Johns Hopkins University Press.

Whittemore, L. W. 1968. *Cop!* New York: Fawcett/Crest.

Wilde, H. R. 1972. *The Process of Change in a Police Bureaucracy*. Ph.D. Dissertation, Department of Government, Harvard University.

Williams, J., L. J. Redlinger, and P. K. Manning. 1979. *Police Narcotics Control*. Washington, D.C.: Government Printing Office.

Wilson, J. Q. 1963. "The police and their problems: A theory." *Public Policy* 12:189–216.

Wilson, J. Q. 1968. *Varieties of Police Behavior*. Cambridge, Mass.: Harvard University Press.

Wilson, J. Q. 1978. *The Investigators: Managing FBI and Narcotics Agents*. New York: Basic Books.

Wilson, J. Q., and G. Kelling. 1982. "The police and neighborhood safety: Broken windows." *Atlantic Magazine* (March), 249:29–38.

Wilson, O. W., and R. McLaren. 1972. *Police Administration*, third edition. New York: McGraw-Hill.

Winch, P. 1958. *The Idea of a Social Science*. London: Routledge & Kegan Paul.

Wittgenstein, L. 1969. *On Certainty*, G. E. M. Anscombe and G. von Wright, eds.; D. Paul and G. E. M. Anscombe, trans. Oxford: Basil Blackwell.

Woodward, J. 1965. *Industrial Organization: Theory and Practice*. Oxford: Oxford University Press.

Yeats, W. B. 1956. *Collected Poems*. New York: Macmillan. Originally published in 1933.

Zey-Ferrell, M. 1979. *Dimensions of Organizations*. Santa Monica, Cal.: Goodyear.

Index